NORMANS AND SAXONS

SOUTHERN LITERARY STUDIES
Fred Hobson, Series Editor

RITCHIE DEVON WATSON, JR.

NORMANS

AND

SAXONS

SOUTHERN RACE MYTHOLOGY AND THE
INTELLECTUAL HISTORY OF THE AMERICAN CIVIL WAR

LOUISIANA STATE UNIVERSITY PRESS
BATON ROUGE

Published by Louisiana State University Press
Copyright © 2008 by Louisiana State University Press
All rights reserved
Manufactured in the United States of America
First printing

DESIGNER: Michelle A. Neustrom
TYPEFACE: Minion Pro, No. 12 Type
PRINTER AND BINDER: Thomson-Shore, Inc.

LIBRARY OF CONGRESS CATALOGING-IN-PUBLICATION DATA

Watson, Ritchie Devon.
  Normans and Saxons : southern race mythology and the intellectual history of the American Civil War / Ritchie Devon Watson, Jr.
    p. cm. — (Southern literary studies)
  Includes bibliographical references and index.
  ISBN 978-0-8071-3312-5 (cloth : alk. paper) 1. Southern States—Intellectual life—19th century. 2. American literature—Southern States—History and criticism. 3. Rhetoric—Political aspects—Southern States—History—19th century. 4. Southern States—Politics and government—1775-1865. 5. Race—Political aspects—Southern States—History—19th century. 6. Anglo-Saxon race—History—19th century. 7. North and south. 8. United States—History—Civil War, 1861–1865—Causes. 9. Confederate States of America—Politics and government. 10. Confederate States of America—Intellectual life. I. Title.
  F213.W38 2008
  973.6—dc22
                                                                    2007034359

The paper in this book meets the guidelines for permanence and durability of the Committee on Production Guidelines for Book Longevity of the Council on Library Resources. ∞

I am grateful to Randolph-Macon College's Walter Williams Craigie Teaching Endowment, which awarded me grants that were crucial to the research and writing of this book.

*To Louis D. Rubin, whose teaching and example
helped to launch me on my critical journey*

CONTENTS

INTRODUCTION: The Brooks–Sumner Caning Incident: Slavery, Honor, and the American Cultural Divide
1

1. Race Mythology, Science, and Southern Nationalism
19

2. *Ivanhoe*, Race Myth, and the Walter Scott Cultural Syndrome
47

3. A Slaveholding Race: Mythology and Southern Polemics
72

4. Race Mythology and Antebellum Fiction
93

5. A Universal Yankee Nation: Northern Racial Mythmaking
119

6. A Proud, High-Toned People Repudiate the Scum of the North
135

7. Northern Vandals versus Southern Ruffians
169

8. Poetry Fights the Civil War
201

CONCLUSION: Race Mythology, the Lost Cause, and Twentieth-Century Southern Sectionalism
235

Notes   253

Index   275

NORMANS AND SAXONS

INTRODUCTION

The Brooks-Sumner Caning Incident

Slavery, Honor, and the American Cultural Divide

On the afternoon of May 21, 1856, Representative Preston Brooks of South Carolina strode down the aisle of the United States Senate, carrying a walking stick, and stood at the desk of Senator Charles Sumner of Massachusetts. The Senate's morning session had adjourned a short time before, and Sumner, virtually alone in the chamber, was busily examining papers. For a moment he was unaware of Brooks's presence. But when he finally did look up, the South Carolinian addressed him with measured, forceful deliberation: "Mr. Sumner, I have read your speech carefully, and with as much calmness as I could be expected to read such a speech. You have libeled my state, and slandered my relation, who is aged and absent, and I feel it to be my duty to punish you for it." Before the surprised Sumner could respond, Brooks began hitting him with the walking stick, the blows becoming progressively harder and more savage. As Brooks later matter-of-factly recalled this astonishing scene, "I . . . gave him about thirty first rate stripes. . . . Every lick went where I intended."[1]

Tall and solidly built, Sumner found himself trapped within the confines of his writing desk, which was bolted to the floor. He was for a number of seconds unable to rise and ward off the blows raining down on him. Finally, through a desperate exertion of strength, he succeeded in wrenching his desk out of its bolts. He staggered up the aisle of the Senate with Brooks continuing to beat him with the now-bloody stump of the snapped walking stick. At last Sumner collapsed unconscious on the floor. "Towards the last," Brooks later observed with undisguised contempt for his victim, "he bellowed like a calf. I wore my cane out completely but saved the Head which is gold."[2]

A few minutes after the attack, Brooks was calmly walking away from the Capitol down Pennsylvania Avenue while a semiconscious Sumner lay on a couch in the Senate anteroom having his wounds attended to by a hastily summoned physician. Afterward he was taken by carriage to his Washington lodgings, his clothes soaked with blood. Before losing consciousness again he remarked, "I could not believe that a thing like this was possible."[3] It would be more than three years before Sumner would reassume his seat on the Senate floor.

* * *

What was the speech that Preston Brooks mentioned in his challenge to Senator Sumner, and how had it libeled Brooks's kinsman and his state? The speech was Sumner's "The Crime against Kansas," an address delivered in the Senate over a two-day period, from May 19 to 20. Its subject was the battle then raging in the Kansas territory between pro-slavery settlers committed to extending the domain of the South's peculiar institution and anti-slavery settlers equally committed to restricting slavery's spread through the Union. These battles had already turned this frontier region into what was popularly known as "Bloody Kansas."

The territories called Kansas and Nebraska had been considered free as early as 1820. In that year the Missouri Compromise, while admitting Missouri to the Union as a slave state, had also forbidden slavery in the Louisiana Territory north of latitude 36 degrees 30 minutes, the modern boundary between the states of Oklahoma and Kansas. Though this compromise had restricted the expansion of slavery north and west of Missouri for over thirty years, it had been repealed by the controversial Kansas-Nebraska Act of 1854. Submitted by Senator Stephen A. Douglas of Illinois and narrowly approved by Congress, this bill provided for the formal organization of the Kansas and Nebraska territories and specified that the question of their being eventually admitted to the Union as free or slave states would be determined by the will, or popular sovereignty, of those settling the territories. Senator Douglas apparently believed that Nebraska would opt to be free and Kansas, adjoining the slave state of Missouri, would choose to be slave. However, abolitionists, furious over the abrogation of the Compromise of 1820 and adamantly opposed to any further extension of slavery, had organized free-soil settlers and sent them into Kansas. The opposition between pro- and anti-slavery forces had inevitably escalated into violence. Indeed, three days after Sumner's caning, on May 24, 1856, an abolitionist named John Brown retaliated against southern depredations in the territory by instigating the "Pottawatomie massacre" of four pro-slave Kansas farmers.

Harvard-educated Charles Sumner, a leader of abolitionist forces in the Senate, interpreted the pro-slavery/anti-slavery strife in Kansas as an unambiguous battle between the forces of evil and good. He believed that the nation had reached a profound juncture, that Kansas must be the place where the growing cancer of slavery was contained. In his powerful "Crime against Kansas" speech he condemned the Kansas-Nebraska Act as "the rape of a virgin Territory, compelling it to the hateful embrace of Slavery," and he called for American citizens to "vindicate Right against Wrong" and to "redeem the

Republic from the thralldom of that Oligarchy" that would enslave Kansas.[4]

Even today, one who reads Sumner's speech can understand why it outraged the southern senators who were forced to listen to it in 1856. The same sense of righteous indignation that provided its powerful anti-slavery substance also imparted a contemptuous and even cruel tone to its description of the supporters of slavery. It was bad enough for southern listeners to hear Sumner identify their region with the antidemocratic and anti-American forces of oligarchy. But when Sumner moved on to repudiate a specific adversary, Preston Brooks's cousin, the venerable Senator Andrew P. Butler of South Carolina, his words became personally abusive. Worst of all, in attacking Butler he held up to ridicule the southern code of chivalry, the foundation of the South's exalted view of itself as an enlightened, cultivated, and aristocratic slave society.

Sumner ridiculed Butler by metaphorically linking him to Spain's mad knight-errant Don Quixote. Like the deluded protagonist of the Cervantes novel, he observed, Butler had "read many books of chivalry, and believes himself a chivalrous knight, with sentiments of honor and courage." However, Butler had chosen an even more morally revolting mistress than Don Quixote: "The harlot Slavery is his 'wench Dulcinea.'" And if Butler could not keep his harlot, Sumner remarked with acid irony, "then, sir, the chivalric senator will conduct the State of South Carolina out of the Union! Heroic knight! Exalted senator! A second Moses for a second exodus!"[5]

It was fortunate that the elderly and frail Butler was not present on the Senate floor, because Sumner concluded his long speech with an even more personal verbal attack. In the words of Sumner's biographer David Donald, "Uncharitably referring to the effects of the slight labial paralysis from which the elderly ... senator suffered," Sumner scornfully described the manner in which Butler had opposed the admission of Kansas as a free state in an address filled with what Sumner called "incoherent phrases" in which Butler had "discharged the loose expectoration of his speech, now upon her representatives, and then upon her people."[6]

Having disposed of Brooks's kinsman, Sumner proceeded to vilify his native state and its "shameful assumptions for slavery." "Were the whole history of South Carolina blotted out of existence," he thundered, "from its very beginning down to the day of the last election of the Senator to his present seat on this floor, civilization might lose—I do not say how little; but surely less than it has already gained by the example of Kansas, in its valiant struggle against oppression." Kansas, he predicted, would one day enter the Union as a free state and would be "a 'ministering angel' to the Republic, when South Carolina, in the cloak of darkness which she hugs, 'lies howling.'"[7]

It would be easy to believe that the Massachusetts senator who delivered this vituperative speech was a mean-tempered individual who despised southerners personally and interacted with them on the Senate floor in a state of permanent hostility. In fact Sumner was a serious man, but not a notably hateful or vindictive one. He personally admired a number of Dixie's senators, including Senator Butler, whose desk had adjoined his own when he came to Washington as a freshman senator in 1851. His feelings for his elderly colleague were affectionate, though tinged with what southerners would recognize, even today, as Yankee condescension. "If he had been a citizen of New England," Sumner once observed of Butler, "he would have been a scholar, or, at least, a well educated man."[8]

One could perhaps best describe Charles Sumner as a person who refused to allow the personal dimension of his life to qualify or compromise his larger political and moral designs. Though personally he liked Senator Butler and even appreciated, to a degree, his combination of courtly manners and erudition, on a more abstract level he felt that the South Carolinian was the spokesman for a social and economic system that was an unmitigated evil and that threatened the very existence of American democracy. In his passionate opposition to slavery, Sumner saw the intrusion of slaveholders into Kansas, simply and powerfully, as a brutal rape of innocence and purity. He was incapable of acknowledging the complexities of the real Kansas territory. In the words of David Donald, he was unwilling to accept "that the Kansas struggle involved not merely freedom and slavery, but also land speculations, bitter rivalries over the location of the territorial capital, and personal ambitions of would-be congressmen from the territory. He did not understand that there was no ineradicable hostility between southern pioneers in this region, virtually all of whom were non-slaveholders, and free-state settlers, who wanted forever to ban free Negroes from Kansas."[9]

Blind to the political complexities of the real Kansas, Sumner was possessed by a savage singleness of moral purpose that would lead him to defame a friend and colleague as a slobbering pimp to the harlot of slavery. Neither appreciating nor fully understanding Andrew Butler's or Preston Brooks's southern notions of personal honor, he could have had at best an imperfect apprehension of the outrage that would compel Butler's kinsman to stand before him on the afternoon of May 21 with cane in hand.

From the point of view of southerners who listened indignantly to Sumner's address, and from that of Brooks, who read it later with an equal sense of outrage, the senator's words were a demonstration not of a lofty sense of moral purpose but of a monomaniacal fanaticism. Indeed, by the 1850s, southerners increasingly believed that such fanaticism was a product of the Puritan inheritance of the northern states in general and of the New England states in particular. Contemporary supporters of Sumner would have undoubtedly agreed with the description of his twentieth-century biographer that he was "the voice of Puritanism in politics."[10] But though many northerners might have associated his Puritan-inflected political vision with lofty moral purpose, southerners viewed it as a sinister force that might destroy the nation.

This southern view of Sumner as a villain of satanic proportions had been articulated by Senator James Mason of Virginia shortly after the Massachusetts senator had finished his speech. Mason had been pilloried as a representative of "that other Virginia, from which Washington and Jefferson now avert their faces, where human beings are bred as cattle for the shambles." In rising to defend himself and his state, Mason repudiated Sumner and his particular brand of Puritan fanaticism as low, vile, and evil, an assessment with which his southern colleagues no doubt heartily agreed. He expressed his disgust in a voice trembling with anger: "I am constrained to hear here depravity, vice in its most odious form uncoiled in this presence, exhibiting its loathsome deformities in accusation and vilification against the quarter of the country from which I come . . . because it is a necessity of my position, under a common Government, to recognize as an equal, politically, one whom to see elsewhere is to shun and despise."[11] In anathematizing Sumner, Mason delivered upon him the worst judgment a southerner could make of an enemy: Sumner was no gentleman, and he was therefore a man without honor.

While they might not have agreed with Mason's condemnation of Sumner as satanic and loathsome, many northern senators felt that Sumner's speech had been intemperate and offensive. Outside the Senate chamber, northern reaction was also decidedly mixed. Writing in his *New York Daily Tribune*, Republican Horace Greeley praised Sumner's effort as "one of the most searching and fearless exposures yet made of the Giant Crime which, in its legitimate consequence, has filled Kansas with violence and threatens now to deluge her plains with blood." A writer to the *New York Evening Post* also approved the speech's "inspiring eloquence and lofty moral tone" and celebrated it as "a triumphant senatorial achievement." But other northern newspapers were troubled by Sumner's harsh personal attacks. The day after the speech, most northerners probably would have agreed with Massachusetts statesman and political moderate Edward Everett. Though he generally approved of Sumner's position on Kansas, Everett also said that he had never heard a speech so offensive in tone "from a man of character of any party."[12]

Reactions to Sumner's speech in the South, as one might expect, were uniformly hostile. The *Washington Star* lamented the "personal vilification and abuse of Senator Butler" and opined that the address had "caused a blush of shame to mantle the cheeks of all present who respect the character of the body before whom it was uttered." Below the Potomac, editorial opinion echoed and amplified the *Star*'s outrage. But the journalistic condemnation paled in comparison with the deadly anger aroused among individual southerners. Not surprisingly, the venom was nowhere more concentrated than in the breasts of South Carolinians. One gentleman of the Palmetto State observed that immediately after the speech he "could not go into a parlor, or a drawing room, or to a dinner party, where he did not find an implied reproach that there was an unmanly submission to an insult to his state and his countrymen."[13]

It was just this sense of implied reproach that impelled Preston Brooks to act to defend the honor of his elderly kinsman and of South Carolina. But how was that honor best to be defended? Northern victims of slander might have resorted to legal action to punish the slanderer. But for an antebellum southern gentleman, such a response would have been considered shameful and even cowardly. As David Donald has observed, "No southern gentleman considered a law suit the proper redress for a slur upon his own good name or upon that of a member of his family." A South Carolina lawyer nicely explained the stigma that attached to litigation: "To carry a personal grievance into a court of law disgraced the plaintiff in the estimation of his peers and put the whole case beneath the notice of society."[14]

Though the notion of legal action never entered Brooks's mind, the idea of challenging Sumner to a duel certainly did. By 1856, northerners had overwhelmingly come to judge the code duello as a crude manifestation of lawlessness, but many southerners still accepted it as an indispensable weapon for defending one's personal honor. Under the unwritten code that had been borrowed from the European aristocracy and superimposed upon a New World plantation society, an insult to a man's honor required a martial response, not the submission dictated by modern legal codes. Most southerners who considered themselves gentlemen would have agreed that in following the code duello one was following the code of honor. In their eyes a challenge to a duel properly transferred a transgression from "state jurisdiction to the jurisdiction of the unwritten code."[15]

In the antebellum South no state was more devoted to the duel than Preston Brooks's South Carolina. An Englishman who traveled to Charleston in the early decades of the nineteenth century claimed that he had been introduced to thirteen gentlemen in that city, eleven of whom "had killed their man each" in duels. Another English traveler, James Buckingham, described an encounter he witnessed in Columbia in which both parties were wounded. "But," he said, "no notice was taken of the affair by the public authorities, and with the community it excited no sensation beyond the passing hour."[16] Given this cultural milieu it comes as no surprise that Brooks, a loyal son of Carolina, seriously considered confronting Sumner and challenging him to a duel.

But even though Brooks briefly entertained challenging Sumner, he quickly dismissed the idea as an impossibility, and his thinking on this matter was particularly relevant to the caning he would administer on the Senate floor. First, as he later explained, "The moral tone of mind that would lead a man to become a Black Republican would make him incapable of courage." Brooks had no expectation that such a coward would respond to his challenge in an appropriate fashion. Instead, he suspected that his adversary would immediately report the incident to the Washington police. Since dueling was illegal within the District of Columbia, he feared that the result of his challenge would be not the satisfaction of his kinsman's and his state's honor but endless courtroom wrangling and "legal penalties" that would make him, Senator Butler, and South Carolina look even more ludicrous and that would compound his region's shame.[17]

The second consideration that made the idea of a duel with Sumner impossible for Brooks to accept was the simple fact that duels were assumed to be engagements between social equals, between gentlemen who possessed a similar sense of honor. Brooks never imagined Sumner to be his social equal. For him, as for James Mason of Virginia, his adversary was a low and vile creature with no understanding of the obligations of a gentleman. Consequently he was not worthy of the respect embodied in the formal challenging of an opponent. As one southerner knowingly explained the code's rules of engagement, "Duelists were social equals from society's first ranks.... A gentleman horsewhipped or, even worse, caned a person of the lower estates."[18]

Brooks apparently spent some of the hours before he entered the Senate chamber wrestling with the nuances of his planned chastisement of Sumner.

He considered with special care the question of the weapon most suitable for the occasion. As he explained later, "I . . . speculated somewhat as to whether I should employ a horsewhip or a cowhide, but knowing that the Senator was my superior in strength, it occurred to me that he might wrest it from my hand and then . . . I might have been compelled to do that which I would have regretted the balance of my natural life." What Brooks would have regretted was a combat akin to a barroom brawl that might have resulted in Sumner's death. Because Brooks considered himself a man of courage, he was not bothered by subsequent northern accusations that he had not given his adversary a fair chance to defend himself. Brooks judged his foe to be a dishonorable creature, one of the lowest of the low, unworthy of claiming a level field of combat. His aim was to beat Sumner as a master might beat a recalcitrant and dangerously surly slave, to within—but only to within—an inch of his life. "It was expressly to avoid taking life," he contended, "that I used an ordinary walking stick."[19] The walking stick served his purpose admirably, almost—but not quite—taking Sumner's life while leaving him for several years a hobbling invalid.

Gentlemen of the South, as we shall see, seemed to appreciate "the delicate shades of meaning implicit in" Brooks's choice of an implement with which to beat his enemy unconscious. But residents of both Sumner's home state of Massachusetts and of the northern states at large did not share Dixie's esteem for its champion's finely tuned chivalric sensibilities. The assault galvanized the entire region. Democrats, Whigs, and Republicans united to condemn it as the cowardly attack of an uncivilized southern ruffian. The newly formed Republican Party was especially energized by the incident. It gave them "the perfectly matched themes of 'Bleeding Kansas' and 'Bleeding Sumner,'" which they would effectively employ in the elections of 1856 to increase their strength in Congress. More moderate northerners were also appalled. They might have disapproved of the tone of Sumner's speech, but they abhorred Brooks's violent response to it. Whig Congressman Robert Winthrop expressed the consternation most tellingly: "How could any high-minded and honorable man, as Mr. Brooks is represented to be in Carolina, have taken such a mode and place of redress, and have proceeded to such extreme violence!"[20]

In the months following the caning, letters of support for the slowly recuperating Sumner poured in and lifted his spirits. Henry Wadsworth Longfellow did his best to console his friend. "I have no words to write you about this savage atrocity," he observed. Historian John Palfrey, writing from England, described to Sumner the reaction of the English. "I can understand better the surprise and consternation with which their disgust is mingled," he wrote, "after all my own intimate observation and experience of the savage power that rules us." If Yankees judged Brooks's attack to be a manifestation of southern savagery, they apotheosized Sumner as a martyr to Dixie's brutality. The words of one admirer echoed the feelings of thousands: "You are glorious now. The crown of martyrdom is *yours*. . . . 'Every noble crown is, ever has been, a crown of thorns' and *you* have been found meet to wear the one the Savior wore—oh thank God and murmur not."[21] If he could have read letters such as these, Preston Brooks would certainly have viewed them as confirmation of the religious and political fanaticism that he and other southerners believed was an inherently dangerous element of the North's Puritan mentality.

Northerners expressed their outrage at Brooks's attack not just in editorials and personal letters but in numerous formal resolutions. One of these, signed by New Englanders Josiah Quincy, Henry Wadsworth Longfellow, Richard Henry Dana, and Edward Everett, included pledges of money to support the Senator's convalescence and praised Sumner's "spotless public and private character" and his "dauntless courage in the defense of freedom on the floor of Congress." It concluded by describing the speech for which Sumner had nearly paid for with his life as a model of "logical acuteness, and Spartan intrepidity in its chastisement of iniquity."[22]

Abolitionist editors like William Lloyd Garrison maintained a relentless focus on the attack and extended their denunciations beyond the barbarity of Preston Brooks's individual behavior to the barbarity of the culture that had produced him. Garrison professed himself astonished by the fact that, although Sumner had been "surprised in his seat, and knocked senseless to the floor," the appalling incident had been represented in the South "as a victory in a fair fight!" Such applause, he believed, indicated "a depth of depravity, a universality of cowardice and ruffianism, a deadness to all sense of shame, and a vulgar scoundrelism, at the South, which exceed all the allegations of the most radical abolitionists." In another editorial, entitled "Southern Degradation," Garrison indignantly observed that South Carolinians had unanimously praised Brooks's deed and had tolerated no criticism of his action. "How she glories in what fills the civilized world with astonishment, indignation and horror!" But what more could one expect, he raged, from such a benighted state as South Carolina: "Without invention, enterprise, art, science, industry, thrift, education, refinement, strength, or promise, how boundless is her conceit, how swollen her pomposity, how active her combativeness, how ludicrous her assumed superiority, how unproductive her head, how evil her heart, how cowardly and brutal her spirit!"[23] Carolinians reading these words may well have concluded that Preston Brooks had laid his cane on the wrong adversary.

Some northerners were so enraged by Brooks's assault that they professed themselves willing to defend their region's honor, even if it meant embracing the South's code duello. Massachusetts Representative Anson Burlingame was one of these firebrands. He delivered a House speech on June 21, 1856, in which he compared Brooks's attack on Sumner with that of Cain on Abel. "There are men from the old Commonwealth of Massachusetts," he warned, "who will not shrink from a defense of freedom of speech, and the honored State they represent, on any field, where they may be assailed."[24] Seizing the opportunity for a proper duel, Brooks immediately challenged Burlingame.

Negotiations over a proper venue for the Brooks-Burlingame confrontation ensued while Charles Sumner agonized over the prospect of seeing a fellow New Englander descending to the South's uncivilized level. "Alas for Burlingame!" he lamented to his friend Joshua Giddings. "He has deliberately discarded the standard of Northern civilization to adopt the standard of Southern barbarism; he turns his back upon the Public Opinion of Massachusetts to bow before that of South Carolina!" Giddings agreed with Sumner, but he was thankful that he, at least, had refrained from joining Burlingame's moral descent. In his own House speech, he pointed out, he had "endeavored to express my views of this different State of Civilization in the free states from that of the Slave States."[25] Much to the relief of Sumner and Giddings, the Brooks-Burlingame duel was eventually cancelled. Intermediaries set up the engagement in Canada, but Brooks refused to travel through the free states to reach the dueling ground.

Of all the northern responses to Sumner's caning, none was more articulate, more filled with moral indignation, or more revealing of the North's own understanding of personal honor than that of Ralph Waldo Emerson. In his "Assault on Charles Sumner" Emerson averred that the entire state of South Carolina could not "offer one or any number of persons who are to be weighed for a moment in the scale with such a person as the meanest of them all has now struck down." While southerners viewed Sumner as a vile creature bereft of a sense of the honorable, Emerson believed that he was a superior man who epitomized the best traits of the northern character. He praised Sumner as an individual "pure" and "exceptional in . . . honor" who had proved his mettle by standing for his region's moral values "a little in advance of all the North, and therefore without adequate support." His honor was manifested in his moral courage, which had "never faltered in [its] maintenance of justice and freedom."[26]

Emerson's celebration of Sumner's "honor" illuminates the profoundly different understanding southerners and northerners brought to this highly charged word. For Preston Brooks, a man's individual honor was inextricably bound to the reputation of both his family and his native state, to his reputation among his peers, and to his avoiding the stigma of shame and reproach that might be visited on him by those peers. As Bertram Wyatt-Brown has explained in his seminal works on this subject, the southern gentleman's understanding of honor closely linked an individual's sense of personal worth to the acceptance of that self-definition by the community at large.[27] For Emerson, community opinion was irrelevant to the attainment of real honor, which was a quality that came from within and that was practically indistinguishable from conscience and godliness. Honor was achieved not by gaining society's approval but by following one's spiritual inner voice "a little in advance" of his society.

For a person possessed of Emerson's Yankee brand of honor, it would have been petty and uncivilized to respond with violence to verbal attacks on one's character, for how could mere words injure the reputation of a man of true honor and conscience? Indeed, Emerson seems to have been blind to the personally vindictive nature of Sumner's speech. Or if he was aware of the abusive tone of "The Crime against Kansas," he seems to have viewed it as a trivial violation of the canons of taste, an instance of excess that was of little significance when weighed against the speech's lofty and honorable moral purpose. According to Emerson, southerners had charged Sumner not with "drunkenness, not debauchery . . . nor rapacity, nor personal aims of any kind; no, but with what? Why . . . that he broke over the proprieties of debate," that he expressed his opinions "with some discourtesy," that "he is an abolitionist, as if every sane human being were not an abolitionist, or a believer that all men should be free."[28]

To Emerson the southern code of honor that dictated Brooks's punishment of Sumner was a manifestation of the barrenness and savagery of southern culture. The assault constituted ample evidence that "the very conditions of the game must always be, the worst life staked against the best. It is only the best whom they desire to kill. It is only when they cannot answer your reasons, that they wish to knock you down." The fact that Brooks had not immediately been thrown into jail and that southern politicians like him were encouraged by their constituents to exhibit intelligence "in reverse ratio" to their "bodily strength or skill with knives and guns" offered ample proof to the

Transcendental sage that it would "only do to send foolish persons to Washington, if you wish them to be safe." As for the region that had molded Preston Brooks and sent him to the nation's capital, clearly it was a place where "life is a fever; [where] man is an animal, given to pleasure, frivolous, irritable, spending his days in hunting and practicing with deadly weapons to defend himself against his slaves and against his companions brought up in the same idle and dangerous way."[29]

The assault on Charles Sumner profoundly altered Emerson's understanding of southerners. Earlier in his life he had assessed them with a combination of admiration, humor, and benevolent condescension. As he had explained to a friend who had moved south after college, "You know our idea of an accomplished Southerner—to wit—as ignorant as a bear, as irascible and nettled as any porcupine, as polite as a troubadour, and a very John Randolph in character and address." Thirty years later, after the Sumner episode, he regarded southerners in a much more sinister light. "The shooting complexion, like the cobra capello and scorpion, grows in the South," he wrote in a journal entry of 1857. "It has no wisdom, no capacity of improvement: it looks . . . in every society, for duels." To Emerson, southerners had become deadly creatures, and he believed that they should be dealt with "as all fanged animals must be."[30] After the Sumner caning, more and more northerners moved toward Emerson's malign assessment of the southern temperament.

If southerners were aware of the storm of indignation that the Brooks assault had precipitated in the North, they seem not to have been much bothered by it. A few southern newspapers, most of them Whig publications, expressed doubts about the wisdom of attacking a man "whilst seated at his desk engaged in writing, and who [had] not had time to place himself face to face with his opponent." However, the great majority of Dixie's editors echoed the sentiments of the *Richmond Enquirer,* which was convinced that "vulgar abolitionists" must be "lashed into submission" like slaves. Since Sumner was "a great strapping fellow, and could stand the cowhide beautifully," the *Enquirer* argued facetiously, he could only be improved by "nine-and-thirty" lashes "early every morning" for the rest of his life. As if seconding the defiant sentiments of the Richmond newspaper, replacement canes were showered on Brooks by his constituents, by a group of Charleston merchants, by the governor of South Carolina, and by students at that citadel of gentility, the University of Virginia. The Charleston cane was inscribed with the words, "Hit him again," and the Charlottesville cane was embellished with an expensive gold knob representing a "badly cracked and broken" human head.[31]

Southerners in Washington rallied to Brooks's defense as enthusiastically as their compatriots south of the Potomac had done. In a letter of May 23, 1856, written to his brother, John Hampton Brooks, Preston boasted that "fragments of the stick are begged for as *sacred relicts*. Every southern man is delighted and the abolitionists are like a hive of disturbed bees." A month later he assured brother Ham that the House of Representatives would never censure him. A censure motion required a two-thirds vote, and Brooks was confident of the solid backing of southerners of all political parties. After the vote failed, he believed that honor would require him to resign his seat, return to South Carolina, and "appeal to my own people." As for the cowardly abolitionists who surrounded him in Washington, "The dogs may bite when I kick them but will never dare assail me, though I have fifty letters saying I shall be killed."[32]

The predictions Preston Brooks made to his brother turned out to be accurate. The House motion to expel him passed 121–95 on July 14, 1856, but it fell well short of the required two-thirds majority. Brooks promptly resigned his seat in the House, returned to his South Carolina district, and was quickly and with near unanimity reelected by his constituents. Ultimately he was convicted of assault in a Baltimore federal court and assessed a fine of three hundred dollars.[33]

Brooks's censure vote revealed a profound and potentially unbridgeable sectional fissure within the nation. Political compromises, such as those of 1820 and 1850, had adjusted with some degree of success conflicting territorial and political claims, but the Brooks-Sumner episode dramatized the opposing notions of justice, of class, and of honor that seemed to be the products of fundamentally different northern and southern cultures. The censure vote suggested that these opposing cultural values could not be reconciled in the political arena. Northern congressmen generally interpreted Brooks's action as a brutal assault on a decent man in response to a speech that had been perhaps intemperate in tone but also strongly moral in content. Regardless of the content of Sumner's speech, they believed the caning to have been a response out of all proportion to any insult Sumner had given Senator Butler and South Carolina. Southern congressman viewed the same assault as the proper chastisement of a bellowing coward who had delivered unprovoked insults impugning the honor of a gentleman and of his native state. Those southern congressmen who entertained misgivings about attacking a man who was seated and unarmed suppressed their doubts in the name of southern unity.

The final vote divided along lines that were almost purely sectional. Northern members voted overwhelmingly for Brooks's censure, while every southern member save one voted against his expulsion. For one troubled representative it seemed as if truth had become a relative concept determined entirely by the arbitrariness of geographic latitude. "Members from the South are rallying in a body to one legal conclusion, while members from the free States are concentrating with like unanimity in the other direction," he complained, "as if there was anything in climate, latitude, or longitude, which ought to control the judgment of a lawyer determining a legal question."[34]

Northerners who looked for signs that their southern brethren were not entirely bereft of a sense of right and wrong could not have been encouraged by the adulation lavished on Preston Brooks when he returned to South Carolina in August. His remarkable reception in the state capital of Columbia was widely viewed north of the Potomac as an egregious display of southern arrogance and insolence. In this city a committee of citizens greeted Brooks at city hall on the evening of August 29, 1856, "for the purpose of receiving some testimonials of their appreciation of your gallant conduct in defending the honor of our State." The crowd inside the building was so large that the meeting had been moved outside, where the hero was presented by the mayor with "a handsome silver pitcher, a goblet, and one of Mr. Peckham's finest hickory canes, with a handsome gold head."[35]

The expensive gifts bestowed on Brooks by the grateful citizens of Columbia expressed their "unqualified approval" of his chastisement of "the notorious Charles Sumner for his wanton abuse and cowardly assault upon the character of the venerable Senator from South Carolina, Andrew Pickens Butler, and the fair fame of his State." Columbia's mayor praised Brooks not only for his "merited castigation" of a "vile slanderer" but also for his gentlemanly conduct in the aftermath of the episode, conduct that had won "the applause of all honorable men" for "one of Carolina's noblest sons."[36]

In his one-hour speech of thanks Brooks described his action as "a deed which was the result of a high sense of duty." "Any man," he said, "who held his honor above reproach would have acted, under similar circumstances, precisely" as he himself had done. Brooks termed the indignant response of abolitionists to his quite "ordinary castigation" of Sumner "curious." He modestly professed that he could not say "that there was no honor nor moral courage at the North; he knew there were some men of as true courage at the North as elsewhere. *But what he wished to say, was, that the moral tone of mind which would lead a man to become a Black Republican would make him incapable of courage, and would involve a loss of all honor and moral principle whatever.*"[37]

His stirring indictment of abolitionists was lustily cheered and was followed by a band serenade and a fireworks display.

If the North needed further proof of the South's incorrigible pride, of its glorying in and affirmation of physical violence, the Columbia reception for Preston Brooks was more than ample evidence, at least for the *New York Daily Times*. In a tone of baffled outrage the newspaper wondered at "a man, returning home to his constituents, after having committed a ruffianly act for which he was fined in a criminal court, and a majority of the members of Congress decided him unworthy to sit among them as an equal; but he is received by the people of his State with the highest honor they can bestow . . . as though he had rendered some important service to the country instead of affixing a foul stain upon its honor."[38] Once again North and South were entertaining the concept of honor and bandying the word about in their speeches and editorials in radically different ways.

Just as northerners and southerners applied profoundly different definitions of honor to their judgment of the Sumner caning, they also articulated opposing assessments of the essential qualities of southern culture that they believed had been embodied in Brooks's action. Southerners viewed the caning as the appropriate response to an "unwritten code" of conduct that every gentleman was bound to follow. This code of conduct was in turn based on the myth, widely embraced in Dixie, "that Southern planters were descended from the aristocracy of Europe and should therefore live in the manner of their legendary ancestors."[39]

The aristocratic myth that provided psychological underpinning for the South's social and economic plantation system encompassed many articles of faith. Chief among these articles was the conviction that the region's slaveholders had descended almost entirely from the English Cavalier aristocracy. Indeed, most southerners believed that the institution of slavery was essential to the preservation of their high and noble genealogical inheritance. They also believed that in caning Sumner, Preston Brooks had expressed the loftiest ideals of his aristocratic culture. They were convinced that he had acted in the only way a southern gentleman could act to defend the honor of his family and of his state and to repudiate a cowardly defamer—a man who possessed no sense of honor and who could not be confronted as an equal by a man of noble sentiments. There is no reason to believe that the citizens of Columbia were anything other than sincere when they lionized Brooks for his conduct. They truly believed that his caning of Sumner was a triumphant affirmation of southern chivalry.

Northerners were well aware that southerners viewed themselves as more aristocratic and chivalrous than their Yankee brethren, and their response to Brooks's attack indicates that they had long chafed under these southern assumptions of superiority. They seized upon the assault as proof of the emptiness of the claims of southern chivalry. Writing in the *New York Daily Tribune,* Horace Greeley made this pungent observation: "No meaner exhibition of Southern cowardice—generally miscalled Southern chivalry—was ever witnessed." In a similar tone of bitter ridicule Henry Wadsworth Longfellow wrote to Sumner that he had just been informed of the beating, which he described as a "great feat of arms of the Southern Chivalry." Abolitionist William Lloyd Garrison gleefully included in his *Liberator* verbatim resolutions of support for Brooks from various South Carolina citizens' meetings under the ironic headline, "More of Southern Chivalry."[40] What the South viewed as a chivalrous rebuke to mean-spirited northern cowardice the North viewed as a barbarous expression of southern ruffianism.

The caning of Charles Sumner by Preston Brooks immeasurably enhanced the feeling that northerners and southerners were profoundly different peoples. "When the two sections no longer spoke the same language, shared the same moral code, or obeyed the same law," David Donald has aptly observed, "when their representatives clashed in bloody conflict in the halls of Congress, thinking men North and South began to wonder how the Union could longer endure." In the aftermath of the Sumner caning, Ralph Waldo Emerson had ceased to wonder. "I do not see," he concluded, "how a barbarous community and a civilized community can constitute one state."[41]

Less than three and a half years after Preston Brooks's caning of Charles Sumner, another violent event would shock the nation, driving deeper the emotional wedge between North and South and propelling the nation forward along the road to civil war. Militant abolitionist John Brown's October 16, 1859, raid on the Federal arsenal at Harpers Ferry, Virginia, would again result in public opinion clearly and bitterly divided along regional lines. Though at Harpers Ferry the roles would be reversed from those in the Brooks-Sumner imbroglio, with northerner Brown in the role of aggressor and the white inhabitants of Harpers Ferry his intended victims, the deeply contrasting responses of northerners and southerners to this attempted insurrection remarkably and ominously mirrored the irreconcilably divided sectional attitudes expressed in 1856 after Brooks's attack on Sumner.

As they had responded immediately after Sumner's inflamed Senate speech, many northerners were initially appalled by the rash audacity of John Brown's failed uprising. But the hysterical southern excoriation of Brown as a conscienceless fanatic, a villain of satanic depravity, and his speedy trial and hasty execution by Virginia authorities produced a remarkable and equally hasty shift in northern opinion. By execution day, December 2, 1859, a solid majority of northerners had come to view John Brown as they had Charles Sumner, as a courageous foe of slavery and a martyr to the cause of freedom. Indeed, Brown's death at the end of a rope purchased him a martyrdom that eclipsed in its power and emotional appeal that of Sumner's brutal but nonlethal thrashing at the hands of Preston Brooks.

If the caning of Charles Sumner had opened American minds to the possibility that North and South might be incompatible societies, John Brown's raid on Harpers Ferry and the nation's deeply divided regional responses to both the nature of his act of insurrection and to the justice of his execution convinced many Americans living both above and below the Mason-Dixon that this cultural incompatibility was real, abiding, and systemic. A northern minister, the Reverend A. Crooks, drew just such ominous conclusions in a sermon he preached to his congregation two days after Brown's execution: "We are a divided people. The Union exists only in form and in name. For the North, the South has no sympathy. They continue the Union only from considerations of policy and of interest. The elements and interests of the North and South, of Liberty and Slavery, are essential and eternal antagonisms. They are natural repellants. Between them there can be no union of sympathy, and in reality none of interest."[42] Crooks's conviction that northerners and southerners were two peoples echoed and amplified the sentiment voiced by Emerson two years earlier that North and South represented two separate communities, one civilized and one barbaric.

Southerners too were pondering the profound differences in attitudes and assumptions that separated the inhabitants of the two regions, and they were reaching the similar conclusion that America was composed of two distinct peoples and two distinct cultures. But, as we shall see, some of Dixie's defenders were willing to go one step further. They were willing to propose that northerners and southerners represented not just a "divided people" but two scientifically distinct races.

During the politically tense and ominous decade of the 1850s—a period highlighted by Brooks's vicious assault on the Senate floor and Brown's abortive but potentially bloody rebellion—the leaders of Dixie's political and journalistic establishments would begin feverishly concocting the myth of the South's aristocratic and chivalric Norman racial inheritance, and it would imagine this newly minted Norman race to be in a fight for survival with an implacable foe: a northern Saxon race descended from the middling commercial and yeoman classes of England and imbued with deeply imprinted racial qualities of Puritan self-righteousness and intolerance that made peaceful coexistence and mutual accommodation within a national framework impossible. Drawing on racial theories of a pre-Darwinian era, molders of southern opinion would apply a superficially scientific gloss to these racial fantasies. They would effectively employ their mythic creation to justify secession and would use it during the Civil War as a rhetorical battle banner, confirming the dawn of a new southern race and a new slaveholding nation.

1
Race Mythology, Science, and Southern Nationalism

In January of 1860, less than one month after John Brown's execution and less than a year before the fateful election of Abraham Lincoln, the influential New Orleans periodical *DeBow's Review* presented for the edification of its readers an article entitled "The Basis of Northern Hostility to the South." In it the essayist advanced a provocative thesis that would explain, he contended, the widening chasm of opinion and sentiment that currently separated the northern and southern states. The article argued that the present-day antagonism between northerners and southerners, which had most recently and dramatically manifested itself in the trial and execution of John Brown, constituted more than a mere disagreement over slavery. Indeed, the writer maintained, Yankees would remain eternally hostile to the South, even if they could be brought to agree with southerners on the issue of slavery, for the dispute between North and South was not only political and economic in nature. It also reflected a deep cultural and racial opposition that had originated over two hundred years before in England in the antagonism between Puritan and Cavalier. "The cavaliers and puritans of that age," the writer observed, "were undoubtedly the ancestors, and, to a great extent, the *prototypes* of this. . . . The puritan hatred of the cavalier was deep and bitter, but neither deeper nor more bitter than that of the mass of the Northern, for the people of the Southern States, especially that portion of the North known as New England."[1]

In pursuing its thesis of the fundamental antipathy of the North toward the South, the *DeBow's* article asserted that "the Southern States had been settled almost entirely from the better and more enlightened classes of Great Britain and France." The people of New England, however, were "lineal descendants of the English puritans; and the other Northern States, especially Ohio, are settled in great part from New England."[2] If northerners and southerners were not precisely delineated in this passage as members of separate races, they were certainly viewed as descending from very different elements within English society. And the writer clearly judged the northern heirs of English Puritans to be inferior to the "more enlightened" and aristocratic Cavaliers who had endowed the South's genealogical inheritance.

For the author of the *DeBow's* essay the strongly contrasting backgrounds of northerners and southerners explained what he considered to be the obvious superiority of southern culture to that of the North. "In our descent," he boasted, "we, of the South, have advanced rapidly on the intellectual, moral, and social development of our ancestors; perfecting the great work they began." The region's impressive cultural advances over a relatively brief period of time could hardly be surprising, given the noble qualities of the South's original Cavalier settlers:

> They were brave, honorable, social; loyal to their king, and loyal to the church. Knowing that earth could not be made a paradise, they did not, therefore, seek to turn the fair footstool of God into a gloomy hell. Failings they had, but dishonor, sordid meanness, and mammon worship, they knew not; and they served their king and their church, with a loyal devotion that history had seldom paralleled. Their intellectual development was then not surpassed in Europe, and their moral culture was at least equal to that of their age.[3]

The *DeBow's* essayist was of the firm opinion that the culture of the Yankee North could never hope to rival that of the South, for northerners had "inherited, with interest, all the characteristics of their puritan ancestors." And what were these unfortunate characteristics? "Misanthropy, hypocrisy, diseased philanthropy, envy, hatred, fanaticism, and all the worst passions of the human heart were," he opined, "the ruling characteristics of the English puritans; and they continue to be the ruling characteristics of New England Yankees." Given such meanness of temper, it was not at all surprising that northerners hated southerners. They were bound to hate and envy Dixie's aristocracy. "They hate us," the writer contended, "because their fathers hated ours; they envy us, because we are happy in our society, and have slaves, denied to them by the coldness of their climate and the sterility of their soil; and they are seeking to deprive us of our social system, apparently for no other reason, than that a similar is unattainable by them. The same fanaticism that impelled their ancestors is urging them."[4]

Though in some parts of this article the contrasting ancestral descents of northerners and southerners were viewed as reflections of the opposing social classes of Puritans and Cavaliers, in other parts the distinction seems to have been understood as a more scientific product of heredity and race. The "gallant, high-spirited, chivalrous" southern Cavaliers represented, in the words of the essayist, a "race of the pure Anglo-Saxon blood."[5] The essayist's choice of the phrase "pure Anglo-Saxon" to describe southern blood was a curious one, considering that by 1860 the term *Anglo-Saxon* had been largely abandoned by the South's polemicists in describing the new southern race. On the verge of the Civil War, the region's apologists were much more inclined to use *Norman* or *Anglo-Norman* to describe the founders of the South's plantation aristocracy. Regardless of the term employed to describe Dixie's progenitors, in the eyes of the essayist the southern Cavalier could boast an ancestry distinct from and superior to that of the northern Puritan. In the *DeBow's* essay this ancestry was sometimes viewed as a product of class inheritance, but at other times it seems to have been viewed as a product of the region's distinct racial inheritance.

The appearance of "The Basis of Northern Hostility to the South" in *DeBow's Review* raises an interesting question: Were northerners and southerners so different from each other in their origins and in their thinking that they were bound to exist in a state of constant enmity? Contemporary historians reject this thesis as a gross distortion of the regional differences that existed in antebellum America. Edward Pessen, for example, contends that the attitudes separating northerners and southerners in 1860 were more than counterbalanced by common beliefs and assumptions. "For all of their distinctiveness," he writes, "the Old South and North were complementary elements in an American society that was everywhere primarily rural, capitalistic, materialistic, and socially stratified, racially, ethnically, and religiously heterogeneous, and stridently chauvinistic and expansionist." David Potter similarly observes that in 1861, southern and northern Americans generally shared pride in the accomplishments of the Revolution, a suspicion and hostility toward Europe, an orthodox Protestant theology, a commitment to hard work and success, a belief in progress and in technological advances, and a profound faith in America's future destiny. "In spite of all the emotional fury," he contends, "there was probably more cultural homogeneity in American society on the eve of secession than there had been when the Union was formed, or than there would be a century later." William R. Taylor agrees that there were no absolute divisions between northerners and southerners. "Southerners," he observes, "engaged in business, speculated on real estate, sought profits, lived in towns and cities, voted for the same national parties and subscribed to many of the same ideals and values as other Americans. What differences they developed, as over the issue of Negro slavery, did not lead many of them to formulate a totally different set of social objectives."[6]

American historians thus agree that antebellum North and South were bound by many similarities of interest and attitude—similarities that more than outweighed their differences. Yet by 1860, northerners and southerners were not thinking realistically, like well-trained historians. Reacting to the political clashes and the intensifying polemical debates of the 1850s, they came to believe that the competing sections were profoundly different. In the opinion of Emerson, they constituted two hostile communities, one barbaric and the other civilized. Conversely, in the assessment of the southern essayist for the *DeBow's Review* they were regions fated by their contrasting Puritan and Cavalier inheritances to eternal hatred and conflict. Taylor brilliantly summarizes the state of the American mind on the eve of the Civil War:

> By 1860 most Americans had come to look upon their society and culture as divided between a North and a South, a democratic, commercial civilization and an aristocratic, agrarian one. Each section of the country, so it was believed, possessed its own ethic, its own historical traditions and even, by common agreement, a distinctive racial heritage. Each was governed by different values and animated by a different spirit. According to a theory then in vogue the North had been settled by one party to the English Civil War, the Roundheads, and the South by the other, the royal party or the Cavaliers. The Yankee was a direct descendant of the Puritan Roundhead and the Southern gentleman of the English Cavalier, and the difference between the two was at least partly a matter of blood. The terminology sometimes varied, but contemporaries generally settled upon some such distinction as "Saxon" or "Anglo-Saxon" for the North and "Norman" for the South. Under the stimulus of this divided heritage the North had developed a leveling, go-getting utilitarian society and the South had developed a society based on the values of the English country gentry. It was commonly felt, furthermore, that these two ways of life had been steadily diverging since colonial times.[7]

Of course, the notion that northerners and southerners were two distinct peoples did not spring forth fully formed in 1860 as if from a vacuum. As early as 1785 Thomas Jefferson had written a letter minutely detailing the differences between the "cool, sober, laborious, persevering, independent, . . . chicaning, superstitious and hypocritical" Yankee and the "fiery, Voluptuary, indolent, unsteady, independent, . . . generous, candid" native of Dixie.[8] The embryonic sectionalism adumbrated by Jefferson during the Federal period had assumed more definite form by 1820 with the debates that accompanied the enactment of the Missouri Compromise. Congress now found itself mediating between the southern conviction that slavery should expand along with the Union and the northern conviction that the institution should be restricted in its growth. Americans began to be aware that the political, economic, and social agendas of northerners and southerners might be fundamentally incompatible.

The Compromise of 1820 stemmed the advance of slavery in the Louisiana Territory, but it did not stem the steadily growing awareness that the interests of the northern and southern states were fundamentally at odds. The sense of unease voiced by a Virginia congressman soon after the forging of the Compromise probably reflected that of many of his fellow southerners. "I doubt whether the calm which has succeeded to this agitating question will be a lasting one," he observed ominously. "The enthusiasm and bigotry which our northern brethren feel on the subject of domestic slavery is not likely to die away."[9]

Southerners were not alone in expressing their fears for the future harmony of the Union. Northerners too foresaw potentially far more serious sectional divisions, but they ascribed this conflict to southern paranoia, not to northern "bigotry." Thirty-three years before the firing on Fort Sumter, New Yorker Henry Van Der Lyn expressed alarm in his personal journal over the growing disposition of southern leaders to dissolve the Union. "They are bound together by the bonds of slavery," he wrote, "and feel extremely inimical to the free states: our very exemption from the curse of slavery is a continued source of disquietude to them, fearing the effects of our free thoughts and example, upon their black population." Van Der Lyn also believed that the South's disquietude was a result of an ever-widening imbalance of power between the regions. "They are not a little apprehensive," he observed, "that as we are far outnumbering them in wealth, population and power, we might ere long interfere by some legislative regulations with the absolute property they claim in their Negroes."[10]

Henry Van Der Lyn was remarkably perceptive in his sense of the South's growing apprehension about its place in the Union. Devoted to the institution of slavery and failing to develop an industrial base comparable to that being established in the North, Dixie began to perceive itself after the Missouri Compromise as part of a nation increasingly dominated by northern economic interests. The growing cultural and political isolation of the southern states was exacerbated by the eventual merging of midwestern with northern economic interests, a union ordained by such technological triumphs as the completion of the Erie Canal, tying the Great Lakes region with New York, and by the subsequent forging of numerous east-west rail links between the

Midwest and the Northeast. As Charles Sydnor notes, by the 1830s the South had begun to think of itself as a region both distinct and beleaguered. "Perhaps the chief product of the troublesome early 1830s," he writes, "was the strong charge of emotion added to matters that had hitherto been on the level of thought and calculation. In the previous decade, something of a Southern platform on national issues had evolved. Clashes over that platform convinced many Southerners that their interests were seldom respected by the rest of the nation and that the fabric of their way of life was being destroyed. A feeling of oppression, of defeat, and even of desperation was engendered."[11]

This sense of cultural beleaguerment in the South produced a corresponding consciousness of and pride in the region's distinctiveness. As part of their defensive response to ever sharper attacks on slavery from the North, southerners became more and more prone to assert the superiority of their planter aristocracy to the more materialistic and ruthlessly competitive Yankee. In the 1830s, English traveler George Featherstonhaugh observed that the great plantation owners considered themselves, "not without some reason, *the gentlemen of America;* looking down upon the trading communities in the Northern States, where slavery does not exist, with that habitual sense of superiority which men born to command—and above all other slaveholders—always cherish when they are placed in competition with men engaged in mercantile pursuits, whom they consider to be, by the nature of their avocations, incapable of rising to their level: to this feeling, the seeds of which are planted in infancy, is added a distrust sometimes amounting to hatred."[12]

Though they were decades away from secession, southerners of the 1830s saw themselves as distinct from northerners and had no wish to be simply lumped with them under the generic term *Yankee* or even *American.* "Even now," Featherstonhaugh pointed out, "there is nothing that a southern man resents so much as to be called a *Yankee,* a term which in the Southern States is applied exclusively to the New England people, and in quite a sarcastic sense." The Englishman found this sense of regional identity nowhere more refined than in South Carolina, the state that had produced John C. Calhoun and that would produce Preston Brooks. In response to Featherstonhaugh's query about his national identity, one planter replied, "If you ask *me* if I am an American, my answer is, no, sir, I am a South Carolinian."[13]

Even though the South's sense of regional identity was firmly established by the 1830s, very few southerners at that time would have gone so far as to assert that they were a separate race of people. Indeed, the overwhelming majority of them remained strongly nationalistic and devoted to the Union and to its expansion. This fervent nationalism dominated Dixie's politics through the 1840s. Southerners were among the most vigorous proponents of the war with Mexico, and they were equally unified in their conviction that the nation was destined to move westward to the shores of the Pacific, for in this movement south and west they saw the potential for the expansion and the survival of their peculiar institution.

During the 1840s, southern periodicals frequently expressed their undiluted faith in America's expansion and in its glorious future. *DeBow's Review* was first among these magazines. The same publication that in 1860 would proclaim the irrepressible hostility of the North for the South relentlessly championed the nation's Manifest Destiny in an 1847 issue. "Westward," it proclaimed, "is the tide of progress, and it is rolling onward like the triumphant Roman chariot, bearing the eagle of the republic or the empire, victorious ever in its steady but bloodless advances." Skeptics, especially New England abolitionists, might argue that in light of the war then being conducted in Mexico the advance of the American empire was hardly "bloodless." But the *DeBow's* editors judged the war to be a glorious event, divinely designed, like the more peaceful settlement of the American plains, to lead "the institutions, the laws, the arts, the commerce of this country . . . step by step, upon the nations south and west of us." And might not northerners view as ominous the expansion of one of these institutions, the institution of slavery, in the direction of Mexico and the Caribbean? The writer acknowledged that with respect to slavery, "some sentiments of distrust and resentment [were] occasionally uttered" outside the South. But he remained confident in a common patriotism that would transcend sectional differences over issues such as slavery. "The mass of the northern people," he asserted, "with all their moral principle, their love of the institutions of the country . . . never will sacrifice the Union for a mere abstract idea of individual liberty."[14]

Within a few years it would become clear to southerners that northerners were far more committed to the "mere abstract idea of individual liberty" than the South had imagined. But through the 1840s the large majority of people in both regions saw their national destiny as a common one, and they saw themselves as members of a common American race. Senator Thomas Hart Benton of Missouri expressed the concept of a single race in 1846 when he celebrated the nation's expansion into the Oregon Territory. "Since the dispersion of man upon earth," he proclaimed, "I know of no human event, past or to come, which promises a greater, and more beneficent change upon earth than the arrival of the van of the Caucasian race (the Celtic-Anglo-Saxon division) upon the border of the sea which washes the shore of eastern Asia."[15] In designating Americans as members of the "Celtic-Anglo-Saxon" branch of the white race Benton was offering an expansive racial definition that included Americans of English, German, Scotch, Irish, Welsh, and French descent. Excepting African slaves, his American race incorporated nearly all ethnic groups then residing in significant numbers in 1840s America. The Missouri senator was essentially proclaiming one white American race spreading north, south, and west from sea to shining sea.

The *DeBow's Review*'s enthusiastic embrace of Manifest Destiny and Thomas Hart Benton's trumpeting of America's common racial origins—pronouncements that commonly characterized southern rhetoric in the 1840s—virtually ceased after 1850. The congressional debates that accompanied the passage of the Compromise of 1850 forced southerners to acknowledge that the prospect of an expanding slave empire made possible by victory over Mexico might prove to be illusory. California, the greatest prize of the Mexican war, now petitioned to enter the Union as a free state. With the admission of California, the slave states lost their parity in the Senate, and they were recompensed only with the uncertain possibility that the territories of Utah and New Mexico might one day choose to enter the Union as slave states. The South's bitter sense that it had gained little or nothing from the Compromise of 1850 was exacerbated by subsequent northern opposition to the enforcement of the Fugitive Slave Act, one of the key sections of the Compromise.

A majority of the South's representatives had opposed the ambitious legislative initiative of Henry Clay and Daniel Webster, and within months of its passage an even greater majority of the South's constituents would have probably endorsed the sentiments of one of the Compromise's most vociferous opponents, Senator Jefferson Davis of Mississippi. Davis warned the Senate that the legislation was but part of a larger northern scheme that effectively represented a declaration of war upon the southern way of life. "A large part of the non-slaveholding states," he asserted, "have declared war against the institution of slavery. They have announced that it shall not be extended, and with that annunciation have coupled the declaration that it is a stain upon the Republic—that it is a moral blot which should be obliterated."[16] For Davis the Compromise was no compromise at all. Its aim was not the balancing of sectional interests but the annihilation of southern interests.

Jefferson Davis's dire conclusions may have seemed paranoid to many northerners, but they reflected the state of mind of many southerners in 1850. The sense of desperation that Charles Sydnor described as part of the southern mentality in the 1830s became much more pronounced in the acrid aftermath of the Compromise of 1850. Three years earlier very few in the South would have invoked the specter of disunion. Beginning in 1850, however, secessionist voices were increasingly raised, and they were seriously entertained by a growing number of southerners. Defenders of the South were more determined that attacks on slavery and on southern culture must, in the words of one essayist, "cease now and for ever—cease, quietly and voluntarily if possible, but if not, then terminate in the night of violence and bloodshed."[17] Benton's vision of a common American blood dominating the continent from Atlantic to Pacific had swiftly been transformed by southern imagination into an American nightmare of bloody civil strife.

The events of the turbulent 1850s did nothing to allay the South's growing anxiety and desperation. The Compromise of 1850 could not maintain harmony between slaveholding and non-slaveholding states; the Kansas-Nebraska Act of 1854 quickly brought "bloody Kansas" to the forefront of the nation's consciousness; and the caning of Charles Sumner in 1856, the Dred Scott decision of 1857, and the raid of John Brown on Harpers Ferry in 1859 ensured that that consciousness would remain continually inflamed and that sectional polemic would become increasingly strident. In reaction to these events the nation's sense of deep and irreconcilable differences between northerners and southerners simply exploded. To measure this shift in sectional identity from a southern perspective, one need only contrast the 1860 *DeBow's Review* article on northern hostility to the South with the journal's enthusiastic 1847 endorsements of Manifest Destiny.[18]

As southerners desperately sought to defend to defend their plantation system from what they perceived as unprovoked northern aggression, it is not surprising that they also sought to define themselves as different from and superior to northerners. What better way to defend slavery than by adducing the superior class of men and women, the planters and their ladies, who were the natural social products of such a system? Indeed, "The Basis of Northern Hostility to the South" suggests that not only the notion of southern class superiority but also a notion of race superiority could be employed as part of an effective apologia for the southern way of life. Thomas Hart Benton's national racial myth, the myth of a common "Celtic-Anglo-Saxon" blood, was soon discarded by the South in favor of a sectional racial mythology that would explain in a seemingly rational and scientific manner both the distinctiveness and the superiority of the southern "race" in America.

During the 1850s, as the South grew ever more alienated from the North, a racial mythology that posited a southern inheritance of aristocratic Norman blood became irresistibly appealing to Dixie's apologists. As Jared Gardner has observed, "Growing regional divisions between North and South prompted metaphors of race to describe distinctions that were regional, political, economic—anything but racial."[19] Northerners were also prone, as we shall see, to employ racial myth to explain regional differences, but southerners more persistently and more flamboyantly cultivated the notion that they were members of a separate and superior race. It was they who, in order to preserve their social structure and their culture, found themselves moving inexorably toward secession, and it was they also who found themselves in the position of having to create a new southern national identity. Racial mythology would be a key element in this flowering of southern nationalism before and during the Civil War.

It is hardly surprising that Dixie's great planters, its social and political elite, would have trumpeted in their most prestigious periodicals a self-flattering Anglo-Norman race myth and would have used such a myth to justify both their peculiar institution of chattel slavery and, ultimately, their determination to secede from the Union. But would the vast majority of southerners, plain farmers who owned few or no slaves at all, have displayed any interest in such a myth? Indeed, might they not have been actively hostile toward a concept employed to buttress a social and economic system that displayed no particular interest in ameliorating the often harsh conditions of their daily lives?

Modern criticism has brought these legions of plain southern farmers into the historical light of day; it has also thoroughly demolished the notion that the nineteenth-century South was a racial and cultural monolith, a concept crucial to those who propagated the moonlight-and-magnolias myth of a Cavalier South suffused with the blood of Norman warriors. Michael O'Brien's recently published *Conjectures of Order* provides a compelling description of the varied ethnic strains that combined to produce antebellum southern culture, a variety at least equal to that which was to be found in the northern states. And David Hackett Fischer has offered a richly detailed account of colonial immigration patterns in America between 1629 and 1775 that throws fascinating light on two discrete waves of settlement that carried to the southern colonies markedly different and sometimes oppositional sets of folkways.[20]

After decades of modern skepticism, Fischer's impressive revisionist history reestablishes the profound significance to the South's cultural formation of the migration from southern England to the colony of Virginia of "a small Royalist elite and large numbers of indentured servants" between 1642 and

1675. The author also convincingly argues that the elite who led this migration brought with them a complex set of folkways that emphasized loyalty to king and established church and to an "elitist, hierarchical" social structure—a folkway fully deserving the appellation of Cavalier. But he also clearly establishes that fewer than 150 of the colony's families could boast an authentically elite English social pedigree and that the overwhelming majority of immigrants who entered the Old Dominion during the formative middle decades of the seventeenth century were indentured servants drawn from the lower orders of English society.[21] The Royalist and Cavalier culture that this Virginia settlement sowed in America was thus geographically restricted to the lands adjacent to the Chesapeake Bay and to the narrow coastal littoral that extends through the Carolinas to Georgia. It was also a culture imposed from above by an extraordinarily small number of elite planter families.

Of far greater numerical significance to the South was the fourth and final wave of British immigration to America from the north of Britain and Northern Ireland that flooded the colonies from 1718 until the eve of the Revolution in 1775 and settled initially in the Appalachian back country. This immigration consisted largely of "farmers and farm laborers who owned no land of their own, but worked as tenants and undertenants. A large minority were semiskilled craftsmen and petty traders." These immigrants, a people who became loosely known as Scots-Irish, vastly outnumbered the gentry-descended Englishmen who established the Cavalier folkway in Tidewater Virginia; the territory in which they eventually established themselves was also much larger than the relatively restricted dimensions of the Cavalier settlement. Fischer observes that the Scots-Irish became the dominant culture across a swath of land that extended from southwestern Pennsylvania down through the highlands and foothills of the colonial South into the interior of the Old Southwest and eventually across the Mississippi into Arkansas, Missouri, and Texas.[22] Scots-Irish immigrants thus dominated the lands that would eventually comprise the major portion of the southern Confederacy.

Scots-Irish settlers carried with them and reestablished in the South a folkway from the borderlands of northern Britain strikingly different from the Cavalier culture of Tidewater Virginia. It was a way of life characterized by a "militant Christianity" and by social egalitarianism, an unbending sense of personal pride, and contempt for those very ordered hierarchies that had been sown in the soil of the coastal South by Cavaliers from southern England. The settlers who came to dominate the interior South may have been poor in terms of possessions, but not in terms of their sense of self-worth. As Fischer observes, "Their pride was a source of irritation to their English neighbors, who could not understand what they had to feel proud about."[23]

Fischer's comprehensive view of America's colonial settlement, particularly his description of the South's settlement by two markedly different waves of British immigrants with markedly different folkways and cultures, fittingly returns students of southern history and culture to W. J. Cash's groundbreaking twentieth-century study, *The Mind of the South*. In this work Cash highlights Dixie's gigantic social paradox, a paradox rooted in the colonial South and reflected in the tension Fischer records between Cavalier and northern British folkways. The brilliance of Cash's argument lies in his understanding of the bizarre way in which the South's proud and prickly Scots-Irish yeomen suffered a Cavalier culture to be superimposed upon the folkways they had brought with them from the British borderlands.

Cash understood that the essential southerner, "the man at the center," was not the Virginia aristocrat but the back-country pioneer farmer from whom the vast majority of present-day southerners could trace their ancestry. "This simple, rustic figure," he wrote, was "the true center from which the Old South proceeded—the frame about which the conditions of the plantation threw up the whole structure of the Southern mind." As Cash's phrasing suggests, Dixie's dominant population of pioneer farmers, rather than rejecting the hierarchic folkways of the Tidewater South, had allowed their yeoman ethos to be subsumed into the Cavalier ethos, achieving a strange, even grotesque, imaginative synthesis. "In the romantic simplicity of their thought-processes," Cash observed, Dixie's Scots-Irish yeomen "seem to have believed for conscious purposes that in acquiring land and Negroes they did somehow automatically become aristocrats."[24]

Cash recognized that not even the flinty imagination of a Presbyterian pioneer farmer was proof against the appeal of the aristocratic Virginia Cavalier. In the ante-bellum South every farmer was a Cavalier-manqué and every slave-owning planter a de facto aristocrat. These social assumptions became broadly shared articles of faith in the interior South during the decades that preceded the Civil War. Understanding as he did the southern yeoman's "romantic simplicity" of thinking, Cash would certainly not have been surprised by the observations of southern writers such as Henry Clay Lewis, a physician who practiced in the backwoods of Louisiana during the 1830s. "Every farmer," Lewis noted with wry irony, considered himself "a planter, from the 'thousand bailer' to the rough, unshaved, unkempt squatter, who raises just sufficient corn and cotton to furnish a cloak for stealing the year's supply."[25]

Even though the Cavalier ideal exerted a powerful hold over the minds of southerners of widely diverse backgrounds and social status, one still must wonder how the non-slaveholding majority could have so identified themselves with the tiny slaveholding elite that they would ultimately have been willing to sacrifice their property and their lives to defend the plantation system. Was it simply blind emotionalism that led enough small farmers to hurl themselves, in the words of Elizabeth Fox-Genovese and Eugene Genovese, "into a prolonged bloodbath to enable a proudly proclaimed slave republic to sustain itself for four ghastly years"? The Genoveses offer a more pragmatic and more satisfactory explanation for the seemingly quixotic behavior of the southern yeoman in the Civil War. They believe that the common opposition of planter and yeoman to the powerful forces of Yankee merchant capitalism cemented the bond between the two groups. The influence of merchant capital seemed destined to undermine the rural, self-sufficient way of life of both classes. The small farmer of the Alabama hill country might quietly despise the pretensions of his aristocratic neighbor in the Black Belt, but he would have agreed with him that local autonomy was to be defended and that the intrusion of northern economic interests was to be resisted.[26]

In addition to sharing the planters' aversion to outside economic forces, yeomen were often dependent on the large planters for ginning and selling their relatively few bales of cotton. The planters, for their part, were willing to extract their profits from the sweat of their slaves rather than from the sweat of their small-farm neighbors. "So long as the yeoman accepted the existing master-slave relation as either something to aspire to or something peripheral to their own lives," observe the Genoveses, "they were led step by step into willing acceptance of a subordinate position in society."[27]

Viewed from a contemporary historical perspective the subordination of yeoman to planter would not necessarily have been difficult or demeaning. Standing alongside the plantation master and helping him defend his interests was easier when the small farmer felt he was defending his own interests as well, when the planter was a personal acquaintance, a neighbor who lived just down the road, or when the farmer's family was linked—as was not infrequently the case—by ties of kinship with the planter's family. When one adds to this occasional bond of kinship what James McPherson describes as the more enduring "bond of race," the loyalty of the southern yeoman to the established plantation culture seems less quixotic.[28] Common economic interests combined with a common faith in white supremacy to assure that the majority of southern yeomen would remain loyal to the plantation elite, whether that elite resided on the tidal rivers of the Old Dominion, the Alabama Black Belt, or the Mississippi delta, and would subscribe with varying degrees of fervor to the Cavalier ethos that underlay this aristocracy.

It is unlikely that more than a handful of southern yeomen read or were aware of the polemical essays in Dixie's most prestigious periodicals that were trumpeting the region's vision of a Norman-blooded southern aristocracy. These articles, after all, would have been fashioned for the delectation of the more literate members of the South's social elite, and they would have been designed as well to provoke the consternation of northern intellectuals and abolitionists who were attacking southerners as products of a barbaric culture. But though the mass of plain southerners remained blissfully ignorant of the Norman race myth, the majority of them were assuredly conscious and proud of their allegiance to a southern way of life founded on the plantation system and the institution of slavery. They identified themselves—no doubt with varying degrees of intensity—with plantation culture. They may have been largely untouched by a polemical idea like the Norman race myth, but on the eve of the Civil War most of them would nevertheless have enthusiastically embraced a correlative idea: that in any prospective contest between North and South, southern blood would prove itself superior to the blood of skulking Yankee abolitionists.

As the nation moved toward the fateful election of 1860, an article in Richmond's influential *Southern Literary Messenger* joined the *DeBow's Review* essay in blithely ignoring the South's Scots-Irish cultural core and urging upon its readers the idea that the peoples of the northern and southern states represented uniform and starkly different races. Indeed, the articulation of the thesis in the *Messenger* was virtually identical to that of *DeBow's*. The author contended that northerners were primarily descended from the Puritans, who "constituted, as a class, the common people of England . . . and were descended of the ancient Britons and Saxons." These Saxon-descended Puritans were people of vigorous intellect, but they possessed no notion of honor. They were in fact fanatics, incapable of controlling their passions. "Being devotional, they push their piety to the extremes of fanaticism,—being contentious withal, they are led to attack the interests of others, merely because those interests do not comport with *their* ideas of right."[29]

In contrast to this land of inbred extremists, the writer described a "Southron" race descending from the English Norman aristocracy and manifesting that culture's generous, honorable, and elite character. The southern states, and most significantly Virginia, had been settled, by and large, by Cavaliers "directly descended from the Norman Barons of William the Conqueror, a race distinguished, in its earliest history, for its warlike and fearless character, a race, in all time since, renowned for its gallantry, its chivalry, its gentleness and its intellect."[30] For the writer of this essay, as for the writer of the *DeBow's* essay, southerners represented a type of master race divinely ordained by heritage and blood lineage to rule and best qualified to control racially inferior black slaves with humanity tempered by firmness.

In the midst of vexing and perilous events, it must have been pleasant for cultivated southerners to read in their most distinguished magazines these descriptions of a superior southern race in whose veins the blood of Norman conquerors coursed. It remained for another *Southern Literary Messenger* writer to give this racial fantasy an appropriately scientific veneer. In an essay entitled "Northern Mind and Character," the author assigned northerners to "that branch of the human family made up of the Saxons and Britons . . . which, by long isolation from the rest of the Teutonic families, have acquired differences so marked as almost to constitute them a 'permanent variety' in the classification of Race."[31] Biological terminology was now being employed to support the bizarre notion that northerners and southerners were profoundly different—so different that they were a hair's-breadth away from constituting "permanent" subdivisions of the human species.

By 1860, southern polemicists were employing racial arguments on two fronts. As part of the defense of the institution of chattel slavery, they proclaimed the superiority of the white race over the black race. And as part of a defense against northern attacks on the barbarity of southern culture, they advocated a racial myth that demonstrated to the region's satisfaction the superiority of a southern American race over a separately descended northern American race. This racial mythologizing might strike one today as a bizarre cultural and intellectual phenomenon. But as James McPherson has observed, it was for its time merely one of a number of nineteenth-century expressions of "ethnic nationalism," similar to those embraced by Germans, Poles, Hungarians, Greeks, and other peoples who were striving during this period for independent nationhood. And like its European counterparts, Dixie's racial mythology proposed as one of its articles of faith "a belief in the common genetic or biological descent" of the its people.[32]

The South's Norman race myth ultimately became, in McPherson's astute phrasing, "an instrumental construction of a genealogy to serve a cultural or political end." By 1861 that end was clear: the establishment of a sovereign southern Confederacy. "Already dependent upon racial arguments to defend the logic of their social system and their daily lives," writes Drew Gilpin Faust, "southerners eagerly embraced the notion of a racially determined nationalism."[33] By the time southern guns had fired on Fort Sumter, Dixie's newly articulated race mythology had became part and parcel with its nascent nationalism. Together these ideas would help to propel the South into the cataclysm of civil war.

Southern writers and opinion-makers who used respected regional periodicals such as *DeBow's Review* and the *Southern Literary Messenger* as platforms for promoting the idea of a Norman-descended southern race could not have chosen a more propitious moment for concocting such a racial fantasy, for at no point in western history were educated people more inclined to accept the validity of the idea that there were clearly delineated physical, mental, and even moral differences between various races—distinctions that could be measured by scientific methods. As a result of remarkable advances in biological and human sciences between the late eighteenth and early nineteenth centuries, human physical and mental characteristics were understood by a growing number of scientists to be biologically determined. By the 1850s, most educated Victorians had come to believe that we could, in the words of Kwame Appiah, "divide human beings into a small number of groups, called 'races,' in such a way that all the members of these races shared certain fundamental, biologically heritable, moral and intellectual characteristics with each other that they did not share with members of any other race."[34]

The idea that race was a result of biological inheritance had been virtually unknown before 1800. For thousands of years racial differences had been viewed either in the Greek way, as a product of environmental factors such a soil and climate, or in the Hebrew way, as a reflection of the relationship established by an original ancestor between a people and God.[35] Not until the Middle Ages was the word *gens,* or people, employed to suggest a concept similar to the modern concept of race. But medieval Europeans recognized many different peoples, such as Africans, Romans, Greeks, and Gauls, and like their classical ancestors, they tended to explain differences in physique or character between these peoples as reflections of external influences such as climate and terrain.[36]

The traditional understanding of race as a product of environmental forces remained unchallenged through the sixteenth and seventeenth centuries— centuries during which the great scientific advances were in the areas of physics and astronomy. Indeed, the devotion of the great minds of the eighteenth century to the concept of human equality was a reflection of the scientific understanding of that period. Democratic doctrine rested, according to William Stanton, "upon biology, the descent of all men from the Creation; it rested upon morphology, the similarity of men's bodies; and it emphasized the importance of environment in shaping men's biological and mental structure."[37] Thomas Jefferson, a distinguished product of the Age of Enlightenment, would have agreed with the great botanist Linnaeus. All races of men were one species. Such differences as existed between these races were attributable to environmental influences.

In 1800 the monogenism of Linnaeus and Jefferson, the idea that all men were members of a single human species, was a universally embraced article of scientific faith. By the opening decades of the nineteenth century, however, the doctrine was being questioned by an increasing number of scientists, who were subjecting human beings to the same kind of biological investigation and classification that had been trained on plants and animals in the eighteenth century.[38] At the same time as biologists began to turn their attention to the human species, explorers were penetrating the last undiscovered portions of the globe and were discovering an ever-greater number of races with significantly different head shapes and sizes, skin colors, and characters. If the Creation had occurred in 4004 B.C., as Archbishop Usher had confidently announced in 1650, more and more scientists were beginning to doubt that such marked differences in human morphology and human nature could have been produced by environmental forces alone over such a relatively short period of time.

As the nineteenth century advanced, support for monogenism steadily declined among scientists. By 1860, many if not most members of the English scientific community embraced the counterdoctrine of polygenism, the idea that "the human races were separated from each other by such profound mental, moral, and physical differences as to constitute separate biological species of human kind." Polygenism rejected the idea that all men had descended from common male and female ancestors, and it consequently brought science into direct conflict with the Genesis account of the Creation. Regardless of scripture, Scottish anatomist Robert Knox believed that physical evidence carried reputable scientists to an unavoidable conclusion. In his highly influential *The Races of Man*, published in 1850, Knox proclaimed, "With me race, or hereditary descent, is everything; it stamps the man." He further asserted that human beings ought to be viewed "scientifically . . . as they now exist, divided as they are, and seem always to have been, into distinct races."[39]

Though they were separated by three thousand miles of ocean from the monogenesis-polygenesis debates in England and on the Continent, American scientists shared a keen interest in the subject and even made their own considerable scientific contributions toward settling the questions of man's origins. In 1839 Dr. Samuel George Morton's *Crania Americana* measured significantly different average cranial capacities between the skulls of eighty-seven Caucasians, eighty-three Mongolians, eighty-one Malays, eighty American Indians, and seventy-eight Ethiopians. Though he did not comment directly on the sensitive question of polygenesis, Morton did believe that the significant differences in the average brain capacity of the five races he had measured could not be entirely accounted for by environmental influences; he speculated that the morphological differences his study had quantified might have been established by God at the time of the biblical Dispersion. Readers who fretted about the potential conflict between Morton's findings and Genesis were perhaps mollified by the fact that the Caucasian race could claim an average cranial capacity larger than any of the other races he had measured.[40]

Five years after *Crania Americana*, Dr. Morton published *Crania Aegyptiaca*, in which he directed his talent for measurement toward the skulls of ancient Egyptians and their Nubian slaves. Here he concluded that the average cranial capacity of Egyptians exceeded that of their Negro slaves and that the descendants of the Pharaohs were themselves a composite race combining Caucasian, Semitic, Austral-Egyptian, and Negro influences. Particularly unsettling to orthodox Christian readers was Morton's assertion that the Egyptian skulls were significantly older than the 4004 B.C. date of Bishop Usher's Creation.[41]

Despite the growing alarm of Christian intellectuals roused by the publication of works such as Morton's, the tendency of American science reflected that of Europe. Scientists in both the Old and the New World were inclined to identify ever-larger numbers of distinct races. American physician Charles Pickering, in his 1848 work entitled *Races of Man and Their Geographical Distribution*, meticulously described eleven separate racial groups. Though like Samuel Morton he tried to steer clear of a direct confrontation with Christianity, asserting that all of his eleven races had descended from "one common parent," he also called the basic premises of monogenesis into question by declaring the existence of these races to be a "phenomenon independent of climate."[42] Pickering thereby implicitly affirmed the position of the polygenists by suggesting that racial differences were the result of biological inheritance.

In the three decades preceding the Civil War, southern scientists were heavily involved in espousing the new doctrine of polygenesis. Indeed, one of its most effective and controversial exponents was Dr. Josiah Clark Nott, a native of South Carolina who became a leader in the intellectual circles of Mobile, Alabama. In 1844 Dr. Nott published *Two Lectures on the Natural History of the Caucasian and Negro Races,* in which he brought to bear his theory of separately descended human races on a subject close to the hearts of nearly all white southerners: the degree of difference between white men and black men. In this work Nott contended "that there is a genus, Man, comprising two or more species—that physical causes cannot change a White man into a Negro, and that to say this change has been affected by a direct act of providence, is an assumption which *cannot be proven.*"[43]

Clearly anticipating the opposition of orthodox Christians to the concept of multiple creations of separate human species, Josiah Nott was intent on persuading his southern readers of the utility of polygenesis. If whites and Negroes were indeed biologically distinct species, this fact invested the cultural and social separation of the races and even the institution of slavery itself with a sort of scientific imprimatur. Viewed through the lens of polygenesis, slavery might even be seen as a philanthropic enterprise. "If there be several *species* of the human race," Nott conjectured, "if these species differ in the perfection of their moral and intellectual endowments—if there be a law of nature opposed to the mingling of the black and white races—I say if all these things be true, what an unexplored field is opened to the view of the philanthropist!"[44]

Emboldened by a climate of opinion increasingly receptive to polygenesis, in 1854 Nott published *Types of Mankind,* written with his colleague George Gliddon. This work expressed unambiguously the elements of the new theory. "In speaking of Mankind," Nott wrote, "we regard as *Types* those primitive or original forms which are independent of Climatic or other Physical influences. All men are more or less influenced by external causes, but these can never act with sufficient force to transform one Type into another." For Nott and Gliddon, human types clearly represented separate biological species. "We recognize," they affirmed, "no substantial differences between the terms *types* and *species*—permanence of characteristics belonging equally to both."[45]

The cause of polygenesis received valuable support from another member of Mobile's scientific community, Henry Hotze. In 1856 Hotze, a polemicist and southern apologist who during the Civil War would serve as the Confederacy's premiere propagandist in England, translated and contributed an "Analytical Introduction" to a work by French diplomat, writer, and racial theorist Count Arthur de Gobineau, entitled *The Moral and Intellectual Diversity of Races*. This work was a distillation of the ideas de Gobineau had presented in his four-volume *Essay on the Inequality of Human Races* (1853–55). In this widely read ethnological study, de Gobineau had anticipated the Nazi theories of the twentieth century by dividing mankind into three races—white, black, and yellow—and by proclaiming the white or "Aryan" race superior to all others. *The Moral and Intellectual Diversity of Races* set forth as "established beyond dispute" the proposition "that a certain general physical conformation is productive of corresponding mental characteristics." "A human being, whom God has created with a negro's skull and general *physique*," de Gobineau contended, "can never equal one with a Newton's or a Humboldt's cranial development, though," he concluded with pleasing piety, "the soul of both is equally precious in the eyes of the Lord."[46]

De Gobineau's ideas comported easily with those of the Mobile advocates of polygenesis. Indeed, Hotze used the introduction of his 1856 translation to proclaim the victory of the theory of separately descended races in scientific circles: "The distinguishing physical characteristics of what we term races of man are recognized by all parties, and whether these races are *distinct species* or *permanent varieties* only of the same cannot affect the subject under investigation. In whatever manner the diversities among the various branches of the human family may have originated, whether they are primordial or were produced by external causes, their permanency is now generally admitted."[47]

Nott and Gliddon's *Types of Mankind* appeared three years, and Henry Hotze's translation of de Gobineau five years, after the death of Samuel Morton, the man whose measurements of human skulls had originally advanced the cause of polygenesis in American scientific circles. By the time of Morton's death, scientists from all parts of America, but most notably the South, embraced the new theory. As William Stanton observes, by the 1850s "the principal tenets of the doctrine that was coming to be called 'polygenism' had been established. If not all American naturalists had been captured, at least none now openly opposed the doctrine."[48]

By the 1850s, polygenesis prevailed in scientific circles from Boston and New York to Charleston and Mobile, as it did in Paris and London, because in a pre-Darwinian era it seemed to be a theory more consonant with observable physical phenomena than monogenesis. But there is little doubt that the idea of multiple human species was also appealing because it obliquely affirmed the superiority of the Caucasian race over all others. As Nancy Stepan has pointed out, by the mid-nineteenth century "a very complex edifice of thought about human races had been developed in science" that was "implicitly" racist in its social implications. After all, the facts of average racial cranial capacity spoke for themselves. And if anyone questioned the significance of the Caucasian's superior brain size, he had only to consider the triumph of Western science, technology, and culture, which in the nineteenth century was sweeping all before it. Kwame Appiah has shrewdly observed that science in the Victorian period validated and gave intellectual respectability to attitudes that would be deemed blatantly racist today: "The notion that all races were equal in their capacities was a distinctly minority view. Even those who insisted that all human beings had the same rights largely acknowledged that non-white people lacked either the intelligence or the vigor of the white races: among which the highest, it was widely agreed, was the Indo-European stock from which the Germanic peoples emerged."[49]

If the theory of polygenesis appealed to both Europeans and Americans by implicitly affirming white superiority, it also came with liabilities. Chief among these was its not-so-implicit repudiation of the biblical account of the descent of man through Adam and Eve. Proponents of the theory tended to finesse the problem by soft-peddling or ignoring its challenge to the Bible and emphasizing instead its "arguments for innate mental and physical differences between races," arguments that enjoyed widespread acceptance at the time. This tactic was particularly effective in the South, where polygenesis, in the words of Reginald Horsman, "permeated all types of periodicals—literary, political, agricultural—at the earliest date and assumed the strongest form." Southerners, not surprisingly, gravitated toward any scientific theory about racial distinctions that might justify the institution of chattel slavery "by proving that the Negroes were innately incapable of benefiting from freedom."[50]

In 1839, the same year that Samuel Morton published his cranial measurements, the *Southern Literary Messenger* was busily engaged in enumerating distinct races and trumpeting the superiority of Caucasians. This tendency to favor the new racial theories was apparent in all major southern periodicals. The *Southern Quarterly Review* published in 1845 a spirited defense of Nott's *Caucasian and Negro Race*. The fact that the magazine felt it necessary to publish a defense suggests that not all southerners were willing to accept an understanding of race that undermined biblical authority. But in the end, how could the region's intellectuals resist a theory that led to such an exalted view of the white race? Polygenesis proffered the separate biological development of Caucasian man who, in Nott's opinion, differed "from all other races: he is humane, he is civilized, and progresses. He conquers with his head, as well as with his hand.... [The] Caucasian has been often master of the other races—never their slave.... All the great sciences are of Caucasian origin; all inventions are Caucasian; literature and romance come of the same stock.... No other race can bring up to memory such celebrated names as the Caucasian race. The Chinese philosopher, Confucius, is an exception to the rule."[51]

By the 1850s, southern periodicals were thoroughly devoted to the theory of polygenesis. In his enthusiastic assessment of Nott and Gliddon's *Types of Mankind,* an 1854 reviewer for *DeBow's* aligned himself solidly in the authors' camp. "All history and all science declare for a plurality of origins," he declared. "We can discover no time, however remote, in which men and animals were not just as they are now; nor is there a solitary case on record of one race or species being transformed into another, by external causes." As for the conflict between polygenism and Genesis, "true religion," he benignly affirmed, "will ever be found going hand in hand with science." In the same issue another writer magisterially dismissed monogenesis as a serious scientific theory. "The doctrine of the Unity of Race, so long believed by the world, is ascertained to be false," he announced. "We are not all descended from one pair of human beings. This fact is now as well established in the scientific world as that a horse cannot produce a cat or a lion a mouse." The *Southern Literary Messenger* joined in declaring the demise of monogenesis. "Ethnology," it proclaimed, had "settled this question" in favor of polygenesis.[52]

Of course it is essential to remember that if the South's most distinguished periodicals were promoting the Norman race theory to a relatively small and elite group of southern readers, they were advocating polygenesis to an even tinier audience: those few intellectual southerners who combined an interest in scientific method with a skeptical attitude toward biblical revelation. By the 1850s W. J. Cash's "man at the center" was far more likely to be a Presbyterian, Methodist, or Baptist farmer from the clay hills of the region's interior than a tolerant, casually observant Episcopal planter from the Virginia or Carolina Tidewater. And although it was true, as Elizabeth Fox-Genovese and Eugene Genovese have recently observed, that during the colonial and Revolutionary periods the South's coastal elite had commonly displayed religious attitudes distinctly flavored by "Deism and skepticism," such casual and condescending attitudes toward established Christianity were fast disappearing by the 1830s. With its peculiar institution under increasingly virulent attack from the North, southerners of all classes and religious persuasions drew together to present a common conservative theological front. Casual and Deistically inclined religious opinions were discouraged and suppressed. By the 1850s "the sedate style of the low country Episcopalians and the shouting Baptist and Methodist congregations of the frontier displayed a common theological orthodoxy and social conservatism."[53]

Polygenesis could be enthusiastically advocated by southern periodicals in the midst of an increasingly conservative religious climate in part because the audience of readers for such opinions was so small. But though polygenesis and orthodox Christianity could never have been completely compatible in the antebellum South, the absolute unity between southern advocates of polygenesis and southern Calvinists on the matter of white racial supremacy guaranteed that polygenesis and religious fundamentalism would coexist on relatively comfortable if not entirely friendly terms. For southern apologists, science as well as biblical exegesis would be crucial in justifying Dixie's peculiar institution.

From Louisiana lawyer John Fletcher to Virginia Presbyterian divine Robert L. Dabney, some of the South's most formidable intellects would be employed in constructing equally formidable Christian defenses of slavery, using copious support from both Old and New Testaments to demonstrate that the holy scripture conveyed a clear truth: "that the relation of master and slave is perfectly lawful and right, provided only its duties be lawfully fulfilled." To this scriptural support of slavery southern theologians added the bleak necessity of the Calvinistic theological perspective. Dabney recognized in the most fiercely Presbyterian way that though slavery might not be "the *beau ideal* of the social organization," there was "a true evil in the necessity of it." This true evil, however, was not the institution itself "but the ignorance and vice in the laboring classes, of which slavery is the useful and righteous remedy." Ultimately, then, for the southern Calvinist "the propriety of slavery" rested upon "the fact that man is depraved and fallen."[54]

Implicit in the southern Christian's assertion of the depravity of man was the corollary racist assumption that of all depraved men, the black slave was the most inferior and bleakly fallen. Absent the theological concept of man's being "fallen," Dixie's forward-looking scientific rationalists and its Bible-thumping Calvinists were in near-perfect agreement on the Negro's physical, mental, and moral inferiority. For southern scientist Josiah Nott, such inferiority made separation of the races, and implicitly slavery, a scientific "law of nature." For southern Christian John Fletcher, it confirmed the Creator's intention that the master "secure to the slave that protection and government which the slave is too degenerate to supply himself." For Nott, no other race could boast such "celebrated names as the Caucasian race." Fletcher was correspondingly intrigued by the idea of a "curious experiment" that would determine how many generations "under the most favorable treatment" it would take for blacks to produce a "Moses, or a David" or even a "Newton."[55] Racial assumptions of the region's scientists and of its religious apologists fit like hand to glove, and if polygenesis affirmed Dixie's vision of white racial mastery over biologically inferior black slaves, rank-and-file southerners were generally willing to ignore the impiety that lay at the heart of the theory.

For those southern readers who squirmed at the subversion of the Creation myth by the new theory of multiple descent, the *DeBow's Review* and *Southern Literary Messenger* were quick to remind them of the utility of polygenesis. If it was indisputably true that a "horse could not produce a cat or a lion a mouse," it was also just as certain that a Negro "till the end of time will still be a Negro, and the Indian still an Indian." The southern version of polygenism thus made the separation of the races not only morally right but also scientifically necessary: "Cultivation and association with the superior race," the writer affirmed, "produce only injury to the inferior one." The *Literary Messenger* expressed the implications of the new ethnology more bluntly. "Two races so essentially different in education, intellect, habits, tastes, cannot occupy the same territory as equals," the writer declared. "The inferior caste must be in subjugation to the higher."[56]

Under the banner of polygenesis, Dixie's learned men of science produced scholarly articles in which, to contemporary eyes, the most base and low-minded racial prejudices were clothed in scientific vestments. Writing in the *New Orleans Medical and Surgical Journal,* Dr. S. A. Cartwright assured his audience that the black race carried within its biological inheritance "a natural fondness for alcoholic drink and tobacco. They need no schooling, as the fair skin races do, to acquire a fondness for either." He also asserted that the Negro's secretions, flesh, membranes, and blood were darker than those of the white race and that Africans consumed less oxygen than whites. Cartwright believed that his less-oxygen theory was supported by the "uncontested" fact that the Negro's movements were "proverbially much slower" than those of their white masters, as was their "mental capacity."[57]

To southern exponents of the theory of fixed and discrete human species even such abstract and nonphysiological traits as "will" were biologically determined. Cartwright believed that Caucasians possessed "exaggerated will," while "the primordial cell germ of the Nigritians [had] no more potency than what [was] sufficient to form a being with physical power." In his essay entitled "Slavery in the Light of Social Ethics" Chancellor Harper added substantially to Cartwright's list of biologically heritable and racially inferior Negro character traits, including "indifference to personal liberty," "want of domestic affections," "insensibility to the ties of kindred," and absence of "noble sentiments."[58]

Polygenesis was thus a potent scientific addition to the stew of ideas that southern writers would serve up in the 1850s in defense of the South's plantation system. In giving indirect aid and comfort to racism, it was a theory that did damage wherever it was embraced. But the damage was particularly severe in the South. Here it became a scientific prop holding up the rickety edifice of chattel slavery. A few years later it would serve as the cornerstone of a nascent southern confederacy, a new nation founded, in Alexander Stephens's words, "upon the great truth that the negro is not equal to the white man; that slavery, subordination to the superior race, is his natural and moral condition."[59]

Southerners employed polygenesis first and foremost as a scientific confirmation that the white race was both distinct from and absolutely superior to the black race. But they also used the theory to impart a rational veneer to the argument that the South had been settled by a Norman-descended race far surpassing in culture and refinement the Saxon-descended Yankees who had settled New England and the other northern states. The new scientific theory thus helped to create an intellectual climate that was congenial to the development of the South's Norman-Saxon racial theory, as it had helped to assure intellectual validity for the idea of white supremacy. Discriminating between two white American races might have seemed both difficult and more scientifically suspect than establishing a clear division between blacks and whites. But as the nineteenth century progressed, advocates of polygenesis proved themselves willing to make ever more subtle and subjective racial distinctions in the name of science.

The history of polygenesis is the history of a scientific movement that tended toward the identification and description of a larger and larger number of human races. In 1839 Samuel Morton had identified five such races, and in 1848 Charles Pickering had described eleven—an increase of six races in nine years. Among these eleven the Caucasian race, which was termed by Pickering the "White or Arabian" race, must have struck the nineteenth-century mind as a remarkably heterogeneous collection of peoples. Given contemporary science's commitment to dividing humans into separate species, the division of the white race—composed, according to Pickering, of peoples as diverse as Arabians, Italians, Irish, English, and Scandinavians—into racial subclasses seemed both natural and logical. This subclassification of races is precisely what advocates of polygenesis proceeded to do.

No scientist spoke with more authority on the distinctions between European races than Robert Knox. In *The Races of Men* he clearly subscribed to the notion that temperament and character as well as physical characteristics such as skin color and hair type were part of a race's biological inheritance and were thus impervious to environmental modification. For Knox this biological determination of a race's character was most vividly in evidence in the contrast between the Celtic and Saxon races. He believed that the Saxon or Scandinavian race had been possessed from its inception to the present day with "inordinate self-esteem," "love of independence," and a "hatred for dynasties and governments." And he proclaimed that Saxons were "the only democrats on earth, the only race that truly comprehends the meaning of the word liberty."[60]

Knox was decidedly less favorably disposed toward the Celtic race, under which rubric he included the Scottish, Irish, Welsh, and French peoples. To this race he ascribed the anachronistic institutions of "feudality and primogeniture" as well as the curses of "dynasty and aristocracy." Though southerners might bask in the glow of their aristocratic Norman descent, for Knox this branch of the Celtic race had added little to the progress of civilization. Indeed, he considered the Norman conquest of England to be "the greatest calamity that ever befell England—perhaps, the human race." As for the notion that racial characteristics such as a tendency toward "feudality" and "dynasty" might be modified over time by environment, Knox averred that in Ireland "700 years of absolute possession" had not "advanced by a single step the amalgamation of the Irish Celt with the Saxon-English." Even in the United States the Celt was "distinct from the Saxon to this day," a fact that carried dire implications for the new nation. Knox did not believe that the Celt would ever understand "what we Saxons mean by independence; a military leader he understands; a factional fight; a fortified camp, for a capital is his delight."[61]

Southerners reading *The Races of Men* would certainly have taken exception to its condescending description of the Celtic race. But beyond the specific limning of Saxon and Celt there was an idea of great value that they could carry away from Knox's work. This was the idea that Normans and Saxons were in fact distinct racial subclasses with distinctive racial temperaments. Of additional value to southern race theory was the proposition that the Norman French combined with the Scots, Welsh, and Irish to make up the Celtic race. Under Knox's expansive definition nearly all southerners might be scientifically described as members of the same racial subdivision. Knox might rail at the feudality and aristocracy that he seems to have believed were biologically inherent in the Celtic temperament, but southerners proudly claimed these very qualities. Dixie's sectional apologists could and would use Knox's study to support their belief that they were a single distinctive race of people, more aristocratic and cultivated than the churlish Saxons who predominated north of the Mason-Dixon Line.

The appearance of Knox's influential work in 1850 was particularly propitious for the fabrication of a new southern race mythology. Prior to 1850, southerners would have had little use for Knox's Saxon-Celtic racial classifications. Indeed, as we have seen, in the 1840s Dixie's spokesmen were largely content to identify themselves with Americans living north of the Mason-Dixon Line as members of a single grand Anglo-Saxon racial stock. America's vanquishing of the Indians, its conquest of Mexico, and its enslavement of Africans were proofs of the superiority of this race. In 1843 a writer for the *Southern Quarterly Review* explained the imperial triumph of the white man both in North America and throughout the world by pointing out that the Anglo-Saxon race had retained "much of its energy and activity" while "long settled aborigines" had surrendered to enervation and yielded "without resistance to the enfeebling influences of a hot climate." The Anglo-Saxon's extraordinarily strong racial fiber prompted another *Quarterly Review* writer in 1846 to rhapsodize over the "sternness and robustness which characterize the German or Teutonic race." Indeed, he observed, one of the glories of nineteenth-century historical scholarship was that it allowed the scholar to "expatiate to his heart's content upon the greatness and excellence of our race!"[62] In the 1840s that race was generally defined as Teutonic, and it included nearly all white Americans, northerners as well as southerners.

If most southern writers were content to identify themselves with the nation's Manifest Destiny in the 1840s, by the 1850s a significant transformation was taking place within the region's psyche. Responding to ever more bitter political conflicts and to increasingly virulent attacks from northern abolitionists, southerners began to imagine themselves not as members of a common white American race but as members of a distinct southern race endowed with Norman English blood. A *Southern Quarterly Review* article on the "Mines of California," published in 1850, is a particularly telling commentary on this sudden shift in racial perspective. The essay views America's movement into California as a victory over a "degenerated" Spanish people. The writer concludes by expressing his thankfulness that "the Anglo-Normans . . . are the dominant race of this continent; and under Providence, may attain to universal moral dominion, at least."[63] *Anglo-Saxon*, the term hitherto preferred by the *Southern Quarterly Review*'s writers, was now eschewed in favor of *Anglo-Norman*. The writer celebrates America's Manifest Destiny, but the victory of a dominant American race is described in the same terms that would soon be used by the *Southern Quarterly Review* and by other southern periodicals to articulate a divisive regional racial mythology.

Dixie's concoction of a Norman-descended "southron" race was the inevitable product of bitter and dangerous sectional tensions. But the South could never have trumpeted its racial fantasies so confidently had not contemporary science furnished those fantasies with both a vocabulary and a rationale. Thanks to the contributions of scientists like Samuel George Morton and Josiah Nott, by the mid-nineteenth century race was understood to be, in the words of Nicholas Hudson, "an innate and fixed disparity in the physical and intellectual make-up of different peoples."[64] Measurements of human crania combined with the compilation of Europe's cultural, intellectual, and scientific achievements to demonstrate to the satisfaction of most educated people that the Caucasian race was superior to all others and that in fact it probably represented a separate human species. Works such as Robert Knox's carried the scientific enterprise of human classification even further, subdividing the Caucasian race into peoples such as Saxons or Teutons and Celts and endowing these peoples with distinct and unchanging physical, mental, and moral characteristics. Out of this peculiar scientific milieu came the South's vision of its lofty Anglo-Norman racial inheritance.

The fabrication of a southern race mythology in the tumultuous decade of the 1850s would provide crucial intellectual support for the region's movement toward secession and Confederate nationalism. By the time southern states began passing ordinances of secession in 1860 and 1861, scientifically sanctioned racial explanations of all kinds of human behavior had, as Boyd Shafer observes, "multiplied and [become] a standard explanation for the establishment of nations and for the kind of nation racialists thought ought to be established. The nation was or should be, so the racialists claimed, really a family held together by ties of blood, and each nation therefore had its own peculiar character and destiny."[65] To facilitate the establishment of a new nation, southerners needed to believe that they possessed in common their own unique blood inheritance. The Anglo-Norman racial myth invested the South with the exalted blood bonds that most southerners believed were essential to the establishment of their Confederacy, while nineteenth-century science invested the journalistic advocates of this aristocratic fantasy with the appearance of rationality and intellectual substance.

2
Ivanhoe, Race Myth, and the Walter Scott Cultural Syndrome

On September 2, 1845, the *Richmond Enquirer* printed the following dispatch from the Virginia resort of Fauquier White Sulphur Springs, dated August 26: "Tomorrow the long expected Tournament which has been preparing for some time will come off, and from appearances, the costumes and skill of the riders and knightly horsemen will rival any previous display of the kind, and do honor to those days of Chivalry." The tournament being announced so portentously in the *Enquirer* was a "Tournament of Knights," and Rollin Osterweis, in his *Romanticism and Nationalism in the Old South*, has provided a full account of the event that Richmond readers so eagerly anticipated. The objective of the competing Cavaliers was to spear from the back of a galloping horse a small ring that dangled from a cord eight feet above the ground. The knight who successfully speared the ring presented it to his lady and crowned her the "Queen of Love and Beauty." Competitors included gentlemen with the assumed names of Brian de Bois-Guilbert, Wilfred of Ivanhoe, and the Knight of La Mancha. They were urged on by a crowd of genteel spectators, who shouted, "Love of ladies—glory to the brave!" The reporter who described the pageantry at Fauquier White Sulphur Springs praised it as "the richest scene" he had ever observed "enacted on any theater." "It far surpassed," he concluded, "any Tournament we ever had."[1]

The Virginia tournament described in such admiring detail by the Richmond newspapers was typical of a number of such equestrian competitions that were held throughout the upper South in the 1840s and 1850s. Indeed, it can be understood as a symptom in antebellum Dixie of what might be described as the Sir Walter Scott cultural syndrome. It was a syndrome that easily blended with the Norman race myth, and it achieved full flower during roughly the same time period. Like the South's conceit of its aristocratic blood lineage, its knightly competitions were manifestations of what Osterweis has described as a unique type of romanticism, one that generated as "its most ambitious impulse" the concept of southern nationalism.

In his groundbreaking study of the antebellum South's cult of medievalism, Osterweis also argues convincingly that no writer was more fully or more enthusiastically incorporated into antebellum southern romanticism than Sir

Walter Scott.[2] Goaded by attacks from the North, accused of maintaining an inhumane and immoral social institution, southerners turned in their literature to Scott's romantic rendering, in ballad and novel, of medieval English and Scottish society. In these colorful period pieces the South found not only an escape from increasingly bitter sectional tensions but also an implicit justification of its own way of life. In southern eyes, Scott's courageous and honorable feudal lords and Scottish chiefs had been reborn in the nineteenth century in the form of the plantation aristocrat. The planter's slaves, like the medieval lord's serfs, were necessary to nurture the flowering of the region's aristocratic society.

So pervasive was Scott's influence on the southern imagination that many of the region's writers sought determinedly, if rather bizarrely, to incorporate his word coinages into their vocabulary. Thus, in many formal essays, "the Chivalry" came to stand for the southern planter, and Yankees became barbarous "Saxons" and "Goths." By the 1850s Scott's "southron" had become, according to Osterweis, "a borrowed badge of nationality." Even in the roughest and most remote sections of the Old Southwest, the cult of chivalry was grafted on to the original cultural stock of frontier folklore that had furnished the flamboyant and comic subject matter of southwestern humor. Osterweis observes that Scott's fictional characters "supplied the names for steamboats, canal barges, and even stagecoaches . . . between New Orleans and Tennessee."[3]

In stressing the importance of Sir Walter Scott's poetry and fiction to the development of the romantic imagination of the Old South, Osterweis was in some respects simply elaborating on an influence that critics of southern culture had long recognized as an important one. In 1917 Hamilton Eckenrode asserted in the *North American Review* that Scott had "beyond doubt" given "the South its social ideal, and the South of 1860 might be not inaptly nicknamed Sir Walter Scottland." W. J. Cash, in his seminal *The Mind of the South*, asserted that the Scottish bard had been "bodily taken over by the South and incorporated into the Southern people's vision of themselves."[4] All of these assessments were, in turn, derivative to some degree of the observations that had been made in the postbellum period by the South's greatest nineteenth-century writer, Mark Twain.

In his *Life on the Mississippi* Twain provided the most entertaining and humorous, if not the most accurate, estimate of Scott's influence on the southerner's self-image—an influence he believed to have been both profound and catastrophic. "But for the Sir Walter disease," he opined, "the character of the

Southerner—or Southron, according to Sir Walter's starchier way of phrasing it—would be wholly modern, in place of modern and medieval mixed, and the South would be fully a generation further advanced than it is." "It was Sir Walter," he went on to observe, "that made every gentleman in the South a Major or a Colonel, or a General or a Judge, before the war; and it was he, also, that made these gentlemen value these bogus decorations. For it was he that created rank and caste down there, and pride and pleasure in them. Enough is laid on slavery, without fathering upon it these creations and contributions of Sir Walter." For Twain the baleful influence of Scott's romantic claptrap could be viewed all too clearly in the Mardi Gras celebrations of postbellum New Orleans. To him such spectacles merely represented the South's continuing emotional enslavement to second-rate romantic clichés and "enchantments." The pernicious poetic and fictional enchantments of Walter Scott, he concluded, had done "measureless harm; more real and lasting harm, perhaps, than any other individual that ever wrote."[5]

Mark Twain was a master of satiric hyperbole, and there is good reason to believe that his denunciations of Walter Scott as the author of the South's inflated sense of aristocratic pride were as much expressions of the writer's mischievous imagination as they were of his serious critical convictions. It is doubtful that Twain fully believed that Scott's works had single-handedly created the South's infatuation with the myth of aristocracy. But beneath the wicked hyperbole and the subversive humor there was a hard kernel of truth in his attack on Sir Walter. Twain's remarkably acute understanding of the antebellum southern psyche detected the extraordinary empathy between what he considered to be Scott's outlandish artistic fabrications and the South's desperate and equally outlandish need to see itself as a highly cultivated society. He also understood that the region's defense of the institution of slavery was founded to a significant extent on notions of inherited social class and honor that derived not so much from southern realities as from southern fantasies, fantasies inspired by works such as *Ivanhoe*.

Despite the nuances of Twain's hyperbolic assault on Scott, a number of twentieth-century critics have taken his satiric attack at face value and seen fit to offer their own sober critical correctives. In *The South in American Literature* Jay B. Hubbell absolved Scott of most of the sins Twain imputed to him. "The influence of Scott may have had something to do with the growth of the Cavalier legend . . . and perhaps with the increased use of the phrase 'Southern chivalry.'" "But," he concluded, "the southern farmer had too keen a sense of realities to turn to *Ivanhoe* as a guide to living in the nineteenth century. . . .

Slavery, tobacco, cotton, and a warm climate were far more important factors in determining his way of life than anything he read."[6]

Some years earlier than Hubbell's landmark study of southern literature, G. Harrison Oriens had pointed out that Scott had been incredibly popular in the first half of the nineteenth century in all parts of America, not just in the South, and that southern reviewers had been just as liable to detail his fictional flaws as their northern counterparts had been. He maintained that though the Bard of Abbotsford "may have been a decorative influence in Southern life, [he] was certainly not a dictating force either in the preservation of an old order or in the defense of southern institutions." More recently Michael O'Brien has called into question both Twain's and Osterweis's assessments of Scott's influence on the mind of the Old South. He suspects that antebellum southerners read "Scott better than did Rollin Osterweis, that they, too, found his Scottish novels superior to his medieval." As for their enthusiasm for Scott's work, "they found him congenial," he believes, "because his standpoint so matched their own situation, buckling down to modernity while shedding a tear for the old ways. In short, Scott was resonant, not because he justified a static quasi feudalism, but because on balance he endorsed progress, and Southerners unquestionably felt themselves to be living in a progressive society."[7]

Southerners, as O'Brien contends, may have believed themselves to be members of a progressive society, but the emotions and sentiments that drew them to their knightly tournaments were anything but progressive. Indeed, in the mind of one southern gentleman who delivered the charge to competing cavaliers at an 1859 tournament in Hampton, Virginia, the days of chivalry had not passed away, at least not below the Mason-Dixon Line. While the orator acknowledged that no "courtly knight" went forth in modern-day Hampton "to shiver his lance in defense of his 'ladye love,' yet," he observed, "when my eye rests upon the galaxy of beauty and manliness here present, the scene tells me the days of chivalry are not gone." This chivalric spirit would survive in the South as long as southerners preserved "inviolate the faith and tradition of our fore-fathers—while we hold sacred the ties which now bind us together, 'honor in man, purity in women, and sanctity in religion,' the age of chivalry can never depart—no, never!"[8]

The gentleman who consecrated the endeavors of the Hampton knights seems to have sincerely believed, as did the spectators who cheered his remarks, that the character of the modern southern gentleman had been formed, "in great measure, upon knightly traditions." He observed:

Feudalism gave us the clay model; later civilization has produced the finished statue. It elevated the fair sex, and gave woman a position from which she has since steadily advanced until now we recognize her as a noiseless but important element in civilization. It gave to the passion of love a degree of refinement unknown to the world before its rise and elevated women while it softened our ruder sex.... Thus, in the elegant language of Sir Walter Scott, the institution of chivalry may be looked upon as "a beautiful and fantastic piece of frost-work which has dissolved in the beams of the sun; though we look in vain for the pillars and vaults, the cornices, and the fretted ornaments of the transitory fabric, we cannot but be sensible that its destruction has left upon the soil valuable tokens of its former existence."[9]

Clearly in the mind of the speaker and his Hampton audience some of the most valuable tokens of the chivalric spirit evoked by Scott's novels could be found on modern southern soil.

Perhaps southerners did believe, as Michael O'Brien argues, that they were members of a progressive society. But their tournaments and their oratorical charges indicate that they were also addicted to medieval-inspired fantasies of chivalry, aristocracy, female purity, and masculine honor that were drastically out of sync with the prevailing commercial spirit of America's burgeoning laissez-faire capitalism. In a rapidly industrializing nation, slavery was an increasingly glaring anachronism, and the defense of the institution required not an embracing of pragmatic and progressive realities but a retreat into what Mark Twain has aptly termed "enchantments." These Scott-inspired cultural enchantments were enacted against what was for the South an increasingly ominous historical backdrop.

The layout of the front page of the January 14, 1859, issue of the *Richmond Enquirer* that contained the account of the Hampton tournament graphically reveals the way southern medieval romanticism was being employed as an antidote to bitter and disturbing political realities. On the same page as the "Charge to the Knights in the Late Tournament at Hampton" there appears an article filled with dire and remarkably prescient warnings of the coming "elevation of an abolitionist to the Presidential chair" and the consequent consolidation of northern political power and "demoralization at the South."[10] One of the ways Dixie could respond to what seemed to be the inexorable rise of northern abolitionist power was by retreating into an idealized world of tournaments in which the region's courtly manliness was on display and over which the chaste spirit of the southern lady brooded. Scott's colorful historical canvases provided a perfect avenue of escape for a besieged slave-owning culture.

Given their increasing predilection for retreating from a troublesome present, it is not surprising that southern readers were early enthusiasts of Scott's ballads and historical romances. In 1820 a Kentucky reviewer of *Ivanhoe* admiringly observed that the Bard of Abbotsford was "known to almost every class of reader." Indeed, the writer observed that in Dixie "the avidity with which his works are sought for and perused immediately on their publication, is a sufficient proof of the estimation in which they are held." As the South drew ever closer to secession, it maintained its infatuation with Scott's works. In 1860, more than forty years after the publication of *Ivanhoe,* the *DeBow's Review* asserted, "Johnson, and Burke, and Sir Walter Scott, should have statues in every Southern capitol. Thus would our youth learn what are the sentiments and opinions that become gentlemen and cavaliers."[11] For this writer the region's ideal cultural triumvirate combined Samuel Johnson's neoclassical aesthetic conservatism and Edmund Burke's political conservatism with Walter Scott's romantic fictional resurrection of a chivalric medieval past. Together they constituted for the *DeBow's* critic a solid intellectual foundation for the perpetuation of the southern plantation culture.

The notion that the South could learn from Scott's works sentiments and ideals befitting a southern Cavalier was not merely an idle journalistic abstraction. At the beginning of the Civil War James Chesnut found in his favorite Scott novel, *The Bride of Lammermoor,* a paradigm for the behavior of the southern soldier in the battles to come. "As Ravenswood rode away," he wrote to his wife Mary Boykin Chesnut, "he passed his foes on the lawn, the lover who had supplanted him and the brother who had insulted him. He raised his hat in mute salutation as he looked them steadily in the eye. And they returned his bow with grave politeness. That is my idea of behavior to a foeman. I mean behavior worthy of the chivalry."[12]

The idea that the South embraced the work of Sir Walter Scott because he implicitly confirmed the region's sense of its social progressivism is a much more serious distortion of his influence than Twain's satire in *Life on the Mississippi.* Twain understood acutely the crucial link between Dixie's chivalric "enchantments" and its cultural self-intoxication and Scott's poetry and fiction. Could the knightly tournaments at Fauquier White Sulphur Springs and Hampton have been imagined without *Ivanhoe*? Would James Chesnut's notion of martial behavior been quite so refined had he not read works such as

The Bride of Lammermoor? One is tempted to the conclusion, closely approximating that of Twain, that had Scott not existed, the South would have found it necessary to invent him.

There is little doubt that in the years preceding the Civil War the writings of Sir Walter Scott profoundly influenced the South's image of itself as a socially stratified and highly cultivated slave society, one founded on the chivalric code of bravery, honor, and reverence for the sexually and racially pure southern lady. And there is also little doubt that the development of the myth of a distinctive southern race was also deeply influenced, both in its substance and in its terminology, by Scott's writing. Of all his works *Ivanhoe* had the strongest impact on the expression of southern race mythology in the 1850s. The Norman-Saxon racial paradigm that was articulated with increasing frequency in the decade preceding the Civil War was indebted almost as much to this medieval historical romance as it was to the scientific discourses of Josiah Nott and Robert Knox. Indeed, had Scott not written *Ivanhoe*, proponents of southern race theory would have been deprived of the operative terminology that so vividly expressed their belief in both the duality of America's racial inheritance and the superiority of southern blood.

Ivanhoe was for decades after its 1819 publication among the most admired of Scott's novels in the South. Southern readers would undoubtedly have agreed with antebellum Dixie's eminent novelist and critic William Gilmore Simms, who praised the work as "one of the most perfect specimens of the romance that we possess." Simms believed that it was not until *Ivanhoe*'s publication "that the general reader had any fair idea of the long protracted struggle for superiority between the Norman and Saxon people. Nay, it was not till that stately creation of art, with all its towers and banners, blazed upon the eyes of delighted nations, that the worthy burghers of London and Edinburgh were made aware that there had been any long continued conflict between these warring races."[13]

Simms was not entirely accurate in maintaining that before the appearance of *Ivanhoe* the English had been unaware of the conflict between the Norman and Saxon "races." Michael Banton's study of the history of race theory reveals that as early as the seventeenth century the Norman-Saxon racial dichotomy had provided intellectual buttressing for the defenders of the Parliamentary cause. Seeking to prove that they were the inheritors of the true English racial stock, Roundheads turned to the theories of Richard Verstegan. An English Catholic, Verstegan was forced to flee England in 1582, living in exile, first in

France, and later in Antwerp. Though he was a Catholic, his *Restitution of Decayed Intelligence* (1605), which passed through five editions by 1673, ironically became a valuable weapon in the polemical arsenal of English Puritans. The book asserted a proposition congenial to Roundheads: that the English people were descendants not of the Norman lords of William the Conqueror but "of the German race and were heretofore generally called Saxons."[14]

Verstegan believed that there was no real distinction between Germans and Saxons. "That our Saxon ancestors came out of Germanie, and made their habitation in Britaine" was, he contended, "no question." Having established the unity of German and Saxon, Verstegan went on to show "what a highly renowned and most honorable nation the Germans have always been, that thereby it may consequently appear how honorable it is for Englishmen to be from them descended." He proceeded to quote extensively from the Roman historian Tacitus's admiring descriptions of the Germans, quotations that highlighted that race's courage, honesty, nobility of character, devotion to monogamy, and hospitality.[15]

Of the many fine qualities of the German race, Verstegan believed the most admirable to be their tendency toward egalitarian social structures and their hostility toward absolute rulers. Certainly the Saxon ancestors of the modern-day Englishman recognized social classes, but, Verstegan observed, "if any of any the inferior degrees did through his vertues deserve well, or by honest industry attain unto riches, enabling himself thereby to assist the commonwealth, he was then advanced higher." Unlike the Norman conquerors, who maintained social and economic privilege through primogeniture, Saxons "suffered not their lands to descend to the eldest son only, but unto all their male children." Most significant to Verstegan was the fact that England's Saxon progenitors had refused to allow absolute power to reside in a single monarch. He approvingly described their democratic instincts in the following passage:

> For the general government of the country, they ordained twelve noble men, chosen from among others for their worthiness and sufficiency. These in the time of peace rode their several circuits, to see justice and good customs observed, and they often of course, at appointed times met all together, to consult and give order in public affaires; but ever in time of war one of these twelve was chosen to be king; and so to remain so long only as the war lasted; and that being ended; his name and dignity of king also ceased; and he became as before.[16]

For Verstegan and for the Roundheads who would later combat the arbitrary power of the Crown and would support his *Restitution* through five editions, the genius of these Saxon-descended English was the genius for democracy and representative government that they shared with all Germanic peoples. Assuredly among these peoples the authority of kings had never been "unlimited." Indeed, Verstegan asserted, "on minor matters the chiefs [deliberated]: on larger questions the whole tribe."[17]

In establishing a link between Anglo-Saxon-descended Englishmen and the respect for individual liberty, Roundheads were implicitly but clearly drawing a contrast between their party and the Cavalier party. They viewed King Charles's supporters as aristocrats of Norman blood, men with no appreciation of or respect for those political institutions that were products of a historically democratic Saxon spirit. Bitter religious and political conflicts climaxed by bloody civil war and regicide confirmed the widespread feeling among the English in the latter half of the seventeenth century that their nation was the uneasy product of two conflicting racial stocks. Not surprisingly, Cromwellians believed that their Saxon stock, with its inherent propensity for representative democracy, was superior to the Norman race, with its propensity for arrogance and absolutism.

With the Hanoverian ascendancy the bitter and bloody conflicts between Cavalier and Roundhead faded from the nation's consciousness. By 1800 the opposition between commoners and lords, between Saxons and Normans, had been largely forgotten. Scott's *Ivanhoe* rediscovered this historical conflict, but Scott sought to approach the subject in his fiction without the bias of Verstegan and the seventeenth-century Roundhead apologists. As he explained in the introduction to his novel, "It seemed to the Author that the existence of the two races in the same country, the vanquished distinguished by their plain, homely, blunt manners, and the free spirit infused by their ancient institutions and laws; the victors, by the high spirit of military fame, personal adventure, and whatever could distinguish them as the flower of chivalry, might, intermixed with other characters belonging to the same time and country, interest the reader by the contrast, if the Author should not fail on his part."[18]

The terms Scott employed in his explanation of the conflict between the Norman and Saxon races indicate that he recognized merits in the temperaments of both. In praising the Saxons for their "free spirit infused by their ancient institutions and laws," he seems to have accepted Verstegan's theory that these original Englishmen expressed the propensity of their race for representative democracy. But he also recognized the strengths of the Norman race, with its "high spirit of military fame, personal adventure, and . . . chivalry" (ix). From the beginning, therefore, Scott seems to have approached the subject matter of *Ivanhoe* in a determinedly unbiased manner.

Perhaps the highest demonstration of Scott's authorial objectivity can be found in his treatment of the knightly Norman nobles. A less scrupulous writer of historical romance would have invested these characters with their full complement of medieval pomp and glamour. But one of the most remarkable aspects of *Ivanhoe* is that despite the colorful and romantic detail with which he surrounds his Norman knights, the author never loses sight of their extraordinary cruelty and barbarism. He examines characters such as the Norman lord DeBracy through anything but rose-colored lenses. After DeBracy kidnaps the Saxon maiden Rowena—determined to possess his lovely captive by fair means or foul—Scott pauses in his account of the action to render this sober assessment of William the Conqueror's descendants: "It is grievous to think that those valiant barons, to whose stand against the crown the liberties of England were indebted for their existence, should themselves have been such dreadful oppressors, and capable of excesses contrary not only to the laws of England, but to those of nature and humanity." Not content to censure DeBracy alone, Scott adds to his narrative a long passage from the *Saxon Chronicle* that gruesomely details the tortures the Norman race inflicted on their hapless victims, and he concludes with the shocking example of Empress Matilda. "Though a daughter of the King of Scotland, and afterwards both Queen of England and Empress of Germany, the daughter, the wife, and the mother of monarchs, was obliged, during her early residence for education in England, to assume the veil of a nun, as the only means of escaping the licentious pursuit of the Norman nobles" (212–13).

The unrestrained cruelty of the Norman conquerors is indeed the principal cause of the enduring antipathy between them and their Saxon subjects, as Scott makes clear in the opening chapter of *Ivanhoe*. "Four generations," he writes, "had not sufficed to blend the hostile blood of the Normans and Anglo-Saxons, or to unite, by common language and mutual interests, two hostile races, one of which still felt the elation of triumph, while the other groaned under all the consequences of defeat." Overbearing Norman kings had "shown the most marked predilection for the Norman subjects; the laws of the chase, and many others, equally unknown to the milder and more free spirit of the Saxon constitution, had been fixed upon the necks of the subjugated inhabitants." The complete Norman discounting of the Saxon language had in Scott's view compounded the humiliation of the conquered race. At the royal court as well as in courts of law "Norman-French was the only language employed." The author concludes, "French was the language of honour, of chivalry, and even of justice, while the far more manly and expressive Anglo-Saxon was abandoned to the use of rustics and hinds, who knew no other" (4–5).

Given Walter Scott's frequent verbal bashing of his Norman lords in *Ivanhoe* and given the fact that the hero and source of his novel's title is himself a Saxon, it may seem surprising that southern readers avoided identifying themselves with the novel's Saxon characters. After all, in the decades following the publication of this historical romance southerners had been ever more inclined to view themselves as an oppressed minority, increasingly at the mercy of a powerful, unscrupulous, and rapacious Yankee race. Why should they not have seen their culture's noblest traits bodied forth in the principled and determined resistance of Ivanhoe's father, Cedric the Saxon, to the brutal Norman hegemony? What could they have seen in the ruthless lust of the Norman lord DeBracy, the cruel avarice of Reginald Front-de-Boeuf, or the cynicism and villainy of Sir Brian de Bois-Guilbert that would have prompted them to associate themselves more and more emphatically in the 1840s and 1850s with members of a Norman race? And how could they have so frequently and enthusiastically referenced *Ivanhoe* as a novel representing the highest qualities of a chivalrous Norman aristocracy, an aristocracy whose blood they were proud to claim?

The answer to these questions probably lies in Scott's authorial objectivity. His honest assessment of Norman brutality is balanced by an equally honest estimate of Saxon culture, which he judges to be decidedly more primitive and less sophisticated than the Norman. This view informs the author's description of Cedric the Saxon's rudely built manor house, a structure that starkly contrasts with the oppressive but much more formidable Norman castles to which the reader will be introduced later in the narrative. Scott observes that the roof of Cedric's house, "composed of beams and rafters, had nothing to divide the apartment from the sky excepting the planking and thatch; there was a huge fireplace at either end of the hall, but, as the chimneys were constructed in a very clumsy manner, at least as much of the smoke found its way into the apartment as escaped by the proper vent.... The floor was composed of earth mixed with lime, trodden into a hard substance, such as is often employed in flooring our modern barns" (25). Such "rude simplicity" even characterizes the more luxurious quarters of the novel's chaste heroine, Rowena. "No fewer than four silver candelabras, holding great waxen torches, served to illuminate this apartment," he writes. "Yet let not modern beauty envy the magnificence of a Saxon princess. The walls of the apartment were so ill finished and so full of crevices, that the rich hangings shook to the night blast. . . . Magnificence there was, with some rude attempt at taste; but of comfort there was little" (51).

In Scott's depiction, the Saxons are as rude and simple in their manners and conduct as they are in their dwellings. At Prince John's post-tournament dinner the contrast between Norman and Saxon manners is particularly striking:

> With sly gravity, interrupted only by private signs to each other, the Norman knights and nobles beheld the ruder demeanour of Athelstane and Cedric at a banquet to the form and fashion of which they were unaccustomed. And while their manners were thus the subject of sarcastic observation, the untaught Saxons unwittingly transgressed several of the arbitrary rules established for the regulation of society. Now, it is well known that a man may with more impunity be guilty of an actual breach either of real good breeding or of good morals, than appear ignorant of the most minute point of fashionable etiquette. Thus Cedric, who dried his hands with a towel, instead of suffering the moisture to exhale by waving them gracefully in the air, incurred more ridicule than his companion Athelstane, when he swallowed to his own single share the whole of a large pasty composed of the most exquisite foreign delicacies, and termed at that time a "karum pie." When, however, it was discovered, by a serious cross-examination, that the thane of Coningsburgh . . . had no idea what he had been devouring, and that he had taken the contents of the "karum pie" for larks and pigeons . . . his ignorance brought him in for an ample share of the ridicule which would have been more justly bestowed on his gluttony. (138–39)

Scott is admirably clear and objective about the implications of the scene he has constructed. He understands that the rules of social etiquette may be arbitrary, but that only the truly knowledgeable can violate them with impunity. A society that places more value on table manners than on the character of the man sitting at the table may be an unfair and superficial one, but Scott acknowledges the reality that such unfairness characterizes many if not most social constructs. Cedric possesses more integrity and natural grace than his insolent Norman hosts, but they have more power and more sophistication. And in Walter Scott's historical world, power and sophistication inevitably prevail. Simplicity and rudeness of habit will never validate the restoration of Saxon authority that Cedric so fervently desires.

Scott's banquet scene demonstrates that though the author acknowledged Norman despotism, he also recognized that the conquering race was superior to the Saxon race in both its cultural and technological sophistication. Even more significant, he identified the Norman aristocracy in *Ivanhoe* with the chivalric ethos that would stamp European civilization for hundreds of years to come. A similar thesis would be advanced six years after the publication of *Ivanhoe* by the prominent French historian Augustin Thierry in his *History of the Conquest of England by the Normans*. Almost certainly prompted by the amazing popularity of *Ivanhoe*, Thierry's work proposed that the Norman invasion of England, which the author described as a "great movement of destruction and assimilation," was historically "inevitable." This aggression also demonstrated to the French historian the clear superiority of Norman over Saxon culture. Indeed, Thierry went so far as to argue that however "violent and unlawful" the action of William and his Norman lords had been "in its principle," the ultimate result of the Norman victory had been the present-day flowering of the "civilization of Europe."[19]

Though *The History of the Conquest of England by the Normans* went through a number of editions in both France and England, southern readers also seem to have been acquainted with the book. In his praise of *Ivanhoe* written for the *Southern and Western Magazine* in 1845, William Gilmore Simms observed that those with an interest in medieval times probably had Scott's novel to thank for "the very charming history of the Norman conquest and sway, from the pen of Monsieur Thierry."[20] He thus directly linked *Ivanhoe* to a historical work with which he assumed many of his readers would be familiar. Contemporary historical scholarship therefore confirmed for southern as well as for English literati Scott's understanding of chivalry as a product of Norman culture, and southerners were increasingly determined to link themselves to such a culture. By the 1840s many of them fancied their plantation society to be an island of aristocratic order harking back to medieval times, striving valiantly to survive the rising tide of Yankee commerce and materialism. Southerners thus were strongly inclined to see themselves reflected in *Ivanhoe*'s Norman aristocracy, no matter how brutal and villainous individual Norman characters in Scott's narrative might have been.

If southern readers were willing to ignore the deformities of the Norman characters they encountered in Scott's novel, they were doing no less than imitating the predilections of their English kinsmen. Whatever the appeal of the Saxon racial myth had been to the Puritans of the seventeenth century, by the nineteenth century it had been supplanted in England by the aristocratic allure of Norman blood. As Mark Girouard has observed in his *Return to Camelot,* the revival of the cult of medieval chivalry and the consequent elevation of the Norman cultural ideal served a distinct social purpose for the English aristocracy. It was employed as a kind of talisman to ward off the unpleasant realities of rapid industrialization, democratic political reform, and the threat of social extinction that these changes posed for the old order. Among these privileged gentlemen the influence of Walter Scott's poetry and fiction was profound. Girouard argues persuasively that the Bard of Abbotsford's works brought "chivalry up to date" and "encouraged aristocrats and country gentlemen to build castles and cram their halls with weapons and armour."[21]

The fictional appeal of Scott's medieval subject matter beyond the aristocracy to a broader English middle class would seem to be a puzzling phenomenon, but Augustin Thierry provides shrewd insight into the English class-consciousness and social snobbery that fueled the myth of Norman racial superiority in the nineteenth century as well as the mass appetite for novels such as *Ivanhoe.* Thierry understood that in the five hundred years that had followed the Battle of Hastings, racial distinctions between these two peoples had gradually disappeared. "There are now," he concluded, "neither Normans nor Saxons, but in history." Still, he wittily observed, contemporary Englishmen loved "to deceive themselves respecting their origin, and to consider the sixty thousand men who accompanied William as the common ancestors of all who now bear the name of English. Thus a London shopkeeper, or a Yorkshire farmer, will talk of his Norman ancestors." And why this middle-class obsession with Norman ancestors? Thierry believed that the answer lay in the stubborn persistence of a racial myth, a myth that supported the popular opinion that "the high personages of this land [had been] descended from the Normans, and the men of low condition from the Saxons."[22] Though *Ivanhoe* certainly did not create such a racial myth, much of its surface texture seemed to endorse this popular nineteenth-century view of Norman racial superiority.

Southerners who embraced *Ivanhoe*'s Norman aristocracy were essentially following the lead of their English cousins. Like them, they tended to associate social prestige with any genealogy that could trace itself back to an Anglo-Norman source. Susan Dabney Smedes's introduction to the *Memorials of a Southern Planter* contains a perfect illustration of the way the Norman ideal was enlisted in the cause of southern social snobbery. Though a native of Mississippi, Smedes spends much of her time in her introduction boasting of the illustrious pedigree of her father's Dabney kin in Virginia. She also provides an exhaustive genealogy that auspiciously links these Tidewater Dabneys to "the old Huguenot name and family of d'Aubigne," thereby grafting onto the stout ancestral tree of the Virginia gentry a more exotic Old World Norman line of descent. In the antebellum South such genealogical graftings were useful in establishing the social position of the plantation aristocracy. Indeed, southerners like Susan Smedes were determined that this aristocracy be seen as representative of what she termed "the best class of English people."[23]

The idealizing of the cult of chivalry and of the Norman racial inheritance served the southern planter aristocracy in much the same way that it served the English aristocracy, as a kind of talisman. In England it helped to numb the irritation produced among the landed aristocracy by the industrial despoliation of the rural landscape and the agitation for democratic political reform. In a similar manner, medievalism such as that on display in *Ivanhoe* offered southern planter-aristocrats a kind of antidote for the psychological pain occasioned by the steady erosion of their region's economic and political power in the Union. Southerners incorporated the trappings of the medieval revival on glorious display in *Ivanhoe* into their justification of a social system that was being ever more vigorously attacked in the North as outmoded, barbarous, and antithetical to American political and social ideals.

Southern readers of *Ivanhoe* were determined to see themselves reflected in the novel's Normans, and this determination resulted in readings that ignored not only the barbarity and turpitude of most of these characters but also the narrative's broader underlying tensions. The political and social exigencies of the antebellum period made it impossible for even the most sophisticated southerners to read *Ivanhoe* in a way that recognized and appreciated the novel's ironies and thematic tensions. They turned a blind eye to the subtleties of Scott's text and read the novel arbitrarily, using it to validate fantasies of a chivalric and exquisitely honorable southern culture related in both spirit and blood to that of its Norman forebears.

In identifying with the Norman chivalry, southern readers were obliged to overlook the ironic fact that their increasingly perilous economic and political situation in the Union was more analogous to Scott's Saxon characters than to his Normans. They could never have allowed themselves to acknowledge that their determined embrace of slavery had made their culture, like that of Cedric and his Saxons, an economic, technological, and social anachronism. Of all Scott's characters, Cedric—a man "proud, fierce, jealous, and irritable" who "stands up . . . sternly for the privileges of his race, and is so proud of his uninterrupted descent from Hereward" (21)—most closely approximates the proud and choleric southern planter of legend. It is in fact Cedric—fighting stubbornly, fiercely, and futilely against Norman domination and dreaming impracticably of a restitution of Saxon authority—who seems today to embody most fully the defiant southern attitudes that ultimately would lead the region to civil war. it is Cedric who expresses this quintessential southern spirit of defiance, not Ivanhoe, a young man who pragmatically acknowledges Norman hegemony and smoothly accommodates himself to its code of chivalry. There was no place, however, in southern fantasies for a character like Cedric the Saxon.

Southern readers might be forgiven for overlooking the fact that Rowena, the fair object of Ivanhoe's chivalrous solicitude, is also, like her guardian Cedric, a full-blooded Saxon. With her "purity of complexion, and the majestic yet soft expression of a mild blue eye" (21), Rowena evokes a physical beauty that is distinctly Germanic. But its ethereal quality allows her to transcend Norman-Saxon racial categories, just as Ivanhoe transcends them with his flawless chivalry. Though southerners preferred their manly heroes with the stamp of Norman character, they favored ladies with more Nordic characteristics. Rowena's flawlessly white skin and liquid blue eyes were features that could be easily associated with the sexual and racial purity that so thoroughly engaged the southern mind, and heroines of the scores of plantation romances that followed and were inspired by *Ivanhoe* would share the same complexion and the same eyes.

Given the South's preference for pure, white, and softly appealing heroines like Rowena, it is hardly surprising that they ignored the beautiful but dark-skinned Jewess, Rebecca. A young woman of extraordinary intellectual capacity, she possesses prodigious medical knowledge, having "been heedfully brought up in all the knowledge proper to her nation, which her apt and powerful mind had retained, arranged, and enlarged, in the course of a progress beyond her years, her sex, and even the age in which she lived" (256). Indeed, she employs her medical expertise to save the life of the seriously wounded Ivanhoe. As a precursor and prototype of the modern woman, Rebecca is a much more interesting character to modern readers than the wooden Rowena. But few of Scott's nineteenth-century southern admirers, male or female, would have allowed themselves to admire deeply or take seriously Rebecca's character, for she represented qualities that were totally antithetical to the ideal of the southern lady.

And what qualities did the South expect its ladies to strive to attain? Anne

Firor Scott, in her pioneering study *The Southern Lady: From Pedestal to Politics,* has observed in that properly bred belles were expected to be pure, submissive, modest, self-denying, and pious. Indeed, the personal qualities demanded of them were the same as those possessed by Walter Scott's fair Rowena, qualities that made her an appealing character to southern readers of both sexes. Of course, the concept of the pure, submissive, and modest woman was, like the medieval-flavored chivalric ideal, widely subscribed to in England and in the northern states as well as in the South. But the notion of the submissive woman was articulated with greater frequency, intensity, and fervor in the southern states than in England or in any other region of the United States, and Anne Scott's analysis astutely explains why the South was so concerned with exacting submissiveness from its fair sex. The plantation system and the institution of slavery fostered the development in Dixie of an extraordinarily strong patriarchal family structure. "Women, along with children and slaves, were expected to recognize their proper and subordinate place and to be obedient to the head of the family," Scott writes. "Any tendency on the part of any of the members of the system to assert themselves against the master threatened the whole, and therefore slavery itself."[24]

Historians have subsequently confirmed Scott's understanding of the crucial link between the South's embracing of a plantation social structure founded on slavery and the region's trumpeting of the exquisite submissiveness of its ladies. Elizabeth Fox-Genovese has also concluded that "the distinctive forms of male dominance in the South developed in conjunction with the development of slavery" and that the plantation system "guaranteed the power of men in society, even as measured by nineteenth century bourgeois standards." Recent scholars have advanced somewhat more revisionist views of the position of southern women in Dixie's male-dominated antebellum social system. Elizabeth Varon, for example, has effectively argued the Virginia's "elite and middle-class women" assumed "active" and "distinct" roles in the Old Dominion's political culture, roles well removed from those of the ideally submissive and modest plantation matron mounted on her pedestal. But Varon also acknowledges that those elite women who took an active part in the political life of their state were overwhelmingly complicit "in a political system founded on inequality," that they "rejected abolitionism and feminism," and that "they did not seek to topple the racial and gender hierarchies that undergirded Southern society."[25] Even when the lady occasionally stepped down from her pedestal, she continued to profess unalloyed faith in the planter aristocrats who had insisted on placing her there.

The institution of slavery was thus inextricably linked to the South's view of women as pliant and submissive. It was also linked to the region's obsession with the southern lady's sexual purity, for the miscegenation that inevitably resulted from the day-to-day contact between white masters and their black female chattel made it necessary for the region to trumpet ever more insistently the ideal of racial purity, symbolized by the untainted southern lady. W. J. Cash has observed that if racial mixing was to be denied on the one hand, southern women had to be compensated on the other: "The revolting suspicion in the male that he might be slipping into bestiality [must be] got rid of, by glorifying her; the Yankee must be answered by proclaiming from the housetops that Southern Virtue . . . was superior, not alone to the North's but to any on earth, and adducing Southern Womanhood in proof."[26]

In 1836 Nathaniel Beverley Tucker expressed just such an exalted concept of Southern Womanhood in his novel *The Partisan Leader*. For Tucker, southern women walked traditionally "in the steps of their chaste mothers . . . safe in that high sense of honor which protects at once from pollution and suspicion." He believed that they represented a social line of defense through which the sexual and moral promiscuity of the lower classes—Tucker termed them "the gangrene of the social body"—could never penetrate.[27] A region that insisted on turning its white women into symbols of absolute virtue and racial purity and that demanded of them an attitude of absolute submission to a patriarchal hierarchy could hardly be expected to embrace with enthusiasm a character like Walter Scott's Rebecca, with her dark, eastern beauty and her inquiring and brilliant mind.

Rebecca's proficiency at administering aid to the gravely wounded Ivanhoe was no doubt disconcerting to those who embraced the southern-lady ideal, for Scott made clear in his narrative that her skills were those of a doctor, not of a nurse. "Her knowledge of medicine and of the healing art had been acquired under an aged Jewess," he writes, "the daughter of one of their most celebrated doctors, who loved Rebecca as her own child, and was believed to have communicated to her secrets which had been left to herself by her sage father at the same time, and under the same circumstances" (256). Southern readers could certainly not have seriously entertained the idea implicit in Scott's characterization of Rebecca: that at least a few brilliant women were capable of taking their places alongside men in professions such as medicine. Such a notion was anathema to the writer of an article for a southern periodical entitled "Women's Rights." For this gentleman, a southern woman had only one right: to love a man. "Love," he contended, was "her destiny, and the sum of her duties." Women who would presume to ague for equal rights with men were not woman at all, but "men-women . . . wonderful quacks invariably," but not people to be taken seriously. Though this writer expressed merely a condescendingly satirical attitude toward assertive women, other southern writers were more harsh and threatening in their insistence that there was no place in Dixie's society for women who would assert their rights to higher education and to the franchise. Nathaniel Beverley Tucker acidly advised these unsexed fanatics to leave the South and "go North, write books; patronize abolition societies; or keep a boarding school." Such females were no longer ladies, and they were certainly "no longer fit" to be the wives of southern gentlemen.[28]

Bound by their allegiance to a plantation patriarchy, most southern readers would have found it virtually impossible to appreciate Rebecca's intelligence and strength. Conversely, northern readers, not so ideologically bound, found it easier to recognize and respond positively to the force and appeal of Scott's characterization. The observations of a reviewer for the Philadelphia periodical *The Port Folio* were typical of the northern critical response. As this writer pointed out, "The true interest of this romance of the days of Richard is placed neither in Richard himself, nor in the knight of Ivanhoe, the nominal hero—nor in any of the haughty templars or barrons who occupy along with them the front of the scene, but in the still, devoted, sad, and unrequited tenderness of a Jewish damsel—by far the most fine, and at the same time the most romantic creature of female character the author has ever formed: and second, we suspect, to no creature of female character whatever that is to be found in the whole annals either of poetry or of romance."[29]

Such a sympathetic and nuanced understanding of the importance of Rebecca's character in *Ivanhoe* was impossible for most southern reviewers. One of them in fact singled out Rebecca, not the marmoreal Rowena, as the novel's most blemished character. "She is," he complained, "too near perfection. In an age when men were so illiterate that scarcely any one could be found able to write his name, it could hardly be expected that we should meet with a female, in so humble a station as this Jewesss, possessed of such extensive information and so well cultivated."[30] It is ironic but hardly surprising that southern critics who were not otherwise notably critical of Scott's historical accuracy should have faulted him in his development of Rebecca, the novel's strongest and most individualized character.

Conservative though Walter Scott may have been, his genius as a writer is evidenced in *Ivanhoe* by his creation of a female character who, had she found a place in the southern imagination, would have existed there as a nightmare. Rebecca implicitly repudiated every attitude about women that southerners held dear. There was simply nothing that southern readers could do with such a character but dismiss her. This they could more easily do because Scott conveniently offered them a contrasting female—the blond, beautiful, chaste, and submissive Rowena, embodiment of the pure, white essence of Dixie's dream.

Southern readers embraced Rowena because she epitomized those feminine qualities that ladies formed by the chivalric code were bound to embody and that gentlemen formed by the same code were bound to adore. They were evidently so captivated by her and by her gallant lover that they ignored the fact that at a crucial point in Scott's novel the concept of chivalry to which Ivanhoe and Rowena unquestioningly subscribe is the object of a remarkable and rigorous verbal assault. And this attack comes not from a man but from a woman who lives beyond the pale of aristocratic society, the subversive Rebecca. She may truly love Ivanhoe, but in a scene of high tension the author allows her to question intently and cogently the chivalric ethos that motivates the man she loves and that is the very foundation of Scott's narrative.

During the ferocious battle for Torquilstone, where Ivanhoe lies wounded and unable to fight, Rebecca is obliged to stand at a window and describe to him the grisly combat unfolding before her eyes. She faithfully limns the terrible action taking place below the window, but she is mystified and slightly repelled by Ivanhoe's excited response to details that to her are almost too ghastly to be put into words. "How couldst thou," she asks, "hope to inflict wounds on others, ere that be healed which thou thyself hast received?" Ivanhoe's response to Rebecca's question is both heartfelt and condescending. "Thou knowest not," he tells her, "how impossible it is for one trained to actions of chivalry to remain passive as a priest, or a woman, when they are acting deeds of honour around him. The love of battle is the food upon which we live—the dust of the *melee* is the breath of our nostrils! We live not—we wish not to live—longer than while we are victorious and renowned. Such, maiden, are the laws of chivalry to which we are sworn, and to which we offer all that we hold dear" (275).

One might have expected Rebecca to be silenced by such high-flown idealism. Nineteenth-century southern readers would certainly have been more than satisfied with Ivanhoe's response, but Rebecca is not. What is chivalric renown, she asks him, "save an offering of sacrifice to a demon of vain glory, and a passing through the fire to Moloch? What remains to you as the prize of all the blood you have spilled . . . of all the tears which your deeds have caused, when death hath broken the strong man's spear." To this question the amazed Ivanhoe cries out, "Glory, maiden—glory! Which gilds our sepulchre and embalms our name." In the face of what is to a modern sensibility an almost hysterical assertion of manly valor, Rebecca bravely persists in arguing her case. Glory, she contends, is "the defaced sculpture of the inscription which the ignorant monk can hardly read to the inquiring pilgrim." And is such decayed remembrance sufficient reward "for the sacrifice of every kindly affection, for a life spent miserably that ye may make others miserable" (275)?

By now Ivanhoe has become thoroughly exasperated with Rebecca's forensic tenacity. In desperation he resorts to what most of his contemporary readers would have considered two annihilating rebuttals. First, Rebecca is a mere woman who speaks "of thou knowest not what." "Thou wouldst," he observes somewhat acidly, "quench the pure light of chivalry, which alone distinguishes the noble from the base, the gentle knight from the churl and the savage." Ivanhoe is also forced to remind Rebecca that not only is she a woman, she is also "no Christian . . . to thee are unknown those high feelings which swell the bosom of a noble maiden when her lover hath done some deed of emprize which sanctions his fame" (276). The notions that chivalry separates the higher social orders from the "base" and that only white Christian ladies like Rowena can be expected to understand and appreciate its finer nuances must have been particularly consoling to conservative southerners who embraced the doctrine in the name of their plantation aristocracy.

To Scott's credit, he does not allow Ivanhoe's assertion of masculine and Christian superiority to silence Rebecca. She responds proudly that she has indeed "sprung from a race whose courage was distinguished in the defense of their own land, but who warred not, even while yet a nation, save at the command of the Deity, or in defending their country from oppression." Though on the surface she displays no contrition, she sorrows deeply within. The knight she loves imagines that in her heart "cowardice or meanness of soul must needs be its guests, because I have censured the fantastic chivalry of the Nazarenes" (276).

The flourishing of knightly tournaments in Dixie in the decades following the publication of *Ivanhoe* suggests that southern readers of Scott's novel were largely responsive to his hero's strained and idealistic defense of chivalry. To a modern sensibility, Rebecca's skeptical attitude toward this ethos seems both more intelligent and more humane than Ivanhoe's fervent and unquestioning embrace of the concept. Today it is difficult to admire the arrogant warrior's arguments, especially when those arguments express such transparently sexist and racist attitudes. Antebellum southerners, however, experienced little difficulty identifying with their fictional hero's point of view. Ivanhoe represented for them the epitome of those noble qualities that they believed animated their region's own chivalry.

If southerners were unwilling to entertain the questions about chivalry advanced by Rebecca, it is hardly surprising that they also seem to have ignored one of the basic themes of *Ivanhoe*. Scott's novel is ultimately not about the triumph of a superior Norman race over a base Saxon race; it is about the union or assimilation of these two conflicting cultures. Ivanhoe—the Saxon youth who accepts Norman hegemony, embraces Richard the Lion Hearted, and becomes a paradigm for the chivalric code—symbolizes what Scott obviously understands as a necessary historical uniting of peoples. Conversely, his father Cedric represents all the reactionary attitudes that would resist such assimilation.

Cedric fiercely resents his son's loyalty to King Richard, and he views Ivanhoe's love for Rowena as an equal betrayal. His ambition is that his ward should marry Athelstane of Coningsburgh, descended "from the last Saxon monarchs of England" (69), and thereby guarantee a pure Saxon succession to the throne when Norman power is overthrown. However, Cedric's plan to restore Saxon authority is a mere fantasy. The impossibility of such a restoration is suggested by nickname bestowed upon Cedric's would-be king: Athelstane the Unready. Regarding the prospects of a Saxon revival, Athelstane ultimately shares Scott's clear-headed pragmatism. Thought to have been killed at the Battle of Torquilstone, he is resurrected at the novel's conclusion as a realist who announces that, contrary to Cedric's ambition, he will "be king in [his] own domains, and nowhere else." He successfully appeals to Cedric to restore Ivanhoe to his favor and allow him to marry Rowena. "The Lady Rowena cares not for me; she loves the little finger of my kinsman Wilfred's glove better than my whole person" (424).

In the end Cedric bows to reality, forgives his son, and blesses his marriage to Rowena. The nuptials that conclude *Ivanhoe* clearly represent the beginning of the merging of Norman with Saxon culture. Celebrated in "the most august of temples, the noble minster of York," Ivanhoe's marriage is witnessed by an approving King Richard and "by the attendance of the high-born Normans, as well as Saxons, joined with the universal jubilee of the lower orders, that marked the marriage of two individuals as a pledge of the future peace and harmony betwixt two races" (443). Far from suggesting a continuation of the racial antagonisms that have marked his novel's action, Scott affirms that in succeeding centuries Normans and Saxons have become "so completely mingled that the distinction has become wholly invisible" (447).

Ivanhoe's conclusion clearly supports Michael O'Brien's contention that Walter Scott's historical fiction ultimately "endorsed progress." But O'Brien's parallel assertion—that such a progressive understanding of history resonated with Scott's southern readers and was a major reason for his popularity in Dixie—seems much more tenuous. Had Scott's southern audience had been as pragmatic and progressive as O'Brien imagines, they would surely have understood differently the relevance of *Ivanhoe* to their antebellum cultural predicament. They would have recognized and accepted the fact that their besieged southern culture was more akin to the proud but relatively backward Saxon than to the insolent but more powerful Norman. They would have seen value in Scott's historical thesis that weaker, less technologically sophisticated cultures must adapt and accommodate themselves, not adamantly oppose themselves, to those stronger cultures. But there is no indication that southerners read *Ivanhoe* this way. Instead they arbitrarily identified their culture and their racial stock with Scott's Norman characters. They used Scott's novel to validate not his progressive view of history but what they believed to be the deeply chivalric spirit of their own plantation aristocracy. They ignored Scott's broader themes, and they feasted on *Ivanhoe*'s medieval trappings, bizarrely translating specific details such as its jousting tournaments into a contemporary southern social setting that was anything but medieval in texture.

The South was able to incorporate *Ivanhoe* so felicitously into its Norman racial fantasy because the novel was in certain respects remarkably obliging of nineteenth-century racism. For example, Scott seems never to have doubted that his Normans and Saxons constituted separate races. Michael Banton has remarked upon this "striking feature" of *Ivanhoe*, "that Scott presents the opposition between Saxon and Norman as a struggle between two races." Scott uses the word *race* fifty-seven times in the course of his narrative, referring mainly to Normans, Saxons, and Jews. In this sense his novel can be understood as a faithful reflection of its nineteenth-century intellectual milieu. As Kwame Appiah has observed, it depends "not only . . . on the assumption of the naturalness of racial feeling but also on the maintenance of certain racial boundaries."[31] These boundaries are vividly present at *Ivanhoe*'s conclusion.

Here the novel is unambiguous in its conveying of the idea that while races such as the Normans and Saxons may combine, people such as the Jews cannot be allowed to cross the racial divide.

Walter Scott is so intent on maintaining proper nineteenth-century racial boundaries that he expediently employs his strongest character, the Jew Rebecca, as a humble spokesperson for attitudes that today would be labeled by most readers as racist. Though he has allowed her in the middle of his narrative to question the philosophical and moral foundations of chivalry, at the end she is not free to question the attitudes that automatically award the man she loves to Rowena and send her into convenient exile. The brave and intellectually forceful Rebecca is reduced to a girl who humbly requests that Rowena lift her bridal veil and allow her to gaze upon the flawless Nordic features that it conceals. She then abases herself before the Saxon maiden's exquisite beauty, an abasement of which Scott seems to approve. Rebecca reverently observes that in Rowena's face "there reigns . . . gentleness and goodness; and if a tinge of the world's pride or vanities may mix with an expression so lovely, how should we chide that which is of earth for bearing some colour of its original?" She blesses God that Ivanhoe has been united with his lady. And to Rowena's entreaty that she remain under their protection in England she firmly responds, "It may not be—there is a gulf betwixt us. Our breeding, our faith, alike forbid either to pass over it" (449).

The Rebecca who stands worshipfully before Rowena at the conclusion of *Ivanhoe* is not the Rebecca who earlier in the novel boldly disputed the merits of chivalry and stood in proud defiance with her oppressed people. But Scott was willing to compromise his novel's most complex and appealing character in the interest of validating what was for him the crucial idea of racial separation. In his fictional world it was not possible that a Jew could marry or even desire to marry a gentile, and in affirming this racial order and its implicit notion of gentile superiority, Scott required that Rebecca defer to the gentile ideal.

Scott's conviction that boundaries between races were both natural and necessary was on vivid display at the conclusion of *Ivanhoe,* and it could not have been calculated to appeal more profoundly to southern readers. The unbridgeable racial gulf that Rebecca acknowledged in her final interview with Rowena was one that southerners could easily invoke for their own purposes. The natural superiority of gentile to Jew could be also expressed as the natural superiority of white to black or of southerner to northerner. *Ivanhoe* accorded perfectly with the South's fantasy of a Norman-descended plantation aristocracy that was superior both to the mass of chattel black slaves over which it ruled and to the Saxon-descended Yankees with whom it was locked in a fierce political struggle for survival.

The facility with which southern polemicists were able to incorporate *Ivanhoe* into their racial mythology is vividly illustrated in J. Quitman Moore's "Southern Statesmanship," written for *DeBow's Review* on the eve of Lincoln's election in October 1860. In his essay Moore argued that "individualism" was "the principle of barbarism and the sustaining power of despotism." As opposed to a barbaric Yankee culture that placed a high premium on such individualism, southern culture had revived "the genius of the medieval civilization," but it had surpassed this medieval society "by making *ethnology* the basis of social science." The South's plantation society, in other words, represented to Moore a superior culture founded on a medieval sense of social gradation and order and a modern sense of precise and scientific racial distinctions. Moore fervently hoped that Dixie's plantation aristocracy would remain untainted by the "commercial spirit" that dominated the North and that, combined with an excessive individualism, was "inherently hostile to the principle of subordination and the institution of ranks." Such commercialism, he warned, would have a fatally "injurious influence upon the social and domestic relations that lie at the basis of Southern society, which, being established on the principle of the *natural* inequality of *races,* makes Gurth the perpetual thrall of Cedric the Saxon."[32] At long last southerners had acknowledged Cedric. But they had subverted him as they had subverted other elements of Walter Scott's fiction. They had made him, like his Norman antagonists, a symbol of southern racial superiority.

3
A Slaveholding Race
Mythology and Southern Polemics

In 1847 a writer for the New Orleans–based *DeBow's Review* modestly proposed to his readers that the South commit itself to a moderate diversification of its plantation economy in order to stimulate the accumulation of commercial capital. He qualified his proposal with assurances to his audience that he was not advocating the radical abandonment of Dixie's historically agrarian pursuits in emulation of a northern economic model. "It is not desired," he asserted somewhat superciliously, "that our planters should leave the cultivation of their fields to engage in the business of the counting-house. All that we would propose is, that they should set apart a portion of their annual surplus, and invest it in commerce."[1]

Appearing as it does in a magazine that had for years trumpeted the commercial potential of the nation's vast Mississippi valley, this appeal for a more diversified southern economy sounds strangely timid. By the late 1840s, even magazines like *DeBow's* that had been devoted to progressive industrial themes were beginning to temper their pro-business rhetoric. Indeed, advocates of southern industry were forced to address the contention of a growing number of northern politicians and intellectuals that the region's plantation system was incompatible with the vigorous development of industrial capitalism. Unlike their northern critics, most southerners—even those who strongly advocated the commercial development of the South—could not imagine a southern economy that did not incorporate as its foundation the slave production of agricultural staples. They believed that the survival of their economy depended on their defending the plantation. And defend that system they did, embracing chivalric medievalism in their literary and social realms and, in the political and economic sphere, ignoring or casting vaguely disapproving and haughty glances toward the counting houses and factories that were beginning to transform the economies of the northern states. By the 1850s, *DeBow's Review* was directing more and more of its journalistic energies to championing the South's plantation-dominated commercial status quo.

Typical of the New Orleans journal's increasingly conservative economic tone was an article by Ellwood Fisher, entitled simply "The North and the South." In his essay Fisher addressed and attempted to refute the widespread perception that since the founding of the Republic the South had declined in population and prosperity relative to the northern states and that this decline had been caused by the region's embrace of the plantation system. In fact, the writer argued, if southern slaves were subtracted from the general population totals and considered as property, with an assessed value like that of the planter's land, the economic picture brightened considerably for the states below the Mason-Dixon. Readjusting population statistics this way, Fisher concluded that the South had not declined in prosperity vis-a-vis the North "in proportion to the number of their *citizens* respectively."[2] The writer was willing to cede the point of the South's relative decline in population in order to affirm its continued relative prosperity.

In article after article from the late 1840s into the 1850s, *DeBow's* abandoned what had once been its standard commercial boosterism to publish essays arguing that the South's prosperity was destined to depend on agricultural wealth alone. Indeed, Fisher contended that the region had successfully "encountered and conquered" the historical tendency for wealth to be associated with urban cultures. In an ironic distortion of Jeffersonian agrarianism, he boasted that the application of slave labor had made agriculture "for the first time in the history of the world, so profitable and attractive as to render rural life the favorite of wealth as well as of the mass of the people—to make the country, instead of the towns, the abode of elegant manners and refined taste." Another *DeBow's* writer, John Forsyth, observed that the South's "soil and institutions" had made it "rich and prosperous, without resorting to the multifarious pursuits" of the more frenetic Yankee businessmen to the North.[3]

In the turbulent years following the Compromise of 1850, polemical writers like Fisher who enlisted themselves in the defense of Dixie's economic system and of its peculiar institution would repeatedly boast of the uniqueness of the South's economic and social institutions, a uniqueness that expressed itself in a culture far superior to that of the North. Aligned with this sense of the South's economic and cultural uniqueness was a developing sense of the racial uniqueness of the white southerner. Indeed, this southern racialism was articulated in polemical writing with more and more frequency as the region moved toward civil war.

The idea that southerners constituted a distinctive race can be detected as early as 1849 in an article written for the *Southern Quarterly Review*. Here the writer boasts somewhat defensively of the superiority of southerners to northerners: "The race cannot be called inferior that has furnished . . . a Washington, a Jefferson, a Madison, a Monroe, a Randolph, the Rutledges, the Pinckneys, a Patrick Henry, a Sumter, a Marion, a Lowndes, a Cheves, a Clay, a Calhoun, a Crawford, a Troup, a Hayne, a Turnbull, a McDuffie, a Preston, and hundreds of others who will rank with the very best their free soil has produced or ever will produce."[4] Already, in the eyes of this writer, Americans have divided into two camps, slave and free soil. What is implicitly disturbing about this division is that the honor roll of southern political heroes are viewed as products of a "race" implicitly superior to what the writer imagines as a competing race of free-soil men.

Four years after constructing its Pantheon of southern heroes, the *Southern Quarterly Review* remained committed to the vision of a distinct southern race. "There is no nation of the white race," it proclaimed, "that has more peculiar *characteristics* than the South. . . . There is none whose condition and character more require nationality, and would better constitute a proper and firm basis for it." By the 1850s, assertions of the existence of a unique southern white race were beginning to be ominously yoked with a parallel concept of southern nationalism. The advantage of such a yoking for southerners of a secessionist persuasion was plain, for who could deny that if the southern people constituted a distinctive race, they were deserving of their own national identity? One year after this extolling of Dixie's racial uniqueness the *Richmond Enquirer* entertained its readers with visions of a slave empire holding sway over Cuba and the Caribbean all the way to the Amazon. Though this empire was rather perfunctorily described as an American one, the *Enquirer*'s vision was clearly regional, not national. And it was inextricably linked to southern racialism. "If," the editor boasted, "the slaveholding race in these States are but true to themselves, they have a great destiny before them."[5] Despite the assertions of the *Southern Quarterly Review* and the *Richmond Enquirer,* most southerners in 1854 would have been uncomfortable with the notion that they constituted a separate race of people within the United States. By 1861, however, they would greet the idea with much more enthusiasm.

Contributing to the increasing inclination of southerners to imagine themselves as a race distinct from northern Americans was their widely embraced conceit that they had retained a more homogeneous racial composition than had their Yankee brethren. In this context the relative decline of the South's population in national censuses could be given a positive spin, for if Dixie's population was smaller than the North's, the region was also largely free of the invasions of immigrant hordes that, in southerners' increasingly xenophobic view, had vitiated the English stock north of the Mason-Dixon Line.

Indeed, this sense of racial homogeneity prompted many southerners to boast that they were more purely American in blood and more deeply American in spirit than their Yankee neighbors.

James DeBow gave full expression to this assumption of southern racial purity when he declared that the South had "been enabled to maintain a more homogeneous population and show a less admixture of races than the North." He also articulated the corresponding sense of the region's profound Americanness: "Our people partake of the American character, and are mainly the descendants of those who fought the battles of the Revolution, and who understand and appreciate the nature and inestimable value of the liberty which it brought. They are not Mormons or Spiritualists, they are not Owenites, Fourierites, Agrarians, Socialists, Free-lovers, or Millerites. They are not for breaking down all the forms of society and of religion and reconstructing them; but prefer law, order and existing institutions to the chaos which Radicalism involves."[6]

DeBow clearly links the South's intellectual stability with its racial homogeneity, and he also suggests that the mongrelizing of the northern population has produced a corresponding destabilization of faith, intellect, and social cohesion. Though he pays lip service to the "American character," he sees southerners alone as embodying that character's strengths. His essay conveys a sense of two American races, not one—one southern and pure, the other northern and impure.

And from what source had this homogeneous southern "slaveholding race" descended? In defining their region's demographic origins, most southern polemicists appealed to the myth, well established by the mid-nineteenth century in America, that northerners were largely descendants of Puritan or Calvinist ancestors while southerners were primarily descended from Cavalier forebears. A writer for the *Southern Literary Messenger* provided a detailed description of this distinctively aristocratic "southron" race: "The convulsions of Europe which drove the English Puritan, the Scottish Covenanter and the trading Hollander to the Northern Provinces, sent to these Southern shores the plundered Cavalier, the younger son of 'the fine Old English gentleman,' the Jacobite, honorable for his steadfast though misplaced loyalty, the Huguenot exiled from his beautiful France; and to Maryland the British or Irish Catholic, whom we must also honour for his sincere though misguided faith."[7] This writer obviously felt himself constrained to apologize for the "misplaced loyalty" of the South's Jacobite forebears and for the "misguided faith" of its Catholic ancestors. But he was just as obviously willing to accept these political and religious handicaps as long as he and his fellow southerners could lay claim to the aristocratic cachet that attached itself to all things royal and all things French.

The southern myth of a Cavalier-descended race was not only a boost to a region whose self-esteem was being battered by the increasingly malign attacks of northern abolitionists. It was also a notion that was marvelously congruent with the South's defense of slavery and the plantation system. Who could better control the energies of masses of inferior blacks than an aristocratic white race of signally noble character, born to rule with firmness and fairness? Indeed, southern polemicists commonly argued that their plantation system sustained the high culture and elevated character that the South's original Cavalier settlers had bequeathed to the region. Edmund Ruffin, a Virginian who became one of the South's fieriest defenders, frequently observed that although free societies displayed "much industry" and impressive wealth, their citizens were commonly "rude in manners, and greatly deficient in refinement of feeling and cultivation of mental and social qualities." Southern culture, in contrast, "by confining the drudgery and brutalizing effects of continual toil to the inferior race . . . [gave] to the superior race leisure and other means to improve mind, taste, and manners." So intoxicated was George Fitzhugh by this vision of southern aristocracy that he claimed that Dixie's planter aristocracy exceeded even the noblemen of Europe in pride, self-command, and authority: "The nobility of Russia do not hold such despotic sway over their serfs, as we do over our negroes, and are themselves mere slaves to the Emperor, whilst our slaveholders have scarcely any authority above them."[8]

In their pell-mell rush to defend the plantation system from attacks to the north, most southern apologists seem to have ignored the fact that the aristocratic ethos they were so enthusiastically promoting was profoundly antithetical to the ideal of equality that had been an animating force of the Revolution. Some southern writers, however, faced the implications of their aristocratic racial mythmaking head on. James Hammond, one of South Carolina's eminent antebellum political leaders, understood clearly that to affirm slavery as "the corner-stone of our Republican edifice" one would have to reject the ideal of the equality of all men. He therefore repudiated as "ridiculously absurd, that much lauded but nowhere accredited dogma of Mr. Jefferson, 'that all men are born equal.'"[9]

George Fitzhugh was, like Thomas Jefferson, a loyal son of the Old Dominion. But he was a member of an antebellum generation of extremely conservative Virginians, and, like James Hammond and other leaders of the Deep South, he had been shaped in his political and social thinking by the increasingly acrimonious sectional debates of the 1840s and 1850s. Like so many of his generation, he lacked the sophistication, the catholicity of taste, and the liberal spirit that had activated Virginians of the Revolutionary and post-Revolutionary period—men such as Washington, Wythe, Henry, Marshall, Jefferson, Madison, and Monroe. For Fitzhugh, Jeffersonian political principles were merely secondhand borrowings from European sources. They were, he declared, alien to the southern spirit and "at war with our institutions." In the eyes of Fitzhugh and of many Virginians of his day, Jefferson, the framer of the Declaration of Independence, was a mere "enthusiastic speculative philosopher." "Men," he observed cynically, "are not 'born entitled to equal rights!' It would be far nearer the truth to say, 'That some were born with saddles on their backs, and others booted and spurred to ride them,'—and the riding does them good."[10]

Southern racial mythmaking, the idea that inhabitants of the states below the Mason-Dixon Line were members of a distinct, Cavalier-descended white race, was thus easily put to the service of promulgating what Fitzhugh termed a "new philosophy" of white supremacy. This philosophy carried Fitzhugh to the remarkable conclusion "that about nineteen out of every twenty individuals have 'a natural and inalienable right' to be taken care of and protected, to have guardians, trustees, husbands, or masters; in other words, they have a natural and inalienable right to be slaves. The one in twenty are as clearly born and educated or some way fitted for command and liberty."[11] Fitzhugh's vision of a paternalistic plantation aristocracy fit like hand to glove with the notion of a Cavalier-descended southern race.

Southern race mythology also melded smoothly with the region's enthusiasm for Walter Scott and for feudalism. As we have seen, a devotion to chivalrous conduct and a commitment to a feudal-style social and political order were two of antebellum Dixie's most fondly cherished concepts. J. Quitman Moore of Mississippi, writing in *DeBow's Review*, lamented the decline of the feudalistic spirit in America and linked this decline, like Hammond and Fitzhugh, to the dangerous theories of Mr. Jefferson. It was, he contended, "from the speculative philosophy of the French revolutionaries" that the Sage of Monticello had "imbibed many of those extreme and radical notions of government." Luckily, however, Jefferson's pernicious thinking had not obliterated the feudal influences that happily continued to linger in the South. Here the "genius of Chivalry and the spirit of fealty" had found a "refuge in the manners and sentiments of the descendants of the Cavaliers of Charles II."[12]

Of course, not all southern intellectuals were committed to the region's Cavalier racial mythology. Alabama native Daniel R. Hundley was one of those who dissented most articulately from such mythmaking. In his *Social Relations in Our Southern States,* published in 1860 on the eve of the Civil War, Hundley acknowledged that the South could accurately boast of a significant number of aristocratic planters. But he also argued that the tendency of northern social critics to focus their attention as well as their opprobrium on these plantation owners had resulted in their ignoring three other classes of southerners, each far more numerous than the planter class. This distorted focus, he believed, had produced a correspondingly distorted picture of the South's social structure.

One of Hundley's overlooked southern classes, the class that constituted "the greater proportion of [the South's] citizens," was a middle class composed of merchants, teachers, doctors, artisans, and, more numerously, farmers. These farmers, many of whom owned small numbers of slaves, were largely descended from what Hundley termed "sturdy Saxon" stock and were neither so polished nor so physically graceful as the Cavalier planters in the class above them. Still, they were hard workers who formed an agrarian middle class that bore favorable comparison with "the more well-to-do and intelligent farmers of New England." Beneath this rural middle class was an almost as numerous non-slaveholding yeoman class, comparable in manners and possessions with the small farmers of the North and West, and a smaller but still significantly numerous class of landless poor whites. This last and lowest southern class combined laziness and poverty with "hard shell" religiosity, heavy drinking, and "downright envy and hatred of the black man."[13]

Social Relations in Our Southern States marked a rare and refreshing departure from the writings of apologists such as Ruffin, Hammond, and Fitzhugh. One of the book's most interesting details was its author's frank if disdainful acknowledgment of the existence of poor whites. This was a class that most of Dixie's polemicists, in their intoxication with the myth of a Cavalier-descended southern race, simply pretended did not exist. Equally at variance with the South's vision of itself as a highly cultivated plantation aristocracy was Hundley's thorough and convincing description of the fundamentally middle-class/yeoman texture of southern society. Since the only significant difference between middle-class farmers and yeoman farmers, in Hundley's view, was the possession of slaves and since he described both classes as descending from "sturdy Saxon" stock, the picture he painted was of a region predominantly populated by people who drew their values from the yeoman tradition and their blood inheritance from Saxon forebears. In short, Hundley depicted a South that was not separated from the North, as most southern polemicists had argued, by deep social and racial divisions.

Southern reviewers were generally respectful of Hundley's work. After all, the author was himself a Harvard-educated product of the Deep South's plantation aristocracy. Though they might have preferred it had he not acknowledged and described the poor whites, they could comfortably share his disdain for this southern underclass. Still, they took exception to what they considered his scanting of Dixie's Cavalier planters. Alabamian J. T. Wiswall, in a commentary on *Social Relations* written for *DeBow's Review,* expressed the prevailing sentiment of southern readers when he chided Hundley's tendency to underestimate the importance of the region's aristocratic planters. After all, he argued, it was "the wealth, brains and refinement of aristocracy, that formed, and now controls and preserves" southern freedom. In his view Hundley had failed to do justice to a class of men inferior to none on earth. Though they could not match in wealth the plutocrats of "the Fifth Avenue," the author was convinced that the South's aristocracy was "infinitely more polished, learned, and graceful" than these New York Yankees. Indeed, how could that city's glorified shopkeepers match the "cheerful tempers and generous natures" of a landed class brought up on the principles of honor and noblesse oblige? Wiswall concluded that "the exclusion of emigration, and the conservative influences of African slavery" had enabled southern aristocrats "to retain the habits and peculiarities of character, and . . . the stout physical prowess of our transatlantic cousins" of old England.[14]

Like so many other southern writers, Wiswall ignored Hundley's impressively detailed examination of the South's broad middle class. In response, he appealed to the prevailing racial myths of the 1850s, myths that were being given such fulsome expression by writers like James Hammond and George Fitzhugh. These myths championed a unique southern race descended from English Cavalier blood, more homogeneous than and superior to the racial composition of the northern states. In this fantasy of aristocratic descent there could be no room for a middle class or a yeoman class, much less a poor-white class. And there was certainly no place in the scheme for Hundley's "Saxon" blood.

If southern polemicists were willing to apotheosize a race of high-minded gentlemen, they were also determined to do no lesser service in praise of the lordly planter's lady. Maria McIntosh, writing in a Nashville women's magazine devoted to "religion and literature," embraced the standard argument of writers such as Edmund Ruffin that slavery had vouchsafed the planter "leisure for the cultivation of his mind, and the practice of all the gentle courtesies of life." Like Ruffin, she agreed that it was just this cultivation and courtesy that marked the South's landed aristocracy as clearly superior to the "rude, laborious North." McIntosh also believed that the peculiar institution that had produced southern men of such aristocratic timbre had produced southern women of equally high quality who combined "in a rare degree, refinement and simplicity." This extraordinary combination of feminine virtues was, in the writer's opinion, the natural expression of a stable plantation culture in which "changes of property are less frequent and violent . . . than in a commercial country."[15]

J. T. Wiswall was one of a host of southern male writers who endorsed Maria McIntosh's observation that the southern lady uniquely and felicitously yoked simplicity and modesty of character with intelligence and refined sophistication. The southern Cavalier's lady, he observed, was nearly always distinguished by her "wit and grace of conversation." Armed with these qualities she was fit to "appear among queens and nobles" with "quiet confidence and ease." And what sort of women had the northern race produced? In Wiswall's opinion these females were commonly characterized by "nervousness, fanaticism, and superstition," qualities that deprived them of the grace and refinement of the southern lady. As we shall see, many southerners were inclined to attribute what they deemed the fanatical, restless temperaments of northern women to their Puritan racial inheritance. Wiswall was also waggishly willing to view their instability as a product of "sedentary life through long winters over hot stoves."[16]

Though apologists such as Quitman Moore and J. T. Wiswall were content to describe the South's unique "slaveholding race" of ladies and gentlemen with the general term *Cavalier*, not all were satisfied with this somewhat romantic historical appellation. After all, the ethnology that flourished in the scientific climate of the mid-nineteenth century demanded more precise racial tags. And as we have seen in chapter 1, southern writers of the 1850s had begun to avoid *Anglo-Saxon*, the term that had been employed throughout the 1840s to describe white Americans from all sections of the nation. Political clashes and the increasingly virulent rhetoric of the North-South sectional debates convinced more and more southerners that they did not want to be lumped along with Yankee abolitionists into a single Anglo-Saxon American race.

In order to define more precisely the South's newly evolving racial identity in a manner that properly acknowledged that southern race's uniquely aristocratic pedigree, the term *Anglo-Saxon* was largely abandoned in favor of *Anglo-Norman*. A writer for the *Southern Quarterly Review* employed the term in 1850, and other writers quickly picked it up. In the same year that the *Southern Quarterly Review* article appeared, Hunter Garnett boasted that "Divine Providence" had delivered the slaves "from the barbarous idolatries of Africa, and brought them within the blessings covenanted to believers in Christ." "At the same time," he continued, it had "provided the whites of the Anglo-Norman race in the Southern States with the necessary means of unexampled prosperity." Garnett believed that God had given to these superior Anglo-Normans "a distinct and inferior race to fill a position equal to its highest capacity, which, in less fortunate countries, is occupied by the whites themselves."[17] It must have been pleasing for polemicists like Garnett to employ the burnished and newly coined *Anglo-Norman* in the service of southern racialism and white supremacy.

By the 1850s the term *Anglo-Saxon* had lost its appeal even among older southern writers who had formerly subscribed to American nationalistic principles. The semantic transformation of William Gilmore Simms was typical of these authors. Reginald Horsman has observed that although in the 1840s Simms had been "aligned with the nationalistic young America group," in the decade that followed he became "a defender of southern nationalism." As his attitudes changed from American national to southern regional, he came to prefer "to use Anglo-Norman to describe his race rather than Anglo-Saxon."[18] By the 1850s, southern writers young and old were beginning to sport a new racial consciousness. They were also brandishing a new term, *Anglo-Norman,* to define the lordly "slaveholding race" born of Dixie's mythic Norman inheritance.

Integral to the efforts of southern apologists to define a distinct southern race was the defining of a separate Yankee race that inhabited the states north of the Mason-Dixon. This northern race served southern nationalists from the beginning as a convenient foil, its debased character highlighting the exalted racial qualities of the southern people. Dixie's polemicists were particularly skillful in subverting the North's most obvious strength, its enthusiastic and phenomenally successful commitment to commerce and industry, by linking the region's economic prosperity to traits of selfishness, acquisitiveness, and greed that in turn were viewed as expressions of the northerner's inherent racial temperament.

As early as 1853 a writer for the *Southern Quarterly Review* remarked that the "bustling competition" that had given the North its enviable prosperity had also bequeathed "a hard and selfish energy to a people, which becomes reckless of means to attain results." The essay was among the first of many to appear in a southern periodical excoriating northerners for their presumed rapacity and amorality. In an essay entitled "The Almighty Dollar" J. N. Maffit attacked the North's manic devotion to the "spirit of trade." The moral climate of such a commercial culture, he argued, was one in which "every virtue [floundered] in a deluge of barter." Edmund Ruffin observed that northerners had focused on the accumulation of wealth at the expense of self-culture. They had become a mean and parsimonious people who had continued "to labor as steadily, and to live nearly as rudely as when under the pressure of [their] early poverty."[19]

And what was the racial source of this parsimony and meanness of spirit that southern writers were so fond of imputing to northerners? There was no doubt in the mind of the essayist for the *Southern Quarterly Review* that the qualities of base expediency that threatened to infect the entire nation's moral and political fiber sprang from and could be historically linked to *"the race of Yankees."* Maffit likewise traced the origins of northern avidity to "the eastern Yankee" who, he disdainfully observed, would compulsively swap "horses until his last exchange . . . too poor to swap, is sold for a jackknife."[20]

Maffit's reference to "the eastern Yankee" suggests that some southern polemicists continued to associate the Yankee character primarily with the New England states, as southerners had done since the early years of the Republic. However, the phrase "race of Yankees" that appears in the *Southern Quarterly Review* indicates that by the 1850s other southern writers had begun to expand the definition of that term, using it to describe more than simply people living in New England. Indeed, in the decade preceding the Civil War *Yankee* would acquire increasingly pejorative connotations in the southern vocabulary, and southerners would employ it more and more frequently to describe all people living in the Northeast and Midwest. After all, were not the people of the northern and midwestern states largely descended from New England ancestry? Claudian Northrup expressed this broader and more inclusive sense of the word when he declared that the Yankee "spirit of selfishness" and "custom of trade" dominated the culture and habits of Americans living in all the states to the "North, and East, and Northwest, both of the cities and praedial population."[21]

As sectional debates sharpened in the years preceding the Civil War, southerners became more and more convinced that while they were descended, in the words of an essayist for *DeBow's Review,* "almost entirely from the better and more enlightened classes of Great Britain and France," the Yankees who had settled New England and subsequently spread throughout the East and Northwest were largely "lineal descendants of the English puritans." In the southern mind, *Yankee* and *Puritan* became nearly synonymous. If *Yankee* was the term preferred by southern polemicists assailing the northern race for its grasping selfishness and materialism, *Puritan* was the term preferred by critics aiming at the North's political and social culture. In the opinion of the *DeBow's* essayist, the "politico-religious fanaticism" of the English Puritans constituted "the very worst developments of human nature—excelled by the French Jacobins only." And the followers of Oliver Cromwell had carried this horrible fanaticism with them to the New World, where to the present day it continued to be "the ruling characteristic of New-England Yankees." Another *DeBow's* writer made the following distasteful observation after a visit to the northern states: "The odor of Puritanism still clings around much of the population." He was convinced that the fanaticism that permeated New England culture was one that pretended to philanthropy. In the hearts of these philanthropic Puritans, he observed bitterly, there was only a desire to "hang a shroud of despair around all peace, all enjoyment, and all earthly happiness."[22]

No southern writer satirized Puritan fanaticism more keenly than George Fitzhugh. In his *Sociology for the South* he linked the North's laissez-faire economic principles and its "every man for himself" social principles to an avid and intolerant mentality that had originally manifested itself in the persecution of witches. "Our Pilgrim fathers being denied the opportunity of practicing to its full extent the divine precept—'Love thy neighbor as Thyself' —removed to America, and here proved to the world that they had not degenerated since the unctuous days of Knox and of Cromwell." Fitzhugh proceeded sardonically to describe the fruits of this Puritan religious enthusiasm: "Many tokens of their zeal and affection were soon seen pendant from the elms of New England; and with a delicate discrimination, that affection selected the ugliest and oldest of the weaker sex, on whom to lavish its embraces."[23]

Fitzhugh was convinced that the same Puritan fanaticism that had precipitated the persecution of witches in colonial times had produced the North's present fractured and frantic religious and intellectual climate. "Why," he railed, "have you Bloomer's and Women's Right's men, and strong-minded women, and Mormons, and anti-renters, and 'vote myself a farm' men, Millerites, and Spiritual Rappers, and Shakers, and Widow Wakemanites, and Agrarians, and Grahamites, and a thousand other superstitions and infidel

Isms at the North?" For Fitzhugh the answer was clear. The Puritan temperament had always been and would always be one that fatally gravitated toward spiritual hysteria and extremes of opinion. As he put it, "This unsettled, half-demented state of the human mind" was "coextensive" with a society of Puritan-descended free thinkers. An essayist for the *Southern Literary Messenger* professed that he was resigned to the emotional anarchy of northerners. What else, he observed gloomily, could one expect from a region that stood "allied by ties of blood and race" to Cromwell's rebellious and brutal Roundheads, men whose deeds would "forever stand a living *absurdity* on the page of English history"? Unlike southern Cavaliers, northerners were descended from "rude and vulgar men—men, who by habit and by *race,* were ignorant of the amenities which should ever attend upon the enforcement of power."[24]

Southern apologists, not surprisingly, viewed abolitionism as the most pernicious and evil fruit of Puritan fanaticism. They scoffed at the notion that men like William Lloyd Garrison were motivated by a sincere desire to help the slave. They condemned abolitionists as troublemakers, and they accused them of being religious hypocrites motivated not by genuine moral concerns but by an obsession with prevailing on the issue of slavery at all costs, by a Cromwellian determination to impose their moral yoke upon the South. Thundered one writer for the *Southern Quarterly Review,* "Is the South to sit content with this dispensation, not of Providence, but of Puritanism?" A writer for a Richmond newspaper fumed that "every dispute from which the Republic suffered in its interests or its honor has been engendered of the corrupt intellect and morbid morality of New England." There was, he warned, an inherent "principle of evil in Puritanism" that was poisoning the nation. There was "not a false religion, a false philosophy, a false literature, or a false system of politics in the country, of which the origins may not be traced to New England."[25]

South Carolina poet William John Grayson reserved special contempt for abolitionists in his neoclassical apologia for slavery entitled *The Hireling and the Slave.* In attacking them he drew skillfully on popular southern prejudices concerning Yankees and Puritans. He pilloried abolitionists like antislavery congressman Joshua Giddings as fools who combined the fanaticism of a foaming-at-the-mouth Puritan with the instincts of a common Yankee peddler:

> There Giddings, with the Negro mania bit,
> Mouths, and mistakes his ribaldry for wit,

> His fustian speeches into market brings,
> And prints and peddles all the paltry things.

When Grayson took on Horace Greeley, he tagged him with the blind intolerance laced with moral hypocrisy that southerners assumed to be the animating quality of Puritan-descended northern extremists:

> He damns all creeds and parties but his own,
> Brawls, with hot zeal, for every fool and knave,
> The foreign felon and the skulking slave.[26]

Goaded on by such inflamed anti-Yankee and anti-Puritan rhetoric, southerners were hardly inclined to abase themselves before the altars of Puritan rectitude and New England culture. One Alabama congressman expressed "sovereign contempt for the memory of the Pilgrim Fathers," and he dismissed their religion as one "of fanaticism, of intolerance, of infidelity, of bigotry and hypocrisy." Southerners also delighted in casting contempt on New England's most esteemed writers. Longfellow epitomized "laborious mediocrity," and Emerson's work feebly attempted "an awkward affectation of German Transcendentalism." A Theodore Parker sermon expressed the "phrenzied utterance of an infernally inspired intellect." For one southern polemicist, the only writer of substance the Puritan race had produced was Nathaniel Hawthorne, and Hawthorne had achieved artistic success primarily because he had "employed the best energies of his incomparable genius in discrediting the source of New England civilization."[27]

If the Puritan-descended Yankee race had produced few men of noble character, it had produced, in the jaundiced opinion of the South's essayists, even fewer ladies of grace, refinement, and simplicity. How could grace and refinement flourish in a laissez-faire society in which there was "no chivalrous devotion to the weak and helpless female, no generous and manly protection of her, but all is calculating, cold, and heartless, as the metal they worship"? And how could simplicity survive among a people who encouraged their women to abjure "the delicate offices of their sex" and to desert "their nurseries" so that they might "stroll over the country as politico-moral reformers, delivering lewd lectures upon the beauties of free-love and spiritualism"?[28]

Southern apologists were particularly fond of titillating their scandalized readers with accounts of northern "free-love" societies. Writing in *DeBow's Review*, Mr. A. Clarkson of Alabama noted that such groups thrived above the Potomac "in abundance" and served only to promote "brutal lust, and the complete degradation of both sexes." They were led by fake spiritualists who played upon "the superstitions of the female mind, forcing her with pretended spiritual commands to pander to their lust." Clarkson believed that, in abdicating their gentlemanly responsibility for caring for women and protecting their honor, northern men had forced their women out of a sense of self-protection "to demand civil and political, as well as social equality, with man." "How deplorable," he wrote, "must be the moral degradation of that society where woman is driven so entirely out of the sphere assigned her by God!"[29]

For most southerners living in the fractious 1850s, Harriet Beecher Stowe epitomized the freakish, intellectualized Yankee "she-male," and her *Uncle Tom's Cabin* was condemned as pure fiction, an agglomeration of distortions and vicious falsehoods. It was the inevitable product of a disordered female imagination, one that had been wrenched by Puritan fanaticism out of its natural feminine sphere. For William John Grayson, the intellect of female Yankee reformers like Stowe was tainted, like that of their male counterparts, with hypocrisy and a sordid love of money:

> Snuffs up pollution with a pious air,
> Collects a rumor here, a slander there;
> With hatred's ardor gathers Newgate spoils,
> And trades for gold the garbage of her toils.

Whatever else Harriet Beecher Stowe may have been, she was not, in Grayson's view, a lady. She was, rather, a perfect example of the "pedantic, masculine women" who in George Fitzhugh's opinion held sway among Yankees. Men of the southern race were bound to turn away in disgust from such unsexed female abolitionists. "We would infinitely prefer," Fitzhugh sneered, "to nurse a sickly woman, to being led about by a masculine blue stocking."[30]

In cataloguing the debased characters of both men and women of the northern race, Southern polemicists were usually content to identify that race as Yankee or Puritan, as they were normally content to identify their own race as Cavalier. But the same pseudo-scientific influences that prompted them to use the terms *Norman* or *Anglo-Norman* to describe more precisely their newly fashioned racial identity caused them frequently to employ the term *Saxon* to define the northern people. One writer for the *Southern Literary Messenger* articulated an even more nuanced definition of the Yankee race. While the blood that flowed through southern veins was largely of Norman origin, he believed that the great majority of northerners were products of the unfortunate union of two racial strains notable for their proclivity for intemperance and violence: the Saxon and the Celtic. This essayist argued that there was "a strong infusion of Celt in Northern society, and where ever there is Celt there are revolutions, disorders and violence, far beyond even such tendencies in the Saxon; and when combined, each but makes the other worse."[31]

In referring to the North's strongly Celtic racial strain the writer for the *Southern Literary Messenger* apparently had in mind Scots, Scots-Irish, and Irish immigrants. Irish immigrants were of course widely disparaged and looked down upon in both North and South, but Scots and Scots-Irish settlers were viewed with much more favor and constituted a significant component of the southern as well as the northern population. The essayist was not blind to this reality. He admitted with a hint of reluctance that in the South there was "a certain *Celtic* element ... among us." But he neatly finessed this potential racial complication with the facile assurance that Norman blood had always dominated the South and with the equally facile assertion that it would continue in future to set the tone of southern culture.[32]

The southern fantasy of a pure or nearly pure Norman race was matched by the specter of a debased Saxon or Celtic-Saxon northern racial stock made even more inferior by invasions of racially suspect immigrants from the sewers of Europe. Dixie's reactionary defenders thus viewed massive immigration not as a sign of progress but as one of racial and social decay. Edmund Ruffin was among those southerners who professed themselves satisfied with the South's relatively slow population growth, and he was proud of the part slavery had played in restraining this growth. By discouraging new settlers, Dixie's peculiar institution had directed to the northern states "the hordes of immigrants now flowing from Europe." In general, he maintained, these immigrants were of "lower intelligence" than the lowest of "native citizens" and "immeasurably inferior" in education and in "appreciation of the principles of free government." The implications of Ruffin's remarks were clear, and they probably reflected the convictions of most educated southerners in the years leading to the Civil War. The northern race was becoming increasingly mongrelized and debased, while the institution of slavery was assuring that the southern race remained pure and white and ethnographically sound. It was no wonder that God approved of slavery. It was, in Ruffin's words, a part of God's "wise and benevolent design," and it had fostered the creation of a highly cultivated, noble, and superior race of people.[33]

It is ironic that while northerners of the 1850s tended to view themselves as victims of a brutal, barbaric, and powerful slave-owning race, southerners likewise saw themselves as victims of an aggressive and fanatical race of Puritan-descended Celtic-Saxons. This sense of southern helplessness in the face of northern extremism was given poetic expression in "The Northman's Cause," published in the *Southern Literary Messenger* on the eve of the Civil War. Here a southern persona stands on the streets of Boston observing citizens whose ancestors had rebelled against British tyranny. The observer is filled with the rueful understanding that these same people who fought tyranny in the past aim in the present to extend a tyranny of their own devising across the modern South. Aggressive abolitionism has become the creed of a people who in their fanaticism plunge heedlessly into the future, committed to no value but change for change's sake. The southerner watches in helpless horror as these Puritan-descended fanatics thoughtlessly draw the nation into the maelstrom of civil war:

> Cast to the billow chart and compass all!
> Portless we voyage time—the Maelstrom looms,
> The warring surge we near, and swift we rush.
> And round the vortex whirling downward sweep!
> —So tends the Age![34]

Like the author of "The Northmen's Cause," many southerners viewed themselves as victims of an aggressive and fanatical northern race. But they were confident that their superior racial fiber equipped them to respond more than adequately to the armed conflict that seemed every month to grow more and more inevitable. Claudian Northrup expressed the sentiments of these southerners when he observed that the "spirit of selfishness" and the mania for trade that had served northerners so well in peacetime commercial expansion were "inconsistent with that self-forgetting public spirit, which is necessary to inaugurate and conduct so grand a movement as a war.... Will they venture to assail the South, with nothing to gain but a barren propagandism of social and political theories, which the great majority are too selfish even to have seriously examined?" He could not imagine that a hodgepodge of inferior races devoted to trade and petty farm enterprises were capable of mounting a serious military threat against the southern states. Northerners, he contemptuously observed, had been "and are yet too busy, in clearing land, building log cabins, pressing cider and cheese, raising corn and wheat, and making flour and bacon, and a numerous little progeny of German and Irish-American boys and girls, to be very eager about enlisting as soldiers or campaigning in the sultry South. Puritanical fanaticism, or trembling and pragmatic mammon, may buy steel pikes, and preach sympathy for a few ruffians like John Brown; but whence will the men come to handle those weapons, or rescue the desperate?"[35] For Northrup and for southerners who had committed themselves to their region's new racial mythology, it was laughable to imagine that a mongrel mob of northern troops could ever prevail in a contest with the South's noble Norman warriors.

In 1854 George Fitzhugh posed a portentous question to southerners. Were they "willing to remain mere colonies and plantations for the centres of trade," or were they ready to throw off these economic shackles and choose to "preserve their separate nationality?"[36] Although by the early 1850s secessionists were growing in number, it is unlikely that a majority of southerners at that time would have chosen to define themselves as a "separate nationality." However, by 1861 most of the South's white population supported the establishment of an independent Confederacy and were willing to go to war to defend it. The Cavalier-Norman racial myth fabricated by southern polemicists in the 1850s provided the perfect propagandistic support for the region's growing nationalistic sentiments. In essay after essay nobly articulated assertions of the South's ethnological uniqueness and superiority glowed beneath a varnish of pseudoscientific terminology, complementing the idea of a new southern nation with the idea of a new southern race.

The expression of this Norman-Saxon race mythology was frequent and widespread in the decade preceding the Civil War, appearing in Dixie's most influential periodicals and newspapers. However, the thesis probably received its fullest and most provocative articulation in an essay published in *DeBow's Review* entitled "Southern Civilization; or, The Norman in America." This essay's central thesis was that the current conflict in the United States between northerners and southerners was an extension of a conflict that had originated in England hundreds of years earlier in the opposition of Saxon to Norman. The essayist proposed that the Saxons who had come to England from the Germanic north had brought with them a distinctive racial character. He asserted that "true to the ideas and instincts of his Northern origin, the Saxon [had] clung to that fierce and lawless individualism in state, and that stern, gloomy, and impracticable idealism in Church, which his rude Teutonic fathers brought with them from the wild Hercynian forests." These anarchic and dark racial traits had not disappeared in the hundreds of years since the Saxons had arrived on English shores. On the contrary, after the establishment of the English Church under Henry VIII "this Saxon element [had become] the fortress and arsenal of that violent and fanatical party of political and religious revolutionists, known as Puritans, Independents, or Presbyterians."[37]

Having established the link between Saxon and Puritan England, the essay went on to link this violent race of men to the rise during the Renaissance of "all that restless, selfish, arrogant and ambitious class, which commerce had elevated to sudden importance" (5). During the seventeenth century the original racial characteristics of the newly prosperous class of Saxon-descended merchants had turned from "lawless individualism" and "gloomy idealism" into grasping avidity and Puritan piety. But the avidity belied the piety. In the writer's opinion, Puritan religious zeal had cleverly masked the real ambition of this ascendant class: "to wrest from the Norman the scepter of empire, making religious fanaticism only the cloak for concealing his political designs" (5).

Against the determined politico-religious assault of England's Saxon-Puritans, her Normans had proved worthy opponents, for the genius of this noble race lay in its instincts for social order and command. "Aristocracy, based upon the feudal relation," the essay observed, was "the natural expression of the political thought of the Norman" (6). The stage was thus set for the decisive battle in England between "Teutonic" and "Norman." The division was, as it had always been, racial as well as political. In the words of the *DeBow's* essayist, "The originally hostile races—Norman and Saxon—now assumed the shape of two equally hostile parties—the Cavalier and Puritan" (6).

Was the bloody English Civil War that ultimately ensued between Cavaliers and Puritans unavoidable? The *DeBow's* essay contended that the King's followers would have been able to compromise in the interests of social concord. After all, the Cavalier was "the builder, the social architect, the institutionalist, the conservator—the advocate of rational liberty and the supporter of authority." These Norman-descended aristocrats were "chivalrous in sentiment and magnanimous in deed." "Honor" was the essential "touchstone" of their characters. "Courtly in his manners and splendid in his tastes," the Cavalier practiced a "knightly generosity," even toward his foes (8). To preserve social order these inherent aristocrats might have forged a compromise with their lowly foes. "But the Roundhead," the essay contended, "at once a religious fanatic and a political agitator and reformer, could conceive of no government but the rule of the Saints, and form no other idea of the principles of civil liberty than what the leveling philosophy of the Covenant taught" (7). In the face of such Puritan bigotry and fanaticism, no compromise was possible, and England consequently descended into bloodshed and regicide.

By the time "Southern Civilization" launches into its description of the English Civil War, its thematic direction has been clearly established. The seventeenth-century conflict between Saxon-Puritan and Norman-Cavalier is viewed as a rehearsal for the even more destructive nineteenth-century racial collision between Saxon and Norman in the United States. "These were the parties that met on Naseby Field under the hostile banners of Fairfax and Rupert," the essayist concludes, "and from which have sprung two nationalities that now divide the empire of the American continent" (8–9). The conflict between North and South is directly linked to the abiding, centuries-old conflict between Puritan and Cavalier. The writer views the antagonists as separate races with drastically opposing temperaments and values, and he uses the English Civil War to validate his contention that the two peoples can never peacefully coexist within the same nation.

"Southern Civilization" conveniently assumed that Saxons resided en masse above the Mason-Dixon Line and that Normans resided almost entirely below it. In advancing the thesis of a Norman-descended southern race the essayist, like other southern polemicists, was forced to acknowledge the obvious fact that his supposedly homogenous southern race was composed at least partially of non-Norman elements. But like these other apologists he finessed the subject of the South's racial diversity without grappling with it. He followed his brief and perfunctory description of the non-Norman elements of the southern population by peremptorily proclaiming the dominance of both Norman blood and culture in the South. "Excepting the French and Spanish in Louisiana and Huguenots in South Carolina," he asserted, "the States of the South were founded almost exclusively by colonists owing allegiance to the British Crown." He conceded that "Ireland, Scotland and Wales [had] contributed equally with the softer Latin Races of Andalusia and Languedoc to the formation of a composite Southern nationality" (9). But he insisted that the Cavalier had "become early the controlling and informing element" of Dixie's racial inheritance, with Maryland, Virginia, and the Carolinas forming important colonial "centres of Anglo-Norman culture" (10). The writer assured his readers that despite a limited Celtic influence, the South's Norman inheritance had definitively molded the character of its people.

Spreading south and west from its original home along the southeastern seaboard states, the Anglo-Norman race had also sown the seeds of its "master passion" through the Gulf and interior regions of the South all the way to Texas. And what was this passion? The essayist believed that it was "an abiding attachment to landed possession and territorial power, which is the secret of the universal dominion and ascendancy of the Norman Race." This remarkably strong attachment had laid the foundations of Dixie's "great, agricultural empire" (12). But while the southern Norman had spread his aristocratic land-centered values toward Texas, the Puritan-Saxon had disseminated a countervailing ethos throughout the eastern and northwestern states, a fanatical obsession with tyrannous majority political rule. The political principles of the American Puritan, like the religious principles of his English Puritan ancestors, cloaked a "grasping and rapacious" mercantile policy (12).

The *DeBow's* article concluded by enumerating five fundamental and defining characteristics of southern civilization. "Domestic servitude," agricultural pursuits, a tropical climate, and staple production ranked second through fifth on this list. At the head of these four stood "the Norman Race" (14), and its preeminent position was fitting, for it was Dixie's uniquely Norman racial inheritance that had blessed it with an ordered and peerless social structure "not unlike" that of medieval Europe. Its lordly Cavalier aristocrats constituted, above all of Dixie's other formative elements, "the Doric pillars and Corinthian capitals" of the region's grand "social edifice" (17).

A modern reader who did not know the publication date of this remarkable *DeBow's Review* essay would probably assign it to the period between 1859 and 1861, when sectional passions had risen to a fever pitch and the South was moving toward secession. In fact, "Southern Civilization; or, The Norman in America" was published in the January–February 1862 issue of the New Orleans magazine, almost a year after southern cannons had fired on Fort Sumter. As we have seen, Anglo-Norman race mythology had been an important element of arguments proposing an independent southern nation. However, the myth was not laid aside after the establishment of the Confederacy, and the Norman-Saxon racial dualism did not disappear from polemical writing during the Civil War. As the *DeBow's* essay suggests, Dixie's wartime defenders continued to employ the racial myth that had been fabricated in the 1850s to convince southerners of the depravity of the inferior northern race they were fighting, of the historical inevitability of conflict between these two entirely incompatible peoples, and of the rightness of the southern race's noble cause.

4
Race Mythology and Antebellum Fiction

As we have seen, the articulation of the South's Norman racial myth was informed, at least superficially, by prevailing mid-nineteenth-century scientific theories regarding the development of distinct human races. Southern race mythology thus often sported a pseudoscientific intellectual veneer, and the most common venue for its expression was the literary and political journal, where it was presented in essay form as part of a broader defense of southern culture. Unlike these nonfiction essayists, the South's writers of belletristic fiction were not directly connected with this popularizing of the South's new racial mythology. However, they were indirectly but nonetheless powerfully involved in creating in their romantic plantation novels a congruent image of Dixie as a culturally and racially unique part of the new American nation. Indeed, southern fiction had been about the business of romantically celebrating the region's alluring distinctiveness decades before southern polemicists embraced the idea of its unique, Norman racial inheritance.

From its inception, southern literature had had at its disposal a myth that glorified the South's origins and affirmed its cultural superiority to the North—a myth based on the Cavalier character ideal. This ideal had rooted itself earliest and most deeply in the plantation society of colonial Tidewater Virginia. It affirmed the aristocratic origins of colonial Virginia's leading families; and it rested on the belief that the Old Dominion's culture had been primarily and profoundly influenced by the immigration to the colony from England of large numbers of Cavalier supporters of King Charles II, who had fled the victorious Puritan ascendancy of Oliver Cromwell in the 1660s and 1670s. By the nineteenth century the notion that Virginia's leading families had descended directly from aristocratic English ancestors was so solidly established in the South that the Virginia romance novelist John Esten Cooke, writing a popular history of his native state, pronounced it ex cathedra as historical fact. "One of the highest authorities in American history," he observed, "has described the Cavalier element in Virginia as only 'perceptible.' It was really so strong as to control all things,—the forms of society, of religion, and the direction of public affairs. The fact was so plain that he who ran might read it."[1]

Was the fact of the Old Dominion's aristocratic foundation as abundantly plain as Cooke insisted? How closely aligned was the Cavalier myth to the historical realities of Virginia's settlement? Until recently modern historians generally agreed that the social origins of most of the landed families who came to constitute what would be popularly known as the Virginia aristocracy were not, in fact, aristocratic. The great majority of the young men who endured danger and hardship to establish themselves in the new colony were products of the English middle class—sons of yeoman farmers, minor gentry, and merchants. These men were by no means products of the lower English social orders, but neither were they lords and aristocrats. In his seminal study of Tidewater society, entitled *Myths and Realities,* Carl Bridenbaugh termed the ruling class that these men established in Virginia a "unique bourgeois aristocracy." And in a later analysis historians Robert and Katherine Brown went even further in distancing the colony's dominant planters from the aristocratic Old World ideal. They emphasized the relative fluidity of class structure in colonial Virginia and concluded that the colony's upper class could not accurately be defined as an aristocracy. Mid-twentieth-century historians thus returned to the conclusions of one of the Old Dominion's earliest chroniclers, native Virginian Robert Beverley, who in his *History and Present State of Virginia* (1705) refused to endorse the Cavalier myth. The colony, Beverley astutely observed, had received very few criminals or Cavaliers alike. The great majority of settlers, he contended, were of low or modest circumstances. "Nor was it hardly possible it should be otherwise," he realistically reflected, "for 'tis now unlikely that any Man of plentiful Estate, should voluntarily abandon a happy Certainty, to roam after imaginary Advantages, in a New World."[2]

As observed in chapter 1, David Hackett Fischer's *Albion's Seed* runs counter to the prevailing stream of twentieth-century historical analysis and makes a convincing case for the dominant presence of the English gentry among the Old Dominion's largest and most powerful planters. But though they undoubtedly exercised a powerful and formative influence on Tidewater colonial society, these gentry-descended planters were remarkably few in number when compared with the large numbers of indentured servants and settlers of low or modest social standing.[3] This was a demographic fact that romantic celebrators of pre-Revolutionary Virginia's Cavalier inheritance completely ignored.

Despite Robert Beverley's observations about the modest circumstances of the colony's settlement, the early development of a plantation tobacco economy dependent on indentured and slave labor helped to turn New World Virginians into colonials who self-consciously and determinedly embraced the Old World social pattern of the rural squire, whatever their social origins in England might have been. Indeed, this embracing of the ethos of the gentry—with its conceptions of gentility, cultural refinement, and social stratification—distinguished in a striking way the culture of the colonies of Maryland, Virginia, the Carolinas, and Georgia from the northern colonies. Here a harsher climate discouraged the cultivation of tobacco on large holdings of land and encouraged smaller farm holdings tilled by yeomen, and here the Cavalier ideal did not take root.

The colonial plantations that clung to the shores and tributary rivers of the Chesapeake Bay and to the narrow southern coastal littoral were the only places in English North America where, through the accumulation of land and slaves, a man might hope to establish a lifestyle and social position akin to that of the gentry of Old England. The appeal of this Old World social pattern was particularly strong in Virginia. Louis Wright eloquently expresses the powerful impression of the idea of gentility on the settlers of Tidewater Virginia:

> As social-climbing citizens [in England] sought to imitate the landed gentry, so Virginia colonists who had the opportunity of acquiring land and accumulating wealth attempted to duplicate the manner of life led by that most envied of mortals at home, the proud and powerful country squire.... While they developed an independence of spirit and became Virginians instead of Englishmen in a distant colony, they had a dream of being Virginians like the fine gentlemen of the older civilization. That dream helped to shape the thinking and the cultural ideals of the Virginia ruling class throughout the seventeenth and eighteenth centuries.[4]

Virginia did indeed develop a social pattern dominated by the planter-aristocrat ideal, but the notion commonly bruited by the region's post-Revolutionary novelists that the colony had been largely settled by aristocratic Cavaliers was more myth than fact. Nonetheless, Virginians ambitious of emulating the social pattern of the English gentry embraced the aristocratic ideal fervently, and it marked their characters so strongly that visitors from the northern colonies were soon commenting unfavorably on the pride and pretensions of the Old Dominion's wealthy planters. An interesting critique of the snobbishness and vanity of the Virginia gentry can be found in the pages of Philip Fithian's diary. Fithian, New Jersey born and Princeton educated, lived for about one year at Robert Carter's Nomini Hall in the early

1770s as tutor of Carter's children. He came to know intimately and to admire the Carter family, one of Virginia's finest. Yet though he enjoyed his time on the Carter plantation, Fithian preferred life in New Jersey, where he felt there was a comparatively level distribution of wealth and where thrift and industry purchased a man's ticket to social acceptance. In Virginia, he noted, "such amazing property . . . blows up the owners to an imagination, which is visible in all, but in various degrees according to their respective virtue, that they are exalted as much above other Men in worth and precedency, as blind stupid fortune has made a difference in their property."[5]

A more damning indictment of the aristocratic pretensions of Virginia's colonial gentry is contained in a manuscript by James Reid that remained unpublished until the twentieth century. Reid has been provisionally identified as an indentured servant of Scottish origin who in the 1760s lived on the Sweet Hall plantation of the Claiborne family in King William County, probably employed as a tutor. In his manuscript, entitled "The Religion of the Bible and the Religion of K[ing] W[illiam] County compared," Reid observed bitterly that money, slaves, and land entitled even the dullest and crudest to call himself a gentleman. This self-anointed Virginia aristocrat, he complained, inflated with self-esteem, "drinks, fights, bullies, curses, swears, whores, games, sings, whistles, dances, jumps, capers, runs, talks bawdy, visits Gentleman he never saw, has the rendez-vous with Ladies he never spoke to, writes Billets-dou to filles des joies whom he stiles women of Quality, eats voraciously, sleeps, snores, and takes snuff. This comprehends his whole life, and renders him a Polite Gentleman." Noting that a slave master "commonly impregnates his own wenches," Reid concluded that "an ignorant, vicious, rich Gentleman differs in nothing from his ignorant, vicious, poor Negro, but in the colour of his skin, and in his being the greater balcguard *[sic]* of the two."[6] Allowing these vituperative descriptions to be the product of a sour and perhaps unconsciously envious Calvinist mentality, it is probable nevertheless that Reid's satiric broadside tells us more about the manners and morals of the Old Dominion's colonial Cavaliers than the romantically embellished fictional portraits of Virginia's nineteenth-century romance novelists.

Historical analyses and the contemporary accounts of visitors to colonial Virginia combine to suggest that the Old Dominion's self-styled Cavaliers were not polished and cultured descendants of the English aristocracy. The pronouncements of Virginians on the subject of social class, however, clearly indicate that they assumed or preferred to believe that they were epitomes of genteel refinement. This inflated self-image is on clear display in the poems and essays that adorn the pages of the *Virginia Gazette,* published in Williamsburg from 1736 to 1778. One writer complains of hearing "the Word *Honour* frequently profaned in the Mouths of the Vulgar and inferior sort of people." Another bemoans the degeneration of the Virginia gentleman. He attacks the excesses of gaming, cock-fighting, horse-racing, drinking, and blasphemy that are currently tolerated among the leading citizens and fears "lest the term *gentleman* sink into absolute contempt." From the *Gazette* of April 4, 1751, comes the tragic story of a young lady "of noble Extraction, but, it seems, not of noble sentiments [who] forgot her Rank so far as to fall in Love with one of her Footmen."[7]

Despite the small number of gentry-descended planters and the rough-hewn nature of a Tidewater culture that until the Revolution remained poised perilously near a wild frontier, history confirms that the colony produced a significant number of men who owned large, sometimes vast, estates and lived on them in a lavish style unmatched elsewhere in America. The notion that these men descended from aristocratic English blood was often an exaggeration. Still, the aristocratic ideal was a powerfully present in colonial Virginia, and it dominated the thinking and the self-perception of all those who were or strived to be grand planters. Except on the rice and indigo plantations of coastal Carolina, no other colony could match the impressive accretion of land and wealth of Virginia's elite planters. And these would-be New World Cavaliers used their wealth to fashion a refined lifestyle of which their Old World models might be proud.

Berkeley, Shirley, Westover, Carter's Grove—the stately mansions that still line the north bank of the James River—bear witness that colonial Virginia at the peak of its affluence developed into something more than merely a rural society of pretentious, socially striving middle-class farmers. These surviving houses remain impressive expressions of architectural and decorative taste and proportion. William Byrd II personally supervised the building of his Westover plantation, with its fine stone chimneys, its exquisite doorways, its carefully handcrafted gates and mantelpieces, its elegantly formal garden. He amassed one of the largest and most diverse collections of books in the New World, a collection large enough to require the services of a full-time librarian. Bryd's beautiful house stands today as a visual symbol of that felicitous fusion of wealth and taste that few societies, least of all frontier societies, attain. Westover and the other great plantation houses that today overlook the banks of Virginia's tidal rivers bear physical witness to the intoxicating appeal of a Cavalier myth that shaped both the behaviors and the tastes and aesthetic sensibilities of the colony's eighteenth-century ruling class.

The Cavalier myth not only strongly informed the attitudes of the Old Dominion's great planters. It also infused the thinking of the mass of Virginia's smaller farmers, most of whom seem to have given fealty to the colony's plantation elite. Historian Charles Sydnor argues convincingly that the political power of the colony's planter aristocracy rivaled that of England's rural gentry, despite the more democratic orientation of Virginia's government. Although property qualifications were not restrictive and nearly all landowners could vote, the dominance of the great planters was clearly displayed in the county courts, where appointed justices of the peace with lifetime tenure wielded wide executive, judicial, and legislative authority. These justices owned an average of nine hundred acres of land and twenty-five slaves, statistics suggesting that the typical county justice was drawn from the upper rather than the middle or lower planter class. Moreover, certain families tended to be represented again and again on the county courts. In the twenty years before the Revolution, 25 percent of Virginia's county justices came from fifty-five families, and 75 percent were chosen from fewer than four hundred families. "In most elections," Sydnor observes, "all the candidates were members of the gentry. . . . In effect, the gentry provided the candidates and the freeholders made choice among them."[8]

Sydnor's statistics indicate that colonial Virginians were inclined to accept a relatively stratified political structure that reflected, in turn, acceptance of a relatively stratified social structure—what Fischer would term an expression of the Cavalier folkway. Their willingness to defer to the authority of the gentry was probably linked to the widespread assumption among them that the blood of aristocratic Cavaliers coursed through their leaders' veins. The success of the planter aristocracy in capturing the allegiance of the yeoman farmer would seem to explain the distinctively elitist ambiance that a French visitor, the Marquis de Chastellux, detected in the Old Dominion at the time of the Revolution. Here Chastellux observed a willingness of the masses, unlike those of other colonies, to be led by the few. He offers as illustration this statement of support made by Virginia citizens to Benjamin Harrison, Richard Henry Lee, and Thomas Jefferson before they left to attend the First Continental Congress in Philadelphia: "You assert that there is a fixed intention to invade our rights and privileges; we own that we do not see this clearly, but since you assure us that it is so, we believe it. We are about to take a very dangerous step, but we have confidence in you and will do anything you think proper." Such implicit confidence in the colony's leaders led Chastellux to conclude that though "the government may become democratic, as it is at the present moment . . . the very spirit of the government, will always be aristocratic."[9]

By the time of America's independence, Virginia and Tidewater Carolina had embraced a Cavalier myth that would prove itself inherently hostile to the evolving national ideals of social and political equality. This marriage of plantation system and Cavalier would have fateful consequences for the rest of the South in the decades to come. Wherever the plantation flourished in the Deep and Middle South in the first half of the nineteenth century, so too did the Cavalier ideal, with its vision of aristocratic southern lords and ladies ruling benignly over hordes of inferior but contented Negro slaves. And wherever the ideal established itself, a literature evolved that celebrated and implicitly defended the Cavalier ideal in the form of the plantation romance novel. Not surprisingly, the first expressions of this genre came from Virginia. These early Virginia romancers would ultimately be followed by romancers from the Middle and Deep South, who would translate the character ideal to the newer terrain of cotton and sugar plantations.

The earliest Virginia plantation novels date from the 1820s—not coincidentally the decade during which sectional antagonism between North and South first began to manifest itself to a significant extent. George Tucker's *The Valley of Shenandoah* (1824) contained one of Virginia fiction's first descriptions of the state's Cavalier aristocracy. These were men who, in the author's eyes, were "remarkable for their urbanity, frankness, and ease," men who possessed "a nice sense of honour; a hatred of all that was little or mean." They were "great epicures at table; great lovers of Madeira wine, of horses and dogs; free at a jest, particularly after dinner; with a goodly store of family pride, and a moderate portion of learning . . . kind and indulgent, rather than faithful husbands."[10]

Unlike the fictional portraits of later Virginia writers, Tucker's Virginia gentleman is no paragon of moral perfection. There are cracks in the Cavalier's armor, particularly in the suggestion of his less-than-complete fidelity to his lady. But the description is ultimately defined by its warm and sentimental tone, and the author's assessment of the Cavalier figure admits no serious or critical flaws. In short, Tucker's Virginia gentlemen possess "luxurious and social habits" that give them "all that polished and easy grace, which is possessed by the highest classes in Europe," without the numbing formality and restraint of the European type.[11] In the Old Dominion's earliest plantation novel, the Cavalier seems far more akin in spirit to aristocratic Old World character ideals than to egalitarian American ones. Indeed, the Virginia squire Tucker admiringly describes would be perfectly at home in a Henry Fielding novel.

Edward Grayson commands the role of hero in *The Valley of Shenandoah*, and he is the most completely developed Cavalier in Tucker's romance. To show Edward to best advantage the novelist draws a deliberate and sustained comparison with the low-minded Yankee villain of the novel, James Gildon, who, professing to be Edward's friend, travels south to visit his Shenandoah Valley plantation. Tucker draws an explicit contrast between his Cavalier and Yankee characters in the novel's opening pages. Edward is described as a handsome young man, tall, thin, and blond, who reflects in his deportment and bearing a character guided by a "refined and high-minded standard of right." He is the perfect southern gentleman, "reserved, somewhat haughty in his manners to those who were not acknowledged inferiors (to whom he was all mildness and condescension), and possessed of the most scrupulous and fastidious honour." In contrast, James Gildon is shorter and more stout than Edward, with a florid complexion, black hair, and black eyes. He is witty, lively, and cheerful, with what the narrator describes as "genteel and insinuating manners."[12] From the beginning of the novel there is a suggestion, through his contrasting physical appearance and the reference to his "insinuating" temperament, that the Yankee visitor is a glib and possibly treacherous poseur, with not a fraction of Edward's strength and nobility. The author's foreshadowing of Gildon's baseness is confirmed later in the narrative when he ruins and betrays Edward's sweet, pure, and equally fair sister, Louisa. James Gildon would be the first, but by no means the last, Yankee serpent to invade Virginia's fictional plantation Eden.

Ultimately *The Valley of Shenandoah* celebrates the superiority of its southern hero's noble passion to its Yankee villain's scheming lust. As in novels of the Virginia tradition that were to follow, the Cavalier best expresses his superior qualities in the pure and worshipful wooing of the only object worthy of his interest: the equally refined, pure, and exquisite Virginia belle. In this novel the belle is a member of an unpretentious, middle-class farming family, but this social inconsistency seems not to bother Tucker. This daughter of a yeoman farmer displays the refinement and exquisite sensibility of the highest-bred of plantation belles. In one excessively dramatic scene she gives her lover a locket containing a curl of her hair as a token of her affection. Edward forthwith experiences, in Tucker's words, "that delight which can be known only to those whose feelings have been refined and sublimated by sentimental love." He ecstatically kisses "little present again and again, with the most rapturous joy."[13] The author apparently judges his hero's effusive and, to modern taste, amusing response an appropriate way for a Cavalier to express his love for and his submission to his lady.

Though George Tucker chose to present the action of *The Valley of Shenandoah* in Virginia's present, the novelists who followed him preferred to view the Old Dominion's peerless aristocrats through the more rose-colored lenses of retrospection. In *Edge-Hill; or, The Family of the Fitzroyals* (1828) James Ewell Heath provided an excellent indication of things to come in antebellum Virginia fiction by moving his setting back in time to the exciting conclusion of the Revolutionary War. His novel's title is taken from the name of the James River plantation of Launcelot Fitzroyal. Launcelot is an "opulent" royalist and a descendant of the plantation's original founder, Sir Rupert Fitzroyal, "a loyal Cavalier and gentleman of wealth and family" who named his plantation Edge-Hill for the battle in which he nearly died fighting for his beloved King Charles. Much more explicitly than Tucker, Heath highlights the aristocratic backgrounds from which his Virginia gentlemen are descended. Launcelot expresses precisely his Cavalier's socially refined if politically reactionary point of view: "I venerate those worthies of the olden time . . . those true Cavaliers, who were firm supporters of Church and State against the leveling assaults of roundheads and puritans."[14] Heath does not fully exploit the anachronistic posture of his character, and he essentially ignores the irony inherent in the contrast between Launcelot's Tory political sentiments and the Revolution raging around his cherished plantation. Indeed, his picture of Revolutionary Virginia is so slanted toward an Old World Cavalier vision that one must struggle to remember that the greatest leaders of the American Revolution were in fact Virginia gentlemen.

Four years after *Edge-Hill,* John Pendleton Kennedy published a less grandiloquent but much more popular fictional account of Virginia plantation life entitled *Swallow Barn* (1832). Presiding over Kennedy's plantation setting is the genial if provincial spirit of its hero, Frank Meriwether. Unlike the narrator of Heath's stilted romance, the narrator of *Swallow Barn* does not view his hero as an aristocratic paragon. In fact, he pokes gentle fun at the pride, narrow-mindedness, and resistance to change of the novel's Virginia squires. But beneath this genial reproof runs a deeper vein of admiration, as is revealed in the description of the boundary dispute between Meriwether and Isaac Tracy, neighboring squire of "The Brakes."

Isaac Tracy has for decades been pressing a suit against Frank Meriwether that disputes ownership of a few worthless acres of swampland. On one level Kennedy clearly expects his readers to view this fatuous dispute as a demonstration of the Virginia aristocracy's quixotic and outmoded sense of values. But on another level the author invites these same readers to examine and admire Tracy's tenacity and dedication to principle and the grace, good manners, kindliness, and tact that Meriwether displays in response to Tracy's suit. However absurd the dispute, Kennedy would have us admire certain abstractly noble qualities in his characters. "Never," he writes, "were there, in ancient days of bull-headed chivalry, when contentious monk, bishop, or knight appealed to fiery ordeal, cursed morsel, or wager of battle, two antagonists better fitted for contest than the worthies of my present story."[15] Tongue in cheek? Most certainly. Going into battle over a worthless piece of land, Tracy and Meriwether carry their code of conduct like the tattered flag of a dying way of life. There is an edge of condescension in Kennedy's portrayal of his protagonists, antique Cavaliers who have somehow stumbled onto nineteenth-century American terrain, hopelessly unequipped to deal with a modern world that demands progressive vision and flexible personal standards. Yet by the conclusion of *Swallow Barn* the reader senses that the narrator is by no means certain that the antique values his affectionately rendered Cavaliers embrace are necessarily inferior to the modern values that are replacing them. Thus, though Kennedy's characters are objects of gentle satire, their underlying nobility remains unquestioned.

Swallow Barn affirms the conventional romantic proposition that Virginia society is permeated and dominated by aristocracy. "Her population consists," the author assures his readers, "of landholders, of many descents, unmixed with foreign alloy." In such a society the forms of government may be democratic, but, echoing the Marquis de Chastellux's earlier conclusions about Revolutionary Virginia, Kennedy insists that "in temper and opinion, in the usages of life, and in the qualities of her moral nature, she is aristocratic."[16]

As a Maryland native with Virginia relatives, Kennedy often visited the Shenandoah homesteads of his Pendleton kin. There his sharp eye would have registered the reality that the majority of Virginia's landowners were small farmers who owned few slaves or, more likely, no slaves at all. He would have been equally aware that the earlier English composition of the Shenandoah Valley, and indeed the demographic composition of all parts of Virginia, had been significantly diluted by substantial Scots-Irish and German immigration. However, in the end Kennedy chose not to violate the orthodoxies of Virginia plantation fiction. The demographic survey he sketched in *Swallow Barn* was accordingly oversimplified and distorted to yield the properly romantic picture of an Old Dominion dominated by large landowners of august, aristocratic English ancestry.

Two years after the publication of *Swallow Barn* the Virginia plantation novel swung back in the direction of an even more opulently aristocratic colonial past. The genre achieved its fullest romantic flowering to date with the appearance of William Alexander Caruthers's *The Cavaliers of Virginia* (1834). Set in Virginia's early colonial period, this romance features a Cavalier hero loosely drawn from the pages of Virginia history, Nathaniel Bacon, who leads a rebellion of the colony's planters against the arbitrary and dictatorial rule of the royal governor. Like all Virginia Cavaliers, Caruthers's hero is activated not by political ambition but by highest and most honorable principles. And like George Tucker's Edward Grayson, Bacon's aristocratic instincts are most apparent in his wooing of the novel's fair belle, Virginia Fairfax. In this courtship he assumes the conventional Cavalier role of reverent and humble acolyte to his divinely pure mistress, a role that, nineteenth-century Virginia romance writers unanimously agreed, expressed most fittingly the relationship between gentleman and gentlewoman. In an oration tailor-made to suit the more sentimental and mawkish tastes of readers, Bacon surrenders his affections to Virginia. "Mould them as you will," he proclaims, "reject me if you must, they are still yours. I swear never to profane the shrine of this first and only love by offering them upon any other."[17]

In addition to the reverential wooing of the lady, *The Cavaliers of Virginia* also introduces what would become another staple of plantation fiction, the code duello. As is proper in romantic fiction, the duel arises from the struggle between the hero and an unscrupulous adversary for the hand of the lovely Virginia. In an attempt to save her true love from possible death, Miss Fairfax promises to marry Bacon on the condition that he refuse to engage in the sword fight that looms before him. Bacon, responding as any true aristocrat would, is horrified. "You cannot, you will not, require me to promise this," he cries. "One evidence I must and will give to the calumniator . . . that I come of no churl's blood."[18] Here Caruthers's New World Virginia hero expresses an Old World concept worthy of a Richard Lovelace lyric. His identity as a gentleman and his worthiness as a lover are absolutely dependent upon the maintaining of his personal honor by means of a duel with his "calumniator."

With its focus on Cavalier Nathaniel Bacon and his belle, Virginia Fairfax, *The Cavaliers of Virginia* becomes an unabashed celebration of the Old Dominion's rich aristocratic past—a past that historians know today to be largely mythical. In his zeal to aggrandize Virginia's history Caruthers even transforms the little seventeenth-century settlement of Jamestown into a "city" of "very imposing and romantic appearance." The novel's romanticized portrait bears no resemblance to the village that archaeologists and historians have recently restored. The inhabitants of this romantically concocted "city" are divided neatly into two classes, aristocrats and nonaristocrats. On the anniversary of the Restoration, Caruthers describes the daytime festivities of the city's plebeians. The night, however, is reserved for the Virginia aristocracy, who "roll along the streets in their carriages" toward the magnificent governor's ball.[19]

Caruthers not only gave colorful and dramatic literary expression to the myth of Virginia's aristocratic settlement, but he also assured both his northern and southern readers that the aristocracy still prevailed in Virginia into the nineteenth century. The "generous, foxhunting, wine-drinking, dueling and reckless race of men" who had founded the Old Dominion still gave a distinct cast to its society. Nathaniel Bacon may have died long ago, but he had founded, in Caruthers's opinion, a race of men who continued to influence "the destinies of the Ancient Dominion from that day to the present."[20] In *The Cavaliers of Virginia* Caruthers unabashedly celebrated the birth and triumph of the Cavalier ideal as an essential component of Virginia's mythical past.

It was significant and probably inevitable that this first full-blown fictional apotheosis of the Virginia Cavalier appeared during the 1830s, a decade that historian Charles Sydnor has described as increasingly "troublesome" for the South. By this time conflicts between northern and southern interests focusing on the emotionally volatile issue of slavery convinced increasing numbers of southerners that their social institutions and their very way of life was under Yankee attack.[21] The siege mentality that was beginning to grip the South was given early literary expression in 1836 by Virginian Nathaniel Beverley Tucker in his *The Partisan Leader*. This ominously prescient novel was the first to employ the Cavalier ideal as a key element in the advocacy of southern secession from the Union.

The Partisan Leader is set in the near future, 1849. After twelve years of Andrew Jackson–Martin Van Buren political hegemony, during which Van Buren has acquired the power of a de facto monarch, the states of the mid- and lower South have broken from the Union, formed a Confederacy, and quickly concluded a favorable commercial treaty with Great Britain. The Old Dominion remains undecided, her leaders intimidated by the stationing of large numbers of federal troops in the state. Against this background Virginian Douglas Trevor, a federal officer, renounces his allegiance to the Union and eventually leads his partisan guerrilla bands into battle against the occupying army.

Despite its almost complete deficiency of characterization, Tucker's novel makes abundantly clear that the foundation of the plantation system—which states to the south of Virginia have determined to protect through the act of secession—rests upon the noble and chivalric personal qualities of the region's planter aristocracy. In contrast to President Van Buren, whose genteel exterior masks a rapacious and totally unprincipled character, the reader is presented with a number of distinguished southern gentlemen, chief among them Douglas Trevor. Trevor's chivalric nature is epitomized by the incident that eventually causes his dismissal from the Union army. When an unmannered unionist insults a southern lady by damning her secessionist father to her face, Trevor threatens the man—who is, naturally, a coward—with a duel and forces him to apologize to the lady. She is properly impressed by "the delicacy which, at once, veiled and adorned his chivalrous character."[22] This same delicacy compels Trevor to resign from the army to avoid giving the lady's name at a formal inquiry into the incident. Trevor's northern superiors—Martin Van Buren chief among them—cannot understand his refusal to testify because, not being southern gentlemen, they cannot appreciate the dishonor that would justly accrue to a man who stooped to "the public use of a lady's name." Expelled from the Union army, Trevor heads south to align himself with true gentlemen who are more sensitive to the intricacies of the chivalric code.

Beverley Tucker's Douglas Trevor earns the distinction of being the first fictional Virginia Cavalier to go to war against the Saxon hordes of the North. He would not, of course, be the last. Beneath the surface of its polemic, *The Partisan Leader* clearly indicates the manner in which the chivalric ideal was being employed as early as the 1830s to justify the southern plantation system. Of course, in 1836 few Virginians or southerners favored the expedient Tucker proposed in his novel—secession. Twenty-five years later, however, armed with both their Cavalier myth and their Norman racial fantasies, most of them did.

By the 1840s Virginia's romance novelists were drawing ever more idealized portraits of their Cavalier forebears. Eleven years after publishing *The Cavaliers of Virginia* William Alexander Caruthers added to the state's gilded colonial lore with *The Knights of the Golden Horse-shoe* (1845). In this narrative the colony's aristocratic Governor Alexander Spotswood leads the knights of the Old Dominion's great plantations on a momentous expedition across the Blue Ridge to lay claim to the wilderness beyond. The governor firmly believes that if the British colonies are to avoid being hemmed in from the west by the French, Virginia must dispatch an exploratory party to press beyond the Appalachian peaks and enter the vast, unclaimed tramontane region. Although the more conservative planters scoff at his ambitious proposal, Spotswood tenaciously fights for appropriations from the burgesses. "Just as sure as the sun shines to-morrow," he declares, "I will lead an expedition over yonder blue mountains, and I will triumph over the French—the Indians, and the Devil, if he chooses to join forces with them."[23] The governor's unflagging determination finally wins him the support he needs from the government as well as the backing of most of the colony's young Cavaliers.

Though on its surface Spotswood's expedition claims the western wilderness for England and the Crown, on a deeper level the novel contrives to make the governor a spokesman for the nineteenth-century American doctrine of Manifest Destiny. The narrative attaches profound significance to the novel's knightly quest, seeing it as the first symbolic step forward in America's conquering of a continent. And it favorably compares Spotswood's achievement with the later accomplishments of other American explorers such as Daniel Boone. The march of Spotswood and his Virginia knights is, the narrator observes, but the beginning of a grand procession that, renewed generation after generation, "would transcend the Rio del Norte, and which in half that time may traverse the utmost boundaries of Mexico."[24]

Though Caruthers published *The Knights of the Golden Horse-shoe* on the eve of the Mexican-American War, the novel's vision of an American empire encompassing "the utmost boundaries of Mexico" anticipated the South's strong support for the conflict then looming on the nation's horizon. If Manifest Destiny suggested to northerners in 1845 the surge of the nation's borders westward to the Pacific, it suggested to southerners like Caruthers the sweeping south of these borders far into Central America. And it likewise anticipated a vast southward expansion of the institution of chattel slavery, an expansion that would assure the survival of the South's slave empire.

Caruthers's account of the first English exploration west of the Blue Ridge projects a romantic vision of Manifest Destiny, but it is a vision warped by regional southern ambitions. Its articulation in *The Knights of the Golden Horse-shoe* is strongly inflected by the author's implicit loyalty to the southern plantation system and to the Cavalier myth. Given this particular inflection, it is hardly surprising that Caruthers chooses aristocrat Alexander Spotswood as his fictional spokesman for America's preordained movement west. The yeoman figure of Daniel Boone would have been a more appropriate symbol of the American democracy's westward sweep. But it is impossible for the author to embrace and highlight such a down-to-earth frontier character in a novel so thoroughly absorbed with Virginia's aristocratic heritage and with the vision of an expanding southern slave empire. Alexander Spotswood thus of necessity serves as the aristocratic voice of the narrative's oddly shrunken and distorted southern conception of Manifest Destiny.

Caruthers's novel ends on a grand note with Spotswood's investiture of his Cavalier adventurers as "Knights of the Horse-shoe." Lee, Page, Randolph, Byrd, Carter, Wythe, Washington, Pendleton, Beverley, Bland, Fitzhugh, Dandridge, Ludwell—each flower of Virginia Cavalierdom receives a golden horseshoe inlaid with precious stones. The governor challenges his young adventurers to carry their tokens to King George and to tell him of the new empire they have added to his dominion. "He will recognize you," Spotswood proclaims, "as part of the chivalry of the empire—of that glorious band of knights and gentlemen who surround his throne like a bulwark."[25] Caruthers does not directly say so, but one takes away from his novel the distinct impression that but for the unfortunate intrusion of the Revolution, the descendants of the Old Dominion's chivalrous first families might have remained happily clustered around England's royal throne.

By the 1850s Caruthers's romances of the colonial Old Dominion were being superseded by those of John Esten Cooke. In Cooke's gracefully written novels antebellum Virginia plantation fiction would achieve its most assured and polished form. Cooke's narratives embrace the lushness of setting and the exaltation of the Cavalier hero of their fictional predecessors. In *The Virginia Comedians* (1854), a prime example of Cooke's romantic coloratura, the author regales his readers with traditional scenes of plantation life: the imposing estates with lush parks sloping gently to tidal rivers, the grand entry hall hung with portraits of noble English ancestors, the plantation balls where noble mansions blaze "from top to bottom with a thousand lights" and "chariots constantly" roll up and deposit "beautiful dames and gallant cavaliers," who dine "in state" and dance and feast and make merry.[26]

But Cooke combines with these standard romantic elements of Virginia fiction an element of elegiac sadness that is uniquely his own. The author's pronounced sense of loss is vividly expressed in his description of racing day in colonial Williamsburg: "Where are they now, those stalwart cavaliers and lovely dames who filled that former time with so much light, and merriment, and joyous laughter? Where are those good coursers, Selim, Fair Anna, and Sir Archy; where are black and white, old and young, all the sporting men and women of the swaying crowd? . . . What do we care for all those happy maiden faces—gallant inclinations—graceful courtesies—everything connected with the cavaliers and dames of that old, brilliant, pompous, honest, worthy race."[27] The wistful tone of Cooke's lavish description reads almost like a reproach to his readers and to the pallid realities of contemporary Virginia life. Could it be that the writer's elegy to the Old Dominion's colonial past is also indirectly an elegy to its plantation present, a response to his native state's ever more turbulent political struggles in the 1850s? It is possible that Cooke wrote flamboyant romances such as *The Virginia Comedians* haunted by the specter of the imminent violent collapse of the plantation system and the immolation of its Cavalier hero.

If Cooke was obliquely sensitive in his fiction to the ominous political developments of the 1850s, he seems also to have been sensitive to the new Norman racial mythology that was being trumpeted in southern periodicals during the same decade. Evidence of this influence can be found in *Henry St. John, Gentleman* (1859), a novel published just two years before the Civil War. Here Cooke describes his plantation belle as "a sparkling, mischievous little maiden of about seventeen" with a finely molded oval face "of that pureblooded Norman type which so fascinated the kings and princes of the middle ages, and led to so many bitter feuds and bloody wars."[28] In this passage the writer artfully yokes the Cavalier ideal with the more specific concept of Norman blood that formed the core of the South's suddenly fashionable racial mythology. On the eve of the Civil War the historical Cavalier myth and the racial Norman myth had finally united on the pages of a Virginia romance.

Plantation fiction was slower to develop in the states of the interior and Deep South, and the reason for this retarded development is not hard to discern. When the earliest Virginia romances were appearing, in the 1820s, the states of the Old Southwest were still essentially frontier societies. Even into the 1830s and 1840s places like Mississippi retained a roughness of social texture that betrayed their recent frontier origins, a point that William Faulkner has brilliantly dramatized in novels such as *Absalom! Absalom!* and *The Bear*. Such societies could not have been expected to produce much in the way of belletristic writing. Indeed, not until the decade preceding the Civil War did the interior South become the setting for plantation novels. And when they did finally appear, these novels blazed no new artistic paths. They remained absolutely faithful to the clichés of Virginia plantation fiction. They subscribed fervently to the Cavalier myth of the Old Dominion originals, simply transferring the myth intact to the raw soil of the Deep South cotton plantation.

The plantation novels of the antebellum Southwest faithfully mimicked those of the Old Dominion because the inhabitants of the interior South had by the 1830s thoroughly embraced the plantation system that had first been established in Tidewater Virginia. They had adopted Virginia as the model for their evolving social structure, and they would seek to link their blood to that of the great Virginia aristocratic families. In his descriptive narrative entitled *The Southwest, by a Yankee* (1835), recently arrived New England settler Joseph Holt Ingraham noted that Mississippi claimed Virginia as her "mother country." Because southwesterners believed that the Old Dominion boasted "a nobler ancestry from England's halls than any other" state, planters with social aspirations were inclined to defer to those who claimed to be FFVs, First Families of Virginia, even if their outward material circumstances seemed to belie their assertions of social superiority. "A Virginia gentleman (poor and living on starved lands though he may be) is," Ingraham pronounced in another of his works, "*the* gentleman of the age!"[29]

The mythic appeal of Virginia blood to the imagination of the Old Southwest was so powerful and enduring that more than one hundred years after Ingraham's homage to the Old Dominion, William Faulkner stood before students and faculty of the University of Virginia in the attitude of a semibarbaric colonial emissary to an imperial court. "Compared to you," he humbly confessed to his audience, "my country—Mississippi, Alabama, Arkansas—is still frontier. Yet even in our wilderness we look back to that motherstock.... There is no family in our wilderness but has that old aunt or grandmother to tell the children as soon as they can hear and understand: your blood is Virginia blood too ... so that Virginia is a living place to that child long before he ever hears (or cares) about New York or for that matter America."[30]

Given the Old Southwest's veneration for the Old Dominion and its Cavalier ideal, it is not surprising that the newly settled region's romance writers opted to embrace without question the established conventions of the Virginia romance. One of the most popular and successful translations of Tidewater plantation fiction to a Deep South setting was achieved by Caroline Lee Hentz in *The Planter's Northern Bride*. Published in 1854, Hentz's novel was penned to defend the plantation system against what she judged to be the libels of Harriet Beecher Stowe's popular masterpiece, *Uncle Tom's Cabin*.

In order to respond effectively to Stowe's novel, it was necessary for the author of *The Planter's Northern Bride* to mount an effective fictional defense of slavery. This defense rested squarely on the idealized figure of the Cavalier represented in the novel by its hero, Russell Moreland. Moreland, in the course of a New England tour, falls in love with a lovely Yankee miss and gently pries her from the reluctant arms of her parents. They send her forth "as a missionary" to help reform the errant South.[31] Little do they suspect that this beautiful northern emissary will quickly be converted to a southern point of view.

Russell Moreland has much to do with his wife's rapid conversion to southern values, for, like the earlier Cavaliers of Virginia fiction, he combines strength, honor, and firm manliness with courtesy, kindness, and noblesse oblige toward men of lower social rank. This hero's superior breeding is displayed early in the novel when an earnest but unmannerly New England innkeeper insists that the planter's body servant sit next to his master at the dining table. Russell betrays no anger or discomfort; he simply preserves his dignity by giving the servant his own place and leaving the room. The slave later tells his master that dinning with common Yankees was an unpleasant experience for him because, as he superciliously observes, "they are no gentlemen."[32]

Again and again *The Planter's Northern Bride* stresses its hero's chivalric temperament. In courting his future bride, Moreland assumes the properly reverent attitude of the suppliant knight that was so firm a fixture of Virginia fiction. Even later in the novel the most trivial of his dealings with his wife are marked by a quality of worshipful adoration. In one scene he returns from the hunt, entering the plantation hall dressed in a green hunting outfit and holding before him a brace of partridges. "Here, Eulalia," he announces, "I lay my trophies at your feet."[33] Is it any wonder that Hentz's delicate and sensitive northern bride has turned her back on her emotionally pinched Yankee suitors and followed her Cavalier lover to the sunny Southland?

Like the earlier novels in the Virginia plantation tradition, *The Planter's Northern Bride* features a conflict between an idealized aristocratic southern hero and a Yankee villain. This villain presents himself in the innocent guise of a minister, but he secretly preaches insurrection to Moreland's slaves while availing himself of the planter's liberal hospitality. When the hero discovers the disguised abolitionist's treachery, his sense of honor demands a formal confrontation. But though the Cavalier is skilled in the use of pistols, his adversary is not. In deference to his foe Moreland eschews firearms for the more dangerous hand-to-hand combat. His decision highlights the essential cowardice of his abolitionist adversary and epitomizes what Hentz terms Moreland's "chivalry of . . . nature."[34]

Critic Michael Kreyling has observed that Russell Moreland becomes in the course of Hentz's novel a hero in the manner of classic epic figures such as Aeneas, who embodies the highest ideals of his race—in this case a Virginia-descended race of southern aristocrats. He becomes the living symbol of a hierarchically structured plantation society, and his superior qualities of character, which represent the superiority of an entire class of southern planter-aristocrats, are instinctively acknowledged by members of the lower classes, both black and white, just as they are in the epic tradition. Even a northern servant in a New England household instantly recognizes Moreland as "a real gentleman. . . . I'd as lieves wait upon him as not. He's as handsome as a pictur, and he don't look a bit proud neither, only sort of grand, as t'were." Such admiring observations are later echoed in the South by a slave named Kizzie. "He's a gentleman, a raal gentleman. Tain't no sham, nuther. It's sound, clean through. Black folks knows it as well as white folks."[35]

The recognition by the lower social orders of Russell Moreland's inherent superiority elicits from Hentz's slaves due submission to a social order dominated by the benignly patriarchal Cavalier. Such submission is most fulsomely dramatized in Moreland's return to his plantation from the North, when his field hands swirl around him "eager to get within reach of his hand, the sound of his voice, the glance of his keen, protecting, yet commanding eyes."[36] In *The Planter's Northern Bride* Caroline Lee Hentz triumphantly affirms the plantation system and the system of chattel slavery that sustains it by apotheosizing her Cavalier hero as fully as the most romantic of her Virginia fictional predecessors.

So spirited is Hentz's defense of the plantation system and so unalloyed her enthusiasm for its lords and ladies that one might reasonably assume that she was southern born and bred. In fact she was a Massachusetts Yankee who moved to the South with her husband when she was in her mid-twenties. Her enthusiastic conversion to a southern point of view was scarcely unprecedented. Dixie's most eloquent fictional defenders were often emigrants from the North, not uncommonly New Englanders like Joseph Holt Ingraham and Caroline Lee Hentz. Other pro-southern writers lived only briefly in the South; some of them never lived there at all. But after the publication of *Uncle Tom's Cabin* northern novelists sympathetic to the slave states rose to repudiate what they, along with a fair number of their Yankee brethren, believed to be Harriet Beecher Stowe's scurrilous abolitionist lies.

Vermont native William L. G. Smith was one of these distant northern converts to Dixie's cause. In *Life at the South; or, "Uncle Tom's Cabin" as It*

Is (1852) he sketched an idealized Virginia plantation whose noble proprietor boasts to his admiring northern guest, "We are proud, sir, of our lineage, and customs, and polity, and we would record it—*all* of it, for the benefit of our descendants."[37] Among the customs and polity with which he proudly and defiantly identifies is the institution of slavery, which in Smith's novel is a benignly paternalistic system far removed from the horrors of *Uncle Tom's Cabin*.

Northerner Robert Criswell moved his fictional setting south from Virginia to Charleston in his *"Uncle Tom's Cabin" Contrasted with Buckingham Hall, the Planter's Home* (1852). Here Colonel George Buckingham is proud to claim an "ancestral blood, which, he often boasted, had *not* 'crept through scoundrels ever since the flood,' but was pure and aristocratic in its descent." The Colonel's genealogical link to the English Dukes of Buckingham justly produces, in the eyes of the admiring narrator, the "haughtiness and unbending pride of his character."[38] Like Russell Moreland in *The Planter's Northern Bride*, a young Buckingham Cavalier ventures North and woos and wins the fair daughter of a northern gentleman who is strongly opposed to slavery, but who is reconciled to the institution after visiting and being cordially entertained at Buckingham Hall.

In 1852, the same year that Smith and Criswell published their plantation romances, Pennsylvanian Charles Jacobs Peterson, writing under the pseudonym J. Thornton Randolph, penned one of the decade's most lavish celebrations of southern aristocracy entitled *Cabin and Parlor; or, Slaves and Masters*. Imitating the flamboyant fictional tradition of Virginia writers like Caruthers and Cooke, he ensconces his FFV aristocrats within their "courtly mansion" with its "noble hall" and magnificent staircase "said to have been copied from an ancient manorial hall in England." Such architectural elegancies are complemented with furniture imported from Paris, a large and tastefully selected library, and a dining room whose pictures, "though few in number, were each a masterpiece."[39]

Presiding over this stunning plantation mansion and its "hereditary acres" are the aristocratic Courtenay family, whose lineage is as purely Norman as it is exquisitely refined. Indeed, the narrator assures his readers that "a Courtenay had entered England with the Conqueror; two several Courtenays had followed Richard of the Lion Heart to Palestine; Courtenays had fought in the Wars of the Roses and Courtenays, known to be of the same stock, though not but remotely connected, were still found among the nobility of England." Peterson thus joins English with Virginia aristocracy as neatly as any southern romancer might have done, taking care to emphasize that the "the arms of the Courtenays, quartered with those of the gentry with whom they had intermarried, may yet be seen, carved on tomb-stones, in many an ancient grave-yard of the Old Dominion."[40] The South's most starry-eyed romancers could not have composed a more lavish or evocative picture of the region's planter aristocracy or linked it more felicitously to the Norman racial myth then being bruited in Dixie's periodicals.

As the nation drew ever closer to the Civil War, the Deep South's romance writers remained as determined as their Virginia fictional mentors and their northern fictional allies to link the planters of the newly settled slave states with the aristocracy of Old England, replicating the fictional bond that had been established between Virginia's great planters and the English nobility. In *The Sunny South; or, The Southerner at Home* (1860) Joseph Holt Ingraham uses the sympathetic point of view of a Yankee governess to establish his Tennessee setting as a modern equivalent of aristocratic merry old England. When Catherine Conyngham first glimpses the impressive "double storied portico" of the Tennessee plantation called Overton Park Lodge, she imagines herself "approaching the mansion of some English Baronet." Indeed, as she stresses more than once in letters to her northern friends, Tennessee "bears a striking resemblance to . . . the best part of England." Having received the civilizing impress of the plantation, the original wilderness has been transformed into a countryside "whose broad patches of light and shade look like scenes in Claude Lorrain's pictures" and whose cultivated sward is "*so* green and soft" it might well represent "the work of trained English gardeners."[41]

Presiding over this verdant patch of England-in-Tennessee is the plantation master, Colonel Peyton. He is first viewed emblematically, seated on his fine horse like some feudal lord, "a rifle laid carelessly across his saddle, and two fine deer-dogs standing by his horse's forelegs and looking up wistfully into their master's face." With his "manly features and silver gray locks," with his "decided military air," the magisterial colonel is the epitome of the patriarchal planter-aristocrat.[42] He is a superior man of great personal power who demands, like Hentz's Russell Moreland or Caruthers's Alexander Spotswood, instinctive recognition and obedience—be it from deer dog, slave, or plantation belle. In short, he is the idealized English Cavalier come via Tidewater Virginia to Tennessee.

Ingraham's text makes abundantly clear that submission to a plantation master like Colonel Peyton is more joy than duty, for beneath his firm and magisterial exterior lies a heart softened and humanized by the influences of Christianity. Overton Park Lodge boasts a house of worship modeled on "an exquisite chapel which the colonel saw on the estate of the Earl of C——, when he was in England."[43] Within this architectural gem both master and slave are called to worship.

As in *The Planter's Northern Bride,* all those who live under Peyton's control find his yoke an easy one. Contented slaves live in neat, whitewashed quarters. It is well that they are content, for the narrator assures us that their servitude is essential "to the happiness and comfort of the beautiful daughter or aristocratic lady of the planter." Without slaves, how could the planter's highly bred daughter find time to read aloud to her beloved father, with a nearly faultless French accent, Madame de Stael's *Corinne,* or to play classical compositions on her harp or on her beautiful rosewood piano?[44]

To make his fictional portrait of the sunny plantation Southland even more appealing, Ingraham invests his Tennessee landscape with a feudal ambiance that is directly derivative of Walter Scott's novels. Indeed, in one description of the master's return from a hunt with his retinue, Conyngham remarks that the scene reminds her of "a similar description Scott has in one of his romances." If Colonel Peyton's plantation seems to Conyngham's eyes the recreation of a baronet's estate, Ashwood, the neighboring ancestral home of the Polk family, is depicted as an even more impressive "princely domain." The governess concludes that "the lordly proprietors" of these Tennessee plantations "live more like feudal nobles than simple farmers."[45]

Princely domain, lordly proprietors, feudal nobles—Ingraham's medieval-flavored terminology was employed in scores of other novels and essays by the South's antebellum romance writers. Landon Carter, for example, penned this description of the Virginia planter: "The barons of old were scarcely more despotic over their immediate demesnes, than were the proprietors of these noble mansions, with their long train of servants and dependents; their dicta were almost paramount to law throughout their extensive and princely possessions."[46] Whether the plantation was set on the Rappahannock River or in the rolling hills of Tennessee, the intentions of the Deep South's writers were the same as those of their Virginia cousins: to associate southern society with the elegance of seventeenth-century Cavalier society and with the magnificence of the English nobility of the Middle Ages as Walter Scott had described them in his historical romances.

This wave of medieval-flavored plantation romance swept the South to the threshold of civil war. In 1861 South Carolinian Mary Howard Schoolcraft ignored the gathering clouds of conflict to apotheosize her native state's planter aristocracy in a plantation novel entitled *The Black Gauntlet*. In her view the Palmetto State had been "the pet of royalty" from "its earliest origin," and its 1674 colonial charter had been "of an almost sovereignly aristocratic character." Given her fictional assessment of South Carolina's history, it comes as no surprise that her fictional setting includes no small farmers, merchants, or professionals—only gentlemen who "mount their richly-caparisoned horses" and ladies so delicately bred and slender that "the extended hand of their several kneeling knights was the pedestal on which each Hebe placed her coquettishly-shod, tiny little foot." Schoolcraft assures her readers that the knightly obeisance of her colonial Carolina gentlemen to their fair ladies was natural, for these "descendants of the lordly Cavaliers of England" were "always under subjugation to beauty." After all, veneration of well-bred ladies was an intrinsic part of the ethos of a culture that had been founded by "the direct descendants of the chivalrous, gay cavaliers of Charles the Second's reign."[47]

Schoolcraft's exquisite descriptions of Cavaliers and ladies are not simply frothy fictional concoctions. They are part of the writer's more serious concern, revealed in her novel's preface: a defense of slavery. If, as she contends, slaves are representatives of "an inferior race" that carries a mark "as distinctive as that on Cain," who could be better equipped to manage and govern such people than Cavalier-descended aristocratic planters combining manly vigor and a lordly instinct to command with natural magnanimity, gentleness of character, and a sense of noblesse oblige? Schoolcraft's sense of her region's exalted aristocratic destiny merges into a frenzied vindication of slavery. "It is a high moral vocation," she asserts, "to civilize and Christianize the heathen, brought to our very doors in the South by the providence of God;—I am so satisfied that slavery is the school God has established for the conversion of barbarous nations, that were I an absolute Queen of these United States, my first missionary enterprise would be to send to Africa, to bring its heathen as *slaves* to this Christian land."[48]

By the eve of the Civil War tributary narrative currents from both the interior South and the northeastern states had materially augmented the stream of Virginia plantation fiction. Regardless of whether these novelists hailed from above or below the Mason-Dixon, all affirmed in their novels the idea that the region's great planters had descended from aristocratic English lineage. And all joined in celebrating and romanticizing the Cavalier character ideal, casting their heroes in this mythic mold. By the 1850s, writers from the Old Dominion and from all other parts of the South and of the nation as a whole were creating scenically lush, richly romantic, highly idealized tales of plantation life. They were also contributing measurably to the popular conception that southerners were a noble, fine-grained people, free from the rank materialism, avidity, and fanaticism of ill-bred Yankees. This literary mythmaking perfectly complemented the racial mythmaking of the South's polemical essayists.

As a rule, romance writers of Virginia and the South were concerned with advancing a Cavalier myth that celebrated a planter class descended from the English aristocracy, the more sharply focused myth of the South's Norman racial inheritance being a product of 1850s polemical essayists. Every rule, however, has its interesting exception. Among antebellum writers of the South there turns out to be one who presented in 1841 a work of fiction that strikingly anticipates the Norman racial mythmaking of the following decade. Paradoxically, this writer was not an American but a Bohemian immigrant named Charles Sealsfield [Karl Postl]. Sealsfield arrived in America in 1823 at the age of thirty, became a naturalized citizen, traveled throughout the new nation for twelve years, and then returned to Europe, retaining his American citizenship and writing a number of works in German about his adopted country.

Of all Sealsfield's publications, the one most intriguing to scholars of the antebellum South is *The Cabin Book,* published in 1841 as *Das Kajutenbuch.* Beginning in Louisiana, this series of fictional sketches follows its European protagonist to the Texas frontier. Here Sealsfield describes and celebrates both the New World spirit of the Texas frontiersmen that is inexorably pushing America west and the more specifically southern vision of the plantation, which will ultimately turn this frontier into a new Eden. Significantly, Sealsfield associates both the frontier drive that created Texas and the plantation ideal that promises to give this new society its civilized form with the idea of Norman blood inheritance. He asserts the idea in the boastful voice of a Texas judge whom the narrator encounters on his journey into the prairie.

According to this judge, the irrepressible spirit of Texas is a Norman spirit. "Without the Norman," he insists, "there would be no Great Britain, no United States, no Virginia; the whole world would have been a miserable puny world." The judge goes on to liken the Norman subjugation of England to the conquest of the New World by their modern descendants. The first great Norman, William the Conqueror, was constrained to "earn something for himself with his own arm. But his arm was powerful." It was an arm that "had nothing at home to lose, and everything to win in a strange land." The judge avers that the adventurous Norman spirit embodied in the conquests of King William produced "the hardest, most blood-thirsty tyrants that ever held scourge over a people." And he is unapologetically proud that this same "rude, powerful" blood in the form of the English aristocracy has subjugated the New World, moving from "the West Indies to our America, there to seek adventures with our Indian chiefs in Virginia, to wrestle with bears, wolves, and howling Indians."[49]

According to Sealsfield's boastful Texan, the Norman forebears who imposed their character and their culture from Virginia to Texas were "downright licentious fellows, who all together had no more piety, godliness, modesty, than would go into the coat pocket of one of our Quakers." He unashamedly asserts the commanding, though libertine, spirit of the southern Norman over the macerating pieties of northern Quakers and New England Puritans. It is this masterly blood heritage, free of effete moral scruples, that has enabled the South's nobly descended settlers to establish their great slave empire. "Because they depended upon themselves for everything, [they] also accomplished everything, and not only founded the greatest, most powerful kingdom of the earth, but also kept themselves as the masters, the lords, of that kingdom, up to the present day." Norman-descended Texans like this proud, imperious judge are therefore "just as good and just as free to make ourselves what we can as any one of the Capets or Plantagenets; are as little subject to any one as they."[50]

The judge concludes his disquisition on the South's Norman inheritors by asserting their clear superiority to the Anglo-Saxon (he terms them "German") inhabitants of England, whose servile spirit was carried to America with the Puritans. "Herein," he contends, "lies the difference between the Normans and the Germans—at first both were men; but the Normans remained men, the Germans became menials."[51] Southern polemicists would assert some years later the same conviction: South and North had been stamped by contrasting bloods—a dominant and martial Norman and a servile and inferior Saxon.

Charles Sealsfield's *The Cabin Book* is an intriguing work for students of antebellum southern culture for several reasons. The ruminations of its Texas judge on Norman versus German blood clearly anticipate the later, more ostensibly rational and scientific opinions of the purveyors of the South's Norman race myth. More important, perhaps, the judge's boastful racial assumptions indicate that something akin to a Norman race theory was an element of southern popular thought as early as the 1830s, more than twenty years before the Civil War. *The Cabin Book* suggests that in propounding their Norman race theory, southern polemicists were expanding on established and widely embraced prejudices that affirmed the distinctiveness and the superiority of southern blood.

5
A Universal Yankee Nation
Northern Racial Mythmaking

It is not surprising that southerners were more assiduous than northerners in developing and trumpeting the myth of their unique Norman racial inheritance. After all, it was they who, as the nineteenth century progressed, felt themselves ever more alienated from other sections of the nation. They also felt increasingly constrained to repel what they considered scurrilous abolitionist attacks, and they were more and more inclined to believe that in order to preserve their peculiar institution and their way of life, they would have to leave the Union and assert their own nationhood. But they were not alone among Americans in feeling the need to assert their racial uniqueness. In 1822, two years after the Missouri Compromise had exposed the political fault line between slave and free states, Philadelphia journalist Robert Walsh issued a call for the rise of a "Universal Yankee Nation" as a counterforce to the South's overweening "Virginia Race." This breed of southerners, he contended, had "unhesitatingly proclaimed and invariably pursued the maxim of being 'true to themselves.'" Unfortunately "the race of New England" could not "be blamed for imitating [the Virginians'] example."[1] Unless they discovered and began to act upon their Yankee identity with pride and confidence, Walsh warned, they would continue to be subject to the political dominance of the Virginians and of those southerners descended from them.

Eventually northerners did begin to express, as Walsh had urged, a spirited sense of their own racial identity. As Reginald Horsman has shown, from the 1830s on they "became interested in, and advocates of, the Germanic and Anglo-Saxon divisions of the white race" from which they proudly claimed descent. In the 1830s and 1840s, as we have seen in chapter 1, northerners shared this common assumption of Anglo-Saxon superiority with southerners. But by the 1850s a sharp divergence developed between North and South on the subject of racial inheritance. The South's writers, compelled to defend slavery and the plantation system and sensing a decline in their region's political power within the Union, turned abruptly away from the idea of America's common Anglo-Saxon blood toward the Cavalier myth and the congruent notion of Dixie's Norman racial descent. By contrast, northern writers, and particularly New England's writers, remained enthusiastically committed to the idea that Americans had largely descended from the German or Anglo-Saxon race. As Horsman observes, "The idea of a Teutonic race imbued with the great idea of freedom melded well into [the North's] search for a guiding spirit in American democracy and the American nation." New Englanders consequently joined with residents of the Northeast and Midwest in "prophesying the ultimate triumph of an American Anglo-Saxon Christian civilization."[2] This was cultural banner they would carry into the Civil War against what they believed to be the forces of an aristocratic and oligarchic South.

By the 1840s the North's trumpeting of its Germanic racial inheritance was in full flower. In 1843 George Perkins Marsh used his work, entitled *The Goths in New England*, to advance two primary arguments. He contended that the "ideal of the perfect citizen" had been "first and most perfectly realized by the communities of New England" and that the "intellectual character" of the Puritan forefathers who had established this civic ideal was "derived by inheritance from our remote Gothic ancestry." This "Gothic" proclivity for freedom and democratic citizenship had manifested itself in England in the Puritan revolution that had liberated Englishmen from the shackles "which the spiritual and intellectual tyranny of Rome had for centuries imposed upon it."[3]

Marsh viewed the English as a people historically divided by the conflict between a "Gothic" democratic ethos and a "Roman" aristocratic ethos. But he argued that England's highest cultural triumphs, its "moral grandeur" and its "intellectual power," derived from its Puritan Gothic racial strain. This strain was not, as defenders of aristocracy had often contended, barbaric and backward, and it was certainly not avaricious, narrow-minded, and materialistic. For Marsh the greatness of New England resided in the fact that it had been settled almost exclusively by English Puritans of Gothic stock. New England had thus escaped the abiding struggle in the mother country between her aristocratic and democratic elements. And the United States had also been fortunately delivered from the hierarchical order of the Old World, for the large-minded, morally upright, and democratic traits of Puritan New Englanders had stamped the new nation and now characterized "in different degrees, the whole American people."[4]

Critic Audrey Smedley has pointed out that the cultural and racial ideas that Marsh advanced were drawn from England, where they had been articulated and widely embraced in the eighteenth century before the advent of romanticism, the Walter Scott historical novel, and the Gothic revival: "The Anglo-Saxons, it was said, had developed advanced political institutions before the Norman conquest." They were also popularly believed to have demonstrated from the beginning of their history a racial propensity for independence, freedom, and democracy. As Smedley observes, eighteenth-century Englishmen widely assumed that their Anglo-Saxon ancestors had "derived the excellence of their social system from German forebears." Thus "glorification of the German past became a prelude to the history and greatness of the Anglo-Saxons."[5] Marsh's use of the term *Gothic* reflects the influence of these eighteenth-century English racial assumptions.

Though not going so far as to declare Americans one single Anglo-Saxon race, Marsh asserted the dominance in the new nation of the Germanic racial strain—a strain he denominated as "Gothic"—that had been bequeathed to the Republic by the descendants of America's Puritan forefathers. He recognized the formidable power of the counterethos of England's Norman—designated by Marsh "Roman"—aristocracy in the Old World. But he discounted the influence of this racial strain in the New World. He posited one American people distinguished by its glorious Anglo-Saxon inheritance. His work appeared before the sectional conflicts that would tear at the nation's social and political fabric after the Compromise of 1850. It did not anticipate the Norman racial mythmaking that would begin to absorb southerners within the next decade and that would undermine his notion of a common Anglo-Saxon American race.

In 1843, the same year Marsh published *The Goths in New England*, Transcendentalist Ralph Waldo Emerson included among five lectures focused on his native region one entitled "Genius of the Anglo-Saxon Race." This lecture substantially echoed the racial sentiments of fellow New Englander Marsh by associating the Puritans with an Anglo-Saxon racial pedigree and by using this pedigree to explain and affirm the "distinguishing traits" of New Englanders, what Emerson termed their "conscience and common sense." The devotion to conscience had manifested itself in a "culture of the intellect," which, Emerson proudly affirmed, had resulted in New England's furnishing "preachers and school-masters for the whole country." The devotion to common sense had produced a people and a region devoted to hard work and trade, traits that had through the centuries been "conspicuous in the Anglo-Saxon mind." Emerson professed himself to be as proud of the New Englander's common sense as he was of his conscience, for he was convinced that the one trait nourished the other. "Behold," he boasted, "the result in the cities that line the Atlantic coast and the intellectual circulation they nourish."[6]

Because he was a powerful, introspective, and often contrary thinker, Emerson was not entirely complacent about New England's Anglo-Saxon racial inheritance. He admitted that the region's "ambition" sometimes ran to excess and consequently overpowered "sentiment," and that "repose which is the ornament and ripeness of man" was rarely to be found in its culture. He also believed that in the field of arts and letters the Anglo-Saxon mentality had produced writers who were "receptive, not creative." "We go to school in Europe," Emerson ruefully observed, echoing the sentiments of his seminal and powerfully influential essay "Self Reliance."[7]

Yet despite his recognition of certain deficiencies in the Germanic temperament, Emerson fundamentally endorsed in his 1843 lecture what he conceived to be New England's positive and formative Anglo-Saxon traits. Though Saxon-descended Puritans had developed a culture that was too derivative of Europe, there remained "an ethical element in the mind of our people that will never let them long rest without finding exercise for the deeper thoughts."[8] It was this racial propensity for deep thinking that portended greatness for America's culture and for the nation's destiny. "Genius of the Anglo-Saxon Race" firmly linked the guiding concepts of American culture with an Anglo-Saxon and Puritan "culture of the intellect"—a genius that Emerson believed expressed itself in energy and enterprise fruitfully combined with spirituality and moral purpose.

Toward the end of the 1840s Emerson's fellow transcendentalist, reformer Theodore Parker, articulated a finely nuanced and provocative description of a Saxon race that, he agreed with Emerson, had been primarily responsible for forming the cultures of both England and America. In an address entitled "The Destination of America" (1848) Parker stressed the remarkable continuity of the Saxon people. "They are," he observed, "yet the same bold, hardy, practical people as when their barks first touched the savage shores of Britain."[9] The Puritan descendants of these hardy people, he proposed, had bravely carried these same character traits to the savage shores of New England.

Though Parker's racial speculations agreed with Emerson's on a number of points, his portrait of America's Saxon forebears was distinctly less admiring. Most notably he declined to endorse the notion that the Anglo-Saxon temperament had fostered a "culture of the intellect." Parker's pragmatic Saxons tended toward "experiment, facts, precedents, and usages." They were not "philosophical, but commercial . . . material, obstinate, and grasping, with the same admiration of horses, dogs, oxen, and strong drink; the same willingness to tread down any obstacle . . . the same impatient lust of wealth and power; the same disposition to colonize and re-annex other lands; the same love of liberty and love of law."[10]

Ironically, the traits of materialism, cupidity, implacability, and aggression that Parker imputed to the Saxon temperament were the very ones that southern polemicists highlighted in their diatribes against the overweening Yankee race. But it was undoubtedly the trait the Transcendentalist speaker mentioned last, the Saxon's "love of liberty and love of law," that for him expressed that race's character in its best and highest sense, for it was this quality that had produced the most democratic as well as the most enterprising nation in Europe. Parker believed that throughout history the Saxons had maintained their love of liberty and law, stamping their devotion on English institutions. The aristocrat Normans who had conquered the Saxons might have taught them "to wear cloth" and "to drink wine," but thankfully they had not altered the essential nature of the people they had subdued. "England has received her kings and her nobles from Normandy, Anjou, the Provence, Scotland, Holland, Hanover," he observed. "Yet the sturdy Anglo-Saxon character held its own, in spite of the new element infused into its blood. . . . John Bull is obstinate as ever, and himself changes not; no philosophy or religion makes him less material."[11]

Parker acknowledged in his address what he considered to be the negative as well as the positive traits of the Anglo-Saxon temperament. And he believed that the race that had formed English institutions had also, for better or worse, formed America. But, like Emerson, he was clearly of the opinion that in both nations the Saxon influence had on balance been for the better. As it had done in England, the race had imprinted on the United States "the most marked characteristic of the American nation . . . love of freedom."[12] Parker made no distinctions in his address between northern and southern Americans, and, like George Perkins Marsh, he did not associate southerners with a Norman racial inheritance. He judged the Norman influence on both the English and the American character to be superficial, and he emphasized a common American character and racial composition that, with both defects and virtues, descended primarily from the Anglo-Saxon race.

As the 1840s gave way to the more politically contentious 1850s, northern assertions of America's proud Anglo-Saxon heritage became both more forceful and more self-consciously responsive to southern attacks on the Yankee character. Ralph Waldo Emerson's *English Traits* (1856) displayed this more combative tone. In this work Emerson laced his praise of the Anglo-Saxon race with rather malicious aspersions on the character and temperament of England's Norman conquerors. His strategy suggests that he was acquainted with the more unsavory Norman characters of Walter Scott's *Ivanhoe* and that he was aware of and testily responsive to the boastful assertions of racial superiority issuing from the pens of Scott's southern admirers. "The Normans," he provocatively maintained, "came out of France into England worse men than they went into it one hundred and sixty years before. They had lost their own language and learned the Romance or barbarous Latin of the Gauls, and had acquired with the language, all the vices it had names for." "These founders of the House of Lords," he continued, "were greedy and ferocious dragoons, sons of greedy and ferocious pirates. They were all alike, they took everything they could carry, they burned, harried, violated, tortured, and killed, until every thing English was brought to the verge of ruin."[13] Emerson's description of a piratical people made more vicious by its deracination may well have struck him as a just riposte to the South's prating on its noble Norman blood.

While Emerson attributed the baseness of the Norman race to its corruption by "Latin" races, he celebrated the uncorrupted purity of an Anglo-Saxon character that had continued to shape the English people to the present day. "The Teutonic tribes," he observed, "have a national singleness of heart, which contrasts with the Latin races. The German name has a proverbial significance of sincerity and honest meaning.... [Add] to this hereditary rectitude the punctuality and precise dealing which commerce creates, and you have the English truth and credit."[14] Clearly what drew the transcendental sage to the English were those same Anglo-Saxon virtues of character he believed had formed the American character.

Emerson's admiration for the English character extended to its military and commercial triumphs abroad. It was undoubtedly flattering to English readers to hear him praise their nation's imperial mission in stirring and typically Emersonian rhetorical fashion. "The moral peculiarity of the Saxon race,—its commanding sense of right and wrong, the love and devotion to that,—this is the imperial trait, which arms them with the sceptre of the globe."[15] English readers may not have been fully aware that Emerson and other Americans were simultaneously using this same triumphal Anglo-Saxon racialism to buttress their own nation's continental aspirations, its Manifest Destiny.

The thrust of Emerson's essays in *English Traits* was clear. Englishmen and Americans were bound by a common and exalted Anglo-Saxon racial heritage. The Norman influence on the molding of the English nation's character, when it was noted, was peremptorily and contemptuously dismissed. And it was likewise dismissed in Emerson's exegesis of the American character. "I chanced to read Tacitus' 'On the Manners of the German' not long since, in Missouri and the heart of Illinois," he wrote, "and I found abundant points of resemblance between the Germans of the Hercynian forest, and our *Hoosiers, Suckers* and *Badgers* of the American woods."[16] Nowhere in these essays did Emerson mention southern backwoodsmen. Apparently he was content to allow them, if they so chose, to claim the Norman racial inheritance he had execrated as cruel, rapacious, and piratical. He proudly claimed the rest of America, from the New England seacoast towns and cities to the prairies and woods of the Midwest, for the Anglo-Saxon race.

Defenses of the North's Anglo-Saxon character such as those mounted by Emerson were accompanied by defenses of the region's Puritan forefathers. Indeed, since by the 1850s both northerners and southerners generally accepted the idea that Puritans had descended from the Saxon-composed middling and lower English social orders, the terms *Anglo-Saxon, Puritan,* and *Yankee* were on the eve of the Civil War virtually synonymous in their connotations. Henry Ward Beecher's lecture on "Puritanism" is an abundantly clear demonstration of this fusion of terms. Delivered in Philadelphia on December 21, 1860, before the New England Society on the eve of the 240th anniversary of the Pilgrim landing at Plymouth Rock, Beecher's stirring oration proposed that all of the nation's thirty-three states, not just the New England states, had been immeasurably enriched by Puritan influences indistinguishable from the Anglo-Saxon influences that Marsh, Emerson, and Parker had earlier celebrated.

Like Emerson, Beecher paid tribute in his lecture to the Puritan capacity for common sense, pragmatism, and dedication to duty and hard work, and like the Sage of Concord he believed that these traits had made America great. "When a railroad needs method, when a bank needs keen sagacity, when iron or stone, wood or clay, are to be moulded, or water called from waste to usefulness, or steam subdued to industry—there," he grandly proclaimed—echoing Robert Walsh's phrase of 1822—"you shall find the universal Yankee." And what of the southern notion that northern Puritans had been lowborn? Beecher proudly embraced these middling social origins. "If you will follow them back to their homes, you will now and then find a mansion, never a castle, but almost always a yeoman's house, or a labourer's hovel. At home the Puritans were weavers, cobblers, tinkers, merchants and mechanics." It was precisely these middling origins, Beecher insisted, that had instilled in them the love of liberty, and it was "for liberty of conscience" that these "firm-faced" men had forsaken home and hearth to stand resolutely "on bleak wintry Plymouth rock."[17]

Beecher agreed with Theodore Parker that there had been flaws in the original Puritan design, but he assured his listeners that these past flaws were being amended in the present. "They were narrow where we have grown broad," he observed. "They were rude and hard, while we have clad ourselves with a few graces." Beyond this admission of weaknesses, which he believed to be products of historical exigency, he refused to accept the southern charge that today's Puritan-descended northerners were vulgar in manners and actions. "The Puritan is pronounced vulgar. But by whom? Not by men who work, not by men whose worth comes by character rather than station." On a higher, more spiritual level, Beecher suggested that Puritans were far more attuned to the scriptural imperatives of the New Testament than their haughty southern detractors. Like Christ, the Puritan "was the prophet of the common people, and was not ashamed to call them brethren."[18]

By 1860, nearly forty years after Robert Walsh had issued the call, northern writers like Henry Ward Beecher were proudly proclaiming the "Universal Yankee Nation." They were wisely articulating not a regional New England vision but a national vision of a hardy, freedom-loving American people descended from an equally hardy and freedom-loving Anglo-Saxon race. They presumed that this race had given birth to the Puritan revolution in England and that it had actuated the Puritan migration to the New World. They believed that the genius of this Teutonic people had expressed itself through history in pragmatic action, duty, conscience, and love of liberty. Though not quite so persistent or as vocal as their southern counterparts, northern writers in the 1840s and 1850s were countering the South's Norman racial myth with a powerfully appealing Anglo-Saxon racial myth that was national, not regional, in scope.

English geologist Charles Lyell was visiting Washington in 1846 when the dispute with England over possession of the Oregon Territory threatened to erupt into armed conflict. Lyell asked a New England politician, Would the United States indeed go to war? No, he answered bitterly. "We are governed by the South, and our southern chivalry will put their veto on a war of which they would have to bear the brunt." And how, Lyell wondered, had the South managed to achieve such political dominance in Washington? The New Englander replied that southern dominance of the national government was partially the product of the southerner's "high bearing, which, in Congress, often imposes on northern men much superior to them in real talent, knowledge, and strength of character."[19]

Twenty-four years after Robert Walsh's admonitions regarding the ascendancy of the arrogant "Virginia race" in Washington, northern politicians continued to chafe under the South's presumption of cultural and political superiority. But by the 1850s more and more of them were rising to repudiate both the institution of slavery and the myth of southern aristocracy that underlay slavery and that also contributed to the northerners' oft-mentioned sense of political inferiority. William Seward issued one of the earliest and most effective salvos in the rhetorical warfare between North and South with his famous "Higher Law" speech to the Senate in 1850. In this address he forcefully opposed any compromise concerning the question of California's admission to the Union as a free state that would allow for the possible extension of slavery in other territories. To support such a compromise, he argued, would require the abject surrendering of one's "exercise of judgment and conscience." As for the institution of slavery, Seward was convinced that "in just proportion to the extent that it prevails and controls in any republican state, just to that extent it subverts the principle of democracy, and converts the state into an aristocracy or a despotism."[20]

Seward's rhetoric suggests how northern writers in future would assault both slavery and the notion of aristocracy that southerners used to justify the institution. His speech implicitly rejected southern assumptions about race—their early employment of Anglo-Saxon racialism to affirm the superiority of the white to the black race and their later fashioning of a Norman racial myth that affirmed their superiority to Yankees. Seward was no doubt aware that northerners also trumpeted their Anglo-Saxon racial inheritance, but he was certainly also aware that they employed this racial ideal very differently from southerners. They invoked Anglo-Saxonism not primarily to proclaim their superiority to black slaves but to affirm America's reverence for freedom and democracy. They also employed the Anglo-Saxon ideal to assert the common racial identity of a nation, not merely that of a region. They refused to subscribe to the notion that southerners possessed a unique Norman blood inheritance. For northerners like Seward, slavery did not arise from the natural assertion of superiority by an aristocratic white race over inferior black chattel. It was an inherently predatory and wicked institution that grotesquely disfigured a state, turning it into a "despotism" ruled by brutal slave owners posing as aristocrats.

As the 1850s progressed, northern polemical writers adopted two approaches in repudiating the idea of southern aristocracy. The first and ostensibly more moderate approach began by admitting that southerners did indeed possess certain appealing aristocratic qualities. For example, a writer for the *New York Daily Times* conceded that the highborn planter was much like a European aristocrat—sensual, brave, reckless, and even violent. These qualities might, the writer admitted, lend the southern gentleman a certain authority and surface appeal. But in their most conservative manifestations the haughty and impulsive slave owners who demonstrated these traits constituted a grave danger to the Republic, for they "hate and despise the Democrats of Europe as much as Francis Joseph himself," he warned his readers. "They glorify Napoleon, and they boast of the contempt with which they were able to treat the humbug Kossuth. . . . They call themselves Democrats, and sometimes Democratic Whigs. Call them what you will, they are a mischievous class,—the dangerous class at present of the United States. They are not the legitimate offspring of Democracy, thanks to God, but of slavery under a Democracy."[21] The *Times* writer, much like William Seward, equated the southern aristocratic ideal with the corrupting influence of slavery, not with the idea of superior blood inheritance.

A second way of attacking the notion of southern aristocracy was simply to hold the very idea up to ridicule, to assert that the South's grand planters were in fact ruffians masquerading as aristocrats. Horace Greeley was particularly adept at this line of attack. In an 1854 issue of his *New York Daily Tribune* he chose as the target of his polemic the state of Virginia, the birthplace of the Cavalier ideal and the place most evocatively associated with the South's aristocratic heritage. The once-mighty Old Dominion, he averred, had "sunk to the level of a mere negro-breeding territory," where one could shamefully observe slaves being bought and sold "within a stone's throw of Mount Vernon or Monticello." In this formerly distinguished birthplace of presidents any "white ruffian" could buy slaves. Then he could hire them out and live indolently on the labor of the unfortunate chattels, "taking their earnings from them by force like a cowardly footpad; disporting his aristocracy at the springs in the summer, and rejoicing in some shabby title of major, colonel, or general." These repugnant activities of a pretentious would-be aristocracy, Greeley indignantly concluded, took place in a state that had been one of the birthplaces of American democracy.[22]

Even when Greeley assumed a more conciliatory tone toward the South, it was so infused with condescension that southerners could have taken no comfort from it. Why, he queried in one of his articles, should there be hatred or distrust between North and South? "True," he admitted, "we believe the *tendency* of the slaveholding system is to make those trained under and mentally conforming to it, overbearing, imperious, and regardless of the rights of others. We believe the habit of living easily and comfortably on the fruits of unrecompensed labor, is unfavorable to a scrupulous sense of justice and to a spirit of active benevolence."[23] How could any rational southerner have objected to Greeley's modest and reasonable reflections on the corrupting influences of slavery on the southern character?

Most abolitionists like Greeley accepted the South's view of itself as an aristocracy. But they deftly substituted negative northern connotations for positive southern associations when they employed the term. If, as Greeley and most northerners believed, the North represented the fullest expression of democracy in either the Old World or the New, the southern slave states represented all that was subversively antidemocratic in American culture. And Greeley was convinced that of all these slave states, South Carolina recognized "the existence of the smallest amount of rights among her own free white men" and exhibited "in its worst form the evils of an aristocracy."[24] In Greeley's view the aristocratic ethos was not the organic expression of a nobly bred people; it was the inevitable and disastrous product of a slave culture that victimized not only chattel slaves but the masses of free whites politically in thrall to the planter elite.

Southern polemicists were fond of justifying whatever antidemocratic tendencies there might exist within their aristocratic society by appealing to the well-bred southerner's refined manners and high cultural tone. Southern newspapers like the *Richmond Enquirer,* for example, commonly boasted of the southerner's being "the impersonation of the high-born aristocrat." To this vaunting Greeley and many other northern polemicists posed a simple but provocative question: Where was the evidence of this high southern culture? Alas, Greeley sneeringly lamented, southern Cavaliers could claim among them no great inventors, or artists, or men of genius. In cultural endeavors Dixie presented to the outside world "one magnificent level." In Greeley's opinion the only items attesting "the brute superiority of the Caucasian over the African" in the South were advertisements for slave auctions and published reward posters for runaways. Contrasting the North's 4 percent illiteracy rate with the South's 17 percent, he concluded that if the slave states could lay claim to "most of the chivalry," they could also lay claim to "very little of the culture of the country."[25]

Greeley's slighting comments on the cultivation of the South's aristocracy, written in 1855, seem in retrospect decorous when compared with the bitter rhetorical attacks unleashed by the northern press after the caning of Senator Charles Sumner of Massachusetts on the floor of the Senate by Representative Preston Brooks of South Carolina. The commentary of the *Boston Chronicle* was typical of the heightened invective that Brooks's assault generated in the North. "The act," the *Chronicle* fumed, "has all the characteristics of the slaveholding chivalry, is in perfect keeping with their past history, and follows legitimately from their principles. It is a cowardly act, and cowardice is the chief trait of Southern chivalry."[26] Like Greeley and other northern polemical writers, this journalist employed the southern term *chivalry*, but he turned it on its head, associating it not with bravery but with cowardice. Nothing could have been more cleverly designed to evoke indignation from southerners—a people who viewed themselves as nobly descended and who associated their nobility of character with precisely those qualities of courage and honor that the writer for the *Chronicle* refused to vouchsafe them.

For Henry Ward Beecher, as for the *Chronicle* writer, the outrages perpetrated by the South's self-anointed chivalry in Bloody Kansas and on the floor of the United States Senate raised questions about the essential nature of southern manhood, questions that could lead only to the conclusion that Dixie's self-proclaimed aristocrats were in fact savages. In his view the confrontation between northerners and southerners was no less than a struggle for the soul of the nation between the forces of civilization and barbarity. "On one side," Beecher contended, "stand men of Liberty, Christianity; industry, arts, and of universal prosperity; on the other, are the waste and refuse materials of a worn-out Slave State population—men whose ideas of society and civilization are comprised in the terms, a rifle, a horse, a hound, a slave, tobacco, and whiskey; beyond these there is nothing but an annual uproarious camp-meeting, where they get just enough religion to enable them to find out that the Bible justifies all the immeasurable vices and wrongs of Slavery."[27]

As Beecher's rhetoric indicates, sectional debate had become so inflamed and vituperative by the mid-1850s that radical abolitionist voices that had been scorned and shunned by northerners a few years earlier were now being listened to with growing respect. Writing in *The Liberator*, William Lloyd Garrison made the most of the times, subjecting the South to his righteous judgment and his withering scorn. For Garrison, southerners who preened and disported themselves as blooded aristocrats were in reality little better than animals. They were blighted by slavery "in the usefulness of their hands and the productions of their brains; in their manners and morals; in every thing pertaining to body, mind, soul, or estate; giving them over to unrestrained licentiousness, filthy amalgamation, incurable laziness, profligate wastefulness, satanic pride, pitiable ignorance, hardness of heart, atrocious barbarity." Garrison gleefully exposed these supposedly lordly aristocrats of the slave states, revealing them to be monsters who blended "the conceit of the peacock with the ferocity of the tiger, and making their condition the most hopeless of any portion of the human race."[28]

If Garrison viewed southerners as unregenerate and spiritually deformed, he was equally scornful of the defenses of slavery mounted by the region's polemical writers. The feisty abolitionist gave a contemptuous reply to George Fitzhugh's boast that no one in the North had denied his theory that chattel slavery was "right in the abstract and in the concrete, the normal condition of the mass of mankind." "The reason why no one has entered the lists against [Fitzhugh] is the same as that which prevents a sane man from attempting to argue with a dolt or a lunatic." Drawing self-consciously on the controversial metaphor that Charles Sumner had employed in his "Crime against Kansas" speech to describe Senator Andrew P. Butler of South Carolina, Garrison proceeded to dismiss Fitzhugh as a demented "Don Quixote of Slavedom."[29]

By the eve of the Civil War abolitionist orators had discovered that they could most effectively wound their slave-owning foes by attacking the ideal of southern gentility and dismissing southern civilization as barbaric. Speaking in the summer of 1860 to the annual meeting of the American Anti-slavery Society, the Reverend J. R. W. Sloane denounced the South's peculiar institution as a "foe to modern civilization." He declared to his cheering audience that "the nature of slavery, its tendency, is to create a set of cowardly, brutal ruffians, who are unfit for the intercourse and society of civilized and refined gentlemen." The Reverend A. D. Mayo drove the rhetoric to an even higher pitch, comparing the conflict between northerners and southerners to the opposition of John the Baptist and Jesus to Herod. "Herod," he proclaimed, "is the type of irresponsible despotism. Every nation is, sooner or later, threatened by the tyranny that consists in the subjugation and use of the weak by the strong for their pleasure."[30] In this analogy the aristocratic southern planter is not-so-obliquely likened to the anti-Christ.

As the Civil War drew ever nearer, northern polemicists were unanimous in their scornful rejection of the idea that their southern adversaries were members of a distinguished and aristocratic Norman race. Most of them had concluded, however, that northerners and southerners were two different peoples, and in this assumption they differed very little from secessionist writers such as George Fitzhugh. William Lloyd Garrison, for example, professed himself in full agreement with the opinion of the *Charleston Mercury* that "the people of the North and the people of the South were never one people, and nothing can ever make them so." Indeed, Garrison appended his own words to those of the *Mercury*. The two peoples differed, he added, "in ideas, institutions, habits, aims, 'wide as the poles asunder.' . . . Why should such attempt to walk together?"[31]

The northern view of southerners as a barbaric and evil people was not one confined to the pages of Republican newspapers and abolitionist journals. By the late 1850s it permeated all levels of society. As Howard Floan has observed, belletristic writers and philosophers from John Greenleaf Whittier, James Russell Lowell, and Henry Wadsworth Longfellow to Ralph Waldo Emerson, Theodore Parker, and Henry David Thoreau, when they described southerners, embraced essentially "the same image of evil which was portrayed by Garrison." Indeed, according to Floan the image of Southern slaveholders projected by New England's literary Brahmins "was more vital, less complex, and therefore more acceptable to the popular mind" than the tendentious arguments of abolitionist agitators like Garrison.[32]

Theodore Parker gave early expression to this demonizing of southerners by the Brahmins in a speech delivered to an anti-slavery convention in Boston in 1850. Parker warned his audience that "the idea of slavery" demanded "for its proximate organization, an aristocracy, that is, a government of all the people by a part of the people—the masters." Such a profoundly un-American idea could no more be reconciled within the Union, he argued, "than the worship of the real God and the worship of the imaginary Devil can be combined and made to coexist in the life of a single man."[33] Parker's indirect relegation of southern slave owners to the Devil's party merged with abolitionist sermons such as the one delivered by Reverend Mayo that linked them to the forces of the anti-Christ. This kind of eschatological rhetoric astonished and outraged southerners. They viewed what they considered the rhetorical excesses of the North as confirmation of their charge that Saxon-descended Puritans remained, as they had been in Cromwell's time, Christ-besotted fanatics.

For transcendentalists like Emerson, such harsh moral condemnations of the southern character as Parker's were not dangerously hyperbolic. They expressed a deep understanding of the corrosive moral effects of slavery, an understanding natural to a Saxon race known through history for its high ethical perceptions, its "culture of the intellect," and its love of freedom. Emerson believed that under the baneful influence of their peculiar institution, southerners had fallen away from these racial ideals. He was certain that slavery had decomposed and stupefied the "moral sense" of slave owners, resulting in a "moral injury" that was "infinitely greater than its pecuniary and political injury." Generous numbers of the South's aristocracy, he observed, had made their way to New England to be "educated here in our institutions." Yet they had obstinately resisted the truths that northern culture had so generously offered them. They had returned to Dixie and surrendered to "ophthalonia, this blindness, which hides from them the great facts of right and wrong." Despite southerners' incessant assertions of their nobility and their superior racial heritage, the North's cultural elite were more and more inclined to dismiss southern culture as second rate, morally blind, and even barbaric. As Henry Wadsworth Longfellow observed with grim humor in a letter to Senator Sumner in 1860, the Union was now divided between the "United States" and the "Benighted States" of America.[34]

By the time Preston Brooks struck down Charles Sumner on the Senate floor, northern writers had had enough of playing second fiddle to the "Virginia Race." They were proudly proclaiming the genius of a "Universal Yankee Nation" that had sprung form sturdy Puritan and Anglo-Saxon roots, and they were in no mood to kowtow to men claiming to be Norman-descended southern Cavaliers. Emerson was quick to interpret the attack on Sumner in these racial terms. "Our position of the free states," he wrote in his journal, "is very like that of Covenanters against the Cavaliers." In his "Assault on Charles Sumner" he rhetorically annihilated the self-appointed defender of Cavalier honor, dismissing Preston Brooks as "some caviller" who had brutally attacked a man without warning "for having had the audacity to write his Senate speech before it was delivered.[35] The implications of Emerson's remark were not hard to discern. Yankees thought before they spoke; brutish, nitpicking southern "cavillers" like the honorable Preston Brooks did not think at all.

As civil war loomed on America's horizon, formerly moderate anti-slavery writers like Emerson had come to believe that freedom and slavery were absolutely irreconcilable within the Union. As for the white people living in the free and slave states, Emerson was not prepared to say that they constituted two separate races. However, he seems to have been willing to accept that the United States was now divided into two nations, North and South, composed of peoples so fundamentally different that not even the elimination of the vexing question of slavery could bring them into harmony. In 1851, nine years before the exchange between Garrison and the *Charleston Mercury*, he had concluded in his journal that "the North and South are two nations. It is not slavery that separates them, but climate. Without slavery they do not agree." After the Brooks-Sumner episode Emerson's sense of this profound regional difference grew even more bleak. Southern Cavaliers like Preston

Brooks were not men but deadly animals like cobras and scorpions. They were lethal and scarcely human, with "no wisdom, no capacity of improvement," looking about everywhere for duels. "With such a nation or a nation with a predominance of this complexion," Emerson grimly concluded, "war is the safest terms . . . if they cross the lines, they can be dealt with as all fanged animals must be."[36]

6
A Proud, High-Toned People Repudiate the Scum of the North

The election of Abraham Lincoln to the presidency in 1860 climaxed the increasingly rancorous political debates of the 1850s, galvanized the southern people, and initiated Dixie's inexorable movement toward secession. By no means did all southerners immediately jump on to the secession bandwagon. Alexander Stephens, who would later serve as vice-president of the Confederacy, expressed the attitude of a substantial number when he rose at the Georgia Convention to oppose his native state's leaving the Union. What, he wondered, would be the result of the blood and sacrifice that secession would almost certainly entail? He concluded that such a conflict would only assure "the overthrow of the American Government, established by our common ancestry, cemented and built up by their sweat and blood, and founded on the broad principles of right, justice, and humanity." The problem for Stephens and other moderate southerners was that in the months following Lincoln's election, fewer and fewer of the southern people were willing to subscribe to his belief that Americans shared a "common ancestry." Increasing numbers were coming to share the conviction of the secessionist leaders of the state of South Carolina that the passing of time had "totally altered the relations between the northern and southern states." They had concluded that the "identity of feelings, interests and institutions, which once existed, [was] gone," that the Union was "now divided between agricultural, and manufacturing and commercial states; between states holding, and non-slaveholding states." And they were ever more inclined to accept the idea that the mutually antagonistic "institutions and industrial pursuits" of the northern and southern states had made northerners and southerners "totally different people."[1]

The writers of the South Carolina secession manifesto had asserted that northern and southern Americans constituted different peoples, not different races. But the distinction was probably not a significant one, either for the polemical writers arguing for a southern confederacy or for their increasingly sympathetic audience of readers. The frequently bruited assertions of southern difference, southern grandeur, and southern nationalism that followed the election of 1860 resonated fully with the Norman-Saxon racial theory that had become a staple of southern polemical writing in the 1850s. The editors of *DeBow's Review* and the *Southern Literary Messenger* would certainly have been pleased by the assertion of Jabez Curry after Lincoln's election that "the possession of the Government by a hostile, sectional party" had placed southern "destinies under the control of another and distinct people." "To the slaveholding states," he asserted, "it is a *foreign government,* which understands not our condition, defers not to our opinions, consults not our interests, and has no sympathy with our peculiar civilization."[2]

In their concern for the survival of the South's "peculiar civilization" within a Republican-dominated Union, southern writers were quick to claim for their region the distinctively aristocratic qualities of gallantry and refinement that they believed had been vouchsafed them by their Norman racial inheritance. Thus the writer of a Charleston broadside judged the election of a Republican to the White House to be the last in a "long, dark catalogue of wrongs, on the part of the Northern . . . States, against their gallant, high-spirited . . . brethren of the South, who so largely helped to found the Republic, and contributed so largely to its renown." The *Richmond Dispatch,* in its defiant justification of South Carolina's secession, argued that the Palmetto State had been forced into its course of action by a "long career of injustice and wrong, of spoliation and aggression, of rapine and blood, which has compelled the South to make a final stand for self-preservation, and irritated a proud and high-toned people beyond the capacity of further endurance."[3]

Among those favoring the creation of an independent confederacy, the idea of Dixie's racial homogeneity was an especially effective rhetorical weapon, and it was frequently drawn from their arsenal. Amid the deliberations of the Old Dominion's political leaders, the *Southern Literary Messenger* reminded its readers that Virginians, "in the main," were "homogeneous with the Southern States in race." The states of the lower South, it boasted, swarmed "with Virginia's sons and her sons' sons. Can the mother forsake her children and think of preferring an alien race (comparatively) hostile to her and her interests, to her own offspring, who would perish to defend her?" As far as the *Messenger* essayist was concerned, Virginia's course of action was ordained by the fact of her racial union with the greater South. "Our race is there," the writer affirmed. "They are bone of our bone, and flesh of our flesh. Therefore, whom God has joined together let us not put asunder."[4]

The *Southern Literary Messenger* was by no means alone among the region's periodicals in emphasizing Dixie's unique racial inheritance. As it had done in the previous decade, *DeBow's Review* led the way in the project to convert the conflict between North and South from a political struggle over slavery into a drama of conflicting races. In its January 1861 issue it proclaimed a bizarre link between the southern American race and the exalted Mediterranean races of Greece and Italy that had given birth to Western civilization. In the face of assertions of northern cultural superiority and southern barbarism, *DeBow's* argued that the most distinguished races and cultures were inevitably products of warmer climes and latitudes. "We habitually undervalue ourselves, and slavishly imitate the heavy, dull, coarse, clumsy, tasteless, races of the North," the *DeBow's* writer complained. "Civilization is an exotic in all cold latitudes. It belongs naturally to temperate climes. It is about to resume its normal, natural, and historical localities." The magazine confidently prophesied that following the creation of the Confederacy, the southern people would produce a culture rivaling and perhaps surpassing the great Mediterranean cultures of Europe. In a final frenzy of chauvinism it crowed that "the country south of Mason's and Dixon's line" was "the true and only seat of high civilization—the only region in which man ever did, or ever will arrive at fully developed, intellectual, moral, and physical maturity." And it ended by boasting that "France, Italy, Greece, Spain, Cuba, Brazil, and our own Southern Confederacy, [were] in the ascendant."[5]

Though the notion defied logic, the coupling of southerners with Mediterranean races enjoyed a brief vogue in southern magazines and newspapers during the rhetorically inflamed months before the firing on Fort Sumter. The *Charleston Mercury,* for example, observed indignantly that "the boys in the Northern schools and colleges" had been taught "that the destiny of Southern nations is to be conquered and overrun by Northern races, just as the Germans overran the Romans." To this assertion southern writer Ellwood Fisher replied that he had "read history very differently" from Yankees. "The civilized world has been conquered seven times—five times by Southern men, and twice by Northern," he observed. "The Greeks, led on by Alexander, were Southerners and slaveholders; as were the Romans, under Caesar; so the Arabs, under Mahomet; the Spaniards, under Philip; and the French, though not slaveholders, are Southerners. I need not tell you what they did under the great Napoleon." Though Fisher urged northerners to "lay to heart history taught by historians who are not Yankees," today one can only be amazed by the distortions of this peculiarly southern view of history.[6] Fisher seems to have seriously entertained the idea that American southerners could be classified with the Greek, Roman, Spanish, and Arab races and that the unifying characteristic of these dominant peoples was that they all were slaveholders.

After such outlandish and unconvincing racial fabrications, it remained for *DeBow's Review* to turn its readers toward the more familiar and less exotic historical terrain of Cavalier versus Puritan that had underlain the Norman racial myth from its inception. Indeed, the January 1861 issue that postulated a link between a southern American race and the races of the Mediterranean also included an essay attributing the failure of the American Constitution to the initial victory of the Puritan North over the Cavalier South in the Constitutional Convention of 1787. According to this thesis, "The Roundhead and Cavalier that had crossed swords under the hostile banners of Fairfax and Rupert, met again, on American soil: and when the battle was fought, in the convention of 1787, the victory, as of old, remained with the saints of the covenant." In this "fatal contest," the writer contended, "the banner of the Cavalier first went down, in his concession to the enemy of the right to regulate the basis of Southern representation, by striking two fifths of the numerical power of the South from the map of the Constitution."[7]

By agreeing to accept its slave population at three-fifths' the numerical value of its free white population for purposes of determining its numbers in the House of Representatives, the essayist believed, the South's Cavaliers had submitted themselves to a flawed political document that would ultimately fail to maintain the union between northern and southern states. The Constitution had been fatally compromised, not only by its refusal to accommodate fully the institution of slavery but also by its excessively democratic foundations, "bottomed upon universal suffrage." The *DeBow's* writer proceeded to explain that a government such as that established by the Constitution, "commencing in democracy, must end in anarchy, despotism, and ruin." If southern Cavaliers had only determined to eschew the Puritan-inspired political union of 1787, they might have fashioned for themselves a southern constitution "originating in the aristocratic, or monarchical principle" that would have guaranteed a vital, glorious, and noble slaveholding nation. Instead, a superior southern race had consented to enter into an unnatural union with inferior Puritan fanatics. This yoking of irreconcilable political values, cultures, and races had led to the current "spectacle of a permanent aristocracy, founded upon the natural diversity of races, patiently subjecting itself to the wildest schemes of democratic theory"[8]—schemes that had resulted in the disastrous election of Abraham Lincoln.

Even as early as the American Revolution, the *DeBow's* essayist concluded, "two systems of civilization" had existed "on the western continent—uniting, but never mingling . . . separate, distinct, antagonistic, and repellant, and forced into the presence of each other by the absence of that greatest of political necessity—an efficient government." From its very foundation, therefore, the Republic had been a political illusion, and from its inception the United States had been composed of "two distinct peoples—two separate nationalities."[9] The composition and disposition of these two peoples were now as they had always been: Norman-descended Cavaliers to the south of the Mason-Dixon and Saxon-descended Puritans to the north.

The antagonism between Puritan and Cavalier evident in the constitutional debates of 1787 was, in the opinion of the *DeBow's* essayist, abiding and irremediable, and it had accompanied American colonists from seventeenth-century England to the New World. As the original Cavaliers had endured the tyranny of Cromwell's Puritan Roundheads, so the contemporary New World offspring of this Norman-descended aristocracy had found themselves subject to Yankee political hegemony. "Twenty years," the writer raged, "the English people endured the absolutism of Cromwell . . . twenty years the Southern States have submitted to the persistent encroachment and lawless usurpation of a fanatical majority, and the two civilizations now find their histories written in the parallel." The only recourse of a noble southern race was to win its freedom from a fanatical Puritan race that adamantly rejected the fundamental southern proposition "that *persons* are *property*" and that was "by force of numbers" preparing to impose upon the South its own "dogma" of "permanent tyranny."[10]

Reading the *DeBow's* article today, one is forced to recall that southern slave owners like George Washington, Thomas Jefferson, and Andrew Jackson had been crucial to the creation, articulation, and expansion of the American democracy that the writer was now so scornfully rejecting. The article indicates the extent to which, by 1861, many southerners had alienated themselves from the democratic spirit and the national vision of these earlier generations of Dixie's political heroes. The profundity of that alienation is suggested by the essay writer's apparently serious admiration for "aristocratic" and even "monarchical" political principles and his contemptuous dismissal of the "schemes of democratic theory" on which he believed the Constitution of 1787 had been founded. In the hysterical political climate that prevailed after Lincoln's election in which secessionist sentiment increasingly thrived, many southern writers seem to have been willing to embrace both the myth of the South's Norman racial supremacy and the Old World, aristocratic political ethos that complemented it. In the process of embracing these reactionary ideas, they recklessly abandoned the Jeffersonian principles that had actuated the Revolution, the Constitution, and the Union.

The word *tyranny,* which had been strategically employed in the *DeBow's* essay, was frequently employed by other southern polemicists to express the South's sense of wrong and outrage. Over and over, southern propagandists articulated a virtually identical grievance. For a noble and aristocratic race of white people to be subjected to tyrannical forces was terrible enough. But for the instruments of tyranny to be placed in the hands of lowborn Puritan fanatics was for aristocratic southerners a horror beyond description. Langdon Cheves was convinced that "a popular tyranny of fanatics and low-minded politicians—a tyranny so much the worse, because it is many-headed—a popular tyranny, even when composed of less foul elements than the present, is more degrading than the tyranny of a monarch."[11] If southerners had been subjected to the unjust authority of a king, Cheves implied, they might at least have had the consolation of knowing that they battled a worthy adversary.

Alas, southerners had been granted no such worthy antagonists. Instead they were facing a Puritan-descended race that, exhibiting the fanatical temperament of its English forebears, had perverted the principles of democracy and destroyed the nation. The *Charleston Mercury* wrathfully observed that northerners had developed a concept of law entirely subject to "the shifting will of the mobocracy, guided by interest or passion alone." Indeed, in "eighty short years" they had converted the Republic "into one vast mob—a ranting, reckless, lawless mob—shrieking for liberty amidst blood, and freedom in plunder." Yankees were bigots and hypocrites like their Roundhead ancestors, bent not on freeing slaves but on having "Southern fields upon which to make their descent and to pillage, [that] they may keep their hands from each other's throats and pockets."[12]

For such a debased race the election of Abraham Lincoln—a vulgar, cloddish rail-splitter—was a perfectly natural choice. Writing in the *Richmond Examiner* editor John M. Daniel acidly dismissed the president as "a King of Shreds and Patches." "In the first of 'Free Presidents,'" he continued, "we have the delightful combination of a western country lawyer with a Yankee barkeeper." Accompanying Lincoln into the White House, he predicted, would be "slang, rowdyism, brutality, and all moral filth . . . all the tag and rag of Western grog-shops and Yankee factories."[13]

As one by one the southern states opted for secession in the early months of 1861, Dixie's editorial writers began to face the likelihood of civil war. But most of them publicly professed little doubt that the outcome of such a conflict would be victory and vindication for the Confederacy and the high-toned southern race that constituted it. The *Richmond Dispatch* was typical of the southern media, prophesying that the aggressive avidity that had stood Yankees in such good stead in the political and commercial arenas of the past would prove a liability in the coming struggle with aristocratic southerners: "The Yankee people have lost their Yankee natures if they, in fact, have any stomach for . . . war. They are the last people in the world to persist in a course of conduct that 'won't pay.'"[14]

The *Dispatch* editorial hit upon the first of two Puritan character traits that southern propagandists commonly maintained would doom the North in battle: cupidity and cowardice. For these writers, such inborn cowardice had been on clear display in the timid northern response to the firing on Fort Sumter that had guaranteed the Confederacy's first glorious victory. The *Charleston Mercury* was one of many southern newspapers that took pains to point out to its readers the ignominious failure of a large Union fleet to come to the aid of the besieged Charleston harbor fortress. "The Northern officers" in command of the fleet, "having been so carefully selected, for their fidelity to their section and superior trustworthiness in a hostile crusade against the South, were unwilling to incur the risk of running their ships into the harbor, and engaging our batteries. They thought it prudent not to attempt reinforcements in launches." Thus, the writer acidly continued, "the soldiers of Abolitionism were left to their fate, without an attempt to relieve their perilous condition. Their idle allies had the pleasure of seeing them strike their colors to the Confederate States. They are commendable for their gallantry, and we trust that these brave mariners will receive a suitable commendation."[15]

So convinced was the *Mercury* that Yankee cowardice would be matched by Yankee cupidity that six days after the attack on Fort Sumter the newspaper reported a Confederate proclamation announcing that "letters of marque and reprisal" would be issued "to armed vessels cruising as privateers upon the high seas." In one masterful stroke, the writer gleefully asserted, Jefferson Davis had contrived through this proclamation to array "Northern cupidity" against "Northern fanaticism," for "the valorous Yankee, led by the scent of the rich prey, will not long scruple, under the sanction of the Southern flag, to sweep from the seas the commercial marine of his Yankee neighbors."[16]

In the days after the firing on Sumter the *Columbia Guardian* expressed the widely embraced sentiment that it was best for the South that the die had been cast at Charleston harbor, for the only alternative to war was for southerners to become the "tools and vassals" of vile abolitionists, to submit to "a democracy of fanaticism, avarice, vulgarity, and insolence," and to "fall down and worship [the] hideous Baal" of Yankee culture. Echoing the sentiments of Langdon Cheves, the *Guardian* proclaimed that aristocratic southerners could never live with the "infamy and degradation" attending submission to "a many-headed autocrat ... a monster without bowels and without conscience," the pure product of "Northern mobs."[17]

Though most southern editorialists were sanguine about Dixie's prospects in the coming civil war, a few, like the writer for the *New Orleans Bee,* warned readers that the conflict might be a difficult one for the new Confederacy. In issuing his warning he utilized a metaphor that would become a staple of southern war rhetoric. The Yankees descending on the South, he cautioned, were "as numerous as the swarms of barbarians which the frozen North sent from her loins to overrun the Roman Empire."[18] Southern editorial pens were deftly transforming the Saxon-descended northern race into a barbaric horde, determined to lay waste to an aristocratic and highly civilized southern slave empire.

As the early military engagements of the summer of 1861 settled into what seemed destined to be a protracted war, southern periodicals such as *DeBow's Review* remained as firmly wedded as ever to the idea that the dismemberment of the Union had not been the result of deep and irreconcilable differences over the question of slavery but rather the result of a "deeply defined difference in race." Saxon elements of England had followed their severe and gloomy faith to New England. The Norman English, "chivalrous, impetuous, and ever noble and brave," had flocked to the South, where they had "attained [their] full development in the Cavaliers of Virginia and the Huguenots of South Carolina and Florida." The issue of slavery had not caused the Civil War. It had, however, helped to focus and sharpen the fanatically "gloomy and ascetic" temperament of the Puritans and set them forth into political and now military combat with the large-minded and valiant "courtiers and gentlemen" who constituted Dixie's plantation elite. It was these profoundly antagonistic racial characteristics, not slavery, that had made the separation of South from North "unavoidable and absolutely necessary."[19]

In contrast to Dixie's journalists, the northern press in its response to secessionist agitation achieved nothing like the near unanimity of opinion that characterized southern condemnations of a northern race that had conspired to elect the vile Abraham Lincoln. Indeed, as late as February 1861, powerful and influential newspapers like the *New York Herald* opposed the new Lincoln administration and bitterly lamented that the nation was being destroyed—not by southern slave interests but by "abolition fanaticism." In prose that must have been music to the ears of southern propagandists, the *Herald* indignantly observed that "the fertile source of the ever-recurring mischief is the Puritan idea of the superiority of their sect over other men, and a mysterious divine right which they claim to possess of dictating to all mankind."[20]

Though the *Herald* writer made no reference to the assertions of superior southern blood that were being advanced by writers south of the Potomac, he held up for ridicule a sermon that had recently been delivered by abolitionist Henry Ward Beecher—one that indicates that race consciousness could be found north of the Potomac as well as south in the months immediately preceding the Civil War. The *Herald* observed that the Reverend Beecher had advanced a disturbing theme in his homily: "Puritan blood means the blood of Christ." The writer warned all those who supported the Union against the dangerous notion, inherent in Beecher's boast, of "the superiority of Puritan blood . . . and the inferiority of all other blood." Was the abolitionist crusader proposing the inferiority of all southern blood, the writer wondered. If so, how did he intend to explain the contributions to the Republic of southerners like Washington, Jefferson, and Madison?[21]

The problem for the *New York Herald* and other moderate political and editorial voices in the North was that, just like southern moderates, they were gradually drowned out in the months following Lincoln's election by more extreme voices. Radical northern writers thrived on distortions of southern character as gross as the distortions of northern character that were concurrently issuing from the southern press. One of these extreme northern voices, the *Chicago Democrat,* gloried in an election in which "eighteen million freemen" had spoken in unison in a voice loud enough for "even the most stupid secessionists" to hear. As for the threat of "southern braggarts" and "southern chivalry" to leave the Union upon Lincoln's election, the newspaper issued this challenge: "Do it if you dare! . . . Every man of you who attempts to subvert this Union, which we prize so dearly, will be hung as high as Haman. We will have no fooling about this matter." The *Democrat* dismissed as risible the notion that southern chivalry was a force to be reckoned with. "The chivalry will eat dirt. They will back out. They never had any spunk anyhow. The best they could do was to bully, and brag and bluster." Toying contemptuously with the South's revered Cavalier myth, the writer claimed that the ghost of John Brown was "more terrible than an army with banners, in the eyes of every

Southern cavalier. These knights of the Sunny South are just such heroes as Sancho Panza was. They are wonderful hands at bragging and telling fantastical lies, but when it comes to action, count them out."[22]

In the months following Lincoln's victory, northern attacks on the notion of southern gentility increased in both frequency and intensity. The *New York Times* eagerly joined the fray, jeering that the "travelled world" was all too familiar with self-proclaimed southern aristocrats, with "the bow legs of the Georgia corn-cracker, the brutish look . . . and piratical visage of the Gulf-Ruffians, who are now the ruling class there." The *Times* assured its readers that the South's claim to aristocracy was a sham. Southern society was in reality a primitive and debased one in which "negro overseers, negro traders, negro auctioneers, or other odds and ends of a diseased community, are entitled to rank foremost of the gentlemen of the world."[23]

The more vicious the attacks from the North, the more readily the South's secessionist papers reprinted them. The *Charleston Mercury,* for example, quickly picked up the *Chicago Democrat*'s diatribe; and the *Savannah Daily Morning News* obligingly republished the *New York Times* attack. In the months preceding the firing on Fort Sumter, extremist elements of both the southern and northern presses fed off each other. They slowly but surely poisoned the minds of their readers with visions of barbaric southern braggarts and fanatical Puritan bigots. They helped make it possible for southern and northern Americans to view themselves as two completely different peoples, two separate races.

By April 1861 even the South's staunchest defenders within the northern press grimly acknowledged the virtual certainty of civil war. But the *New York Herald* remained convinced that the blame for such a fratricidal conflict lay with the extreme abolitionists of the North. "Future history," it admonished, "will repeat the truth—that all this calamity . . . has been brought upon the North by its own folly. Brought about by giving a license to traitors in the form of abolition exhorters, fanatical preachers, editors, political demagogues, selfish and hypocritical spoilsmen . . . by elevating men to office who preached an irrepressible conflict with the South . . . who made a merit of John Brown's murderous invasion . . . whose clergy denounced its people as barbarians, unfit for church association or recognition even as human beings."[24]

Less than a week after the *Herald* editorial came the attack on Fort Sumter, and all such sympathy for the South was swept away in a torrent of northern outrage and patriotism. Abolitionists like Horace Greeley, sensing that through its foolish aggression at Charleston the South had finally succeeded in unifying the North, lingered vulture-like on the details of the battle and distorted them, refuting southern claims of Yankee cowardice and portraying southerners as heartless monsters whose purported chivalry masked an underlying barbarism:

> Charleston herself was drunk with excitement and joyous exultation. Her entire white population, and her gay crowds of well-dressed visitors, thronged her streets and quays, noting the volume and resonant thunder of the Confederate cannonade.... That seven thousand men, after five months of careful preparation, could overcome seventy, was regarded as an achievement ranking with the most memorable deeds of Alexander or Hannibal, Caesar or Napoleon. Champagne flowed on every hand like water; thousands quaffed, and feasted on the richest viands.... "Damnation to the Yankees!" was drunk with rapture by enthusiastic crowds.... Already, in the ardent imagination of her Chivalry, the Confederacy had established its independence beyond dispute, and was about to conquer and lay waste the degenerate, cowardly North.[25]

The *New York Times* likewise exulted in the final unmasking of southern perfidy, and it celebrated the near unanimity of sentiment against southerners that had followed the bombardment. "The reverberations from Charleston harbor have brought about what months of logic would have been impotent to effect," it declared—"the rapid condensation of public sentiment in the Free States. The North is now a unit." Even the newspaper's own New York City, "the spot most tainted by the Southern poison," was now possessed by "one intense, inspiring sentiment of patriotism" that had "fused all other passions in its fiery heat." For months, the *Times* observed, New Yorkers had refused to believe that "the country really held men so insane, so suicidal, as to attempt to transform such threats as theirs into deeds." The attack on Fort Sumter had finally unmasked "the sheer demonism" that marked "the programme of social construction put forth by the Slave Power."[26]

In the weeks following the surrender of Fort Sumter, northern editorial writers challenged the notion that their southern adversaries were a gallant, aristocratic people. They were particularly sensitive to the southern charge that the events at Charleston harbor had established beyond doubt the bravery and determination of the southern warrior and the ineptness and cowardice of the Yankee. One writer protested that "the chivalry and even bravery of the South, has been altogether over estimated." In pressing his argument he steered clear of the events in Charleston, preferring to dredge up from the recent past the infamous caning of Senator Charles Sumner. If "the brutal attack from behind . . . upon an unarmed Senator in Congress" was the highest "specimen of this kind of Chivalry," he observed, then the North had best prepare itself to battle savages, not aristocrats.[27]

Another editorialist agreed "that the high-bred and chivalrous 'southron' of whom we have all heard so much, and read so much, and seen so little, is an absolute and universal humbug." Of course, he observed archly, "impelled, as we of the North nearly all are to earn our bread by our own labor . . . it could not reasonably be expected that we should exhibit all the grace and polish of a courtly and imperial race fed by the labor of slaves, and able to devote an elegant leisure to self-culture." When one examined more closely the achievements of the exalted southern gentleman, however, one confronted a much less flattering picture. One saw a man who beat his quadroon mistress in a fit of rage, who swore on the way home from church, and who failed to pay his bills. One also was regaled with the spectacle of those so-called southern aristocrats who had run the departments of the army and navy in Washington and who had, following Lincoln's inauguration, deserted their government and "brought sorrow upon their country, disgrace upon their profession, and then went among their confederates and fairly wallowed in their own shame." In the mind of this writer, treason had converted the southerner's vaulted honor into shame. As for the southern aristocrat's reputed courage, another editorial writer contended that Dixie's soldiers were not brave and knightly warriors but rather "sepoys" whose conduct in battle more resembled "barbarians, maddened by the scent of blood, than Christianized men."[28]

By the beginning of the Civil War many northern opinion makers had reached the conclusion of their southern counterparts that Americans were "not a homogeneous people." They even seem to have agreed with their adversaries that the source of the abiding hostility between regions lay in their contrasting Puritan and Cavalier heritages. In the words of one Yankee editorialist, "What [was] distinctively denominated American civilization" had "streamed across the continent on parallel or nearly parallel lines, from the two centers, Plymouth Rock and Jamestown."[29] Beyond this point of agreement, however, there was sharp disagreement with the South over the characteristics of the Puritan and Cavalier races that had been stamped upon their respective regions.

Northerners naturally refused to accept the southern caricature of the fanatical, avaricious, treacherous, and hypocritical Yankee. They refined and polished the counterimage of a "sturdy Puritan" braving bleak New England winters, hostile Indians, and sterile soil in the pursuit of freedom. Neither did most of them pay obeisance to the figure of the southern Cavalier. They chose to view their slave-holding adversaries not as humane and civilized aristocrats but as "profligate gentlemen" of Virginia, "greedy speculators" who had purchased their opulent and privileged lives at the expense of turning themselves into "tyrannical masters" of their unfortunate slaves. For the North, the genius of Plymouth Rock was a love of democracy and a fidelity to justice and human rights that had spread fruitfully from the shores of Massachusetts to the prairies of Kansas and Minnesota. The genius of the Cavalier race was a diseased love of privilege and a mania for human exploitation that had spread destructively from Virginia through the Deep South westward to the borders of Texas. "The shoots planted early by the bragging and *gentlemenly* settlers of the Southern States have gone to seed now," a northern editorialist remarked with grim satisfaction. "And most villainous seed they are too."[30] Now was the time to destroy the wicked harvest of a depraved Cavalier race.

To what degree were individual northerners influenced in their opinions of southerners by editorials and polemical essays? Letters written during the turbulent months following Lincoln's election indicate that correspondents of abolitionist persuasion faithfully echoed the attitudes and even the vocabulary of the essays and editorials they were reading. These influences were apparent in a letter American Samuel May wrote to English abolitionist Richard Davis Webb on the eve of the presidential election. In this missive May prayed for a Lincoln victory, even if it resulted in the secession of the slave states, for he was convinced that "our union with slaveholders, our joining in a common government with these robbers, plunderers, adulterers, and murderers is a wicked union." The second part of May's letter, written after the election returns had come in, expressed his jubilation over the Republican triumph. In it he predicted, much as the *Chicago Democrat* had done, that the South would make loud threats toward the new administration and then do nothing. "These blustering slaveholders," he wrote, "are cowards, not less than tyrants; and they are surrounded [by those who] will not suffer these braggarts to plunge the South into scenes of insurrection."[31] It is significant that in his letter May used the same term that northern editorial writers had favored in their unflattering descriptions of southern slave owners: *braggarts*.

Northerners hostile to slavery seemed not only willing to accept the idea that slave owners were cowardly braggarts; they also seem to have been receptive to the notion bruited in both regional media that southerners constituted an entirely different race of people. John Bigelow, in a letter written in February 1861, was inclined to the view that warm climate had incapacitated southerners for responsible government, as it had rendered unfit other Latin races. If inhabitants of the slave states were unwilling to submit themselves to a lawfully elected government, he opined, "it must be because our Southern brethren are under those climatic or other influences which have hitherto seemed to disqualify the Latin race in all its branches for the task of self-government." And if Lincoln's vigorous effects to save the Union failed, he wrote, "I shall then conclude that there is some genetic difference between the peoples of the two sections which exacts different political institutions for them."[32]

After the attack on Fort Sumter northerners generally shared the disgust of their editorial writers toward the perfidious South. Writing to the Reverend Samuel May, William Furness observed in phrases reminiscent of the *New York Times* editorial that "the Southern character is being laid bare and stript of every thing looking like honor, honesty, and humanity. All that weak consideration for Southern sensibilities which neutralized the effect of the plainest anti-slave statements and facts is all gone." As for the aristocratic pretensions of the South's people, "what was regarded as a chivalrous aristocracy, and as such dazzled and corrupted the Northern imagination, is now found to be a compound of falsehood, treachery, and brutal ruffianism." How fortunate for the North, Furness averred, that the true villainy of barbarians posing as aristocrats had been exposed by the momentous events in Charleston. "How plain is it now that no direct progress towards . . . abolition was to be looked for until the foul thing was seen. It must be stripped of all its decorations to the last rag of its finery before it could be turned neat and free out of doors."[33]

By the beginning of the Civil War most northerners shared with their polemical writers so jaundiced a view of the southern people that some were even willing to subscribe to the southern notion that the conflict was not primarily about slavery but rather about the irreconcilable hostility between two races. Edmund Clarence Stedman believed that slavery had been "the cause of the War in no sense other than that it has added another distinctness to the line betwixt North and South which climate and race had already drawn." In Stedman's opinion it was the unbearable character of this southern race, "domineering, insolent, irrational, haughty, scornful of justice," that made all compromise impossible. The southerner's false assumption of the "positive rights of a superior race," he wrote, had had more to do with the coming of civil war than any other factor.[34]

Though northerners like Stedman were certain that blame for the Civil War could be placed at the feet of an insolent southern race, southerners were equally certain that secession was necessitated by the unprovoked aggressions of a northern race of Puritan zealots. In his sermon to the congregation of Wilmington's Saint James Episcopal Church, delivered on January 4, 1861, the Reverend Thomas Atkinson warned his listeners about the struggle to come with their Yankee adversaries. He contended that over the years New England had effectively come to dominate the North and define its culture. And he based his criticism of the region on this key assertion: "New England is Puritan, and Puritanism is not reverential." In the decades following the Revolution, he argued, Puritanism had "run to seed." New England's present-day inheritors of this religious tradition had become "enthusiastic, self-confident, but irreverent and destructive, that is, fanatical." He concluded his sermon by urging his flock not to discount their enemy's strength, and he admonished them not to dismiss Yankees as mere mercenaries, as many in the southern press had done. Adopting such a complacent attitude would be a grave mistake, for New Englanders were capable of rabid devotion to concepts such as abolition, and that capacity made them formidable adversaries. They were not so mercenary, Atkinson warned, that they "would [not] go as far as any men on earth, for a mere idea."[35]

The Puritan fanaticism about which Atkinson cautioned his congregation was also much on the mind of the South's politicians. Thomas O. Moore, governor of Louisiana, believed that the danger to the southern states had increased exponentially as New England's zealotry had spread throughout the North. "So long as these interests were confined to scattered and uninfluential and demented zealots in New England," he wrote, "they excited no other feeling than contemptuous commiseration. But they have now perverted the whole structure of social life in the entire northern or free states, and leavened the whole mass." The Republican presidential victory was ample proof to Moore that "a mad and senseless fanaticism [had] taken possession of the northern mind."[36]

Southerners of all walks of life joined their writers, ministers, and politicians in denouncing the fanatical Puritans who threatened to destroy both the South and the Union. Writing to a friend in January 1861, Virginian N. F. Cabell condemned the satanic fanaticism issuing from above the Mason-Dixon and traced it to its English Puritan sources. "What was Puritanism in its origin and most palmy day? It meant this, 'I have a system of opinions on diverse subjects—no matter how come by. You, by inheritance or otherwise, hold a different set, and so I am right and you are wrong—you must come over to my side. In short I want to rule you, and if you will not submit, why then you are the tyrant! I will move heaven and earth (and hell if necessary) to get the ascendancy, and if I get it, will show you that a Minority that dissents from me . . . have no rights!'" Cabell was certain that the rigid intolerance Cromwell's Puritans had imposed upon England had also been bred into those of his followers who had settled New England. "This breed also has been transferred here," he wrote, "and under that or other names still survives; nor has the demon of Fanaticism or Intolerance ever been wholly exorcised."[37] As a result of Lincoln's lamented election, he feared that such unexorcised Puritan demons would soon be vengefully unleashed upon the South.

Over and over, southern corespondents like Cabell excoriated the dangerous and fanatical northern Puritans who were bent on enslaving white southerners to their perverted concept of right. Charles C. Jones, son of a prominent coastal Georgia plantation family, wrote to his parents decrying the "suicidal, outrageous, and exasperating policy" of the "fanatical" Black Republican administration. On their own soil they might, if they wished, "grow mad with entertainment of infidelity, heresies, and fake conceptions of a 'higher law': but Heaven forbid that they ever attempt to set foot upon this land of sunshine, of high-souled honor, and of liberty."[38]

As Lincoln's inauguration approached, southerners pondered the possibility of war with the ascendant zealots of the Black Republican Party. A few maintained a fragile optimism that some sort of accommodation with northerners might be reached, but A. C. Haskell reflected the majority opinion that such optimism was a fantasy. He was convinced that the South could not "hope for any reason or wisdom or justice from the insane God-forsaken fanatics who are in power." If war was indeed inevitable, Charles Jones, like many other proud southerners, refused to consider the possibility of southern defeat. "I cannot," he wrote, "bring myself to entertain even the impression that a God of justice and of truth will permit [victory to] a blinded, fanatical people, who already have set at naught all rules of equality, of right, and of honor." A Yankee victory, he grimly predicted, would replace a southern Age of Gold with a northern Age of Iron that would bring in its wake "refined barbarity, moral degeneracy, religious impiety, soulless honor, and absolute degradation almost beyond belief."[39]

Even though they had initiated hostilities with the attack on Fort Sumter, southerners generally and with apparent sincerity denied that they were responsible for the war that was just beginning. After all, Savannah patrician George Mercer pointed out, before Lincoln's election America had been peaceful and united, and it might have remained so. The truth for Mercer was that the Union had been destroyed not by southern intransigence and treachery but by the "poison of puritan fanaticism" that had spread inexorably from New England and "leavened the whole north." It was the poisonous zeal and religious frenzy of the despicable Yankee race, focused destructively on the question of slavery, that had forced the South to secede in self-defense and inflicted upon the Union the "terrible malady which has penetrated its vitals, and is now convulsing its frame."[40]

Southerners seem to have widely shared the convictions of their polemical writers that the potent fanaticism that had impelled the North to war would be diluted and negated in the prosecution of the coming conflict by Yankee avarice. Henry St. John Dixon, writing to his father, assured him that the southern people could "not be conquered; numerical strength may gain the superiority for a while, but the very people which is waging war against [the South] will be opening its own veins: the supplies of cotton once stopped, the whole of the vast manufacturing class in the North will be turned out of doors with empty mouths and lawless hands." Who, he asked, would feed these unemployed textile workers? His answer was such a ludicrously unlikely one that he had no doubt his father would understand and share the joke: *"Yankee liberality!"* As for formerly sympathetic northerners who had abandoned the southern cause after the attack on Sumter, George Mercer refused to grant that such shifts in loyalty might be related to the North's sense of patriotic duty. Yankees had "no intense and lasting convictions as the southern people have," he wrote in his diary. "Hence their opinions and their friendships are as unstable as water. . . . The free states of the North are true to only one thing—their pockets!"[41]

Southerners grew fond of contrasting Yankee perfidy, lawlessness, extremism, and avarice with their own selflessness. It was indeed a quality that confirmed for them the inherent nobility and the aristocratic sensibility of their race. Mercer praised numerous examples of the southern people's "most exalted patriotism" as they labored to build defensive fortifications for Savannah in the weeks before the attack on Fort Sumter. "Our volunteers work cheerfully at Fort Pulaski, notwithstanding they receive no compensation, lose much time, are removed from their families, and are put to considerable expense." Such noble sacrifice, he concluded, was "the wonderful, indescribable, but deeply felt sentiment of chivalry that makes their patriotism so pure and generous."[42]

When southerners tired of portraying their Yankee adversaries as avaricious and narrow-minded heirs of Oliver Cromwell, they could fall back on another racial caricature of the northern people that they developed with great relish. This caricature substituted for the fanatical, Puritan-descended Yankee an even more debased, racially hybridized Yankee. Those champions of secession who viewed northerners as a lowly hybrids believed not only that Yankees had been bequeathed an inferior Puritan racial heritage but also that this suspect inheritance had over time become so impure as to constitute no coherent racial heritage at all. Thus many southerners concluded that, unlike themselves, Yankees could make no legitimate claim to being a distinct and self-respecting race of people. While the white inhabitants of Dixie frequently boasted of their noble Anglo-Norman descent, they dismissed the people of the North as lowly products of a mongrel mixture of races. As they saw it, the North's original Saxon-Puritan blood, a racial pedigree of questionable quality, had been subsequently diluted by the even more questionable blood of waves of impoverished immigrants who had entered the northern states from some of the most disreputable corners of the Old World.

Given the North's confused mingling of racial influences, southerners did not find it surprising that people living above the Mason-Dixon were entirely lacking in Dixie's fixity of intellectual, social, and political purpose, for they believed that a coherent culture like theirs was the natural product of racial homogeneity. Since the North lacked such homogeneity, they maintained, how could it ever hope to compete with the elevated and finely poised society of the South? This mixture of cultural and racial prejudices was no doubt reflected in the irritated question South Carolinian Laurence Keitt posed to a northern correspondent in March 1861: "Who are these Black Republicans?" Of course Keitt knew the answer to his question. They were, he contended, "a motley throng of sans-culottes and Dames des Halles, infidels, and free lovers, interspersed by Bloomer women, fugitive slaves, and amalgamists." Could a high-toned southern race be expected to submit to such a disgusting assortment of fanatics? "Southerners are an obliging people," Keitt mused, "not hard at driving bargains as the Yankees are; but this is asking too much of their chivalry."[43]

Against such a rag-tag assemblage of debased peoples espousing bizarre causes, southerners did not hesitate to go to battle. Nonetheless, writing on the eve of the attack on Fort Sumter, one Carolina warrior proclaimed himself to be disgusted by the vile and unworthy nature of the South's opponents. "The Pride of our State, the very pick of its best men of all grades and duties," he lamented, "must be brought to bear against hirelings and the refuse of God's creation." One advantage of battling such a degraded assortment of foes, A. McCall of Tennessee believed, was that it guaranteed a short war, for Yankees were at heart "mobocrats," and soon, he predicted, they would be engaging in civil war not only with the South but also with each other. A hybrid race would inevitably set itself at its own throat. Writing to a northern friend in February 1861, he confidently predicted that "Irish Catholics, Jews and all foreigners, except the Hessians will open *a war* in all your cities next fall."[44]

Laurence Keitt shared the ironic view of southern editorialists that the mongrelized Yankee race had found a perfect leader in Abraham Lincoln. Like all well-bred southerners, he was disgusted by the spectacle of the vulgar president-elect exhibiting himself "at railway depots," joking familiarly with the populace, and accepting "kisses bold" from women in "promiscuous crowds" of admirers. How could a race of lordly planters submit themselves to such a buffoon, he wondered. "Did you think," he scolded his northern friend, "the people of the South, the Lords Proprietors of the land, would let this low fellow rule for them? No. His vulgar facetiousness may suit the race of clock makers and wooden nutmeg venders . . . but never will he receive the homage of southern gentlemen."[45]

Keitt's sentiments reflected the more polite ranges of southern thinking regarding the new Republican administration. When Marian Harland, wife of a Presbyterian minister from New Jersey, visited her family in Richmond in March and April of 1861, she was assured by at least six different gentlemen that southern horses would be stabled in Boston's historic Faneuil Hall within three months of the swearing in of the "Springfield ape." But if Lincoln was an ape, her acquaintances in the Virginia capital believed that his running mate, Hannibal Hamlin of Maine, was even worse. Mrs. Harland was "assured over and over and over" that "the Vice-President was a full-blooded negro, or, at the least, a mulatto." And what was the evidence of this horror? "Wasn't his name damning evidence of the disgraceful fact?" Richmonders asked her. "What white man ever called his child 'Hannibal'?"[46]

Sharing such a shockingly low opinion of the Yankee race, southerners were naturally appalled, as their editorial writers had been, by northern ripostes that emphasized the South's barbarity, crudeness, cruelty, and violence. Addressing the Virginia State Convention that was debating the secession question, South Carolinian John Preston protested that those who favored Dixie's independence were not, as northerners delighted to depict them, a "hungry rabble, answering in blood to every appeal to brutal passion." And they certainly were not like the most extreme of their northern adversaries, "canting fanatics, festering in the licentiousness of abolition and amalgamation." They were, he asserted, "grave," "prosperous," "religious" people, "the holders of the most majestic civilization."[47]

Like John Preston, Mary Boykin Chesnut was a South Carolinian. And like him, she considered herself well educated and well bred and was especially wounded and offended by the charges of barbarism being leveled against Dixie in the northern press. In her diary she reflected with acerbic irony on "Mrs. Stowe, Greeley, Thoreau, Emerson, Sumner, in nice New England homes—clean, clear, sweet-smelling—shut up in libraries, writing books which ease their hearts of their bitterness to us." What, she asked, did these airy Transcendental reformers, safely insulated in their studies from the realities of life, really understand about the South? Did they realize that there were southern women like her who "read the same books as their Northern contemners . . . have the same ideas of right and wrong—are high bred, lively, good, pious—doing their duty as they conceive it"? Southern women did not think abstractly about Negro villages like Emerson and Thoreau. "They live in negro villages," she declared. "They do not preach and teach hate as a gospel and the sacred duty of murder and insurrection, but they strive to ameliorate the condition of these Africans in every particular." "Think of these holy New Englanders," she cynically pictured, "forced to have a negro village walk through their houses whenever they saw fit."[48]

To Chesnut, the deep gulf between southern and northern culture was nowhere more clearly defined than in a scene she described in her diary that she had witnessed in a public dining room in Richmond a month before the Sumter attack. One of her party was beginning to make an observation about the South's adversaries: "Now if there be a war and it pinches the Yankee pocket instead of filling it—." Suddenly, Chesnut writes, the "shrill" voice of a northern woman could be heard in the next room, responding to a remark that had not been intended for her but that she had overheard. "Yankees are no more mean and stingy than you are. People at the North are as good as people at the South." Though Chesnut's table was quick to apologize for their inadvertent discourtesy, the Yankee woman continued to harangue them as they sat in embarrassed, well-mannered silence.[49]

For Chesnut, the northern woman had revealed her social inferiority not by speaking in defense of her people. Rather, she had done so by means of her shrill and uncivil manner of expressing herself, her tactless refusal to defuse a tense situation by accepting an apology, and her not knowing when to be quiet for the sake of politeness. Had Chesnut found herself in the North, she would have expected Yankees "to belabor" her people like her friend had begun to belabor Yankees. But unlike the prickly and ill-mannered Yankee woman in the Richmond dining room, she would have known to "hold [her] tongue," like any properly bred southern lady. Chesnut did not conclude that this incident demonstrated an incompatibility between distinct northern and southern races, but she did interpret it as evidence of a profound "incompatibility of temper" between the two peoples.[50] Whether the incompatibility was that of race or temper, southerners like Mary Boykin Chesnut were increasingly drawn to the conclusion that the gulf was deep and unbridgeable and that it justified the separation of South from North.

As events moved closer to armed conflict, southerners drew upon the by-now clichéd Goth-and-Vandal metaphors of their editorial writers to describe the enemy menace. This menace was clearly manifest to George Mercer. He observed in a diary entry of January 25, 1861, that when attempts to reinforce Fort Sumter had been repelled by Confederate guns, democratic representatives from "conservative New York City" blustered "that had Major Anderson reduced Charleston to ashes . . . he would have been justified before the civilized world." Such bloodthirsty sentiments, Mercer maintained, were "worthy of the worst days of the Goths and Vandals." And to these common metaphorical partners he added a third race of barbarians: "The Tarters proposed seriously to convert China into a cattle pasture: the North and West would follow their example."[51]

Against these barbarous hireling hordes, southerners arrayed what they believed to be the flower of their Norman aristocracy. Sophia Haskell wrote proudly in March 1861 of sending three sons to defend the newly formed Confederacy at Charleston. In phrases evocative of Walter Scott's *Ivanhoe* she boasted that her youngest boy had rushed to the city "with all the ardour of the days of chivalry to lay down his life for His God, his Country, and his Lady Love." Her son's first letter to her had contained these stirring and exalted sentiments, which she quoted approvingly: "God save our Country! For such a Country and such a people it is easy to die."[52]

Southern correspondents thoroughly agreed with Dixie media accounts that the surrender of Fort Sumter was a validation of the bravery of Confederate knights and an exposure of Yankee cowardice. Ben Allston, a soldier and witness to the fort's fall, wrote to his father that when the firing began, it had been "the general opinion that the [northern] fleet would at once move to [Major Anderson's] support, and orders were at once sent to all commanders to get all their men ready for action. But, shame be to them, they did not move, tho' they could witness the whole action." "The indignation excited in the camp was intense," Allston angrily observed, "by this, to us, dastardly conduct."

A. C. Haskell was also present at the bombardment as a combatant, and he too was shocked by the behavior of Yankee troops. "We were sure once of a fight from the man of war off the bar crammed with soldiers," he wrote his parents, "but the dastardly wretches disappointed friend and foe alike by not striking one blow for their flag and burning fort."[53]

Spectators watching from the piazzas, piers, and embankments of Charleston shared the same contempt for their lowborn enemy. Adele Allston expressed amazement to her brother that Yankee ships had stood idly by at the destruction of their fort. "Anderson," she wrote, "made a signal to them Friday and they might have come in that night, but there they remained and saw their flag shot down and the fort surrendered without moving! Of course we thank them but we despise them for their cowardice." Allston considered such disgraceful behavior a fitting foil to the magnanimous and chivalric demeanor of General Beauregard upon accepting Major Anderson's surrender. Anderson had sent "his *sword* and *flag* wrapt in a Palmetto flag to General Beauregard acknowledging himself a prisoner of war! But Beauregard refused to consider him as such and gave him permission to leave when he chose and also to salute his flag. Was not that magnanimous?"[54] She might also have observed that it was an action typical of an aristocratic race of warriors.

After Major Anderson's surrender of Fort Sumter there was no turning back from the cataclysm of civil war. Not all southerners rejoiced in the prospect. Writing from her Louisiana plantation, Sarah Butler observed to her sister that although she believed the South should both demand and defend its rights, it seemed to her "*awful* to see *Brethren* arrayed against one another." By the beginning of the Civil War, however, the notion that southerners were arrayed against their brethren was a distinctly minority view in Dixie. Indeed, by June 1861 Mrs. Butler's own doubts about the wisdom of secession had been substantially allayed. She explained her transformation of sentiment thus: "The aggressiveness of the North has done more to reconcile me to things than any thing else." Even in the minds of southerners of a Unionist persuasion, this perceived aggressiveness on the part of the Yankees rapidly turned them into barbaric hordes. George Mercer expressed this dark view when he wrote in his diary a week after the fall of Sumter that Federal troops were "being transported to Washington by water: Vandals from Massachusetts are quartered in the Capitol."[55]

Some southerners were no doubt troubled by the idea that brother was about to be set against brother. Most, however, seem to have shared the conviction of Charlestonian John Coles Rutherfoord, who on the day following the Yankee surrender wrote in his diary that the Confederate victory confirmed the existence of "two distinct nationalities represented by the words—'North' and 'South.'" Charles Jones put the matter in a more specifically racial context. "I have long since believed," he wrote to his father, "that in this country have arisen two races which, although claiming a common parentage, have been so entirely separated by climate, by morals, by religion, and by estimates so totally opposite of all that constitutes honor, truth, and manliness, that they cannot longer coexist under the same government. Oil and water will not commingle." Going one step further than Jones, John Preston of South Carolina placed a religious imprimatur upon the division of northern and southern races that was now to be effected by civil war. He charged that the bigoted fanatics of the North had "with demoniac rage . . . set the Lamb of God between their seed and our seed." God now intended these seeds to remain forever distinct. "Never, never, until by your power, your art, and your virtue, you can unfix the unchangeable economy of the Eternal God," he declared, "can you make of the people of the North and the people of the South one people."[56]

Thus in April 1861 a self-proclaimed southern race, newly minted by southern polemical writers and fervently embraced by southern opinion, marched to the defense of the Confederacy's newly proclaimed independence. Because they believed that their warrior knights had in common with their Norman English ancestors the qualities of bravery, loyalty, and honor, southerners shared the sanguine expectations of victory that had been routinely issued by their propagandists. Senator Louis T. Wigfall of Texas was one of the majority who were confident of the South's chances in the coming conflict. After all, he pointed out, the southern race was clearly superior to a northern race, which "had been corrupted by the greed for money and did not have the individuality and self-pride" of Dixie's warriors. Lieutenant Henry Ewing of Tennessee put the matter even more bluntly. For him it was inconceivable that northerners could prevail in warfare. As he acidly observed, "The scum of the North *cannot* face the chivalric spirit of the South."[57]

The attack on Fort Sumter inflamed northern hostility to the South, and northerners promptly began justifying the coming conflict as one to be fought on idealistic political and moral grounds. They overwhelmingly came to view southerners as treasonous rebels and saw themselves as a virtuous nation fighting to preserve the Union and the democratic principles upon which they believed that union rested. For southerners, however, the question of why they were fighting and what they were fighting for was a more problematic one. After all, what cause could have been so exalted as to justify the repudiation of what many of them would have hitherto considered history's grandest national experiment in democracy? And how could southerners have failed to see the irony that the national experiment they now disowned had owed to a substantial degree its establishment, its articulation, and its survival to the brilliance of earlier generations of southern warriors and statesmen like Washington and Jefferson?

Most southerners implicitly if grudgingly recognized that the maintenance and expansion of the institution of chattel slavery was an idea that could never effectively justify their insurrection and never successfully compete with the northern ideals of freedom, Union, and Constitution as a justification for civil war. Yet it was clearly the survival of the South's peculiar institution that was uppermost in the minds of Dixie's political and social elite as they considered the question of secession. Southern polemical writers were thus most forthright in presenting the survival of slavery as a justification for leaving the Union in the months immediately following Lincoln's election. In this they reflected the convictions of the South's secessionist political leaders that the region's submission to Republican political ascendancy spelled the end of both the institution of slavery and the southern way of life that they believed was founded on that institution.

A Charleston broadside published just days after Lincoln's victory baldly expressed this slavery-based secessionist argument. Lincoln's triumph, it averred, would inevitably result in the abolition of "the domestic institutions of the South," and the destruction of these euphemistically termed "domestic institutions" would lead to the most frightening of prospects. Abolitionists would bring in their victorious wake the elevation of "the negro race to an equality with the free white inhabitants of the country, thus introducing practical amalgamation, to end . . . in after years, in inter-marriage . . . between two races, never designed by Providence to live together, on terms of equality."[58] In the face of such horrors, how could any reasonable southerner choose to remain within a Yankee-dominated Union?

As events moved relentlessly toward their climax at Charleston harbor the *Southern Literary Messenger*, Dixie's premiere belletristic magazine, gave most eloquent and complete articulation to the "Great Issue" that constituted the South's primary justification for going to war. The writer affirmed, forcefully and in no uncertain terms, the propositions that the southern way of life was established on the belief in racial inequality, and that this belief must be defended at all cost. Slavery, the essayist contended, was "indissolubly connected" to two essential southern ideas: "the idea of property of the master in his slave—and the idea that the negro, everywhere and in all conditions, whether bond or free, is the inferior of the white man." Republican hegemony threatened a profound disturbance of both of "these fundamental ideas." It presaged a nightmarish world in which "the master's property [would be] endangered" and "the inequality of the race [would be] questioned." The disturbance of the one idea, the writer maintained, struck "at property," while the disturbance of the other introduced "the odious doctrine of the equality of the white man and the negro. The first is fatal to vested rights of property—the last to the ... sacred supremacy of the Caucasian white, and the absolutely necessary subjugation to him of the African negro."[59]

Given the centrality of slavery to the southern way of life, the writer maintained that the South's course of action following Lincoln's election could scarcely be debated:

> Now, if industrially, socially, morally and politically, slavery has secured such inestimable blessings; if its extinction is fraught with such incalculable disasters; if our civilization, in all its glory, is threatened with overthrow, and our social system trembles beneath the frowning power whose inauguration, within three short months, will put it "in the course of ultimate extinction"; if we are left only to choose between a *slow* and a *violent* death; if our immense property interests must decay or perish; if the equality of the white and black races is an experiment now to be tried; if our inferior race must sink to savage life, and the Southern Saxon become a slave to foreign domination or an exile from his native home ... if these things be so, or any of them, is it not worse than folly to hesitate or falter in our course?[60]

For this essayist and for most of Dixie's leaders, slavery was indeed the "Great Issue" dividing North and South, and secession was unquestionably the South's only possible course if the institution was to be preserved.

Savannah patrician George Mercer gave private expression in his diary to the sentiments that had been given public utterance in the *Southern Literary Messenger*, boasting that the newly established Confederacy would be based "upon two fundamental truths, the inequality of the races, and the fairness and necessity of free trade." Mercer believed that the Confederate States of America had embarked on a "grand mission." "We must conquer the prejudices of the world," he opined, "and prove to Christendom that we are right—that our government is founded upon the truths of the Bible and the nature of man."[61] For Mercer, as for most of the region's social and political leadership, Dixie's *raison d'être* was inextricably linked to the defense and preservation of slavery on both political and moral grounds.

The centrality of slavery to the South's determination to secede from the Union was articulated in less flattering terms by a southern moderate, Percival Drayton. A captain in the United States Navy and a member of a distinguished South Carolina family, Drayton refused to resign his commission and continued to serve his country during the Civil War, a decision that would estrange him from his family in Charleston. In a letter written in May 1861 he despaired over the belligerence and intransigence of his fellow southerners that had led to war. "The fact is," he observed bitterly, "that slavery seems to have turned the feelings of the whole community where it exists to gall towards all those who do not believe it a divine institution, and one without which true civilization cannot exist."[62] As a southerner Drayton recognized all too well that the South had precipitated civil war because it was unable to conceive of compromising with the North over the institution it had come to believe was inseparable from and essential to its cultural identity.

The South's leaders were thus clear in their own minds in the months leading up to the war that secession was the only course that would guarantee the survival of slavery. Indeed, this argument was presented over and over again in the individual state debates about leaving the Union. But though secession as a means of preserving slavery was a persuasive argument in political debates, ordinary citizens and soldiers seem to have found it inadequately inspiring as a justification for the sacrifices of war, and southerners did not often mention it once the Civil War commenced. Southern soldiers did occasionally refer in their correspondence to the fact that they were fighting to defend slavery. However, James McPherson has established that far more of them were inclined to express the conviction that they were fighting "for liberty as well as slavery," the liberty of a high-toned race of southern men. Instead of devoting their eloquence to praise of their region's peculiar institution, Dixie's warriors were much more likely to declaim upon their determination to defend themselves and their families "against their own enslavement by the North."[63] As one might expect from a proud and imperious people who styled themselves heirs of a Norman-blooded aristocracy, it was the prospect of shameful subjugation to the North, not the prospect of a South stripped of its slaves, that tended to capture the southern imagination from the moment of Abraham Lincoln's election to the moment the first shots were fired on Fort Sumter.

The humiliating prospect of submission was uppermost in the mind of the editorialist for the *Richmond Whig* as he pondered Lincoln's war strategy of occupying Virginia with Federal troops. "Shall we," he asked the newspaper's readers, "tamely bend our necks to the yoke and *such* a yoke!" For the *Whig* writer, submission to Yankee occupation would entail the total humiliation of the southern people. Expatiating on the horrors of bowing to Lincoln's rule, he offered this grotesque prospect to his Virginia readers: "The countrymen and kindred of Washington, of Henry, of the Lees, the Randolphs, the Jeffersons, the Harrisons, the Blands, the Nelsons—the vassals of Yankee taskmasters!" "Better ten thousand times," he thundered, "to stake everything—life, liberty, prosperity, altars, and firesides, than endure such degradation." Writing at this same tumultuous moment to his father, Mississippi native and University of Virginia student Henry St. John Dixon echoed the sentiments of the *Richmond Whig*. He believed that "Lincoln's determination to invade our beloved country" left residents of both the Old Dominion and the South in general with a stark choice: "Beyond a shadow of a doubt, no alternative is left but war or slavery."[64] The slavery the young southern gentleman alluded to was not chattel slavery but something much worse: the servile surrender of a noble southern race.

The South's sense of itself as courageously resisting subjugation became, if anything, more pronounced as the war dragged on and hostilities grew ever bloodier. John Lee Holt, a private in a Virginia regiment, expressed the conviction of legions of high-minded southern warriors that submission to Yankees was unthinkable, and he conveyed this heartfelt sentiment to his wife Ellen: "If we should suffer ourselves to be subjugated by the tyrannical government of the North, our property would be confiscated ... and our people reduced to the most abject bondage and utter degradation."[65] For Holt, as for most southerners, the economic devastation that would attend a northern victory and the abolition of slavery would be more than matched in infamy by the "utter degradation" that would attend the humiliating surrender of a proud and noble southern people to a debased race of Saxon-descended abolitionists.

The obsession of southerners like Dixon and Holt with the humiliation of submitting to the North was practically indistinguishable from their parallel obsession with maintaining through force of arms both their personal honor and the honor of their region, an obsession that had furnished the justification for Preston Brooks's brutal assault on Charles Sumner five years earlier on the Senate floor. This southern dedication to honor had an early provenance that can be clearly traced to the settlement of the region's first permanent colony. As historian Louis B. Wright has explained, the concept of honor had been an essential element in forming the values of colonial Virginia's ruling planter aristocracy, an aristocracy that would function as a model for future generations of southern plantation owners. Like the English gentry, whose style and manner of living the Old Dominion's substantial land and slave owners sought to replicate in America, these New World gentlemen variously identified their honor with virtue and with reputation. But though there were slight differences concerning the precise definition of honor among those who aspired to be Virginia aristocrats, there was unanimous agreement that a gentleman's main purpose in adhering to a code of conduct was to establish and maintain his personal reputation as a man respected by all. Virginia's planter aristocracy thus bequeathed to Dixie a definition of character that placed primary importance on the preservation of individual honor, and it linked that individual honor with the gentleman's privileged position in the southern social hierarchy.[66]

Bertram Wyatt-Brown has incisively observed that the concept of honor, as opposed to the inner-directed notion of conscience, tightly binds an individual's sense of personal worth to the acceptance of his self-definition by the community at large. To possess honor, therefore, one must possess the respect of others. One might expect this rather primitive and feudal concept to have been embraced only by the South's wealthiest planters. Yet though lacking the manners and largesse of the more substantial plantation owners, most southern yeomen considered the possession of honor to be essential to their reputations as well. As Wyatt-Brown observes, they too aspired to the gentlemanly ideal because "they had access to the means for its assertion themselves—the possession of slaves—and because all whites, non-slaveholders as well, held sway over all blacks. Southerners, regardless of social position, were united in the brotherhood of white-skinned honor."[67]

This superimposition of the Cavalier mystique of honor upon a yeoman ethos was manifestly on display throughout the South in the decades before the Civil War. And it acquired a distinctly more ominous and volatile tone when nineteenth-century southerners—responding enthusiastically to what Edwin Cady has termed the "glamorized and sentimentalized" chivalric code celebrated by "literary medievalists" such as Sir Walter Scott—resurrected the antique code duello and attached it to their contemporary code of honor. Given the South's proclivity for boasting of its aristocratic Norman racial inheritance, one might imagine the surprise of explorer Henry Stanley when he discovered common farmers of the Arkansas plains and even store clerks upholding a strict code of personal honor, with its attending focus on the duel as a means of defending one's reputation. He noted, for example, that the proprietor of a country store in the village of Cypress Bend, a Jew of German extraction, owned and proudly displayed a fine and costly pair of dueling pistols.[68]

Had Stanley understood southern culture more thoroughly, he would not have been surprised by the Jewish storekeeper's proud display of firearms. On the eve of the Civil War, southern men of varied social backgrounds, professions, and ethnicities shared an intense and often militant concern for the preservation of personal honor. Englishman John Elliott Cairnes, traveling by steamboat down the Mississippi, had his attention directed by a certain "Colonel B" to "a crowd of men of all ranks clustered around a cabin stove." The colonel observed, "Now, there is probably not a man in all that crowd who is not armed; I myself have a pistol in my state-room." The research of modern historian Clement Eaton confirms Cairnes's impressions as to the ubiquity of this southern male obsession with honor. In his analysis of the state of southern consciousness in 1860, Eaton examined the opinions of fifteen men. They represented a fairly diverse cross-section of the region's society. There were political liberals as well as conservatives, and members of the merchant and professional classes as well as the planter class. Despite considerable differences in outlook and opinion, however, Eaton discovered that these men were united by two powerful emotions: a strong consciousness of race and an "exaggerated sense of honor, based on the cult of the gentleman."[69] The aristocratic concept of personal honor was thus an article of the gentlemanly code of conduct avidly appropriated by southerners, whether they were planters who proudly boasted of their Anglo-Norman racial heritage or shopkeepers spawned in European ghettos.

The class-transcending nature of southern honor helps to explain why in the state of Alabama secessionist sentiment was strongest not in areas dominated by the large plantation but rather in small farming communities. It also helps to explain why the South achieved an impressive public consensus respecting secession, despite considerable private misgivings among individual southerners concerning the wisdom of leaving the Union. As Wyatt-Brown explains, "It was a part of the honor code itself that community consensus forced dissenters to surrender to popular decision, even if the dissenters thought the policy foolish. Otherwise, he ran the risk of communal disloyalty."[70]

Robert E. Lee was the most famous southerner, though by no means the only one, to justify his joining the war in terms of maintaining his personal honor. He expressed his decision to resign his commission in the United States Army and join the Confederate Army simply and eloquently: "I could have taken no other course without dishonor." Many northerners viewed Lee's words as a flimsy rationale for treason. Indeed, Judge Charles Daly, visiting the fallen Confederate capital of Richmond in April 1865, refused the offer of an introduction to Lee because he did not consider the South's sainted hero a "man of honor." "Six days before he left for Virginia," Daly complained, "he said that nothing would induce him to desert the United States flag."[71] Daly's northern concept of honor was molded by ideals of civic virtue, ideals he believed Lee had violated. Southerners—understanding honor in the more traditional aristocratic sense of personal reputation in the eyes of one's peers—knew that Lee was anything but a traitor. They believed that his devotion to his home, to the soil of his native state, and to the ethos of his planter class expressed the most highly honorable instincts of a nobly born southern gentleman.

Of course, southerners were not alone among Americans in venerating the ideal of personal honor. Northerners like Charles Daly also embraced the concept, and they commonly mentioned it as a reason for going to war. But Wyatt-Brown is both perceptive and accurate when he observes that, as with the ideals of male chivalry and female purity, men living above the Potomac embraced honor with nowhere near the intensity of their brethren in the South. Being more industrialized and urbanized, more "bourgeois and highly institutionalized," the North had developed a society in which "the strength of other institutions lessened personal dependency upon family and community opinion."[72] Thus honor was not, and never could have been, as absolutely central to the northern experience as it became to the rural, slave-owning South.

So devoutly did southerners worship at the altar of manly honor that it is doubtful that many of them were conscious of the pragmatic psychological and political dividends of their devotion. The South's trumpeting of its honor implicitly validated the racial mythology that the region's political leaders and polemicists had begun formulating during the troublesome 1850s. After all, was not the possession of a refined sense of personal honor, such as had been displayed by the estimable Lee, proof positive that the chivalric sentiments of England's Norman aristocracy had been passed undiluted to its southern descendants? And were not the fanatical abolitionist rants of Yankee Puritans, devoid of the generous and large-minded sensibility inherent in the character of a noble and honorable southern race, proof positive of their inferior Saxon racial inheritance?

In so assiduously defending their honor, Dixie's defenders were also able to deflect their attention from the more pressing but less emotionally stirring issue of defending slavery. This wrapping of slavery in the more appealing garb of gentlemanly honor had been increasingly employed in the South during the same decade of the 1850s when its writers had been developing the Norman racial myth. In 1856, for example, Jason Lyons, president of the Southern Commercial Convention, had linked his defense of slavery with more exalted chivalric concepts when he had warned his audience that the day might well come when the South would find itself "driven to the necessity of exerting ... all her powers, to preserve her rights and honor." As would many southerners after him, Lyons inferred that submission to northerners on the issue of slavery would stain the honor of southern gentlemen. Indeed, he insisted that "the independence of the South equally with that of the other portion of the Union" was as essential to southerners as "life ... honor and happiness."[73]

After Lincoln's election it was probably inevitable that southerners would continue to frame their response to the victorious Republicans in terms of dishonorable submission or honorable defiance. In late November, James Hamilton Couper wrote to a northern friend that he believed the South was "in the position either of passive submission to a powerful, increasing, and hostile enemy, or a prompt and decided resistance." Speaking out publicly in *DeBow's Review*, J. Quitman Moore employed the terminology of the duel to express the necessity of the South's forcefully responding to the Republican ascendancy in a way that would maintain the region's honor. Lincoln's candidacy was more than a mere election; it was a challenge mounted by a deadly adversary. And Moore concluded that this "challenge, so defiantly thrown out, must be, as defiantly, accepted" by all honorable southern gentleman.[74]

On the eve of the fateful presidential election of 1860, Senator James Chesnut, husband of Mary Chesnut, spoke to the concerned citizens of Charleston who had spontaneously gathered before his residence. "Before the setting of tomorrow's sun," he portentously told them, "the destiny of this confederated Republic would be decided." If Lincoln won the election, as he expected, the South would have "two ways before us.... One is beset with humiliation, dishonor, *émeutes*, rebellions—with submission, in the beginning, to all, and at all times, and confiscation and slavery in the end. The other, it is true, has its difficulties and trials, but no disgrace. Hope, duty, and honor, shine along the path."[75] For Chesnut and for the South, the path of secession and war was the path of courage and honor.

Following the dreaded election of Lincoln, North Carolina planter Weldon Edwards wrote to a friend in Virginia that their two states had no choice but to follow the cotton states that were beginning to secede. Otherwise, he predicted, they would be swallowed up and the institution of slavery would be destroyed by the "ceaseless aggression of the wicked madmen" of New England. If Puritan New England had only left the Union first and joined Canada, Edwards opined, the country might have been saved. But the Yankees had hung on, and now the forces of abolition occupied the White House. To remain unified with them was clearly impossible. Secession, he declared, was absolutely necessary: "Our Honor, dignity, self-respect ... demand it at *whatever cost*."[76]

The notion of honor that southerners like Couper, Moore, Chesnut, and Edwards appealed to in their advocacy of secession remained uppermost in the minds of the men who immediately volunteered to fight for the budding Confederacy. Both northerners and southerners rushed to enlist in their respective armies after southern cannons were fired on Fort Sumter. But if Yankee recruits tended to see the cause for which they were fighting in moral terms—defending democracy and abolishing slavery—southern volunteers commonly viewed the conflict as a matter of simple honor. "If we are conquered," one wrote, "we will be driven penniless and dishonored from the land of our birth." For this young soldier, as for most of his compatriots, death in battle was far preferable to seeing the South "dismantled of its glory and independence—for of its honor it cannot be deprived."[77]

James McPherson has observed that the devotion of southern troops to the concept of honor vividly distinguishes their correspondence from that of northern soldiers. Union troops commonly attributed their enlistment to a sense of duty—duty to defend the flag and the Constitution under which they lived. Southerners, however, "were more likely to speak of *honor*: one's public reputation, one's image in the eyes of his peers." Again and again in his reading of southern war correspondence McPherson encountered the opinion that not fighting for the South would have been a dishonorable action, a social disgrace that would have led to loss of face and "public shame."[78]

The southern soldier's heightened sense of responsibility toward his community and his peers was nowhere more nobly and poignantly expressed than in the letter David Pierson of Louisiana wrote to his father on April 19, 1861. In this letter he sought to explain why he was enlisting in the Confederate Army, even though he had vigorously opposed secession as a delegate from Winn Parish to the Louisiana Convention. "I am not acting under any excitement whatever," he wrote, "but have resolved to go after a calm and thoughtful deliberation as to all the duties, responsibilities, and dangers which I am likely to encounter in the enterprise." He added, "Nor do I go to gratify an ambition, as I believe some others do but to assist as far as in my power lies in the defense of our Common Country and home which is threatened with invasion and annihilation." Pierson admitted to his father that he had been opposed to secession because he "thought it would lead to the present difficulties." Now, however, his fellow southerners had made their choice. For him there were "but two alternatives—either to take up arms against the South or in her defense. And between these I am not slow to choose."[79]

Pierson ended his letter by telling his father that he had volunteered "because I thought it my duty to do so." But he was not using the word *duty* as his northern brethren were using it. Pierson's sense of duty was molded by his southern sense of honor. Despite his deep misgivings about secession, he was no more inclined than Robert E. Lee to risk the loss of face and of reputation that would attend the repudiation of his community and his peers. In the end, the chivalric code of honor operated just as effectively in Pierson's decision to join the Confederate army as it did in Lee's. It also determined the decisions of thousands of other southerners, men devoted to the concept of the Union but even more enthralled by the concept of honor.

A careful reading of both the public speeches and essays and the private letters of southerners in the months following Lincoln's election reinforces the historical thesis that the South fought the Civil War primarily for the preservation of slavery, an institution that it deemed indispensable both to its economy and to its way of life. But these same texts also suggest that other motives almost as powerful factored into the southern mental equation during this fateful period. Ultimately the war was more than a conflict over chattel slavery or states' rights. On a more visceral level it reflected what Bertram Wyatt-Brown describes as a "discrepancy between one section devoted to conscience and to secular economic concerns and the other to honor and to persistent community sanctions that eventually compelled the slaveholding states to withdraw."[80]

Had southerners not subscribed en masse to the conduct code of a landed aristocracy, and had they not insisted on idealizing themselves as highborn gentlemen of exceptional honor battling a crass and materialistic Yankee race, they might have been able to acknowledge more honestly their own society's flaws as well as the anachronism of their peculiar institution. They might even have forged some sort of pragmatic political accommodation with northern moderates regarding slavery. But southerners were not entirely pragmatic men when it came to the issues of slavery and secession. They were not, as they contemptuously deemed their northern adversaries, calculating. They were instead Cavaliers cast in a Norman racial mold. And, as Jefferson had accurately observed seventy-five years earlier, they were "fiery" Cavaliers at that—men who, in the words of Weldon Edwards, were determined to preserve their "honor, dignity, self-respect . . . at *whatever cost.*"

7

Northern Vandals versus Southern Ruffians

On July 24, 1861, John M. Daniel, fiery editorial spokesman for the *Richmond Examiner*, triumphantly announced the Confederate victory at the First Battle of Manassas and punctuated his announcement with this contemptuous observation: "The South has suffered long enough from the incursions of the Northern Vandals."[1] Such rhetoric was a clear indication that antebellum polemical exchanges between northerners and southerners playing upon grossly exaggerated racial stereotypes would continue and even intensify during the years of bloody conflict to come. For Daniel and for most of his compatriots in the new southern Confederacy, inhabitants of the northern states were no longer brethren Americans but a savage, debased, and completely alien enemy race. Meanwhile, above the Mason-Dixon, northern writers were taking an equally jaundiced view of their southern adversaries.

Some observers may have been astonished by the rout of the United States Army at Manassas by hastily assembled southern forces. But Daniel professed himself not the least bit surprised. "Every day," he wrote, "we hear it said, and see it written that the people of the North are personally as brave as the people of the South. It is wholly untrue." Indeed, he maintained, "cowardice" had been "carefully inculcated on the Yankee from his birth." Yankees had been "taught that fighting is unprofitable, and therefore to be avoided" and "instructed, at the same time, that cunning and sharpness and cheating are very creditable and very profitable." In phrases of which Preston Brooks would no doubt have thoroughly approved, had he been alive to read them, Daniel concluded that the northerner had been "born like other people" but had become "a coward and a knave from severe training and careful education."[2]

Daniel thoroughly embraced the view of many other southern polemicists that the high character "of the Southern people, of the Cavaliers of Virginia and the Huguenots, and other indomitable spirits of the Carolinas" had been further elevated by the institution of slavery. He understood that "the presence of an inferior race" had influenced and molded "the manners and character of the white man in the South," producing a southern warrior who, trained to command and lead his inferiors, had prevailed on the battlefield of Manassas. How could Yankee troops hope to vanquish Cavaliers of such mettle? "Universal liberty and equality, universal elections, absolute majorities, eternal demagogism and free competition," he contended, "have leveled, degraded, demoralized and debased Northern society. Nobody there sees anyone beneath himself—lower, meaner, or more contemptible than himself. Hence nobody there respects himself. Vain and arrogant Northerners we have seen," Daniel continued, "but have yet to see, to hear of, or read about the first one who, self-poised in his own good opinion, and respecting himself, knows always how to respect others." He concluded, "All Yankees are vain, arrogant and independent, and carry on their visages and in their manners a sort of 'I'm as good as you' assertion simply because they feel that they are not as good as you."[3]

Though in some editorials Daniel seemed content to ascribe the superiority of the southern people to the exalted influences of their plantation culture, in other writings he contemptuously described Yankees as members of a debased and vile race. Such was his rhetorical response to the infamous General Orders no. 28, issued by Union Major General Benjamin Franklin Butler in New Orleans on May 15, 1862, three weeks after its surrender. In response to the hostile snubs and verbal harassment of Union soldiers by the Confederate ladies of that city, this order stated that "when any Female shall, by word, gesture, or movement, insult or show contempt for any officer or soldier of the United States, she shall be regarded and held liable to be treated as a woman of the town plying her avocation."[4]

Months after the issuing of this odious order, Daniel continued to assail "Beast" Butler as the product of a "race which the civilized world, with one consent, acknowledges to be its last and vilest product." He was revolted by the general's triumphant procession through Washington, New York, and Boston, where "the spawn of northern cities" had seen fit "to prostrate themselves before this ... Beast, emerging from his cave filled with dead men's bones." For the tempestuous southern editor, Butler was the loathsome symbol of an equally loathsome race. "He is at this time," he wrote, "the *Representative Man* of a people lost to all shame, to all humanity, all justice, all honor, all virtue, all manhood. Cowards by nature, thieves upon principle, and assassins at heart."[5] It came as no surprise to the indignant editor that the "spawn" of Yankee mobs had lavished their adulation upon such a monster.

Daniel's reference to Yankee "spawn" suggests that the pre–Civil War southern view of northerners as members of an inferior mongrelized race continued to appeal to Dixie's imagination during the war. For one *Richmond*

Daily Dispatch journalist, this mongrelizing was linguistic as well as racial in its dimensions. The war, he declared in an article written in February 1863, was one "between two peoples who are as distinct as the Russians and the Danes, or the Saxons and Dutch. Nor do we speak the same language," he continued. "The language of the South is the English language. The language of the North is English, Dutch, German, Spanish, a compound, in a word, of every known language and dialect in the world. The population of the South is homogeneous. That of the North is more heterogeneous than that of the Austrian Empire." "The great wonder," he concluded, "is not that the two sections have fallen asunder at last, but that they held together so long."[6]

Even more imaginatively potent than the specter of the invasion of a mongrelized northern race was the notion that the South's Cavaliers were locked in a life-or-death struggle with a Saxon-descended race of fanatical Puritans. Indeed, according to the *Charleston Courier* the spirit of Puritanism was directly responsible for the terrible conflict now taking place. It was the Puritan fanatic, "indoctrinated with the conviction that he is the elect vice-regent of God upon earth . . . perpetually intermeddling with the affairs of his neighbor . . . and anathematizing as pagan and pestiferous, whatever may be inharmonious with his own little agitations," who had brought fire and blood and destruction to the fair and unoffending South. Like their antebellum predecessors, Dixie's war writers continued to view northern aggression as a product of Puritan self-righteousness and cupidity. In the words of one of these journalists, it was "the speculating shopkeepers of the North" who were "making money out of the unusual war they have instigated" and who were the "genuine descendants of their ancestors," pharisaic and avaricious heirs of Oliver Cromwell. The *Courier* consequently warned its readers of the "projected campaign of the Roundheads" against "our own Queen City."[7]

The *Richmond Whig* perhaps best summarized the South's journalistic case against its Puritan adversaries. "When the developments, now being made, of the Yankee character, come to be duly appreciated by the world," it observed, "they will be justly held by impartial history to be the vilest race on the face of the earth. Possessed of all the vices which distinguish the Chinese, they have the additional one of pretending to virtues which they do not possess. Bigoted and intolerant, rapacious and stingy, fraudulent and roguish, boastful and cowardly, ostentatious and vulgar, envious and spiteful,—they are an exaggerated embodiment of all the vices of the Puritan and the Blackleg." The writer professed himself to be nonplused regarding "the particular cause, or combination of causes" that had "conspired to produce this odious population." But he was convinced that the "calamity of war" itself was a blessing because it had filled "every Southern bosom . . . with detestation and loathing for this abominable race."[8]

The debased Yankee of southern imagination was a perfect foil for the Norman-descended Cavalier fashioned by Dixie's polemicists and novelists. As it had been before the commencement of hostilities, *DeBow's Review* remained the principal promulgator of this Norman racial mythology during the war. Its January–February 1862 issue, for example, contained an essay entitled "Southern Civilization; Or, the Norman in America," which recited the myth's by-now familiar articles of faith. According to the essayist, the South's planter aristocrats were directly descended from the Norman warriors who "had conquered the Anglo-Saxon, and during the long dynasty of the Plantagenets, maintained his supremacy among the nations, and stood at the head of European civilization." Unfortunately this cultivated aristocracy had been challenged by the rising "commercial spirit under the reign of Henry VIII, and its double alliance with the democratic principle and the genius of a lawless, intolerant and proscriptive semi-religious fanaticism"—the fanaticism of the Puritan Roundheads. The rise of Puritanism and its opposition to King and Church represented, in racial terms, the "attempted conquest of the Norman by the Saxon which . . . finally gained a violent and bloody triumph in the overthrow and execution of the unfortunate Charles Stuart."[9]

Like those who had promulgated the Norman race myth in the decade preceding the Civil War, the writer for *DeBow's Review* interpreted the current armed conflict between northerners and southerners not as a struggle between pro- and anti-slavery forces but as a New World manifestation of the historic Old World animosity between Cavalier and Roundhead, Norman and Saxon. And just as Cromwell's bloody and repressive interregnum had given way to the glorious Stuart Restoration in England, the essay confidently promised its readers that the southern heirs of Britain's Norman aristocracy would achieve "an assured final triumph." With this inevitable victory, it predicted, the "Norman race" would "record, in America, what, with strong hand and ten centuries of domination and power, it has written on the civilization of Europe."[10]

Though normal channels of commerce and communication between North and South were severed during the Civil War, northern journalists and writers remained well aware of invectives against the vile Yankee race issuing from southern pens. Virginia Sherwood, writing in the *Continental Monthly* in September 1862, observed with bitter weariness that hatred "of the abhorred 'Yankees,' scorn and the loathing of 'Lincoln's hirelings,' detestation of the mean, sordid, groveling, mercenary spirit of the Northern masses, have been the burden of Southern oratory and journalism for the last eighteen months."[11] In answer to these southern rhetorical assaults northern polemicists drew from their own ample store of the racial stereotypes they had refined and polished in numerous essays, articles, and speeches during the contentious 1850s.

Chief among these stereotypes was the view of southerners as benighted barbarians and ruthless ruffians. Sherwood asserted that southern opinion was dominated, distorted, and controlled by "slave oligarchs" whose culture and thinking were pervaded by "barbarism, slavery, injustice, ignorance, despotism." In plying their barbarism thesis, Northern writers found it useful to resurrect the potent memory of the brutal 1856 assault on Massachusetts Senator Charles Sumner by Representative Preston Brooks of South Carolina in the Senate chamber, for to them this attack typified the brutality and "ruffianism" of Dixie's so-called planter aristocrats. As hostilities commenced, one northern editorial writer contended that Union forces had little to fear from face-to-face combat with rebels, particularly with those rebels who hailed from Brooks's home state. The southern Cavalier's most dangerous and effective specialty, he jibed, was attacking a foe brutally and without warning: "To cudgel a United States Senator in his seat, off his guard and with no means of defense, beating him with a bludgeon within an inch of his life, while other armed ruffians stand near to see that the job is thoroughly executed, is the height of South Carolina chivalry and daring."[12]

Northern writers felt obligated not only to attack the South's conceit of itself as a noble and chivalrous race but also to defend themselves from the southern charge that Yankees were the detestable offspring of a Saxon-descended race of Puritan bigots and fanatics. One line of defense was to argue, as Evan Evans did in *The New Englander,* that the "distinctive principles of American civilization, namely, constitutional democracy, religious liberty, and free popular education, had their first development in New England." Like Ralph Waldo Emerson in his earlier writings on the character of New Englanders, Evans countered the negative stereotypes cultivated by southern polemicists by emphasizing the positive links between Puritan culture and the development of freedom, education, and enlightened progress in America. He also rejected the notion that southerners were a superior people descended from the English nobility. As he astutely observed, this self-proclaimed southern aristocracy actually consisted of men who had been fortunate enough to rise to wealth "in a country where land [had] cost almost nothing," making it relatively easy "for the most thrifty of the inhabitants to acquire large plantations."[13]

In Evans's opinion, the South's pretensions to aristocracy rested not on the solid foundation of superior blood inheritance but on the more dubious pillars of cheap land and slave labor. "The introduction of Negro slavery," he contended, "served still further to elevate this fortunate class above the common level. Planters with a few hundred acres and a score or two of slaves, began to take pride in aping, in a small way, the old feudal lords of Europe with their broad territories and their thousands of retainers." Southerners would no doubt have been outraged by Evans's suggestion that they were an aristocracy manqué, a society of ambitious immigrants who, by embracing the morally repugnant institution of chattel slavery, had succeeded only in creating a very minor reproduction in America of an anachronistic Old World social pattern. But such mundane and morally repugnant facts, Evans insisted, constituted "the true history of the rise of aristocracy in Virginia."[14]

Standing in vivid contrast to these middling and ambitious early slave owners who had indelibly stamped the South's culture were those equally middling Puritans who had come to America not to attain wealth and emulate an aristocratic European ethos but to pursue an idea of religious freedom: "It was a purely intellectual craving which called them from the comforts of their former homes; and in facing the inevitable sufferings of exile their object was the triumph of an idea." Evans believed that the idealism of New England's founders had been the primary source of the nation's subsequent greatness. It was a quality, he argued, that confirmed the Puritan as "superior to the American Cavalier in social position as well as in character."[15]

Evans's thesis that America's grandeur and its exalted destiny were essentially products of Puritan idealism was one that was effectively employed by other northern polemicists, such as Virginia Sherwood in an essay entitled "Southern Hate of New England." Sherwood was convinced that the South had focused its antipathy on the states north and east of New York because southerners implicitly understood that the "*Northern* idea" was synonymous with the "*Puritan*" idea.[16] She believed that America's national character, which Dixie was in the process of violently repudiating, had been largely defined by those admirable traits embodied in men like Winthrop, Mather, and Edwards and passed on to the Union's future generations.

And what were these noble Puritan traits? Chief among them were enlightened social attitudes and high communal moral principles. Sherwood averred that New England society had possessed from its inception to the present day "a higher standard of morals, a more intelligent adhesion to what is regarded as duty, a more simple social intercourse, and purer social manners and customs, with fewer dissipations and derelictions, than perhaps any other people in the would can boast." Yoked with this rarified moral tone was a strong and genuine piety—a product of the unrivaled purity of the region's gospel preaching—and a *"pure republicanism"* that testified to the democratic impulses of the Puritan brand of Christianity.[17]

Virginia Sherwood was too clever an advocate not to acknowledge that Puritans were in some respects imperfect social specimens, but she contended that their faults were "the exaggerations of their virtues." Their commendable zeal for the true and holy, for example, had occasionally degenerated "into a blind and bitter bigotry." Yet while acknowledging flaws in the Puritan character, Sherwood remained convinced that in the totality of its expression, Puritanism had been "the agency whereby Providence [had seen] fit to inaugurate the ideas which were to form the foundation of our national polity," ideas that had inspired the Declaration of Independence, the Bill of Rights, and the Constitution. She neatly finessed the inconvenient fact that all of these documents reflected the strong influence of Virginia planters such as Jefferson, Madison, and Washington by blithely asserting that these revolutionary heroes were "of the spirit and understanding of the Puritan." Indeed, she ventured, "I suspect that Washington was a Puritan of Puritans."[18]

If Puritanism was so inextricably entwined with America's democratic ethos, why did the South so intensely hate New England? Sherwood answered this question by arguing that the planters who had followed the great generation of Revolutionary-era southern statesmen had suffered a mental stagnation caused by their commitment to chattel labor and resulting in an increasing hostility toward the democratic ideals of the Revolution. While the rest of the nation had moved toward the further refinement of Puritan concepts of justice, social morality, and democracy, the South had heeded the siren song of slavery and retreated into cultural ossification and barbarism. It was inevitable, Sherwood concluded, that "the ignorance and mental darkness of slave Virginia or Carolina should fear and hate above all things the light of knowledge that stems from New England." In light of the righteous struggle then being undertaken by President Lincoln, Sherwood professed herself willing to "let the world judge between the Puritan and the so-called Cavalier."[19]

If southern readers had chosen to peruse Sherwood's essay, they would no doubt have commented on its stridently self-righteous tone, a tone that they believed had historically characterized Puritan polemics. They would also have been disgusted by the almost religious zeal of her assertion that the North carried into battle against the South the banners of "civilization, freedom, justice, education, republicanism, the gladness and gratitude of redeemed humanity, the jubilee of joy among angels." Yet no southern ripostes past or present could disabuse their Yankee adversaries of the conviction that in fighting the Civil War they were about God's business. This certainty that the North was acting as an instrument of God's vengeance against the wicked South had been naturally congruent with the rhetoric of Puritan-descended abolitionists. But during the Civil War it also became part of the language of New Yorkers and midwesterners, and it was probably given most potent expression by Abraham Lincoln. In his second inaugural address, for example, the president expressed the hope that the war would end shortly. "Yet," he proclaimed, "if God wills that it continue until . . . every drop of blood drawn with the lash shall be paid by another drawn with the sword, as was said three thousand years ago, so still it must be said 'the judgments of the Lord are true and righteous altogether.'"[20]

The strategy of wartime polemical writers above the Mason-Dixon was thus to uphold the moral supremacy of a Puritan-descended northern culture while attacking the South's claim to a superior aristocratic racial inheritance. W. H. Whitmore's "The Cavalier Theory Refuted" was an especially effective example of an essay written expressly to repudiate the notion that southerners were "the descendants of the gentry of England, and that the Unionists of the loyal States [had] neither any identity of origin nor a historical pedigree." Whitmore ingeniously employed Robert Beverley's colonial history of the Old Dominion to undermine the Norman racial myth by stressing the heterogeneous nature of Virginia's settlement, which had consisted of Scots, Irish, German, and French immigrants. Even among those settlers who could rightly call themselves English, Whitmore contended, there was "a very large portion . . . of transported felons." Considering the nature of colonial Virginia's population, he concluded that New England could assert a stronger claim "to a purely English ancestry" than could the South.[21]

Whitmore felt it necessary to answer the southern charge that the original Puritan settlement had been debased and mongrelized by successive waves of inferior Old World immigrants. It was true, he admitted, that the North had welcomed "millions of foreigners," but this new immigration could never destroy the "controlling influence" on the national character of Puritan New Englanders whose stock had "invigorated every state of the Union" with its instinct for democracy, progress, and industry. Whitmore went so far as to boast that New England, "colonized by Englishmen, homogeneous in a remarkable degree, has been the only thoroughly pure nationality within our territories."[22]

As for the southern claim of superiority for its Norman-descended Cavalier over the northern Puritan, Whitmore argued somewhat defensively that the Puritan "was as much a gentleman in the technical English sense as the Cavalier." Surveying the great families of Massachusetts with distinguished surnames that included Winthrop and Adams, he avowed proudly in the face of southern insolence and ignorance that "Puritanic New England could always display a greater array of 'gentlemen by birth' than Virginia, or even the entire South." For northern writers like Whitmore, Sherwood, and Evans, the South's assertions of aristocratic refinement and Norman blood were concepts that a proper understanding of history revealed to be fantasies. Ironically, in the process of dismantling southern myths, northern polemicists ignored their own mythical aggrandizement of their Puritan heritage, confirming the long-held southern prejudice that Puritans remained, as they always had been, a race "famous for discerning the mote in their brother's eye, and taking no notice of the beam in their own."[23]

Verbal battles between northern and southern polemical writers thus continued to rage along with battles on the military field as both sides sought to stir up the patriotism of their respective audiences. But what sort of pragmatic impact did this verbal antagonism have on the opinions of the northern and southern people on the home front regarding the nature of the enemy? Letters and diaries suggest that, just as before the war, noncombatants from both regions widely shared and reflected in their private correspondence the prejudices and the inflamed attitudes toward their adversaries of their respective journalistic opinion makers.

Like their polemicists, people living in the North tended to view southerners privately as little more than depraved animals completely alienated from high ideals or considerations of morality. Emerson was one of many who, when writing to friends, took such a dark and even satanic view of southerners. In the early months of the war he zestfully returned in one of his letters to the animal metaphors he had publicly employed at the time of Charles Sumner's caning to describe what he saw as a vicious and morally stunted enemy. Despite the southerner's "suave, cool, and picturesque" manners, he observed, the war had quickly revealed "what a noxious reptile the green and gold thing was." Emerson seems even to have believed at this point in the conflict that Dixie's moral blindness and its aversion to truth were qualities inherent in the genetic composition of its people. "Their detestation of Massachusetts," he wrote, "is a chemical description of their substance, and if a state more lawful, honest, and cultivated were known to them, they would transfer to it this detestation."[24]

New Yorker George Templeton Strong agreed with Emerson that southerners were a people incapable of exhibiting a high moral sense. "Their nerves of moral sensation," he marveled, "seem smitten with paralysis. Their 'chivalry' exults in treachery, bad faith, oppression of the weak, and every thing that distinguishes the churl from the knight." Strong would have completely agreed with those northern polemicists who contended that the South's pretension to aristocracy was a facade constructed to hide the savagery of its culture. After the Battle of Bull Run he responded indignantly to the reported killing of wounded Union troops: "How the inherent barbarism of the chivalry crops out whenever it can safely kill or torture a defenseless enemy! Scrape the 'Southern Gentleman's' skin and you will find a second-rate Comanche underneath it."[25]

Like their polemical writers, northerners were aware of and sensitive to the southern charge that Yankees were an inferior and plebeian people. Historian and Boston Brahmin John Lothrop Motley, writing to Oliver Wendell Holmes about the wounding of his son, Oliver Wendell Holmes Jr., was convinced that despite the younger Holmes's exposure to danger and death, his "brilliant, intellectual, poetical" spirit had taken arms for a "noble cause," demonstrating the highest ideals of the northern people. "The race of Philip Sydney is not yet extinct," he boasted, "and I honestly believe that as much genuine chivalry exists in our free States at this moment as there is or ever was in any part of the world, from the Crusaders down." Behind Motley's proud assertions lay a consciousness nettled by the South's assumption of racial superiority. This same sort of pride edged with defensiveness was apparent in Strong's claim that northern manners were "less showy and splendid than Southern chivalry, but sounder and better, nevertheless."[26]

Although most northerners viewed southerners as a backward and morally depraved people, they did occasionally wonder about the Confederacy's ability to win victory after victory on the battleground, especially in the early years of the war. New England historian and Brahmin Francis Parkman analyzed this conundrum publicly in two letters that he contributed to the *Boston Daily Advertiser* in the summer of 1863. Parkman's first letter argued that the

Union's military defeats were not attributable to a failure of resolve and courage on the part of the common soldier; they represented instead a deficiency in "the principle of military honor" among the North's officers. In Dixie, a region that he described as "a community essentially military," this instinct for command and this military spirit were "rife." In the North, by contrast, "luxury and commerce" had combined to weaken and "sometimes emasculate" the region's martial resolve. Parkman frankly conceded that among the North's social elite "the pride of a good bargain" had often "overborne the pride of manhood." He believed that the excessive influence of commerce on the North's social and political institutions had weakened an otherwise "vigorous and practical race, courageous, indeed . . . but not spurred to acts of courage by the same exacting and unanswerable demand which urges . . . ruder nations."[27]

Parkman was careful to describe the South's superior military spirit as a characteristic associable with a "ruder" people. Still, his remarks must have been disturbing to many Boston readers, for in scoring the macerating effects of the North's devotion to commerce on the manly resolve of its military leaders it seemed to confirm the southern stereotype of the Yankee as a base and cowardly worshiper of mammon and to accept implicitly the preeminence of the southern warrior. It was perhaps a concern for being misunderstood that prompted the historian to submit a second letter to the *Advertiser* in which he further refined his interpretation of the Confederacy's military achievements. In this letter he asserted that the key to understanding what had become a surprisingly equal military contest between two regions of decidedly unequal economic power lay in recognizing that the war was a struggle between a more primitive and militaristic southern "oligarchy" and a less martial but more complex and technologically sophisticated northern "democracy."[28]

As he had in his earlier letter, Parkman began by appearing to accept the South's conception of itself as a uniquely aristocratic people. But like earlier northern polemicists, he turned this seeming positive into a negative. "A truer aristocracy never existed," he wrote, "or a worse one when considered in its origin and foundation," for "from his cradle" the southern "slave oligarch" had been taught that he held "a place of power and peril, isolated, pelted with opprobrium, beset with swarming foes." In the face of sustained attacks on slavery, aristocratic southern pride had been transformed into xenophobia and paranoia. Dixie's haughty planters had excoriated both the North's merchant class, "whom they scorned as the feudal noble scorned the rich burgher," and its politicians and abolitionists, to whose calls for racial reform they had turned a deaf ear.[29]

The same stubborn and autocratic spirit of the South's aristocracy that had impelled the region to secession had also vouchsafed them early military successes. Parkman was confident, however, that the North's superior intellectual and technological vigor would ultimately prevail. "We in New England," he observed, "are a bookish people." But, like other northern polemicists, he believed that this "bookish" commitment to education, culture, and democratic principles would lead to ultimate Union victory. "Oligarchy and Democracy," he concluded, "cannot live side by side. In war we can in time master them." In peace, he prophesied, every advantage would lie "with the concentrated will, the trained and subtle intellect" of the Universal Yankee Nation.[30]

By the beginning of the Civil War northerners were willing to accept the opinion of their polemical writers that the northern and southern peoples were, in the words of Yale-educated Yankee William Chauncey Fowler, "alien to one another in race, in religion, and in political affinities." They were just as inclined as southerners to agree with the notion that New Englanders "were descended from that class of the English, who were Puritan in their religion, and Roundhead in their politics." They even embraced the idea that "the prelatical Cavaliers" of Virginia and the "French Huguenots" of South Carolina had bequeathed to Dixie a unique racial inheritance.[31] But they strongly disagreed with southerners about the ruling characteristics associated with these separate northern and southern races, attributing to their own Puritan ancestors qualities of intellect, cultural sophistication, and idealism and to the Cavaliers of the South qualities of arrogance, moral degeneracy, and barbarity.

Intemperate and scathing as northern indictments of the southern race often were, they paled in comparison with the scorching prose that issued privately from southern pens condemning the damned Yankee race. Given the fact that Dixie was defending its peculiar institution, its way of life, and its newly proclaimed nationhood against invading Union armies, it is hardly surprising that its people took an especially dim view of northern aggressors. Nor is it a surprise that in rhetorically flaying the ruthless invader, southerners would draw upon the by-now familiar Norman race myth that had been skillfully purveyed by the region's antebellum polemicists, viewing themselves as a heroic, aristocratically descended, and honorable people repelling a hybrid swarm of conscienceless barbarians.

The South's sense of racial superiority was perhaps most vividly expressed by Savannah patrician George Mercer in a diary entry of May 5, 1861, in which he described the coming onslaught against the South of three hundred thousand "roughs, a foe beside whom the Goths and Vandals were meek and gentle." Mercer pronounced himself "sad and despondent," not because the Union was in the process of being destroyed but because the Confederacy was being forced to send into battle its "best people" to face "the scum of the earth." And what specific elements composed this northern scum? "Germans, French, Irish and foreigners of all stripes," he declared, were being mustered above the Potomac "to subjugate a free southern people."[32] The imaginations of southerners like Mercer had been fired by the polemical debates of the preceding decade. As the Civil War commenced, they were determined to see their erstwhile American brethren as an alien and inferior race of mongrel warriors.

As the war progressed, the southerner's conviction of his superior blood remained strong. North Carolina judge and secessionist David Schenck looked anxiously toward Richmond in the summer of 1862 as a Yankee force of 125,000 men—bent, he believed, on pillage and revenge—prepared to descend on the Confederate capital. Opposing this "horde of vandals" were 100,000 southern "patriots" who, in Schenck's words, were "composed of the common blood of our country. . . . They are those whose interests and rights are involved—no hireling emissaries of destruction—no fierce and cruel Germans, regardless of moral or political right—no starving Irish, who fight for daily bread."[33] Like Mercer, Schenck had no doubt that a homogeneous and honorable race of southerners was bravely arrayed against a mixed horde of northern mercenaries. For him the Union army was a contemptible racial potpourri not worthy of occupying the field of battle against southern Cavaliers.

As they had done before the War, when southerners tired of depicting northerners as a people debased by racial hybridization, they moved on to denouncing the stereotypical Yankee monster. They continued to view their enemy as an unrefined mob stamped with the Saxon-Puritan mania for money and profit. Mary Chesnut reported approvingly in her diary during the summer of 1861 the remark of one southern gentleman that "Yankees did not fight for the fun of it. They always made it pay or let it alone." Another clever Cavalier made this snide response when informed that a Pennsylvania senator had announced himself ready to go on the warpath: "Then profit will accrue."[34]

Those southerners who fell under northern control in the occupied areas of the Confederacy seemed bitterly pleased to have had their expectations of the Yankee's unrefined materialism confirmed by brutal experience. Martha Matthews's description of the movement of northerners into Holly Springs, Mississippi, in December 1863 was a typical southern portrayal of the barbaric invaders. "Yankee aspirants for competition," she wrote, "were to be found in every branch of commercial enterprise; speculators came swarming like Egyptian locusts bringing their families with them and intruding themselves into houses of private citizens . . . while the rapacious Jews played a conspicuous part in the grand drama." Perhaps most humiliating to Matthews was the fact that this degraded assortment of Yankees and Jews acted as "Lords of the Manor" and regarded the proud southern heirs of the Norman aristocracy "as mere retainers."[35]

If southerners like Matthews believed that the Universal Yankee was possessed by a detestable avarice, they also believed that his rank materialism was matched and even surpassed by his contemptible cowardice. How could such a lowly race of miserly shopkeepers ever understand or appreciate aristocratic notions of noblesse oblige and honor and the sense of personal courage that attended these lofty concepts? The South's conviction that Yankees were a base and cowardly lot had been confirmed by what, to southern eyes, had been the humiliating surrender and evacuation of Fort Sumter in April 1861 and by the disastrous Union defeat at the First Battle of Manassas that had followed soon after in July. For George Mercer, the gaudily clothed New York Fire Zouaves who, despite their brave military finery, had been among the first to break and flee at Bull Run epitomized the pusillanimity of the northern people. "These were the terrible fellows in red breeches," he whimsically observed, "who were bold in killing cattle, pillaging houses, and insulting women and prisoners, and whom the Yankees, with Chinese-like anticipations, expected to frighten the Southerners with their gaudy colors and brutal manners." With a mixture of delight and pride Mercer pointed out that joining the fleeing Zouaves at Bull Run had been "bold Congressmen and Editors" who had run "like sheep from the 'cowardly Southerners,' as those same southerners always expected them to do."[36]

New Orleans native Clara Solomon was just as offended as Mercer had been by the showy affectations of the Union troops who occupied her city in May 1862. On the eighth of that month she had steeled herself, walked to Canal Street, and found it filled with northern Vandals "sporting uniforms with any quantity of brass buttons. Oh! That our streets should be ever so disgraced." Given the common southern opinion that Yankee soldiers were little better than cowardly looters, Clara joined the ladies of the Crescent City in subjecting Union troops to "silent insult." "A car on Camp Street," she wrote, "was hailed by some Federal officers and as they walked in the ladies walked out. As some officers came into their pews in Church they vacated them, and it is said that they seemed to feel the insult."[37]

Benjamin Franklin Butler's infamous General Orders no. 28, which directed that a southern woman exhibiting such disrespect as Solomon had described be "treated as a woman of the town plying her avocation," simply affirmed for southerners their feeling that Yankees were a people bereft of both courage and honor. Solomon's indignation was predictably intense, "The cowardly wretches!" she fumed. "To notice the insult of ladies! And how did they expect to be treated?" The indignation of Dixie's Cavalier warriors was just as intense as that of its belles. In replying to Butler's insult Confederate General G. T. Beauregard thundered this response: "Men of the South! Shall our mothers, wives, daughters and sisters be thus outraged by ruffianly soldiers, to whom is thus given the right to treat at their pleasure the ladies of the South as common harlots! Arise, friends! Drive back from our soil the infamous invaders of our homes, and the disturbers of family ties!"[38]

Though southerners like Solomon and Beauregard scorned both the Yankee's character and his courage, they never doubted his capacity for ferocity. General William Tecumseh Sherman's destructive march through Georgia and South Carolina in the later stages of the war was visible proof to Dixie that a barbarian's capacity for gratuitous destruction lay embedded within the character of the northern race. "What cruel brutes the Yankees are," Confederate Congressman Warren Akin wrote, responding indignantly to Sherman's atrocities. "You doubtless remember hearing me say sometime since—last year perhaps—that the Yankees would become more and more brutal and savage as the war progressed, and this opinion is being confirmed almost daily." Writing amid the ashes of her native city, Emma Le Conte bitterly confessed her naiveté in having given credence to General Sherman's promise not to burn South Carolina's capital city of Columbia. "Strange as it may seem" she wrote, "we were actually idiotic enough to believe Sherman would keep his word! A *Yankee*—and *Sherman!*" Le Conte's bitterness toward northern troops was matched by her righteous indignation at their savagery toward women and children, a savagery that confirmed for her the essential cowardice of the enemy. "This is civilized warfare," she cynically observed. "This is the way in which the 'cultured' Yankee nation wars upon women and children! Failing with our men in the field, *this* is the way they must conquer!"[39]

For southerners the idea that a high-toned, aristocratic people should have found it necessary to defend its culture on the battlefield against a base and villainous race of savages was a repugnant reality. Shielded by their concept of honor, it was impossible for them to conceive of submitting to the authority of such an inferior foe. The southern people yearned for peace as ardently as northerners. But since the conflict had been precipitated by men described by South Carolinian Henry Ravenel as "mad fanatics," they were insistent that peace be achieved "upon terms honorable to us and our rights."[40]

As the war dragged on, however, southerners slowly came to realize that, barring a miracle, they would never achieve a peace that vouchsafed the Confederacy's honor and that their most humiliating nightmare—the subjugation of a noble and proud southern people to a vile and debased Yankee race—loomed as an increasingly likely reality. The horrible prospect of submission almost certainly prompted the South to fight on, even after the military outcome of the Civil War was no longer in doubt. Surrender would bring subjugation, and subjugation would bring, in the words of Congressman Akin, "free Negroes in abundance—enemies at that—while white slaves will be more numerous than free Negroes. . . . Subjugation will deprive us of our homes, houses, property, liberty, honor, and every thing worth living for, leaving for us and our posterity only the chains of slavery, tenfold more galling and degrading than that now felt by our Negroes." Southerners of both sexes were galvanized by the awful prospect of their impending humiliation. Toward the very end of the conflict Kate Stone emphatically presented a short list of the South's most dreaded words: "*conquered, submission, subjugation* are words that burn into my heart."[41]

Within months of the beginning of the Civil War the majority of southerners would certainly have agreed with Ella Gertrude Thomas, daughter of a Georgia planter, that "the Northern and Southern people [were] entirely different," that they were "morally and socially as well as politically the antipodes of each other," and that the war had made "the line of demarcation [between them] broader." Thomas had not characterized the two peoples as different races, but there can be little doubt that as the hostilities grew more bloody, southerners increasingly embraced the arguments of their polemicists that inhabitants of the Confederacy descended from a racial stock different from and superior to that of Yankees. A letter written by North Carolinian Clara Hoyt to her friend Fannie Hamilton on February 1, 1862, vividly illustrates how the traumas of war prompted southerners to demonize northerners as an alien enemy race. "Fannie," she wrote, "I thought I hated the miserable Vandals before, but I never knew how intense, how bitter the feeling was until I saw the boat go by this morning loaded to the water's edge with helpless women and children, obliged to leave so hurriedly their happy homes perhaps forever." Such a scene of suffering filled Hoyt "with mortification and regret that we ever extended the right hand of fellowship to such a set." She could not indeed bring herself to believe that the troops harrying defenseless women and children were "the same people we once fraternized with." She now considered them a separate race, "a new race of desperate unscrupulous savages, lately sprung up, who would overcome us if they could."[42]

Hoyt's letter illustrates not only southerners' willingness to turn northerners into a "new race" but also their preference for the term *Vandal* when denouncing this alien enemy. The word commonly appeared in the southern press. A Savannah newspaper provided one of the more inflamed contexts for its use when it issued this biblically inflected excoriation of the northern people: "We prefer that God should rain down upon us fire and brimstone and consume us as he did Sodom and Gomorrah, to falling into the hands of Yankees, or being in any wise subject to their tender mercies. . . . Yes, let any destruction, or death, befall us all, in preference to being subjugated to the rule of power of the unfeeling Yankee vandals." As we have seen, southerners also used the term frequently in their private correspondence. David Schenck gave the word additional menace when he employed it in combination with the image of a serpent, announcing exultantly in one of his letters that Confederate military hero Stonewall Jackson had been "busy among the Vandals" in his Virginia campaign and that he had "thrust a vital stab into the coil of the huge anaconda."[43]

One might have expected that a racial myth that buttressed the Confederacy by positing a homogeneous race of aristocrats descended from Norman blood would have generated a degree of disaffection among those southerners manifestly unconnected to such a genealogical inheritance. Yet strong support for the Confederate ideal persisted throughout the war among most segments of the South's population, most notably among the region's Jews. Though southerners like Martha Matthews were perfectly willing to lump northern Jews with detested Yankees, most seem never to have doubted the loyalty and worth of the South's own small but influential Jewish community. Even before the beginning of hostilities the *Charleston Mercury* had praised the "Israelites of South Carolina" as "amongst the most faithful and patriotic of the people" of the Palmetto State. The *Mercury* proudly pointed out that both of the Jewish members of the most recent United States Senate, Senators Benjamin and Yulee, had hailed from Dixie. In South Carolina and in the South as a whole, the editorial boasted, "our Israelite fellow-citizens have promptly thrown their whole weight to sustain the State in the great contest in which she is engaged, to save her liberties and institutions from the ruthless despotism of the Northern people."[44]

Southern Jews not only loyally supported secession and the establishment of the Confederacy; they were even capable of imaginatively identifying themselves with the region's wartime myths of aristocracy and racial homogeneity. Clara Solomon was the daughter of a prosperous Jewish New Orleans merchant, but in her diary she expressed a pride, a sense of superiority, and a repugnance of Yankees worthy of the most Norman-descended of southern belles. Just before the fall of the city she claimed that she was "willing to make any sacrifice, to behold our prided city reduced to ruins, rather than it should fall into the hands of the barbarous invaders." Having read a triumphant northern account of the capitulation of her beloved city to what she termed "a barbarous enemy," she unashamedly confessed that her "Southern blood was fired up, and the blush of indignation glowed on my cheeks, and my pulse throbbed high, when I contemplated our fall. . . . Tears suffused my cheeks, and I felt how strong was my love for my beloved country."[45] Clara Solomon was a Jew, but in the throes of defeat her blood became "Southern blood" and the Confederacy became her "beloved country."

Southerners of all orders and ethnic origins were so convinced of their racial and moral superiority to the northern people and so confirmed in their conviction that their Yankee adversaries were members of an inferior race that many of them could neither accept nor fathom what they conceived as God's judgment in giving final victory to the North. As George Mercer observed in a diary entry of April 16, 1865, the southern people were "now passing through a period of deep depression: our vindictive enemies seem successful on every hand, and God seems to smile upon their cause." Even as he questioned God's will in the final days of the conflict, Mercer was ineluctably drawn toward understanding the South's downfall in racial terms. History, he was convinced, was "repeating itself: we are feeling another terrible eruption of Northern tribes recruited from the whole world." In the face of such a barbaric racial aggression he could "not believe that a just god" would allow the aristocratic South "to be overwhelmed, and utterly cast down."[46]

Some southerners tried to qualify their despair at the perverse expression of God's will with some degree of hope for the eventual survival of the southern people. Though Virginian Kate Garland was "not able to comprehend the goodness and greatness of God—in thus allowing our enemy to triumph over us," she continued to "trust in Him, and believe there is good in store for us yet—that He will send us deliverance in some way—and that in the far off coming future we will be a free and happy people." Garland's determined and abstract optimism was, however, an exception to the prevailing tone of southern opinion. Most southern correspondents reflected both the bitterness of Richmonder Lucy Muse Fletcher and her repugnance toward the conquering Yankee. Like Mercer, Fletcher was acutely sensitive to the racial dimensions of the South's catastrophe, and she insisted on viewing the North's victory as a hollow one. "With the resources of the whole world open to them," she bitterly opined, "and hirelings from all lands to help them fight their battles, they were still compelled to seek assistance from the ignorant and degraded Negro."[47]

The occupation of Richmond confirmed Fletcher's worst fears about the coarse and alien race the South had spent four years bravely resisting. She watched in helpless indignation as Negroes streamed freely through the streets of the former Confederate capital to the disgusting music of "Yankee Doodle" and "Old John Brown." Jefferson's noble Capitol Square grounds were littered with "dirty tents" set up "for the sale of cakes and pies and this is *Yankee Civilization!*" The moral tone of the hypocritical Yankee race was just as degraded as a southerner like Lucy Fletcher would have expected it to be. Officers, she observed contemptuously, hitched their horses in front of respectable houses while they sneaked out to visit "some disreputable houses in the neighborhood kept by negroes! ... This is Yankee *morality*—a thing that was never done during the war by our own officers, who without claiming any high degree of morality had yet sufficient *decency* and self-respect to show some consideration for the feelings of respectable people in the neighborhood."[48]

Lucy Fletcher and George Mercer, like countless other loyal southerners, writhed emotionally under what they deemed a brutal and vulgar Yankee yoke, but Virginian Edmund Ruffin refused to submit to such humiliation. At the end of the war the fiery secessionist, who had been given the honor of firing the first shell on Fort Sumter, penned one final entry in his journal in which he declared his "unmitigated hatred to Yankee rule—to all political, social and business connections with the Yankees and to the Yankee race." And he concluded his entry with a proud and defiant reiteration of this anathema: "I here repeat and would willingly proclaim my unmitigated hatred to Yankee rule—to all political, social and business connections with Yankees, and the perfidious, malignant and vile Yankee race."[49] He then seated himself squarely in his chair, placed the muzzle of his silver-mounted gun in his mouth, and pulled the trigger.

In his critical study *The Common Soldier in the Civil War,* historian Bell Irvin Wiley examined the letters, diaries, and journals of hundreds of soldiers from both the Union and the Confederate side and concluded that the similarities between "Billy Yank and Johnny Reb far outweighed their differences. They were both Americans, by birth or by adoption, and they both had the weaknesses and the virtues of the people of their nation and time."[50] Wiley's conclusion about the fundamental resemblance between northern and southern troops, based on his twentieth-century historical perspective, is to a degree an accurate depiction of America's Civil War soldiers, but a reading of Civil War correspondence also makes clear that at the time, soldiers on each side imagined themselves to be both superior to and very different from their adversaries. Civil War hostilities blinded both Billy Yank and Johnny Reb to the reality of their common American identity; therefore, neither was inclined to view his enemy as a brother bound to him by common traits of national character.

Yanks were just as liable as Rebels to condemn their foes as barbarians, and they were equally fond of reporting gruesome evidence of this barbarity in their letters home. One northern soldier assured his family that Confederates were using the skulls of the Union dead as soup bowls. Another averred that Rebels had "no humanity. They kill our wounded soldiers and even our women nurses are said to be shot." General Robert McAllister indignantly described the bodies of seven Union soldiers who had been stripped and shot in the head kneeling in a circle. In a slam at the South's precious myth of aristocracy, he bitterly judged the deed to be murder "in cold blood by the would-be 'Chivalry of the South.'" Others viewed Rebels through the lens of Puritan abolitionism, condemning them as embodiments of pure evil. Pennsylvanian John White Geary informed his correspondent that the enemy's pickets had been placed "close to ours, and I have a daily view of these demons of Satan." Echoing the sentiments of more bloodthirsty northern ministers, Fred Spooner of Rhode Island believed that the war against southern slaveholders was a "holy cause" and that the issue of slavery had to be settled once and for all, "even if the whole South has to be made one common graveyard, and their cotton soaked in blood." He had little pity for the southern people. "They have prospered dealing in human flesh," he wrote censoriously, "let them now take the results of it."[51]

Not all northern soldiers passed such grim judgment on southerners as Geary and Spooner. William Thompson Lusk eschewed the northern invective and made fun of the southern penchant for demonizing Yankees. While serving in the Low Country of South Carolina he wrote home to inform his family that "vile Yankee hordes [were] overrunning the pleasant islands about

Beaufort, rioting upon sweet potatoes and southern sunshine." "Alas," he continued in the same humorous vein, "Yankee hordes, ruthless invaders—the vile Hessians—infest their splendid plantations." Beyond its play of wit, Lusk's letter shows that at least some northern soldiers were capable of appreciating to a degree the finer aspects of plantation culture, particularly those who served in the coastal areas of the South where that society had flowered earliest and longest. In one of his letters Lusk observed, not entirely whimsically, that he had "grown immensely aristocratic since in South Carolina. . . . There [is] something in the air that's infectious." In another passage, marked by a similarly inflected tone, he admiringly described the impressive Beaufort mansions that had been owned by men whose "effervescent exuberance of gentlemanly spirit" had helped bring on the war.[52]

The longer Lusk remained in coastal South Carolina, the less whimsical and more serious about the South he became in his letters home. He could not deny that the fine Beaufort residences the Union officers now occupied, in their "old fashioned Southern mansion style," clearly evinced a society of both "luxury and comfort." Indeed, his awareness that the war was bringing to a violent end this gracious and ample lifestyle prompted feelings of regret and nostalgia. "These were pleasant places that the planters have abandoned us," he wrote, "and though conscious that our victory has been glorious . . . [I] would to God that the war had never visited us, and that the planters were once more peacefully cultivating their pleasant homes."[53]

There was no condemnation of slavery and little evidence of hostility toward the southern people in Lusk's letters. In fact, given the grim portrayal of southern barbarity and ignorance by abolitionist writers, he was astonished at both the content and the tone of the intercepted southern war correspondence he had read, especially by a religious piety that seemed to be both genuine and deep. "There is one thing very conspicuous in all letters from southern soldiers," he observed. "I refer to the deep religious vein pervading them. Their religious impressions seem to be warmer than those of our troops."[54] Southerners had been so demonized by northern polemicists that a man of more open mind like Lusk seems to have been genuinely astonished to discover the Confederacy's soldiers to be, like Union soldiers, men of Christian convictions.

Lusk's letters demonstrate that at least some of the North's soldiers developed through their war experiences a more nuanced view of southerners and of southern culture. This occasional striving for objectivity and fairness in assessing the enemy was probably due to the fact that Union troops were fighting in the South and stationed within the region. They therefore had the opportunity to experience the South at first hand and to evaluate its social system from a close perspective. As the letters of Yale graduate Uriah Parmelee show, even when northern soldiers judged the South less positively than Lusk had done, they not infrequently sought to qualify their criticism by acknowledging that the region possessed at least some social virtues.

Serving in Virginia, Parmelee came to believe that there was "much hospitality, much refinement, and true politeness" in the Old Dominion. The problem, he believed, was that inextricably bound to these admirable qualities was the less admirable quality of "Virginian pride." "If there is any one trait that I have seen illustrated here in desolated Virginia," he wrote to his mother in 1863, "it is—*Pride,* pride of race, pride of State, pride of wealth, pride of rule. It is a pride which is educated to them. It was born in them to begin with and has become a part of their inheritance. To follow its dictates is manly: to resort to bully, to retaliate is to be—a—*gentleman!*" In the complexity of what Parmelee termed a "mixed . . . world," the New England officer was thoughtful enough to attempt to render a balanced judgment of the enemy that few polemicists or soldiers on either side of the conflict were able or inclined to emulate: "Motives and actions are not clearly defined as we might wish them," he ruefully admitted, "and good men espouse bad causes."[55]

Despite the occasionally sympathetic responses of soldiers like Lusk and Parmelee, the great majority of northern soldiers were in no mood to make excuses for the people who they believed had initiated a destructive civil war through their own haughty pride. Because they had listened for years to the South's boasting of its refined culture and its aristocratic blood, they were surprised and delighted to report to their friends and relatives on the low and primitive state of the southern society they encountered. Writing from Tidewater Virginia in 1864, New Yorker Constant Hanks observed smugly that a visitor "from one of our free northern states coming here would naturally come to the conclusion that the people of this state have gone to sleep 150 years ago and have not waked up yet." Connecticut Yankee Henry Thompson made these unflattering remarks in a letter to his wife about the southerners he had met just inside the North Carolina line: "I don't know what kind of description to give now of the inhabitants, only if they send Missionarys *[sic]* from home anywhere I think they had better send them here, for the natives aint more than half civilized and look like ghosts skeletons or flyaways. They're as wild as hawks and don't know a ten dollar bill from a one nor but few know how to make the right change of money. I supposed we were fighting a civilized class of people but I find we are not."[56]

Even in the Old Dominion, the state most associated in popular imagination with aristocratic refinement, Union General Robert McAllister encountered widespread poverty while fighting in the area just south of Washington. Add to this impoverishment, he wrote, "an unusual amount of ignorance and you have a faint description of what inhabitants, including F.F.V.'s, are like along the valley of the Occoquan River." McAllister was not alone in lumping the South's vaunted aristocracy with the other benighted social classes of the region. Nathan Webb found all southerners, "even of the finest society," to be "an ignorant, overbearing, proud, arrogant set."[57]

McAllister directly linked the southern preoccupation with the aristocratic ideal to the region's backwardness and to the fact that Virginians had been "standing still for the last twenty years. They prided themselves on family, and worshipped slavery, and fancied that they were superior to all creation." While Virginians had sunk into the sough of pride and complacency, McAllister proudly pointed out, in phrases echoing those of northern polemicists, that "the North [had] made rapid advancements in refinement, education, and everything that is calculated to raise the scale of civilization and religion." Edward Hall of the Third New Hampshire Volunteer Regiment made observations similar to McAllister's linking of the benighted condition of South Carolina to its obsession with aristocratic pride. "The difference between Yankee industry and the shiftlessness of the southern Chivalry can be plainly seen," he wrote with obvious satisfaction. South Carolina's absorption with its myth of aristocracy had produced a ruling class averse to labor and a southern gentleman "too aristocratic ever to be a Base Carpenter." What the Palmetto State needed, he concluded, was a little more "Yankee energy and thrift, and a little less aristocratic pride."[58]

If the indictments of the Tidewater societies of Virginia and South Carolina were often harsh, the assessments of the culture of the interior South were even more severe. John Geary viewed Tennessee as a "backwoods where the sun of intelligence has never yet beamed, and where it has been the pleasure of the Southern Aristocracy to obscure the mental vision of the people in every possible manner." Like other northern soldiers, he described the state's benightedness in biblical terms. "Truly," he wrote, "darkness prevails, like that which prevailed upon the face of the great deep at the Creation." Suffering in the frost and snow of a Tennessee winter, Geary quickly concluded that the

South was not sunny and that its people were not great. "Southern greatness," he opined, "was always a humbug in my opinion, and more so now than ever before."[59]

With the exception of Robert E. Lee's brief and fateful foray into Pennsylvania, southern soldiers had no real opportunity either to conquer or to observe northern culture. Instead they were obliged to defend the Confederacy against increasingly powerful Union armies that, within a space of four years, had crisscrossed and trampled the sacred soil of the Old Dominion and inflicted a swath of destruction on the interior and Deep South stretching from the Mississippi River through Georgia to the Carolinas. In this context of defeat and devastation it is hardly surprising that measured evaluations of northern soldiers and northern culture were virtually absent from southern war correspondence. From officers to enlisted men, Rebel soldiers drew from the familiar repertoire of stereotypes crafted by their polemical writers in denouncing the vile, savage, fanatical, coarse, and avaricious race of Yankees who were descending like Vandals upon their beloved South.

In his study of the correspondence of Confederate combatants Bell Irvin Wiley concluded that southern soldiers of all ranks and social classes shared a common and unifying hatred of Yankees. They hated them not only because they had invaded and were destroying their homeland but also because they believed their enemy "to be an unsavory sort of people who came from a low and vulgar background." Southern polemical writers had succeeded in convincing the soldiers of the Confederacy that the North was sending to overrun their homeland a mass of debased, savage, and unprincipled invaders who were completely alien from and inferior to them in character and spirit.

South Carolina volunteer Alexander Cheves Haskell reflected the standard prejudices of the southern soldier in a letter in which he discussed the possibility of an attack on the newly established Confederate capital of Richmond in May 1861. "I much fear," he wrote, "that the Yankee horde have forgotten the laws of war and have not *natural honour* and chivalry enough to suggest them on the conduct they enforce." Haskell was just as inclined as his counterparts in the Union army to expect the most savage conduct from the enemy. He predicted that northern troops would "hang or otherwise murder any prisoners they catch at first "and would "keep on at it until fire and sword [had] driven them trembling and suppliant to ask for mercy."[60]

In addition to conveying his low opinion of Federal troops, Haskell's correspondence also shows that if northerners like Emerson could compare southerners to glittering and deadly serpents, southerners were willing use equally unflattering animal imagery to describe Yankees. He was not content merely to condemn them as "savages" descending on Richmond to "glut" on Virginia "plunder." He also compared them to "ferocious monkeys which I believe the Spanish proverb makes the most cruel wicked and capricious of tyrants." North Carolina Confederate Peter Hairston would have agreed with Haskell that there was but one response to the armed aggression of a race distinguished not by its nobility of conduct but by its wolfish ferocity. "I do not wish this war to end," he declared, "until this mercenary horde which has invaded us has been driven back to their dens and learned that lesson of humiliation which we will be sure to teach them and all the southern blood which they have shed shall be fully avenged."[61]

When they tired of comparing Yankees with monkeys or wolves, southern soldiers compared them with the worst and lowest forms of human beings they could think of. Sometimes they echoed the vocabulary of northerners, referring to Union soldiers as "ruffians." Haskell used this term when he boasted that if ever parents were capable of feeling "gratification in having sons it must be when they can be given to protect their country and their homes from the brutal ruffians (for such they really are) who are invading with murder and plunder for their war cry and incentive." In other letters, as we have seen, they referred to Yankee invaders as a "horde," alluding to the legendarily fierce and cruel Mongol army of Genghis Khan that had devastated and subdued medieval Russia. One Confederate soldier, for example, angrily described the Union army that southern forces were about to meet on the field of battle as a "cursed horde of northern Hessians and hirelings."[62]

Of all the derogatory terms employed by Johnny Reb, however, his favorite was the one also favored by the civilian population: *Vandal*. To the southern imagination this word conveyed the essence of the barbaric northern race that had invaded the aristocratic South, just as barbaric northern European races earlier in history had descended upon imperial Rome. Mississippian William Nugent probably had this sort of linguistic provenance in mind when he predicted that despite the early loss of New Orleans, General Beauregard would ultimately serve as an "instrument in the hands of God, to work out our salvation and redeem us from the polluting tread of our Vandal invaders." And North Carolinian H. C. Kendrick expressed the emotions of thousands of his fellow Confederates when, just before his death at Gettysburg, he professed in a letter to his father that he lived "to hate the base usurping Vandals." "If it is a sin to hate them," he avowed, "then I am guilty of the unpardonable one."[63]

Like their polemicists, the South's soldiers were fond of imagining their cursed Vandal enemy as the corrupt and inferior product of the promiscuous mixing of races that had taken place after the Revolution in the northern states. Speaking to his troops on the eve of battle, Confederate General T. C. Hindman reminded them that the enemy they were about to engage had "no feeling of mercy.... His ranks are made up of Pin Indians, Free Negroes, Southern Tories, Kansas Jayhawkers, and hired Dutch cutthroats." Hindman's demographic catalog was an eccentric one, but his purpose in presenting such a list would have been obvious enough to his troops. He wanted to remind them that Yankee soldiers, unlike southern fighters, possessed no racial homogeneity. They were not the armed representatives of a self-respecting people and a coherent culture, and they had entered the war with no real ideals and no concept of soldierly honor. In sum, Hindman thundered to his men, northern soldiers were "bloody ruffians" who had "invaded your country, stolen and destroyed your property, murdered your neighbors, outraged your women, driven your children from their homes, and defiled the graves of your kindred."[64]

The image of northerners as an invading race of mongrels was informed by a corresponding vision of swarms of inferior European immigrants infesting the North's urban slums, eagerly recruited and hurled into battle against the flower of southern chivalry. It was the suspect racial composition of the invading Yankee army that convinced Peter Hairston that the newly established Confederacy required "every man to do his whole duty." Truly it was a duty from which he could not honorably shrink when he realized that by responding to its call he would "assist in shielding North Carolina from invasion by the most merciless horde that ever plundered any country. All accounts from the North represent them as almost frantic and appealing to the lowest and vilest passions of the starving multitudes in their cities to induce them in enlist."[65]

Southern warriors assumed that the racially impure offspring of "the starving multitudes" of the North would fight poorly, and they often expressed scorn for the combat skills and battlefield behavior of northern soldiers, particularly in the early stages of the war. William Nugent conveyed this characteristic scorn in his description of the capture of four Federal officers. "Three of them are 'Germans,'" he observed with casual disgust, "and the other is from Missouri." Nugent seems to have expected these captive officers to display a deficiency of manly resolve, and he was not disappointed in his expectations. None of them, he reported with amazement, knew precisely what he was fighting for, nor did they even seem interested in being exchanged so that they might fight again. For Nugent the dull, hapless Germanized Yankee officers he described with such distaste were contemptible representatives of a culture bereft of all sense of manly courage and nobility. Virginian John Hampden Chamberlayne expressed his detestation of northern soldiers even more superciliously. Yankees, he observed, were "scum, spawned of prairie mud." Incapable of true valor, they had opted instead to become the "world's wonders of brutality."[66]

Like southern civilians, when Dixie's soldiers wearied of excoriating their northern foe as the detestable spawn of a hybridized race, they could shift their point of view with facility and imagine them with equal aversion as the vile offspring of a race of base and fanatical Puritans. Henry Higginbotham's reference to a possible attack on Mobile as the work of "our *'puritan' friends*" reflects the common southern rhetorical coupling of *Puritan* with *Yankee*. And as southerners had been wont to do before the Civil War, Confederate soldiers had no difficulty identifying the two most damning traits of the Puritan character: fanaticism and avarice. Tennessee soldier Sam Watkins battened zestfully on these despicable qualities in this passage from his war journal: "These cursed Yankees are invading our country, robbing our people and desolating our land, and all under the detestable and damning name of Union. Our representatives in Congress have been fighting them for fifty years. Compromise after compromise has been granted by the South. We have used every effort to conciliate those at the North. They have turned a deaf ear to every plea. They saw our country rich and prosperous, and have come indeed, like a gang of robbers, to steal our property and murder our people."[67]

For Watkins, as for many other southern soldiers, northern fanaticism was the direct product of the region's Puritan racial inheritance. And he satirized this intolerance by putting the following absurd pronouncements into the mouth of a representative Yankee: "We came over in the *Mayflower*, and we used to burn witches for saying that the sun rose in the east and set in the west, because the sun neither rises nor sets, the earth simply turns on its axis, and we know, because we are Pure(i)tans."[68] Watkins here faithfully embraced the widely shared conviction that the war the South was fighting had been precipitated not by deeply felt differences over southern slavery but by crazed Puritan intransigence. Like other southerners, he indulged himself with the idea that had Puritans not gone to war abolish slavery, they would have initiated hostilities on the basis of some other equally ludicrous prejudice.

Southern soldiers were thus convinced of the key role Puritan fanaticism had played in fomenting civil strife. Despite the sustained force of such irrational zeal, however, William Nugent expressed the equally strong opinion of southern combatants that this diseased Puritan idealism would be ultimately checked by the Puritan's consuming avarice. Nugent predicted confidently that when Yankees finally began to reckon the frightful costs of the conflict they had initiated with such fervor, the northern will to fight would collapse and the world would ultimately hear the sound of "Southern and Western soldiers marching to the proud emporium of northern trade—New York." Edmund Dewitt Patterson of the Ninth Alabama Regiment agreed that the mammon-worshiping denizens of the North would not bear the burdens of a costly war indefinitely. He was certain that the region, "so long accustomed to receive her countless thousands from the South, would not willingly sacrifice her share in the profits accruing from Southern trade."[69] Fear of financial ruin brought on by the disruption of the profitable cotton trade would finally bring a race of Yankee shopkeepers to its knees.

On the few occasions when southern soldiers actually come face to face with the northern people, they seemed grimly pleased to have had confirmed their preconceptions about the Yankee's meanness of temper and his cupidity. John Hampden Chamberlayne's brief incursion with his Virginia regiment into western Maryland in 1862 convinced him that he had entered not a neighboring state but a "foreign country." It was a land inhabited by a low-minded hybrid race, the unfortunate product of "dutch instincts dashed . . . by Yankee blood." Assuming the posture of a refined Old Dominion aristocrat, Chamberlayne described with a mixture of disgust and condescension a people whose minds disregarded "everything except . . . the pursuit of gain." He believed that for such a coarse tribe of Scrooges a well-functioning and ordered society like that of the South was impossible, and he was convinced that an elevated and humane social tone could not be expected in a benighted place like western Maryland, where people thought about nothing but "work, work, work" and "making money."[70]

Chamberlayne ultimately dismissed his Maryland subjects as a contemptible racial amalgam of German and Puritan, a mixture offering no hope for future refinement. The proud Cavalier scornfully concluded that northerners were united in embracing as a article of their commercial faith the belief "that he is worthiest who most unremittingly toils with his hands" or who withers his imagination "with years of mechanic toil over Day Book and Ledger; any thing else being blank heresy and schism."[71] Like Sam Watkins, he seems to have understood the Civil War not as conflict brought about by the issue of slavery but as one precipitated by the incompatibility of temper between two distinct peoples: an aristocratic, gracious, and high-minded southern race and an inferior northern race, descended from Germans and Puritans and bound by their secular dogmas of avarice, social leveling, and cultural mediocrity.

In taking the field of battle against an inferior northern foe—whether they styled that foe a degraded racial hybrid or a Puritan-descended fanatic—southern soldiers were ever mindful and confident of their own exalted racial inheritance. Indeed, most of them seem to have been absolutely convinced that they were the offspring of England's noble Cavaliers. Sam Watkins communicated this conviction with heartfelt emotion when he described the members of his company readying themselves for their first battle against a better-armed and better-outfitted Union force. "The blood of the old Cavaliers," he wrote proudly, "tingled in our veins. We did not feel that we were serfs and vagabonds. We felt that we had a home and a country worth fighting for, and, if need be, worth dying for."[72]

There is no doubt that the Norman race myth concocted by southern polemicists in the 1850s was a significant element in wartime Cavalier sentiments such as those expressed by Watkins. And it became an integral part of the exhortations that helped to boost morale and propel southern warriors into battle. The myth was neatly encapsulated in a rousing sermon delivered to Tennessee troops that Watkins reported in his war journal. The minister assured his audience that "we of the South had descended from the royal and aristocratic blood of the Huguenots of France, and of the Cavaliers of England." Yankees, by contrast, "were the descendants of the crop-eared Puritans and witch burners, who came over in the *Mayflower* and settled at Plymouth Rock." The Rebel divine argued that two races so distinct could never peacefully coexist. He ended his sermon in a fine fury of religious zeal by vowing to the troops that if southern knights would vanquish the wretched Puritan spawn on the battlefield, "he and his brethren would fight the Yankees in this world, and if God permit, chase their frightened ghosts in the next, through fire and brimstone."[73]

Such rousing rhetoric sent Rebels off to battle. After their military engagements they often celebrated their victories against the despised enemy with more hyperbole, wrapping themselves in the raiment of both the Roman warrior and the medieval Norman knight. In his address to a town he had liberated from Ulysses Grant's forces, Confederate General Van Dorn pulled out all rhetorical stops the celebrate his military triumph, invoking the spirit of Caesar, the providence of God, and the chivalric honor of a Walter Scott romantic hero. "In the language of Caesar," he declared to the enthusiastic townspeople, "*veni, vidi, vici,* and it is done in the name of the God of battles and through the prowess of southern chivalry." In the Scott tradition, Van Dorn described war as a means of illustrating the gallant, honorable, and purely patriotic character of his Rebel troops. "It was love of you fair ladies that urged us to your rescue," he dashingly claimed. "It was love of country," he more somberly declared, "that versed our arms to break the great backbone of Grant's Grand Army."[74]

Even more than love of country, love of honor remained a crucial element in the southern soldier's refusal to submit to Yankee domination. Indeed, southern warriors were convinced that only by stubbornly resisting subjugation could they retain the sense of personal honor that was essential to the characters and reputations of gentlemen who proudly claimed the blood of Norman knights. Both the southerner's belief in his aristocratic descent and his attestation of honor were heartfelt and sincere, but they were also beliefs that conveniently masked the fact that the Confederacy's destructive war for independence was being waged so that it might maintain the institution of chattel slavery. It is telling that the huge reality of slavery was nowhere factored into A. C. Haskell's equation of war. Instead, for him, as for nearly all who styled themselves southern gentlemen, honor was the dominant and most crucial term. Haskell was certain that the Civil War had little or nothing to do with liberty. It was rather a war "of subjugation and extermination" precipitated by "one side," the northern side. The South had nobly taken up arms in "just and righteous defense of *honor* and families." Southerners had never intended to destroy the North, he insisted, but brutal Yankee aggression had "spurred" in their courageous hearts "all the rage and hate that can be excited by the approach of an unpious, piratical, bloodthirsty invader."[75]

William Nugent gave the honorable ideal more personal definition when he wrote to his wife expressing his regret at having been taken away from her by the exigencies of war. In his letter he lovingly conveyed to her sentiments worthy of a Richard Lovelace lyric or a seventeenth-century Cavalier's billet-doux. "If the opportunity could now be afforded me," he told her, "I would give all I have to be with you and fold you in my arms once more. There are, however, duties and responsibilities resting upon me which if I did not properly discharge I should be unworthy of the wealth of love you have bestowed upon me and recreant to all that a man of honor considers noble."[76] It is not hard to find expressions of love and longing like Nugent's in the correspondence of northern soldiers. But nowhere in the letters of Union warriors can one find this particularly southern fusion of romantic love with martial honor. Nugent's sentiments were those of a southern, not a northern, American consciousness.

As a matter of course, southern soldiers assumed that Yankees were incapable of understanding honor and manifesting honorable conduct in war. The dashing and elusive Virginia cavalryman John S. Mosby was amused by the persistent failure of the Union army to capture him, but he was not amused that, "baffled in their attempts," northern soldiers had dishonorably threatened "to retaliate on citizens for my acts." Such dastardly conduct steeled his determination to continue his sneak attacks on the enemy, for he was "not prepared for any . . . degrading compromise with the Yankees."[77]

Given the southern warrior's assurance of his nobility and his aristocratic lineage, it is hardly surprising that he considered himself superior as a soldier to his base Yankee adversary and that he believed vindication and victory on the battlefield to be inevitable. Kendrick advanced the opinion common among southern troops in the early stages of the war that the Confederacy could not lose, despite obvious disparities in population, wealth, and industrial capacity between North and South. How would it be possible, he asked, "for a low, a degraded set of Northern people to be victorious over a noble and respectable squad of Southerners? Men that are fighting through a pure motive?" Even toward the end of the conflict many Confederate soldiers refused to accept the fact that their noble race was headed for ignominious defeat at the hands of the same vile Yankees whose fighting skills they had earlier in the conflict so denigrated. Less than three months before Lee's surrender at Appomattox, Edward Guerrant expressed the bitter and unbending pride of a people who had entered the Civil War possessed by a feeling of their absolute superiority and who were now loath to surrender it. "With a glorious, noble, band of devoted enlightened patriots, especially among the women (blessed women, mothers of all that is great and good) war, eternal war, would be preferable to any compromise of our honor."[78]

Of course, not all southerners faced defeat with their sense of the righteousness of their cause and their hatred of the Yankee aggressor intact. Robert Patrick no doubt expressed the sentiments of more pragmatic Rebels when he made this mordant resolution: "I think I shall make this my motto in the future. Never appeal to arms, if the same end can be arrived at by argument." Years of war had sharpened Patrick's judgment, and he saw clearly that the blood that had been shed in such appalling quantities was on the hands of fanatics from both regions. "If only I had the fanatic of the North and the fire eaters of the South, in equal numbers in a pen together," he vowed bitterly, "I'd make 'dog eat dog.'"[79]

It is significant that Patrick expressed these sentiments in a "secret" diary. Had they been uttered publicly, they would have received a decidedly hostile response from most southerners. They certainly did not reflect the prevailing sentiments of southern war correspondents in 1865. Much more typical were the agonized reflections of Henry St. John Dixon. "Oh god," he wrote to his father a month after surrender, "that I should live to see my colors lowered to such a foe! To see my nation thus pass away!"[80] The South's gallant warriors had been defeated, but that defeat prompted few of them to reassess their opinion of the victorious but, in their minds, still debased Yankee foe. And it prompted few to reconsider whether their violent attempt to create a southern Confederacy and their trumpeting of a unique race of southern Cavaliers had been ultimately an exercise in social fantasy and self-destruction.

8
Poetry Fights the Civil War

In his poem "The Wound Dresser" Walt Whitman adopts a persona and a point of view unprecedented in the annals of war poetry. The voice of Whitman's poem is not that of a warrior; neither is it that of an observer of or a commentator on the conflicts of the battlefield. The speaker is instead a nurse "bearing bandages, water and sponge / straight and swift" to the wounded in his care. And he is followed in his gruesome hospital rounds by an attendant who carries a "refuse pail / soon to be filled with clotted rags and blood, emptied, and filled again." In the course of introducing his readers to one after another of his patients, Whitman's persona brings us to the cot of a young soldier whose hand has been recently amputated. He describes this scene with both shocking clarity and extraordinary empathy:

> From the stump of the arm, the amputated hand,
> I undo the clotted lint, remove the slough, wash off the matter and blood,
> Back on his pillow the soldier bends with curv'd neck and side-falling head,
> His eyes are closed, his face is pale, he dares not look on the bloody stump,
> And has not yet look'd on it.[1]

Modern readers who are acquainted with the repugnant and shocking war descriptions of novels such as Ernest Hemingway's *A Farewell to Arms* or of poems such as Randall Jarrell's "The Death of the Ball Turret Gunner" may not fully appreciate the extent of Whitman's accomplishment in "The Wound Dresser" and in the other Civil War poems that make up his *Drum Taps* collection. The revolutionary nature of these poems lies in part in the poet's refusal to glorify war, his insistence on confronting us with its cruelties and, in the case of "The Wound Dresser," on bringing us into contact with the war not though the eyes of a soldier but through the experience of a humble nurse. Whitman's greatness as a war poet is also manifest in his refusal to allow his poem to be a vehicle of propaganda and his concomitant rejection of simplistic moral distinctions between "good" northern soldiers and "bad" southern ones. The maimed soldier could be any man, black or white, northern or southern. Though Whitman was a passionate opponent of slavery and an equally passionate supporter of the Union, his unerring poetic instincts led him in *Drum Taps* and in *Memories of President Lincoln* to the understanding that in the extremity of war, suffering and courage are not terms specific to a particular nation or region; they are a part of all human experience. Whitman's masterful combining of concretely powerful imagery with deep thematic vision has prompted Edmund Wilson to praise his poems of the Civil War as "the best poetry . . . written during the war on the subject of war."[2]

One might easily carry Wilson's praise for Whitman one step further by asserting that his work represents not only the best but, practically speaking, the only poetry of lasting esthetic merit to come out of America's epic civil conflict. With the exception of a few appealingly ironic and skeptical poems penned by Ambrose Bierce years after he had completed his distinguished service in the Union army, the poetic landscape of the Civil War is a metaphorical wasteland, an artistic terrain of shocking banality. In this context Wilson's observation in *Patriotic Gore* that "the period of the Civil War was not at all a favorable one for poetry" should be read as a masterful exercise in understatement.[3]

How can one explain why a conflict that so completely enlisted the profoundest feelings and the most deeply held ideals of both sections of this nation resulted in war poetry of such paltry quality? One answer may be that the extraordinary intensity of the passions unleashed by the Civil War made it difficult for poets of ordinary and even better-than-ordinary merit to write verse that expressed those passions authentically and compellingly. Ironically, the very strength of America's convictions, whether for slavery or for its abolition, for Union or for Confederacy, probably militated against artistic refinement both above and below the Mason-Dixon. Poets of respectable gifts—from northerners such as Oliver Wendell Holmes and John Greenleaf Whittier to southerners like Sidney Lanier—were so consumed by notions of right and justice that they were incapable of rising above or separating themselves from these notions and examining them with dispassionate irony. They failed to embody in their poetry what F. Scott Fitzgerald has termed the supreme quality of a "first-rate intelligence" (he might also have called it a first-rate creative intelligence): the "ability to hold two opposed ideas in the mind at the same time, and still retain the ability to function."[4]

Poets from the warring sections seem at the time to have been fully aware of the banal quality of the poetic effusions emitting from the opposing side.

Providence newspaperman Howard Brownell expressed the common Yankee opinion that southern poetry was bound to be bad and that the South's warriors were fated to be lowered into the earth absent poetic tributes of lasting beauty. They were, indeed, "gone—aye me!—to the grave,/and never one note of song," for the muse might conceivably "weep for the brave,/but how shall she chant the wrong?"[5] Brownell's depiction of the Civil War poetic scene was only partly accurate. Southern poetry was indeed blighted by its unswerving devotion to the myths and pieties of its culture, but northern critics were in no position to gloat. Whitman's *Drum Taps* was a happy accident, a miraculous expression of a single magisterial and transcendent poetic vision. In reality, northern war poets were crippled by the same enthrallment to cultural myths that blighted the creations of their southern counterparts. Both northern and southern Civil War poetry sank ingloriously into repetitive bombast, rehashing at mind-numbing length the dogmas of the polemical essayists from both regions that had dominated sectional discourse during the contentious decade of the 1850s. Prominent among these dogmas was the myth of an aristocratic Norman southern race in battle with the Saxon-descended heirs of New England Puritans.

From the outset of the Civil War, southern poets were absolutely clear in their minds about the kind of men who were representing their new nation on the battlefield. They were the Cavalier inheritors of a race of Norman-descended Englishmen, and they possessed a superior aristocratic blood that would vouchsafe victory to the newly established Confederacy in its struggle for independence. Mrs. C. A. Warfield of Kentucky presented the basic elements of this race myth in her "Southern Chant of Defiance."

> You have no such blood as theirs,
>   For the shedding:
> In the veins of cavaliers
>   Was its heading.
> You have no such stately men
> In your abolition den,
> Marching on through foe and fen,
>   Nothing dreading!

Warfield's high-blooded southern Cavaliers were engaged in a mortal struggle with a race of English-descended Puritans whose values and aims were totally antagonistic to those of the South. In the words of poet Kate Brownlee

Sherwood, the "tread of war" was now "thundering through the land," and "Puritan and Cavalier" were fatefully "clinching neck and hand." The enemy Puritans of the North might possess superior numbers and greater industrial capacity, but the superior mettle of an aristocratic southern race would be ultimately vindicated in battle. Yankees might win occasional triumphs, but Anne Pryre Dennies was confident that such victories would be "fleeting, for the hour is drawing near / when the war-cry of [the South's] Cavaliers shall strike his startled ear."[6]

Dixie's war poets, like the southern polemicists of the 1850s, were careful to link their aristocratic Cavalier blood to their mythic French-Norman racial inheritance. The author of "A Ballad for the Young South" proudly denied any blood link between the Confederacy's exalted Norman-descended warriors and the fanatical, ill-bred Puritan hordes that sought to destroy the new nation and bend proud and aristocratic southerners to the Yankee's arbitrary will:

> Men of the South! Ye have no kin
> With fanatics or fools;
> You are not bound by breed or birth
> To Massachusetts rules.
> A hundred nations gave their blood
> To feed those healthful springs,
> Which bear the seed of Jacques Bonhomme
> With that of Bourbon Kings.

Though many nations had contributed tithes of blood to the establishing of a New World southern race, the poet asserted that "Huguenotic will" and "Norman grace and chivalry" were among the most important characteristics of a noble people who had no affinity for the Yankee race's "bigot gloom / or pious plunder's art."[7]

Given the South's conviction of its superior aristocratic racial lineage, it is no surprise that the region's war poets celebrated the chivalrous nature of the southern warrior. Such chivalry was the inherent quality of men descended from the knightly legions of William the Conqueror. Dixie's poets waxed rapturously over "The South! The South! My own beautiful South / Land of Chivalry / Home of Liberty!" Indeed, chivalry was believed to mark every aspect of the new southern nation, an assumption on proud display in the inane chorus of a poem entitled "Chivalrous C. S. A.":

> Chivalrous, chivalrous people are!
> Chivalrous, chivalrous, people are!
> In C. S. A.! In C. S. A.!
> Aye, in chivalrous C. S. A.![8]

Not surprisingly, Virginians considered themselves the most chivalrous of all southerners. In Frank Ticknor's opinion, the Old Dominion's warriors who were serving under J. E. B. Stuart in the Shenandoah Valley campaigns were

> The knightliest of the knightly race,
> Who, since the days of old,
> Have kept the lamp of chivalry
> Alight in hearts of gold.

Another Virginian, Margaret Junkin Preston, apotheosized Stonewall Jackson and the troops who served under him as "cool knights, and true as ever drew / their swords with knightly Roland."[9]

Those who hailed from the Old Dominion may have considered themselves a bit more refined than their fellow Confederates, but in truth most white southerners from the banks of the Potomac to the Rio Grande seem to have believed that they were members of a race distinguished for its aristocratic refinement and chivalric instincts. Armed with such chivalry, as the author of a "Southern Battle Chorus" contended, how could southerners not prevail against a "hireling ruffian throng" of Yankee soldiers?

> Southrons on! No stain e'er rested
> On our proud, chivalric name—
> Scoff of yonder race detested—
> On! For vengeance, home and fame!
> On! Our flag waves gladly o'er us,
> Flashing swords our way shall clear,
> God is with us, they quail before us—
> Strike! For all we hold most dear.[10]

Dixie's war poetry provides ample evidence of southerners' determination to define themselves not only as a chivalrous people but also as a noble martial race struggling manfully to fend off scurrilous Yankee challenges to their honor. Indeed, slavery is scarcely ever mentioned in southern war poetry, but the South's apprehension about the threat to individual and regional honor is commonly expressed. For South Carolinian Henry Timrod, the firing of Confederate guns on Fort Sumter had been a responding action clearly precipitated by a northern challenge to southern integrity. In his lyric "Carolina" he urged his people, like their "own proud armorial" ancestors, to "fling down thy gauntlet to the Huns, / and roar thy challenge from thy guns." In "Dixie," Arkansas poet Albert Pike contended that the Confederacy was fighting not primarily to preserve slavery but in response to "faith betrayed, and pledges broken, / wrongs inflicted, insults spoken." Dixie's honor required a manly and noble response to such vile Yankee perfidy. Amazingly, southerners were so obsessed with the threat to their honor posed by Yankee political and cultural aggression that they frequently imagined themselves, not their black chattel, as slaves—slaves of northern arrogance and political domination. The writer of "God Save the South" was typical in his exhortation to the "sons of the South" to bestir themselves and break the bonds of subservience to the North. "Strike till the brand shall break," he urged, "strike for dear Honor's sake."[11]

Like the seventeenth-century Cavaliers whom southerners conceived to be their direct ancestors, Dixie's poets equated the preservation of the Confederacy's martial honor with their reverence for the southern lady, representing in her purity and refinement the highest ideals of the region's plantation culture. In "The Cavalier's Glee" Captain Blackford Mason imagined the war as a soldierly performance staged for the edification of the bright-eyed ladies who faithfully waited for the South's Cavaliers on the home front:

> The path to honor lies before us,
> Our hated foemen gather fast;
> At home bright eyes are sparkling for us,
> And we'll defend them to the last.

In a similar vein Virginian Susan Tally lamented that the Confederacy's knights had been forced to bid adieu to "loving eyes," yet she acknowledged that no genuine southern warrior could linger at home with his beloved "when honor calls." She also implicitly understood that in defending his new nation's honor the southern cavalier was also defending the honor and winning the approbation of those "loving eyes" he had so reluctantly left behind.[12]

There were immense psychological benefits for the South in poetically celebrating the Civil War as a conflict undertaken in the defense of honor, an honor inseparable from the honor of the virtuous and pure southern ladies who were for Dixie's warriors an object of veneration. After all, it was far prettier to imagine oneself fighting for duty and love than it was to accept the more pragmatic explanation that the Confederacy was fighting primarily to preserve the institution of chattel slavery. Too often in the sectional debates that had preceded the war, abolitionists had to the South's vexation insisted on associating with Dixie's peculiar institution the very same vices of materialism and human exploitation that southerners had been so fond of associating with Puritan mammon worship. Chivalric seventeenth-century notions of manly honor and worship of the lady effectively removed the spotlight from the thorny social and moral issues associated with slavery. They provided for the newly minted citizens of the Confederacy a noble and immeasurably more inspiring justification for secession and war.

The propensity of southern war poets to merge love of honor with love of ladies helps to explain why, when reading southern war poetry, one often feels as though transported back in time to the England of Richard Lovelace. In a poem entitled "My Order," for example, a southern soldier promises, like his Cavalier ancestors, to wear his belle's flower beneath his jacket as an "order" to strike boldly against the enemy. In accepting this chivalric injunction the poem's protagonist becomes like the seventeenth-century gallant who charged "home with fiery Rupert / in the van of old England's best blood." A similar directive is promulgated in "The Homespun Dress":

> And now, young man, a word to you:
> If you would win the fair,
> Go to the field where honor calls,
> And win your lady there.[13]

Lovelace's martial lyrics had expressed the same concept much more subtly. But though manifestly less felicitous in expression than England's Cavalier lyricists, the South's war poets seem to have been just as sincere as their English predecessors in their sentiments concerning honor.

The South's preoccupation with preserving its honor and its conflation of that ideal with its idealization of the southern lady help to explain how Dixie seemed sincerely to view its attack on Fort Sumter not as an act of aggression but as an action initiated by stalwart southern warriors in response to a long series of abolitionist aggressions that had culminated in the election of Abraham Lincoln. The most terrible prospect that a society founded on the aristocratic ideal of honor could imagine was the prospect of a noble, slave-owning southern race submitting passively to the insults and aggressions of an inferior northern race of abolitionists and Puritan fanatics. To honor-obsessed southerners, the word *submission* was the vilest in their vocabulary, for how could servile compliance command the respect either of the enemy or of the beloved southern ladies whose honor they had pledged to defend? It was just such compliance and loss of honor that the attack on Fort Sumter had forestalled. One Charleston poetaster captured perfectly the South's sense of pride and relief at having escaped the humiliation of bowing to Yankee insolence: "The fleet turned slowly southward, we saw the last ship go, / we had saved old Carolina from the insults of the foe."[14]

In the fateful months after the fall of Fort Sumter the disgrace of submission continued to be a powerful poetic argument advanced to encourage southerners to remain firm in the face of Lincoln's ominous mobilization for war. Southern poets over and over again equated submission to Yankees with dishonor and bondage. Though slavery was almost never directly mentioned, southern war verse drew a direct link between the emancipation of its slave population and the concomitant enslavement of the region's highborn white race. For the author of a poem entitled "Invocation," the real question for Dixie was not whether southern shackles would be removed from the black race by force of Yankee arms, but whether "northern shackles" would ever be allowed to "disgrace / a proud and noble Southern race." In more specific contexts southern poets invoked the horrors of submission to encourage residents of border states to spurn the Union and join the Confederacy. John R. Thompson refused to believe that Kentucky, "the land / of a Clay," would ever "submit to the brand / that disgraces the dastard, the slave," and he was confident that Kentuckians would successfully resist Yankee control. As he phrased it, "her own sons her own honor shall save." By contrast, Maryland's rapid and relatively bloodless submission to Union rule had, in the opinion of poet James Brewer, left an ignoble stain on the honor of its people. Now, he lamented, the sounds of craven submission echoed throughout the state:

> Hear it in the taunts of cowards,
> Who accept dishonor's stains;
> Hear it in the sullen clanking
> Of a state's ignoble chains.[15]

As the fury of the Civil War increased, the dishonor associated with defeat and submission remained a prominent theme of Confederate war verse. In "The Foe at the Gates" John Dickson Bruns opined that if Charleston was fated to fall to Union armies, then southerners were also fated to "die! As becomes a race of free-born men, / who will not crouch to wear the bondsman's chain." Any man who doubted the South's sacred cause, any who pragmatically questioned the war's eventual outcome, was pilloried as dishonorable and craven and was poetically exiled from the sacred precincts of the southern gentleman. In "Away with the Dastards Who Whine of Defeat" Paul Hamilton Hayne damned as "accurst" such southern vermin:

> The caitiffs who falter and flee from the strife,
> Who would slake at Dishonor's foul cess-pool the thirst
> Of a passion—the meanest and basest—for life![16]

For Hayne, as for most proud southerners, honorable death in battle was infinitely preferable to a life lived under the stigma of dishonorable and submissive cowardice.

There can be little doubt that the southerner's ardent embrace of the gentlemanly code of honor and his corresponding horror of dishonorable submission fired his resolve for war and maintained that resolve long after more practical people would have sued for peace. Only after the fall of Richmond and the flight of the remnants of the Army of Northern Virginia to Appomattox, when it became clear that there was absolutely no hope for sustaining the Confederacy, did Robert E. Lee surrender to Grant. But most southerners seem to have required such futile and last-ditch resistance as proof that they had fought to the bitter end with their honor intact. The eulogy entitled "Virginia Dead," which was offered up to those soldiers from the Old Dominion who had died for the Confederacy, could easily have been offered up to all the South's valiant Cavaliers who had laid down their lives for Dixie's sacred cause:

> Wherever Honor's sword is drawn,
> And Justice rears her head,
> Where heroes fall and martyrs bleed,
> There rest Virginia's dead.[17]

Southern versifiers who sought to trumpet the exalted qualities of their martial and aristocratic race found plentiful numbers of flesh-and-blood Confederate heroes on whom to focus their veneration, and they piously decorated the tombs of all their fallen heroes with chivalric verbal garlands. Dashing cavalry officers, such as Virginians Turner Ashby and "Jeb" Stuart, were particular favorites of the southern reading public, and upon their deaths in battle they were lavishly eulogized as epitomes of southern knighthood. John Reuben Thompson employed allusions to *Ivanhoe* and the Crusades to transform the deceased Ashby into a peerless representative of Norman aristocracy in mortal combat with debased hordes of Puritans:

> Well they learned, whose hands have slain him,
> Braver, knightlier foe
> Never fought 'gainst Moor or Paynim—
> Rode at Templestowe:
> With a mien how high and joyous,
> 'Gainst the hordes that would destroy us,
> Went he forth, we know.

"Dirge for Ashby" was an even more extravagant celebration of the brave and brilliant Virginia cavalryman. This poem favorably compared its deceased hero's mettle with a long line of legendary knights of equal courage and mettle, and it also evoked the polish and refinement that completed the portrait of the perfect noble warrior:

> Bold as the Lion's Heart—
> Dauntless and brave,
> Knightly as knightliest
> Bayard could crave;
> Sweet—with all Sidney's grace—
> Tender as Hampden's face—
> Who, who shall fill the space,
> Void by his grave?[18]

The poetic veneration attending Ashby at his death was surpassed by that lavished on Jeb Stuart after he was killed in battle in 1864. With his plumed hat, his jaunty yet steely courage, his impeccable manners, and his genteel appreciation for beautiful ladies, Stuart was particularly well suited for his Cavalier role, and the South's war poets often enlisted him to play that role to the hilt. In "Riding a Raid" Stuart himself entered the poem and exhorted his soldiers to follow him, not merely on a cavalry raid but on the path to chivalrous honor and glory: "Now each cavalier who loves honor and right, / let him follow the feather of Stuart to-night."[19]

Stuart's death, coming at a time when the South was facing the near certainty of defeat, elicited a strain of veneration that was especially somber and emotional. Winston Fontaine reverently praised him as "the princeliest scion of a royal race" and "the knightliest of his knightly name." Alas, his "imperial brow encrowned by Fame" now lay "pallid" on his mother country's breast.

No more, the poet lamented, would the Confederacy's beloved "courtly cavalier" ride off to "fright the Northman in his tent." Fontaine's poem dramatizes the fervor with which Dixie's poets embraced the myth of southern aristocracy, from the beginning of the war to the bitter end. In a prefatory note the author was careful to remind his readers that "General J. E. B. Stuart sprung from the Royal House of Scotland." His royal blood inheritance explained those knightly qualities that had so distinguished his military career and so embellished Fontaine's lyric.[20]

Even before the South's surrender, Jeb Stuart, like other of the Confederacy's venerated heroes, had left the realm of history and entered the poetic realm of southern legend. This transformation was given striking utterance in John R. Thompson's "Obsequies of Stuart":

> The Spanish legend tells us of the Cid,
> That after death he rode erect, sedately,
> Along his lines, even as in life he did,
> In presence yet more stately:
>
> And thus our Stuart, at this moment, seems
> To ride out of our dark and troubled story
> Into the region of romance and dreams,
> A realm of light and glory.[21]

Stuart now joined other dead heroes whom Dixie's poets were ushering into the southern pantheon well before the ending of hostilities at Appomattox.

Of all the South's military losses, none was so devastating as that of Stonewall Jackson. However, in rushing to eulogize him Dixie's poets were hard pressed to cast him in the mold of Cavaliers such as Ashby and Stuart, for Jackson was anything but an aristocratic Cavalier. In spirit and temperament he was a severe and plain-spoken Presbyterian hailing from the mountains of what is now West Virginia. Facing the challenge of turning Jackson into an idealized Norman warrior, Mrs. C. A. Warfield did her best with the materials at hand, invoking his Scottish lineage and enhancing it with references to Scotland's kings to suggest the enormity of the South's loss:

> Of thee as of the Douglas,
> We say with Scotland's king,
> "There is not one to take *his* place
> In all the knightly ring!"

In contrast to Warfield, H. L. Flash took an exceedingly rare tack in southern war poetry in his tribute "Stonewall Jackson." He eschewed his region's cherished celebrations of its soldier heroes as knights and, drawing on Jackson's stern and Calvinistic temperament, held him up as "the Moses of the South" who, leading God's chosen southern people, had broken "the house of bondage with his hand."[22]

If Stonewall Jackson furnished rather stringy metaphorical meat for Dixie's poetasters, there was heartier fare in the character of the Confederacy's other great general, Robert E. Lee. Though Lee was one of the few southern war heroes denied martyrdom in battle, he nonetheless attained through both his remarkable military genius and his exemplary integrity of character a peerless reputation in the southern mind. Indeed, by the later stages of the war Dixie's admiration had morphed into worship, and Lee, in the words of the author of "General Lee at the Battle of the Wilderness," had become "great Virginia's god-like son/ ... equal of her Washington."[23]

Like Ashby and Stuart, Lee was an appealing model for poets who sought to celebrate the chivalrous qualities of the South's warriors. And, like these fellow Virginians, he was typically draped in a mantle of medieval poetic trappings. Lee was especially useful to poets seeking not only to trumpet southern chivalry but also to discount the role of slavery as a casus belli, for his aristocratic gallantry was enhanced by his personal opposition to the institution of slavery. As the author of "General Robert E. Lee" pointed out, the great general had pledged his loyalty to the new Confederacy out of entirely idealistic motives that had nothing to do with political or social gain:

> As went the knight with sword and shield,
> To tourney or to battle field,
> Pledged to the lady fair and true,
> For whom his knightly sword he drew;
> You offered at your country's call,
> Your life, your fortune, and your all.[24]

For the purpose of idealizing the southern aristocrat, Lee was an even more valuable figure for southern poets than Jeb Stuart, for he epitomized not just the courage, flair, and sprightly chivalry of Stuart but all the more weighty and morally substantial characteristics of a noble, Norman-descended race. Even in the darkest days as the war ground down to its inevitable conclusion, Dixie could take solace in the knowledge that, just as Camelot could boast of King Arthur, their own race had produced an epitome of chivalric nobility, a man motivated not by love of slavery but by honor and a sense of duty to his native state and his new nation. Lee's calm graciousness, his natural dignity of manner, and his sense of family and tradition, combined with his self-denial, his abstinence, and his Christian piety, made him the perfect heir to Dixie's English Norman heritage. Even before Appomattox he had become, in Dixon Wecter's words, "the patriarch and oracle of the shattered South." And with the death of the Confederacy, southerners and their poets were left to wonder how God could ask such a race and such an oracle to submit to such a lowly adversary:

> Oh! Merciful God! Can it really be,
> This downfall awaits our gallant Lee,
> And the cause we counted right?
>
> That Lee at the head of his faithful band,
> The flower and pride of our southern land,
> Must yield to the hateful foe!

The perfect exemplar of the southern race had been forced to enact before General Ulysses Grant Dixie's horrible nightmare of submission.[25]

If Dixie's war poets were of the unanimous opinion that southerners constituted a noble race descended from Norman warriors, they were equally united in their assessment of the detestable Yankee race they were now engaging on the battlefield. Throughout the war southern versifiers parroted the racial mythology of the region's polemical essayists and editors, a mythology perhaps no more bluntly expressed than in *DeBow's Review*. Here an editorial note exhorted readers always to remember that "the Cavaliers, Jacobites, and Huguenots who settled the South, naturally hate, condemn and despise the Puritans who settled the North. The former are master races; the later, a slave race, descendants of the Saxon surfs."[26] By 1861, southern apologists had established a powerfully negative northern racial stereotype, and the Confederacy's poets would enthusiastically draw upon and embellish this grotesque image in their lyrics.

In the litany of vices associated with the degraded race of Yankees, fanaticism—a quality that Dixie believed could be attributed to Saxon-descended Puritans from at least the time of Oliver Cromwell—ranked among the most malignant. In southern eyes it was the northern race's narrow-minded conviction of its utter rightness and its absolute contempt for opposing opinion or compromise, not the South's insistence on maintaining slavery, that had led to civil war. In "South Carolina's Justification to the North," for example, the poet railed against the "base fanatics—canting preachers" who had "long tampered with our slaves," as well as against "northern abolition teachers" who had "southward flocked to find their graves." For this writer, as for countless other southerners, John Brown epitomized the treacherous and dishonorable essence of Puritan fanaticism:

> Old John Brown such welcome courted,
> When with murderous bands he came,
> With our rights and laws he sported,
> And dishonor shrouds his name.[27]

Like most of their compatriots, southern poets were certain that the fanaticism that had produced a demon like Brown had now infected all of New England's Puritans leaders, political and cultural, male and female. A scathing poetic indictment, "A Ballad for the Young South" transformed these moral monsters into a pack of mongrel dogs in rabid pursuit of their prey, the noble South:

> Hark to the howling demagogues—
> A fierce and ravenous pack—
> With nostrils prone, and bark and bay,
> Which run upon our track!
> The waddling bull-pup, Hale—the cur
> Of Massachusetts' breed—
> The moping mongrel, sparsely crossed
> With Puritanic seed—
> The Boston bards who join the chase
> With genuine beagle chime,
> And Sumner, snarling poodle pet
> Of virgins past their prime;
> And even the sluts of Women's Rights—
> Tray, Blanche, and Sweetheart, all—
> Are yelping shrill against us still,
> And hunger for our fall.[28]

The South's detestation of Puritan fanaticism was fortified by its conviction that the high ideals northerners proclaimed with such seriousness and such uncompromising fervor were profoundly tainted by self-interest and hypocrisy. The author of "The Cotton States' Farewell to Yankee Doodle" bitterly satirized the North's predilection for mischief making that, disguised as high idealism, had maliciously sought to destroy an essentially benign and paternalistic southern institution. In this poem Yankees are viewed as self-righteous hypocrites, consumed with the abstract idea of abolition and unconcerned about the deleterious practical effects such drastic action would have on freed blacks:

> Yankee Doodle strove with pains
> And Puritanic vigor
> To loose the only friendly chains
> That ever bound a nigger.
> But Doodle knows as well as I
> That when his zeal had freed 'em,
> He'd see a million niggers die
> Before he'd help to feed 'em.
> Yankee Doodle's grown so keen
> For every dirty shilling—
> Propose a trick, however mean,
> And Yankee Doodle's willing.[29]

The reference to the northern abolitionist's keen interest in a "dirty shilling" suggests another malignant quality of the northern race that, in combination with Puritan fanaticism, southerners believed, produced a particularly odious moral failing: Yankee mammon worship. Indeed, poets who defended the South were quick to note that the same New Englanders who had sanctimoniously condemned slavery had also benefited enormously from the cheap slave-produced cotton they had bought from southern planters to keep their mills profitably spinning. As one southern poet bitterly observed:

> Their parsons will open their sanctified jaws,
> And cant of our slave-growing sin, sir;
> They pocket the *profits*, while preaching the laws,
> And manage our cotton to spin, sir.[30]

Southern war poetry thus faithfully reflected the prevailing opinion in Dixie that Yankee avidity had combined with Yankee fanaticism to bring on the Civil War, and it also reflected the southerner's conviction that this mania for money and profit would ill serve the detested Yankees in their armed struggle with a noble southern people whose racial fiber was infused with honor, courage, and an aristocratic sense of noblesse oblige. Dixie's poets observed with scornful glee that the northerner's passionate devotion to mammon had been of little or no avail to him in his early contests with the South's noble warriors. In a poem "Written after the Battle of Manassas" the author employed a humorous allusion to Byron's "The Destruction of Sennacherib" to accent the victory of southern valor over northern greed and cowardice and to satirize the headlong retreat of Union forces back to Washington:

> "Yankee Doodle" came down, like the wolf on the fold,
> And his cohorts were greedy for plunder and gold,
> But, when met by cold steel and hot lead on the field,
> Mammon yielding to terror, the dastards all wheel'd;
> And there made, 'tis conceded, the best time by far,
> Yet recorded, throughout the long annals of war.[31]

Southern war poetry stands as proof that most southerners believed they were engaged in a fateful life-or-death struggle to preserve their aristocratic culture, their honor, and their way of life against an aggressive, powerful, and materialistic society bent on the destruction of their new Confederacy. Because of these convictions, their poetic descriptions of the enemy were mere caricatures, without the least nuance of psychological complexity or the faintest suggestion that Yankee soldiers might be human beings. Dixie's poets consequently availed themselves of every derogatory word in their possession to describe a craven, hypocritical, and mercenary race of Yankee aggressors. Southern war lyrics variously excoriated northern soldiers as "a batch of knaves," as "Yankee Hessians," as "Huns," as "a hireling Northern band" come "to desolate the land," as wolves "returned to the spoil," and as "Northern scum." These armed emissaries of a loathsome and barbaric race who seemed determined to devastate the South were not human. They were, in the typically overcharged verse of A. E. Blackmar's "The Southern Marseillaise," demons thirsting for southern blood:

> Shall fiends who basely plot our ruin,
> Unchecked, advance with guilty stride
> To spread destruction far and wide,
> With southron's blood their hands embruing?[32]

Such a monstrous and conscienceless enemy could be met and mastered only by the absolute resolve and courage of southern warriors through whose veins coursed the noble "southron" blood of Norman ancestors.

In their less heated and more composed moments when they had tired of demonizing the "Northman," Dixie's poetasters often fell back upon the favored term *Vandal* to describe their Yankee enemy. This word seemed to convey for southerners more fully than *Hun* or *Hessian*, or even *Saxon*, the barbaric nature of the northern race. In "My Maryland," James Ryder Randall exhorted that state's populace not to "yield the Vandal toll":

> Better the shot, the blade, the bowl,
> Than crucifixion of the soul.
> Maryland! My Maryland!

In terms very similar to Randall's, the anonymous author of "War Song" equated submission to a barbarous enemy with the crucifixion of the noble spirit not just of a single state but of an entire country:

> The Vandal hosts oppose us,
> We stand without a fear,
> Than crucify the spirit,
> Better the blade, the bier.[33]

For poets substituting specific for generic representations of Yankee villainy, two northern generals presented themselves as convenient objects of vilification: General Benjamin Franklin Butler and General William Tecumseh Sherman. Butler, popularly known to southerners as "Beast" Butler, had earned his nickname as military governor of the city of New Orleans in 1862 when, in response to the largely verbal abuse his troops had regularly received from the patriotic ladies of the Crescent City, he issued his infamous General Orders no. 28. This proclamation commanded that any "female," who "by word, gesture, or movement" insulted a Union soldier would be "regarded ... as a woman of the town plying her avocation."[34]

Southern reaction to Butler's order was predictably one of intense outrage, an outrage made more profound by the general's having chosen as the object of his wrath the southern gentleman's venerated and undefiled lady. Dixie's rage was further stoked by its sense of impotence, by the fact that there were no brave Cavaliers left in the occupied city to defend the honor of their ladies from such an humiliatingly sexual insult. Who but a ruffian race of Saxon barbarians, a people devoid of all notions of honor and respect for ladies, would have conceived of such an order? In "The Southern Oath" Rosa Vertner Jeffrey rose to hurl her rhetorical challenge to the enemy:

> Think ye, we'll brook the insults
> Of your fierce and ruffian chief,
> Heaped upon our dark-eyed daughters
> Stricken down and pale with grief?

For Paul Hamilton Hayne, as for Rosa Jeffrey, Butler's conduct had exposed northerners before to world as the vile, detestable, and base people that southerners had always known them to be. "We know thee now," he proclaimed with a mixture of joy and revulsion, "we know thy race!" Hayne believed that the Yankee's "dreadful purpose" now stood "revealed / naked before the nation's face."[35]

Though he held sway as the principal northern villain in the Civil War's early stages, by the end of the war Benjamin Franklin Butler had been completely eclipsed as the type of the demonic by General William Tecumseh Sherman. Sherman's destructive rampage through Georgia from Atlanta to the sea in the fall of 1864, followed by an equally devastating incursion into the Carolinas, earned him an enmity among southerners that would endure for generations. During the Civil War's early years Sherman had not been notably distinguished for his ferocity, but by the time his army took Atlanta he had come to an understanding of war that he would thereafter employ ruthlessly and articulate frequently and with powerful concision. With merciless clarity he defined the essence of warfare as "cruelty," a cruelty that he believed no one could hope to "refine." More ominously, he also defined it as "simply power unrestrained by constitution or compact." Charles Royster has observed that Sherman's "accepting the idea of limitless violence and his writing about making war on civilians as if such conduct were inevitable" in war were concepts that foreshadowed the military holocausts of World Wars I and II.[36]

If the Union general's concept of warfare was one that did not fully unfold in modern history until the twentieth century, Georgians and Carolinians could fairly claim to have been among the first victims of its initial and partial application. From the day Sherman's army marched out of Atlanta on November 12, 1864, until the day it burned most of the South Carolina capital city of Columbia on February 17, 1865, Union forces torched or pillaged nearly everything in their path worth destroying or plundering. Even southerners most obsessed by the specter of Yankee barbarism could not have anticipated the ferocity of this army and the thoroughness with which it accomplished its destruction. Sherman's March inflicted a deep and lasting trauma on the southern psyche, and it was a lurid prelude to the fall of the Confederacy.

Of the numerous poetic condemnations of Sherman's March, none was more bitter than Virginia French's "Shermanized." Indeed, the poet's sense of agony and outrage was so intense that it extended beyond Sherman himself to include a God who seemed to have sanctioned the victory of wrong over right, of evil over good:

> Where the golden crown of harvest trodden into ashes lies,
> And Desolation stares abroad with famine-phrenzied eyes;
> Where the wrong with iron-sceptre crushes every right we prized,
> There shall people groan in anguish—God! The right is Shermanized!

There was, however, one southern possession that French defiantly believed neither Sherman nor Satan himself could destroy: the valorous honor of the South's knightly warriors. And she implored the women of the South:

> ... never, *never* fail to weave above our "noble dead"
> The laurel garland due to deed of Valor's high emprize,
> And won by men whom *failure* could not sink, or—*Shermanize!*[37]

The North's poets did not remain silent in the face of the deluge of southern war verse libeling both their political and social ideals and their racial inheritance. Indeed, in response to these attacks northern poets embraced with pride the word that southerners bandied about with such scorn: *Puritan*. As their polemical writers had done in the years immediately preceding the Civil War, their poets answered the lyric invective of the South by glorying in the word and invoking the most exalted qualities they could associate with their Puritan racial tradition. As the nation plunged into civil war, northerners seem to have been almost as committed as southerners to the idea that America was divided into two profoundly different regions, North and South, as well as into two distinct races, Saxon-Puritans above the Mason-Dixon and Norman-Cavaliers below it. They would simply reverse the connotations that southern poets had attached to these racial myths.

Like southern versifiers, northern poets tended to understand the Civil War as a continuation in America of the original seventeenth-century struggle in England between Puritan Roundheads and the aristocratic Cavalier followers of King Charles. But unlike southern poets, they proudly identified with the Roundhead victors of that original civil conflict. For example, the author of "Ho! Sons of the Puritan" infused his northern call to arms with allusions to the great battles that America's Puritan ancestors had fought and won during the English Civil War:

> Ho! Sons of the Puritan! Sons of the Roundhead,
> Leave your fields fallow and fly to the war. . . .
> From green-covered Chalgrave, from Naseby and Marston,
> Rich with the blood of the Earnest and True,
> The war-cry of Freedom, resounding hath passed on
> The wings of two centuries, and come down to you.[38]

These lines clearly indicate why Yankee poets were so proud of their Puritan forebears. They believed that these religious rebels had been apostles of freedom. They also believed that the English Civil War had ultimately expanded the realm of democracy in England, and they were equally convinced that the current civil war, fought by the New World inheritors of these two antagonistic racial traditions, would again be won by Puritans and would again lead to an expansion of democratic boundaries. They were, in short, convinced that history was on their side in the New World, as it had been on the side of Cromwell's legions in the Old.

If history was on the side of freedom's expansion, northern poets concluded, then the Saxon race that had produced the freedom-loving English Puritans could proudly claim a preeminent place in the sweep of history. And if, as many of them averred, the genius of the English people resided in its instinct for freedom, then that racial genius was essentially Saxon, not Norman, in its composition. This Saxon racial myth was a crucial element in a poem by John Greenleaf Whittier entitled "To Englishmen," an appeal to the "English ruling class," which was thought to be generally "hostile or indifferent to the party of freedom" in America:

> Oh Englishmen! In hope and creed,
> In blood and tongue our brothers!
>
> "Thicker than water," in one rill
> Through centuries of story
> Our Saxon blood has flowed, and still
> We share with you its good and ill,
> The shadow and the glory.[39]

The poet was urging his aristocratic audience to imagine their English blood to be Saxon, like the blood of the North, not Norman, like that of the South.

Yankee poets generally accepted the notion that their racial stock could not claim the aristocratic lineage of their southern foes. But rather than being ashamed or cowed by their heritage, they expressed pride in the solid religious, moral, and political values that had sprung from a race of middle-class English workingmen. This pride is evident in Ralph Waldo Emerson's "Boston Hymn," in which God himself speaks to the early Puritan settlers of their destiny in New England:

> I will never have a noble,
> No lineage counted great:
> Fishers and choppers and ploughmen
> Shall constitute a state.

A similar sense of self-respect rings through the lines of Charles Godfrey Leland's "Northmen, Come Out!" as the poet exhorts his fellow Yankees to marshal themselves in their "strength and let them know / how working men to work can go." Leland was confident that just as the haughty followers of King Charles had been surprised by the vigor, courage, and competence of their Roundhead adversaries, their equally haughty southern heirs would receive a similar military comeuppance:

> Northmen come out!
> Come like your grandsires stern and stout;
> Though Cotton be of kingly stock,
> Yet royal heads may reach the block;
> The Puritan taught it once in pain,
> His sons shall teach it one again;
> Northmen come out![40]

Though northern poets might easily have associated their Puritan blood with an aptitude for enterprise and commerce, qualities that had helped to produce amazing prosperity in New England, such an association would have played into the hands of southern poetasters who were condemning northerners as hypocritical mammon worshipers. It was far more convenient and uplifting to link the Yankee race with its rural yeoman heritage, for the sturdy and independent northern farmer would contrast neatly and vividly with the haughty and aristocratic southern slave owner. Thus the North's war lyricists studiedly celebrated the bond between Puritan and yeoman ideals. William Bourne's "The New Reveille" issued a call to battle not to shopkeepers, bankers, or lawyers but to Yankee farmers, evoking in the process the patriotic rural associations of poems such as Emerson's "Concord Hymn":

> Come from the fields, O brave and sturdy yeoman!
> Come from the hearthstones where ye love to sing!
> Now is the hour to meet the bloody foeman,
> Then back victorious all your laurels bring![41]

Given the North's thorough emotional identification with the Puritan yeoman ideal, it is not surprising that the concept of southern honor carried little or no currency above the Mason-Dixon. The South's definition of honor had evolved from the ethos of the Old World landed gentry, and it tightly bound a gentleman's sense of personal worth to the acceptance of his self-definition by the larger community of his peers. Such an anachronistic concept could never have taken firm hold in what Bertram Wyatt-Brown has described as the more industrialized and urbanized, more "bourgeois and highly institutionalized" North.[42] It would be wrong to contend that personal honor was of little or no concern to northern men. But there can be no doubt that they embraced the idea with nowhere near the intensity of their brethren in the South and that their idea of honor tended to be much more aligned to their sense of morality and Christian duty.

One can measure the impact of the yeoman ideal on the northern conception of honor in Josiah Gilbert Holland's "The Heart of the War." Set in "a plain New England home," the poem describes a farmer who could have avoided the war and remained at home with his wife and children, but who chooses the path of duty to his country. As he tells his wife, "I'm sure you'd rather have me die / than not to bear my part." He follows his duty to his death, and the poem ends with this pathetic scene of domestic desolation:

> Peace in the clover-scented air.
> And stars within the dome;
> And underneath, in dim repose,
> A plain New England Home.
> Within a widow in her weeds
> From whom all joy is flown,
> Who kneels among her sleeping babes,
> And weeps and prays alone![43]

Holland's protagonist has chosen what southerners would have termed the course of *honor,* but that word so sacred to southern ears appears nowhere in this poem. The farmer believes his wife would expect him to bear his part, to do his duty. But, unlike southern war poetry, the sense of duty conveyed in this lyric is not primarily linked to the protagonist's sense of individual honor or to his concern for the honor of his wife, but rather to his sense of obligation to his country, his acceptance that he must bear his part in a collective national enterprise. The sensibility of the poem is anything but martial and chivalric. It expresses the sensibility of a common man, and its pathos is bourgeois rather than chivalric.

If, unlike in the South, questions of honor were not significantly involved in the North's decision to go to war, what did northerners believe they were fighting for? Their poetry suggests that most of them were fighting to save the Union, to preserve intact the United States of America. Their conviction that the Union must be saved was bound to an equally strong belief that its dissolution would deliver a potentially fatal blow to the concepts of liberty and justice upon which the national Constitution rested. Francis Janvier was among the most fervent in his poetic expression of these ideas:

> The Union! The Union! The hope of the free!
> Howsoe'er we may differ, in this we agree:
> Our glorious banner no traitor shall mar,
> By effacing a stripe, or destroying a star!
> Division! No, never! The Union forever!
> And cursed be the hand that our country would sever!

William Cullen Bryant was equally determined that nothing be allowed to destroy the sacred compact that bound the states in liberty:

> Knit they the gentle ties which long
> These sister states were proud to wear,
> And forged the kindly links so strong
> For idle hands in sport to tear—
> For scornful hands aside to throw?
> No, by our father's memory, no![44]

Poems like those by Janvier and Bryant provide ample support for Deborah Clifford's thesis that at the beginning of the Civil War "most northerners saw the approaching conflict as a crusade to save the Union." But as the war progressed toward an increasingly certain Union victory. anti-slavery poetic voices grew stronger and more assured. The "chain of the slave," W. W. Story proclaimed, had been "suffered so long." But "striving together" the North would break those oppressive links. In "Bring the Hero Home" General E. D. Baker thundered that "no soil of a traitor" should serve as a grave for the Union's "glorious dead":

> For liberty dwelt in his spirit;
> And free men should fashion his grave
> Beneath free humanity's banner,
> And not the cursed flag of the slave.

It was left to the Union's unofficial poet laureate, Ralph Waldo Emerson, to proclaim abolition as an integral part of the nation's war mission:

> Today unbind the captive,
> So only are ye unbound;
> Lift up a people from the dust,
> Trump of their rescue, sound![45]

The North's pronounced sense of moral duty and of its unique national mission, its understanding of the Civil War as a righteous struggle between the northern forces of good and the southern forces of evil, was nowhere given more powerful expression, and nowhere had a more profound or lasting impact on the nation's consciousness, than in Julia Ward Howe's great and moving "Battle-Hymn of the Republic." A New York native, Howe was living in Washington in the fall of 1861 when a friend suggested that she write more eloquent lyrics to be sung to the popular tune "John Brown's Body Lies A-Mouldering in the Grave." She accepted her friend's suggestion, and she later described the inspired composition of her lines this way: "I awoke in the gray of the morning twilight; and as I lay waiting for the dawn, the long lines of the desired poem began to twine themselves in my mind. Having thought out all the stanzas, I said to myself, 'I must get up and write these verses down, lest I fall asleep again and forget them.'"[46]

Luckily for the nation, Howe sprang up and wrote the stanzas down before going back to sleep. The lines she spontaneously composed that morning were inspired by both Old and New Testament scripture, and they conveyed the North's sense of righteous endeavor more powerfully than any other war lyric of the time by masterfully transforming the armies of the North into instruments of God's divine vengeance. Other northern poets, of course, had viewed the northern people as holy enforcers of Jehovah's will. In "The Watchers," for example, John Greenleaf Whittier had predicted in lines evocative of Howe's images that before the "hopeless quarrel" between North and South could cease, "the rod / must fall, the wine-press must be trod."[47] But Howe's poem was distinguished from poems like Whittier's both by the comprehensiveness of its biblical allusions and the rhetorical power of its utterance.

The sense of the divine wrath that was to be brought down upon the South by the Union army is most vividly presented in stanzas 1 and 3 of the poem. Howe skillfully employs allusions to the final New Testament Book of Revelation in stanza 1's justly famed reference to "the grapes of wrath" and to the opening Old Testament Book of Genesis in stanza 3's reference to the "Hero" who will "crush the serpent with his heel."[48] These allusions combine suggestively to convey the idea of God's omnipresent and active judgment of the wicked through the course of human history from the beginning of his creation to the present-day conflict:

> Mine eyes have seen the glory of the coming of the Lord:
> He is trampling out the vintage where the grapes of wrath are stored;
> He hath loosed the fateful lightening of his terrible swift sword:
> His truth is marching on.
> . . . .
> I have read a fiery gospel, writ in burnished rows of steel:
> "As ye deal with my contemners, so with you my grace shall deal;
> Let the Hero, born of woman, crush the serpent with his heel.
> Since God is marching on."[49]

The appeal of "Battle-Hymn of the Republic" is magnified by the author's decision to move in her poem's final stanzas beyond the concept of God as a divine avenger. The Old Testament God of the first four stanzas pronounces "righteous sentence" on the wicked, sounds forth his final trumpet, and summons the sinful "before his judgment-seat." But he is supplanted in the concluding two stanzas by the resplendent vision of a New Testament Christ, whose sacrificial love for man Howe urges her fellow northerners to emulate:

> In the beauty of the lilies Christ was born across the sea.
> With a glory in his bosom that transfigures you and me:
> As He died to make men holy, let us die to make men free,
> While God is marching on.[50]

To say that Howe's "Battle-Hymn of the Republic" was aptly titled would be an obvious understatement. Though it was published in the *Atlantic Monthly* in February 1862 to little fanfare, within months regiments throughout the Union Army were enthusiastically singing it, for it had touched a deep chord in the emotions of the northern people. Hearing it sung by troops in Washington soon after the Battle of Gettysburg, President Lincoln excitedly called out to them to "sing it again!"[51] In the course of one early winter morning Howe had spontaneously authored the hymn that would usher the North's warriors into holy battle and that would live on to become the beloved battle anthem of a reunified nation.

The Civil War's victorious conclusion, which "The Battle-Hymn of the Republic" had prophesied, confirmed both the northerner's sense of being God's special emissary to the world and his sense of the superiority of his racial inheritance. The triumph of the Puritan-Saxon race in America was given fitting and celebratory poetic utterance by Lowell in his "Ode Recited at the Harvard Commemoration, July 21, 1865." "Who now," the Boston Brahmin proudly boasted to his Harvard audience, would dare to "sneer" at the nation's Puritan ancestors?

> Who dare again to say we trace
> Our lines to a plebeian race?
> Roundhead and Cavalier![52]

Lowell argued that the Civil War had proved that the "best blood" was fluid that "hath most iron in't." It was precisely this iron blood that coursed through the veins of northern Roundhead warriors, not southern Cavaliers. To achieve its victory over the haughty Norman South, Yankees had poured out their resolute Puritan blood "without stint." Supercilious aristocrats from below the Mason-Dixon could no longer emptily boast of their racial origins and sneer at the North's. "Tell us not," Lowell contemptuously proclaimed, "of Plantagenets, Hapsburgs, and Guelf, whose thin bloods crawl / down from some victor in a border-brawl!"[53] The blood that had driven the North to victory was not the depleted inheritance of an Old World aristocracy. It was the vigorous Saxon blood of the Universal Yankee Nation.

In a poem entitled "April Twenty-sixth," presumably composed seventeen days after Lee's surrender at Appomattox, Annie Ketchum Chambers expressed the South's feeling of dazed numbness as it sought to come to terms with the utter defeat of its noble people and the complete failure of its noble cause. In 1861, Chambers observed wistfully, Dixie's dreams had been those of the aristocratically "earnest-browed and eagle-eyed, who late with banners bright / rode forth in knightly errantry, to do devoir for God and Right." But these grand reveries had been brutally shattered by a horde of debased Yankee invaders, and now the refined ladies of a vanquished South, "the women of a desolate land," could only helplessly "weep for the true and brave" Confederate survivors who were struggling homeward. Along with the sense of shock that Chambers's poem conveyed, southern poetry of the postwar period also evinced a bitter pride and a stubborn insistence that despite their defeat the southern people remained a refined race superior in every way to their degraded conquerors. For example, the author of "Lines Written July 15, 1865" contrasted in a stiffly defiant tone the nobility and honor of the defeated southern warrior appareled in his faded suit of gray with the rapacity of the victorious northern soldier, much as southern war poets had excoriated the Yankee invader during the war:

> Their hireling troops let others boast,
> Who fought for spoil and prey,
> Our southern lads we love the most,
> In a private suit of grey.
>
> What honor is in purple pall,
> Or gold and diamonds gay?
> Can they arouse the hearts of all,
> Like a tattered suit of grey?[54]

Postbellum southern poetry amply demonstrates that the South would not be moved by its defeat to question retrospectively its fierce commitment to the institution of slavery or to the idea that the southern people were aristocratic, honorable, and superior in character to the uncivilized northern Philistines who had vanquished them through force of numbers and sheer material superiority. Indeed, these were substantially the same prejudices that had helped to precipitate the region into the war in the first place. Postwar southern poets gave voice to these convictions more moderately than they had done during the war. Vicious and rabid attacks on the Yankee race largely ceased as southerners grudgingly conceded the reality of military defeat—but they conceded little more than that. Margaret Junkin Preston was typical of many of Dixie's poets when she counseled her readers to assume in their subjugation the attitude of the noble and proud Stoics of old:

> Bend, though thou must, beneath his will,
> Let no one abject moan have place;

> But with majestic silent grace,
> Maintain thy regal bearing still!
> Look back through all thy storied past,
> And sit erect in conscious pride,
> No grander heroes ever died—
> No sterner, battled to the last!

Preston's synthesis of stoical endurance and "conscious pride" was echoed in Rose Vertner Jeffrey's poem "Dixie," which boasted defiantly that the North could never entirely eradicate the essential chivalric courage of the southern race :"Forests fade, but acorns springing leave us not of shade bereft;/ nations fall—but not to perish, with a race of heroes left."[55]

There was less trumpeting of Dixie's Norman race myth in southern verse of the Reconstruction period, for it would have been of no benefit in helping the South accomplish the bitter, difficult, but necessary task of reintegrating itself into the Union. Yet even though explicit declarations of Norman supremacy were uttered with decreasing frequency in southern verse, the region's poets proudly and persistently proclaimed after Appomattox a new sectional mythology founded implicitly on the notion of southern race superiority. Father Abram J. Ryan, dubbed by his admirers the poet-priest of the South, was among the first to transmute poetically the great cause for which southerners had courageously fought into a hallowed Lost Cause in this adulatory description of Dixie's vanquished warriors:

> And their deeds—proud deeds shall remain
> And their names—dear names without stain for us,
> And the glories they won shall not wane for us;
> > In legend and lay
> > Our heroes in gray,
> Though dead, shall live over again for us.[56]

The crucial tenets of the Lost Cause myth alluded to in Ryan's poem were more fully set forth in D. B. Lucas's "In the Land Where We Were Dreaming." As rendered by this poet, the Civil War had not been the bloody consequence of southern fears over the future of plantation slavery. It had been, rather, the result of the South's "fair" vision of independence, a vision that had completely united an aristocratic and honorable people, "Godlike" in their simplicity of motive and "single" in their desire for freedom:

> Fair were our visions! Oh, they were as grand
> As ever floated out of Faerie land;
> Children were we in single faith,
> But Godlike children, whom nor death,
> Nor threat, nor danger drove from Honor's path,
> In the land where we were dreaming.[57]

In Lucas's poetic vision of southern history, Dixie's warriors had been as proud "as pride of birth could render" them, and their ladies had been without exception "pure and tender." This noble race of southerners had ruled their chattel with firmness tempered with noblesse oblige, so that "both bond and free" residents had been "content." But though God had been satisfied with his favored people, evil Yankees, possessed by "envy" of the South's social order, had "coveted" this Eden-like land. It was they who had aggressively unleashed the dogs of war and brought "disorder's Chaos" to reign over a hitherto idyllic country.[58]

To oppose what Lucas viewed as a barbaric northern incursion, the Confederacy had sent the flower of its chivalry to wage war under a battle flag that had appropriately represented in its crossed pattern of stars "Chivalry's cross." These brave southern knights had been led by a man "full of grandeur" and "clothed with power," who carried within himself the essence of his race—Robert E. Lee:

> As, while great Jove, in bronze, a warder god,
> Gazed eastward from the Forum where he stood,
> Rome felt herself secure and free,
> So, "Richmond's safe," we said, while we
> Beheld a bronzed Hero—Godlike Lee,
> In the land where we were dreaming.[59]

Given such perfection as Lucas described, the South's defeat could be comprehended only as a terrible dream. But in his emotional evocation of an idealized plantation culture viewed through the imaginative lens of Lost Cause mythology, the poet was emboldened to transcend the nightmare of southern history and to exhort his audience to join him in denying the reality of defeat. His final assertion was a paradox that was no doubt powerfully appealing to the emotions of unreconstructed southern readers, the assertion that the dreamland of the Old South so lovingly articulated in his poem was after all the most permanent of realities:

> And are they really dead, our martyred slain?
> No! dreamers! Morn shall bid them rise again
> From every vale—from every height
> On which they *seemed* to die for right—
> Their gallant spirits shall renew the fight
> In the land where we were dreaming.[60]

In enduring the exigencies of postbellum life, southerners had no recourse but to acknowledge the reality of their defeat, but southern poetry offered its readers a reliable refuge from such harsh and unpleasant actuality. Lyrics like "In the Land Where We Were Dreaming" commonly invited their audience to feast on cultural conceit and historical denial. Sidney Lanier's "The Tournament" was notably one of a handful of southern lyrics that sought to move beyond pure social and political fantasy to analyze seriously the nature and significance for the South of the North's victory. In his poem Lanier denoted the North as a warrior named "Brain" and the South as a knight named "Heart," and he sent them forth to engage in manly duel. The poet imagined Heart to be motivated by the chivalric love of ladies. In contrast to this romantic and chivalric warrior, he emphasized the pragmatic and coldly realistic qualities of his northern adversary by describing Brain's helmet as "bare as Fact—not he / or favor gave or sought." As the knights prepare to advance, Heart cannot resist casting "a glance / to catch his lady's eye"; but Brain looks "straight a-front, his lance / to aim more faithfully." In Lanier's poetic contest between southern chivalric fancy and hardheaded northern pragmatism, there could be but one outcome:

> They charged, they struck; both fell, both bled;
> Brain rose again, ungloved;
> Heart fainting smiled, and softly said,
> "My love to my Beloved!"[61]

Lanier's poem is certainly not immune to the myth of the Lost Cause. True to his region's romantic myths, he nowhere mentions slavery as a motivating force in Heart's armed confrontation with his northern foe. Moreover, he stresses, like more unreconstructed southern poets, the chivalry of his southern knight, and he clearly empathizes with him in his duel with the unemotional and brutally factual northern warrior. But despite employing the clichés of southern romanticism, Lanier is not completely caught up in the moonlight-and-magnolias vision of the vanquished Old South. Part of him is able to stand far enough above the fray to record dispassionately the inevitable victory of Brain over Heart. "The Tournament" implicitly acknowledges the impossibility of a romantically appealing but culturally anachronistic South prevailing against a northern culture that is supremely attuned to the factual and technological impulses of modern history.

Despite Lanier's partial dissociation from the Lost Cause myth in "The Tournament," the poem nevertheless dramatizes the irresistible appeal of that myth to southern poets. Even at his best, Lanier could not substantially separate his poetic imagination from southern mythology, and no other southern poet was accomplished enough even to try to disentangle southern fantasy from southern reality. It was easier for both Dixie's poets and its readers to surrender to the idea of the Lost Cause because giving themselves over to its fantasies made it possible for them to repudiate internally the harsh external truths with which they were forced to live day by day. They thus could conveniently carry within themselves two concurrent though contradictory attitudes, a pragmatic understanding of Dixie based on fact and a poetic understanding based on mythic fantasy.

Fantasy consequently reigned over postbellum poems like "In the Land Where We Were Dreaming," as it governed A. J. Requier's "Ashes of Glory." In this poem the South's glorious cause had "lived with Lee, and decked his brow," though in the present day it slept "the sleep of Jackson now." It had perished, however, not because of a deficiency of southern courage and determination but because noble southerners had been "outnumbered—not outdone." And in their valiant defense of that cherished Lost Cause, southerners could take pride in the knowledge that they had manifested the highest qualities of aristocratic chivalry, qualities unsurpassed by any other race in human history:

> Nor Arthur's knights, amid the gloom
> Their knightly deeds have starred;
> Not Gallic Henry's matchless plume,
> Nor peerless-born Bayard;
>
> Not all that antique fables fame,
> And orient dreams disgorge;
> Nor yet the silver cross of Spain,
> And lion of St. George,

> Can bid thee pale! Proud emblem, still
> Thy crimson glory shines
> Beyond the lengthened shades that fill
> Their proudest kingly lines.[62]

In Requier's vision of southern grandeur, the highborn inheritors of the Norman race who had defended their region's sacred cause were worthy to stand shoulder to shoulder with legendary knights such as Arthur, Bayard, and St. George.

Under the impulse of its Lost Cause mythology, the Old South assumed its place in the southern mind alongside Camelot and all other realms of legend that had, for a brief shining moment, cast their aristocratic light upon the prevailing darkness of history. In "Heroes of the South" South Carolinian Paul Hamilton Hayne nostalgically viewed the momentary wartime splendor of the Confederacy as the last and most sublime expression of an aristocratic race in a bourgeois-dominated century:

> But for a time, but for a time, O God!
> The innate forces of our knightly blood
> Rallied, and by the mount, the fen, the fold,
> Upraised the tottering standards of our race.[63]

Hayne's poem gave evidence that although expressions of the South's Norman race mythology decreased after Appomattox, they would not completely cease.

The laying of the cornerstone for the Robert E. Lee monument in Richmond on October 27, 1887—a profoundly emotional moment for nearly all white southerners—furnished what would prove to be the last grand occasion for dusting off and presenting to public view the Norman race mythology that had played so significant a role in imaginatively girding southerners for the Civil War. In his dedicatory poem entitled "Memoriae Sacrum," James Barron Hope declaimed verses that were heavily laced with references to the South's Norman genealogy. Key to his implicit assumption of a single aristocratic southern race was his poem's suggestion that Virginia, the mother colony of the plantation South, had impressed her Cavalier stamp upon all the states lying below the Mason-Dixon. The Old Dominion had been "first of all Old England's outposts," and, developing in the benign historical shadow of the English aristocracy, the colony had passed on its racial and cultural inheritance to the newer states of the Old South:

> Behind her stormy sunrise shone,
> Her Shadow fell vast and long.
> And her mighty Adm'ral, English Smith,
> Heads a prodigious throng
> Of as mighty men, from Raleigh down,
> As ever arose in song.[64]

Fittingly for a Richmond audience that was dominated by Virginians, Hope apotheosized Robert E. Lee as the exemplar of Dixie's Norman racial heritage:

> His was all the Norman's polish
> And sobriety of grace;
> All the Goth's majestic figure;
> All the Roman's noble face;
> And he stood the tall examplar
> Of a grand historic race.

Yet attached as he was to his vision of a uniquely aristocratic southern race, Hope seemed also to understand that in succeeding decades the Norman myth would possess little or no currency. His poem acknowledged sadly that Lee was the "last" of a race of Cavalier warriors. There would be no more like him in the united and Yankee-dominated America of the future:

> Truth walked beside him always
> From his childhood's early years,
> Honor followed as his shadow,
> Valor lightened all his cares,
> And he rode—that grand Virginian—
> Last of all the Cavaliers![65]

In October 1887 in Richmond, Virginia, the South bade a fond farewell to its myth of racial uniqueness, a uniqueness based on a Norman English blood inheritance. This pseudoscientific conceit bruited with such fervor by southern polemicists and poets both before, during, and immediately after the Civil War would be gently consigned to a dusty corner in Dixie's plunder room of fantasies. But even though the region's view of itself as racially unique would fade away, its view of itself as a people superior to and more refined than northerners would stubbornly persist into the present day. Indeed, by 1887 it had become an attitude inextricably interwoven into the region's Lost Cause mythology. In its death at Appomattox the Old South had assured its survival as an Eden-like land of perfection inhabited by graceful and noble aristocrats—a land that, in the unerringly apposite words of Virginia author James Branch Cabell, could never "be smirched by the wear and tear of existence." The phenomenal success of future works such as Margaret Mitchell's *Gone with the Wind* would validate Abram J. Ryan's poetic prophesy that the Old South, its Cause, and its highborn people would remain alive in the imaginations of the region, the nation, and even the world:

> Furl that banner, true 'tis gory,
> Yet 'tis wreathed around with glory,
> And 'twill live in song and story,
> Though its folds are in the dust:
> For its fame on brightest pages,
> Penned by poets and by sages,
> Shall go sounding down the Ages—[66]

CONCLUSION

Race Mythology, the Lost Cause, and Twentieth-Century Southern Sectionalism

In October 1863 in Little Rock, Arkansas, three months after the devastating Confederate losses at Gettysburg and Vicksburg, Confederate Brigadier General Edward W. Gantt composed an open letter to the people of his state. In this publication he made an unprecedented and unique appeal to his fellow Rebels, calling for a pragmatic and honest acceptance of the South's inevitable defeat and of the end of the institution of slavery. "Let us look these new ideas and our novel position squarely in the face," he urged with grim humor. "*We fought for negro slavery. We lost. We may have to do without it.*" In a similarly wry vein he admitted to having subscribed upon the fall of Fort Sumter to the facile assumption "that the Government was divided, and negro slavery established forever. *I erred.*"[1]

Writing from the far-flung western fringe of the Confederacy, Gantt must have felt himself less bound by the pieties and orthodoxies that dominated southern thought from Richmond to New Orleans. We cannot know how many of his fellow Arkansans or of his fellow southerners privately shared his pragmatic acceptance of Dixie's fate in the fall of 1863. But if there were other published voices raised in support of Gantt's pragmatism, they have not been preserved. Southerners would not publicly admit the possibility of defeat, and they would dedicate themselves to fighting their bloody and hopeless war for another year and a half. Indeed, even after Lee's surrender at Appomattox they would refuse to admit that the war they had initiated with such fervor in Charleston harbor had been a disastrous mistake and that the cause for which they had fought had been irremediably tainted by their commitment to the institution of chattel slavery and white supremacy.

Southern blindness to the reasons for and the consequences of the Civil War, the region's compulsion to idealize its social and political aims and purposes, could be clearly detected in the comments of its military leaders when the war ended. Colonel George Alexander Martin's attitude toward defeat was typical of Confederates of his position. He sorrowfully announced to his men the news of Lee's surrender but proudly maintained that even if henceforth there was to be no Confederacy, "the deeds of its citizens would be handed down to posterity, as bright and unsullied as the rays of the sun above us."

Though he reluctantly recognized that the South must be "consigned . . . to the list of conquered nations," he believed that as long as "patriotism, nobility, courage, fortitude, and virtue [found] eulogy in the human race, these [would be] hallowed at the sacred shrine of the alters of [the] Southland."[2]

As they had done in their war poetry, southern writers and political leaders immediately began a postbellum transformation of the sacred cause for which they had fought into an equally sacred Lost Cause. As William Basinger wrote to George Washington Custis Lee within a year of Appomattox, the "trials and sufferings and dangers" of Dixie's brave knights had been undertaken "apparently in vain; but they fought in a just cause, and if they did not achieve success, they at least deserved it. I await with impatience the day when the world will do justice to our Country and our Countrymen." Basinger expressed unambiguously the opinion of the great majority of southerners that though the South had lost the war, it had not "deserved" to lose it. Indeed, time would not dull the region's conviction that its objectives in initiating civil war had been noble ones. Thirty-five years after the cessation of hostilities, southerners remained enthralled by their rhetoric of heroic sacrifice. William Rasin's language was typical of that of many of his fellow ex-Confederates when he wrote to the director of the Virginia Historical Society in April 1900 praising the memory of a young Marylander who had died in the last charge made by the Army of Northern Virginia at Appomattox on April 9, 1865, and eulogizing him as a "splendid soldier of our *great* and lost *cause*."[3]

By the time the states of the Old Confederacy had been readmitted into the Union in 1868, the articles of faith of the Lost Cause myth were well established, and by the 1880s they had hardened into dogma. Chief among these articles was the conviction that the South had marched to war for principle, not for property. This conviction was given forceful and effective utterance by South Carolinian Benjamin Rutledge in a letter written to Benjamin Williams of Lowell, Massachusetts, on June 24, 1886. Rutledge explained to his northern correspondent that slavery—the institution Yankees had erroneously identified as the prime motivator of secession—had been "merely an agitating cause—a right infringed—which if submitted to in one case furnished a precedent for indefinite infringement." The South Carolinian was convinced that states' rights, not slavery, had been the South's primary concern in 1861. "The Cause of the South," he argued, "was not Rebellion—It was nothing more than each State defending its original unrelinquished sovereignty from invasion and assault."[4]

Rutledge, like nearly all southerners, had by now abandoned the contentious and condescending vocabulary of Dixie's Norman-Saxon race myth, but his letter makes abundantly clear that southern Americans continued to view their genealogy and their culture as thoroughly aristocratic in composition. As he somewhat haughtily lectured his New England correspondent, to have surrendered the rights of one's native state without resistance and to have submitted to what one honestly deemed to be Federal oppression "would have been craven." Such servile submission might be expected from a Saxon-descended varlet, but for a nobly descended southerner it was unthinkable. Since the South's motives in rebelling against Federal authority had been principled and above all honorable, there was nothing in retrospect that need be regretted and nothing for which Dixie need be pardoned. "As to the Right—the Honor—and the Justice of that Cause," Rutledge affirmed, "the men of the South . . . are a unit today." Turning to Jefferson Davis—widely unpopular during the later stages of the Civil War but now rehabilitated and resurrected by the letter writer of 1886 as "the official embodiment of [southern] principles"—and to other more popular objects of Dixie's "veneration," such as Lee and Jackson, Rutledge staunchly asserted that southerners would never repudiate or apologize for the ideals of "patriotism, dignity, fidelity and courage" that these courageous Cavaliers had so sublimely embodied through four years of bloody strife.[5]

As the nineteenth century gave way to the twentieth, many if not most southerners remained imaginatively entombed in the past, pining for the glorious and noble Confederacy of myth-enshrouded memory. Speaking to a class of Charleston schoolgirls on April 12, 1909, Sophia Haskell vividly recalled the day forty-eight years earlier when all five of her brothers had been gloriously engaged in the bombardment of Fort Sumter. She recreated this battle confident that her audience had been properly instructed by their teachers about the Civil War and that these teachers had "explained to you . . . how wicked it was of the Yankees for their own interests to try to force us to remain in the Union." On April 12, 1861, it had seemed certain to Sophia that southerners were destined to be free to live their lives "in the full exercise of our cherished States Rights." Little did she realize that Fort Sumter "was but the prelude to four such years of cruel war, as I hope that none of you girls may ever have to live through—years that left our homes and hearts desolate, our fortunes broken, and our beloved banner furled forever." And yet in the decades following the South's bitter defeat, Haskell proudly averred, she had "never once wished that those years had never been, for they made many heroes—who lived and died for the 'land we love.' And the love of country when you have to suffer for it, as we did, becomes a very pure and sacred passion—and this love was graven upon our hearts forever."[6]

One is struck by two aspects of Sophia Haskell's address to her young female audience. One is the survival into the twentieth century of an intense and defiant southern nationalism. Haskell was not ashamed to announce to her listeners that on the fateful day of April 12, 1861, she had "learned to hate" the stars and stripes, and forty-eight years later to the day she was not afraid to express her feeling that she would "never love" that flag "to [her] dying day."[7] The second striking quality of this unreconstructed southern lady's speech is the total absence in it of any reference to slavery. In her pious iteration of Lost Cause dogma, Haskell completely ignores the South's peculiar institution, casting the southern people in the role of noble victims and squarely laying the blame for the war at the feet of wicked Yankee aggressors.

Well into the modern period that has now been denominated "the American century," southerners felt free to eulogize a Confederacy that, had it prevailed, would have fractured the Union and probably destroyed the very idea of an American national destiny. As late as 1938, seventy-three years after Lee's surrender to Grant, A. Burnett Rhett in a Confederate Memorial Day speech played on the same Lost Cause themes that had dominated southern thinking since Reconstruction. The Confederacy, he declared, had entered "the war on a definite principle—the principle of States' Rights." Indeed, he assured his audience, "the most ardent of the Confederate soldiers had no particular interest in slavery." Though Rhett avoided references to the South's superior Norman blood, the assumption of Dixie's racial superiority was implicit in the reverent amazement with which he described his region's ability to fight and hold at bay numerically superior Union forces for four bloody years. Moreover, he was convinced that the extraordinary mettle of the southern people, exemplified in war by such peerless leaders as Robert E. Lee, had continued to sustain the region through the dark days of Reconstruction, ultimately enabling Dixie to forge a new life for itself that preserved "what could be saved from the old regime" and integrated it with "new conditions imposed by an alien and hostile administration."[8]

The Lost Cause creed trumpeted deep into the twentieth century by voices such as Rhett's continued effectively to sanitize the South's motives for entering the Civil War by isolating southern principles from the nasty and morally problematic issue of slavery. But behind the continued aggressive championing of the purity and nobility of the South's social and political ideals lay an arrogant conviction of the superiority of white southern blood, a racial triumphalism that had been employed frequently by Dixie's leaders over a half century before Rhett's 1938 speech to facilitate the reassertion of white conservative political power, to justify the stripping of political power from newly enfranchised blacks, and to return these former slaves to subservience. Indeed, Rhett baldly and unashamedly linked his lofty Lost Cause rhetoric with the less lofty but more pragmatic aims of the South's high-blooded leaders when, in celebrating the victory of white conservative Redeemers in his native South Carolina during the 1870s and 1880s, he made the following boast to his no-doubt approving audience: "The elimination of the carpetbagger and the scalawag, the removal of the negro from control, and the restoration of local government to the hands of the white citizens of the state was largely the work of the former Confederate Officers, such as Hampton and Gary in this state."[9] Wrapped in such lofty rhetoric, the Lost Cause myth articulated by Rhett continued to console modern southerners with visions of their noble racial inheritance and to validate by insidious means the region's most regressive political and social attitudes.

The Lost Cause myth that continued to flourish in the South long after Appomattox was not directly dependent for its nurturing upon the Norman-Saxon race myth that had so strongly marked southern polemical writing from 1850 to 1865. In reality, southern eulogies to the Cause steadily increased in number and fervor while southern trumpeting of the region's unique Norman racial heritage largely ceased during the postbellum period. After all, what would have been the point in promoting the idea of a separate southern race in a nation so obviously destined to be unified under Yankee rule? Nonetheless, the stubborn survival of Dixie's Lost Cause mentality indicated just how obstinately unreconstructed most postbellum southerners continued to be. And although during Reconstruction they largely backed away from the invective they had directed against Yankees before and during the Civil War, natives of the former Confederacy remained as unwilling to surrender the cherished notion of their racial and cultural superiority to Yankees as they were loath to assess their rebellion as one fought primarily in the defense of slavery.

The end of the Civil War thus did not prompt Dixie to relinquish either its conviction of the sacredness of its cause or its sense of superior racial distinctiveness. Indeed, for a southerner like Lucy Muse Fletcher there was no better way to understand the recently concluded conflict than to view it as the ineluctable result of a profound incompatibility between two peoples who sprang from fundamentally different bloodlines. "It takes blood," she observed, "to compose a long bred quarrel, and there is no formula provided by statesmanship that has even been able to prevent it."[10] Though references to "Normans" and "barbaric Yankees" largely vanished from printed discourse after 1865, many southerners would no doubt have agreed with Fletcher's premise that northern blood and southern blood were markedly different and that southern blood was the more aristocratic of the two. In fact, twelve years after the Civil War the same opinions privately expressed by Lucy Fletcher were publicly bruited in that most quintessentially Yankee of publications, the *Atlantic Monthly*, in an essay entitled "South Carolina Society," written "by a South Carolinian."

The romantic portrait of "the famous Palmetto aristocracy" that appears in the June 1877 issue of the *Atlantic* avoids the specific labeling of southerners as a Norman-descended race, but it otherwise hews closely to the traditional myth of a South Carolina aristocracy directly descended from English nobility. The state's planters are described as "chiefly Cavalier immigrants" who immediately came to constitute in the new colony "a regular landed gentry. They resided on their estates, erected imposing mansions, kept fine dogs and horses, and hunted over their vast demesnes . . . in the true style of English noblemen and squires." As described by the writer of the *Atlantic* essay, the life of the Carolina aristocracy is a nearly exact copy of that of the English nobility from which these aristocrats are descended. "The fashions of England were imported for the ladies," it informs readers, "and the young men were sent over the water to pass through the English universities. Tea, coffee, chocolate, and delicious wines were kept on the tables, and every Sunday the ladies turned out in coaches driven four in hand, with the gentlemen galloping along outside on horseback, to hear their loved Anglican service read in the tasteful rural churches."[11]

The South Carolina nobility limned in this essay are not viewed as merely picturesque characters in a local-color sketch. They are endowed by the writer with a social and cultural significance that extends far beyond the limited boundaries of the Low Country within which they are described as ruling from colonial times. "South Carolina Society" promotes the premise that these Carolina gentlemen eventually joined forces with the "landed nobility in colonial Virginia" to originate "the *antebellum* aristocracy of the whole South, excepting, perhaps, Louisiana."[12] The exaggerated claims that the author makes for an English-descended coastal Carolina aristocracy are thus merged with the myth of the Virginia Cavalier and expanded to include all of Dixie's planters.

Conclusion: Race Mythology and Twentieth-Century Southern Sectionalism 241

Ultimately this rose-tinted portrait of tidewater aristocracy, appealing to the reader in a tone that is as ingenious as it is disingenuous, becomes a seductive and devious apology for the most reactionary southern social and political attitudes. Although the narrator initially seems willing to face the fact that "the old plantation days are passed away, perhaps forever" and although he piously declares that his "principles now lead [him] to abhor slavery and rejoice at its abolition," he also confesses—apparently sure of his readers' approbation—that "in the midst of the heat and toil of the struggle for existence, the thought involuntarily steals over me that we have seen better days." The writer then proceeds to describe in luxurious and, to modern tastes, cloying detail an idealized picture of antebellum plantation life that gives the lie to his initial professions of pragmatism, historical acceptance, and forward-looking liberality:

> I think of the wild rides after the fox and the deer . . . of the long sittings at meals, and the after-dinner cigar; of the polished groups in easy but vivacious conversation in the parlor; of the chivalric devotion to beautiful women; of the pleasant evening drives; of the visits to the plantation, with its long, broad expanse of waving green, dotted here and there with groups of industrious slaves; of the long rows of negro cabins with little pickaninnies playing about them . . . of the wild old field airs ringing out from the cabins at night; of the "Christmas gif' Massa," breaking your slumbers on the holiday morn; of the gay devices for fooling the dignified old darkies on the first of April; of the faithful old nurse who brought you through infancy, under whose humble roof you delighted to partake of an occasional meal; of the flattering, foot-scraping, clownish, knowing rascal to whom you tossed a silver piece when he brought up your boots; of the little darkies who scrambled for the rind after you had eaten your watermelon on the piazza in the afternoon.[13]

Reading this fulsome description of noble southern masters ruling benignly over loyal and happy darkies is a decidedly anachronistic experience, for one cannot help feeling that this highly idealized portrait of "the famous Palmetto aristocracy," excepting the elegiac postbellum variation in its tone, could just as easily have been written in 1857 as in 1877. The great irony is that such an essay would not have been publishable in the *Atlantic Monthly* twenty years earlier. Girding themselves for their confrontation with the South over slavery, northern readers of this magazine would have had little stomach in 1857 for the Carolina author's sanitized vision of Dixie. Just twelve years after the war, however, they were increasingly inclined to overlook the nation's violent past and to join southerners in shedding a tender tear for the vanished felicities of plantation life.

The appearance of "South Carolina Society" in New England's most august publication is a clear indication that northern readers could no longer be counted on to object to the tone of muted apologia flowing from postbellum southern pens. Indeed, not only were northern readers receptive to sympathetic portrayals of the Old Confederacy by southern writers remarkably soon after the Civil War, but northern writers themselves demonstrated in a number of popular novels published as early as the late 1860s what Joyce Appleby has described as "an amazing readiness to let bygones be bygones. Southern postwar characters are depicted as contrite, forgiving, and rededicated to the old Union." These popular works, she concludes, "supplied the Northern reader with a striking alternative to the angry political rhetoric emanating from Congress, the lecture platform, and the Press."[14]

By the 1870s and 1880s the sympathetic rendering of southern subjects by northern writers had assumed a deeper artistic significance. A number of America's most distinguished literary figures were using southerners and southern attitudes as moral references by which the failures of postbellum American society might better be judged. In *The Burden of Southern History* C. Vann Woodward details this employment of southern characters in Herman Melville's philosophical poem *Clarel* (1876), in Henry Adams's *Democracy* (1880), and in Henry James's *The Bostonians* (1886). In each of these works, he observes, "a Southerner, a veteran of the Confederate Army, is introduced in a sympathetic role. His importance varies with the work concerned, but in each of the three works the Southerner serves as the mouthpiece of the severest strictures upon American society or, by his actions or character, exposes the worst faults in that society."[15]

The remarkable degree of sympathy toward the South emanating from northern readers and writers alike was indirectly attributable to the enormous and unsettling changes that were transforming economic and social institutions above the Potomac. Jay Martin has described the rise of new wealth, the extraordinary growth of cities, and the astonishing triumphs of science and technology that marked the latter half of the nineteenth century in America. Yet rapid change brought concomitant anxieties to millions of Americans. Industrialization carried with it new and more complex social problems, such as the creation of large urban slums and the dehumanization and alienation of workers. For many Americans the price of progress seemed too great. As

Martin has observed, Americans "longed for simpler conditions, and made a mythical past embody collective fantasies.," After militarily destroying the South, northerners soon came to accept the South's nostalgic and self-serving assessment of its antebellum culture in part because this idealized way of life seemed to embody the simplicity and purity that the North too had forfeited in its embrace of urbanism and industrialism. Against the materialism and the crass commercial values of the triumphant North, the legendary South held forth a counterimage, the image of a pastoral life whose values were rooted in the land and centered in the family. And the central symbol of this pastoral Eden was the nobly descended patriarchal planter who was associated, in the words of Rollin Osterweis, with "honor, courage, orthodox religion, respect for women, noblesse oblige to inferiors, and white supremacy."[16]

It seems particularly appropriate that the *Atlantic Monthly* paean to South Carolina's aristocracy appeared in 1877, for this was the year when southern Democrats joined with northern Republicans in forging a political compromise that assured the South's support for the election of President Rutherford B. Hayes by removing all Federal troops from the former Confederate states, thus effectively ending Reconstruction in the South and guaranteeing the political hegemony of white supremacist Democrats. By 1877 most northerners, whether politicians or casual readers, had lost interest in reforming Dixie or in protecting the rights of the former slaves they had a few years earlier fought and died to free. They were now in the mood for nostalgia, for visions of southern lords and ladies strolling beneath moonlight and magnolias amid their loyal and contented slaves.

The South had lost the war. Not even the most unreconstructed southerner could deny that fact. But by the end of the nineteenth century it was also hard for those Yankees who retained their idealistic political fervor to deny the fact that Dixie had won the imaginative battle for the hearts and minds of most of the nation's readers. In an essay written in 1888, the lawyer, civil rights advocate, and novelist Albion Tourgée acknowledged the South's fictional triumph when he observed that American literature had become distinctly southern in sympathy. Even the war, he lamented bitterly, was being viewed though southern eyes. "The federal or Union soldier," Tourgée noted with wry humor, "is not decried, but the Southern is preferred." The southern soldier, he complained, was always an aristocratic Cavalier: "So far as our fiction is concerned there does not appear to have been any Confederate infantry."[17]

Throughout the postbellum period the South would gain supremacy in popular romance writing by proclaiming its aristocratic pedigree, just as it had done in the decades leading up to the Civil War. Unlike antebellum polemical writers, however, southern writers of the Gilded Age were addressing a northern audience increasingly sympathetic to their romantic subject and their idealized tone. They were thus mindful of the need not to offend their readers gratuitously, and so they were generally content to celebrate their own noble genealogical inheritance without casting aspersions on that of Yankees. There were, of course, some exceptions to this rule of literary politesse. In 1900, for example, Virginia war veteran John Cussons penned a diatribe against what he considered to be northern distortions of southern history in which he excoriated the "Puritan" spirit of the North in terms strongly reminiscent of 1850s southern polemical writing.

Writing at the cusp of the twentieth century, Cussons remained just as skeptical as his antebellum predecessors had been about the nature of the Puritan Yankee. "He has laid aside his steeple hat and his sour visage and his sad-colored raiment," he conceded, "but at bottom he is the same old Puritan." Cussons was convinced that Cromwell's modern American descendent carried within him the same "inborn passion for regulating other peoples' affairs that he [had] when England vomited him forth to the Continent and when the Continent in turn spewed him to the shores of the New World.... Self-styled as the apostle of liberty, he has ever claimed for himself the liberty of persecuting all who presumed to differ from him."[18]

Northern readers need not have minded the fulminations of a third-rate southern writer whose opinions were published by an insignificant press in the insignificant village of Glen Allen, Virginia. But they probably were more stung by English author Percy Greg's *History of the United States from the Foundation of Virginia to the Reconstruction of the Union* (1887). A rabidly conservative Tory political writer, Greg reflected the same prejudices against Puritan Americans and in favor of aristocratic southerners as had been so frequently expressed by conservative Englishmen during the antebellum period. In his highly tendentious history he argued that New England Puritans, like their Cromwellian ancestors, had always been "intolerant of control from without" and "rebellious against royal or Episcopal authority. They were equally intolerant of intestine license, impatient and contemptuous of individual liberty. Their ideal polity was a searching, severe, all-embracing civil and religious despotism."[19]

Greg clearly implied that it was the inveterate intolerance of the American Puritan that had propelled what to his Tory sensibility had been the wicked and wrong-headed rebellion of 1776. Of course, such a simplistic and biased point of view willfully ignored the crucial and even primary influence of southern aristocrats such as Washington and Jefferson in the American Revolution, but Greg was not concerned with historical subtleties. In his mind the Puritan was the source of all evils in American history, and it was the Yankee's bigotry, religious zeal, and contempt for other opinions that had brought about both the Revolution and the Civil War.

As a foil to the bigoted New England Puritan, Greg's history offered his readers the estimable southern planter aristocrat. Greg never directly described southerners as a distinct Norman race, but like the author of "South Carolina Society" he admiringly viewed them as descendants of the English aristocracy, possessed like their Old World ancestors of a high and noble character and an exquisitely developed sense of personal honor. It was the Yankee's inability to grasp the southern nobility's devotion to the concept of honor, he argued, that had left the North stunned by the disastrous consequences of Lincoln's election in 1860. Greg expressed the Yankee's failure to weigh and respect the knightly southern temperament in this way: "That men so acutely sensitive on the point of honor, that a people high-spirited, courageous and determined to a fault, should tamely eat their words and trail the honour of their states in the dust, none who knew them could deem possible. Unfortunately the North did not know them." Neither, the author contended, had a Puritan-descended people been able to imagine the dauntless courage and the masterful leadership abilities that were the birthright of an aristocratic southern race. Such qualities had sustained the South for four years against Union forces far superior in numbers and matériel, and they been preeminently exhibited by Robert E. Lee, in Greg's words the "typical representative of Southern chivalry."[20]

In its enthusiasm for the Old South, Greg's *History of the United States* came close to arguing that the United States was comprised of two different races of people. Though the terms *Norman* and *Saxon* were never employed in Greg's argument, much of the vocabulary of traditional southern polemical writing, contrasting Puritan with Cavalier aristocrat, was on display in the book, and southerners could hardly have asked for a more sympathetic rendering of their nature and their motives. Not surprisingly, the London edition of Greg's work was followed five years later by an edition printed in Richmond, Virginia. The work stood as proof that the South's defeat in Civil War had not destroyed Dixie's myth of aristocratic racial descent. The idea would continue to exert an irresistible appeal both for American southerners and for political and cultural conservatives of all nations, like Percy Greg. The Yankee might or might not be, in Albion Tourgée's words, "decried." But in romantic fiction and from conservative historical perspectives, the southern Cavalier would be nearly always "preferred."

The pseudoscientific terminology of Dixie's Norman race myth, which had been largely a product of the politically charged 1850s, dwindled away after the Civil War, but unfortunately the South's sense of aristocratic blood inheritance did not. Southerners continued to believe that they were a nobly descended people destined to rule over their inferior former slaves. But behind the idealistically charged Lost Cause rhetoric and the panegyrics to the South's noble Cavaliers lay a brutal and imperfectly disguised racism. Indeed, southerners would use the aristocratic myth to validate their racist social and political agenda. The destructive implications of this race consciousness were on fascinating display in English author William H. Dixon's *The White Conquest* (1876). In this study of the postbellum South the author presents with apparent approval the detailed observations of a South Carolina aristocrat named Colonel Binfield, "a Southern officer, who has studied the Negro Question on the battle-field, in the tobacco grounds, and in the public schools."[21]

Unlike some of his more outspoken and unreconstructed fellow southerners, Binfield pragmatically admits that the South "made a great mistake in parting from our flag; but we have long since seen the error of our way, and we shall not commit that fault again." He has no trust in the policies and aims of Yankee Republicans, southern scalawags, or freed slaves, but he does trust what he terms "the law of life." This law is ordained by nature, and what it ordains is the racial triumph of white southerners. Though Binfield is speaking before the Compromise of 1877, he is supremely confident of the white aristocracy's eventual reassertion of power in Dixie, a confidence tinged with a unique brand of southern arrogance that is on clear display in this striking passage:

> The Negro had his day of power. If he chafed us by his petulance and folly he never awed us by his strength. Even now, when he has a ruler of his own opinions in Columbia, a majority of friends in the Legislature, and the command of all the public forces, we have no fear of him. A European is too strong for any African. Unless he stabs you in the dark, or throws a brand into your room, a coloured man can hardly do you harm. The tussle of a White man with a Negro is the tussle of a man with a woman. It is the same in masses. Plant me one of your Utopias on the Santee or Edisto; set me ten Europeans in the midst of ninety Africans; give each of your hun-

dred settlers an equal share of soil, seeds, implements, and money; start them with a free code and equal rights, and leave them to till the ground, to make laws, and to rule themselves. In ten years the White men will own the soil, the granaries, and the money. Nature has given the White man brain and strength, invention, courage, and endurance of a higher quality, on a larger scale, than she has given these elements to the Black. In spite of accidents the White man must be master on this continent. Why, then, should we provoke an issue in the field? No one but an enemy of White civilization wants a second civil war. We only need to wait, certain to conquer if we wait.[22]

Beneath Colonel Binfield's suave and mannered exterior there is a hard foundation of white supremacy that chillingly anticipates the social Darwinism and fascism that would exert such powerful appeal in the succeeding decades of the nineteenth and twentieth centuries. By 1876 such frankly coarse racial rhetoric could be applied without qualm to the subjugation of blacks, but justification for the continued subjugation of poor and middling white southerners to the former plantation aristocracy required a more idealized and high-toned vocabulary and a more conventional appeal to the aristocratic myth. Thus for the author of "South Carolina Society" the explanation for the reestablishment of aristocratic power in postbellum Dixie was "simple." "While the industrial power of the aristocracy has been taken away, their ancestral distinction and their intelligence and social superiority to the mass of the whites have remained intact," he explained. "They compass the highest circle of Southern society, which is looked up to and copied by all below, with how much awe words cannot tell."[23] If Binfield's blacks were required by nature to submit to the inevitable position reserved for inferior races, the South's more humbly raised whites were accorded the honor of worshiping at Dixie's Cavalier shrine.

Southern Redeemers like the author of "South Carolina Society" and Colonel Binfield were confident that the region's antebellum elite would soon return to power in the states of the Old Confederacy, and they enthusiastically approved of this southern Restoration. They and aristocrats of like mind had only to hunker down and bide their time, buttressed by their region's racial myths, assured of their superiority to base carpetbaggers, scalawags, and freed blacks, and confident of the inevitability of the planter aristocrat's imminent triumph. They would not have to wait long for their vindication.

* * *

The phenomenal worldwide success of Margaret Mitchell's old-fashioned Redeemer romance *Gone with the Wind* (1936) and the equally enduring appeal of Harper Lee's enlightened aristocrat Atticus Finch in *To Kill a Mockingbird* (1960) testify to the continuing hold of the southern aristocrat, in both his reactionary and his more liberal manifestations, on the imagination not just of America but of the world. And how does the concept of the Cavalier aristocrat play among southerners themselves today? Do any vestiges of the region's nineteenth-century race consciousness, particularly the Old South's mania for claiming a Norman English racial descent, survive into the twenty-first century? Tony Horwitz's fascinating *Confederates in the Attic: Dispatches from the Unfinished Civil War* (1998) suggests that the old Cavalier myth retains a distinct appeal for contemporary southerners, especially those who live in the Atlantic tidewater, that original, first-settled, and most atmospheric section of the plantation South that extends from the popular Virginia holiday destinations of Williamsburg and the James River plantations to the tourist meccas of Charleston and Savannah.

On one of his travels through the states of the Old Confederacy, Horwitz converses with a Charleston lady who serves as a guide at the city's Confederate Museum, and in the course of this interview she displays a rather supercilious end-of-twentieth-century pride in her past, her city, and her ancestry that distinctly evokes the attitudes of both antebellum and postbellum southern romanticism of the nineteenth century. "We're not a migrating people," she informs Horwitz, with a scarcely detectable hint of condescension. "We live in our old houses and eat on our old dishes and use the old silverware every day. We're close to the past and comfortable with it. We've surrounded our lives with the pictures of all those relatives hanging on the walls, and we grow up hearing about them."[24] Her conversation—devoid of references either to slavery or to the current state of race relations in Charleston—is not the product of a contemporary American sensibility. It is essentially the expression of a traditionally conservative southern sensibility. And though the Charleston lady is living in the late 1990s, her reflections might just as easily have been voiced by a Charlestonian of the 1890s.

In the contemporary tidewater South, Horwitz learns, people continue to attach primary social significance to a legendary aristocratic English pedigree. For example, his interviewee is careful to point out to him that her family is descended from ancestors who arrived on the "first ship" that brought Charleston's original English founders to the colony in 1670. "When modern-day Charlestonians intimated that their ancestry went back to the 'three ships,'" Horwitz observes with some irony, "they were letting you know, in genteel code, that their blood was of the bluest Charleston pedigree." And like the author of "South Carolina Society" writing more than one hundred years earlier, this contemporary Charleston lady acknowledges a profound kinship between the English-descended aristocrats of the Carolina low country and the English-descended Cavaliers of the Old Dominion. When she sees the author's Virginia address in the museum guest book she exclaims, "You're from Virginia? Oh, we're deeply flattered."[25]

But while the myth of an English-descended southern aristocracy still seems to exert considerable appeal in the seaboard southern states, it apparently wields less power in interior and Gulf State Dixie. One rarely encounters today voices native to the Old Southwest like William Faulkner's, who in the late 1950s chose his Charlottesville venue to evoke with something like reverence the aristocratic mystique of "Virginia blood" and to confirm its seminal and lasting impression on the mind of the Deep South.[26] Indeed, the interior South has in the past few decades produced a new type of thinking about the southern states, described by Horwitz and others as "neo-Confederate," a way of reasoning that completely rejects the traditional, nineteenth century–generated myth of a region distinguished by its noble Norman racial inheritance.

Unlike nineteenth-century southern polemical writers, when neo-Confederates define Dixie's distinctiveness, they don't focus on biologically oriented race theory. Rather, they focus anthropologically on cultural influences. Still, both the nineteenth-century race-based and the twentieth-century culture-based articulations of southern difference share a common sense of the deep gulf between South and North, and for modern-day neo-Confederates that difference seems nearly as pronounced as it was for the region's nineteenth-century essayists. Horwitz summarizes this current school of southern thought: "North and South went to war because they represented two distinct and irreconcilable cultures, right down to their bloodlines. White Southerners descended from freedom-loving Celts in Scotland, Ireland and Wales. Northerners— New England abolitionists in particular—came from mercantile and expansionist English stock." This ethnography, as Horwitz explains, can easily be employed to explain how the Civil War was fought and why the South lost. True to their Celtic blood, "Southerners hurled themselves in frontal assaults on the enemy. The North, meanwhile, deployed its industrial might and numerical superiority to grind down the South with Cromwellian efficiency." In the opinion of "neo-Confederate guru" Grady McWhiney, "Southerners lost the War because they were too Celtic and their opponents were too English."[27]

On one level the cultural theories of the neo-Confederates appear to mark a significant break with nineteenth-century southern racial mythology. These theories, after all, demand nothing less than a cultural and racial redefinition of the American South. Barry Reid McCain insists, for example, that the labeling of southerners as English or Anglo-Saxon "is a colossal case of the misnomer if ever there was one and is perhaps the greatest fraud presented as history. The fraud was born in the anti-Celtic political and social climate of the British world during the time of the expansion of an English-dominated British empire."[28] For McCain and McWhiney the southern people and southern culture are basically Celtic in substance, not English, and this understanding of the South's Celtic heritage explains its profound difference from the North.

Neo-Confederate thinking is salutary in its insistence on recognizing the importance of the Scots, Irish, and Welsh in forming the South's culture and temperament, an importance that Dixie's Anglo-Norman racial mythology completely ignored in its mania for creating an idealized planter aristocracy. But on a deeper level the neo-Confederates offer no valuable new insights that would help southerners to free themselves from their racist-blighted past or to face the future more productively and positively. They continue to view the South as divided by deep differences from the rest of America. The cultural conflict they transpose to the New World is not the mythical nineteenth-century struggle between Puritan and Cavalier, Saxon and Norman, but it is essentially the same nineteenth-century battle, with the new terms *English* and *Celt* substituting for the old terms *Norman* and *Saxon*.

The American terrain that Grady McWhiney and his fellow neo-Confederates survey remains distinctly bifurcated by culture and racial heritage. In words that distinctly and rather chillingly evoke the South's antebellum polemicists, McWhiney argues that "British immigrants—English and Celt—brought with them to America their habits and values as well as their old feuds, biases, and resentments." Though significant numbers of Celts immigrated to the northern colonies and the English were especially prominent in the coastal South, "the tendency, by and large," McWhiney writes, "was for Celts and other non-English people in the North to become Anglicized and for Englishmen and other non-Celtic people in the South to become Celticized." The dominance in North and South of two antagonistic cultures, one English and one Celtic, created a "sectionalism that . . . ultimately exploded into the War for Southern Independence."[29]

And so into the opening decade of the twenty-first century, southerners like McWhiney continue striving to define the difference that separates Dixie from the rest of the nation and to explain and defend the South's distinctive culture and "way of life" to the rest of America. They likewise continue to use the idea of southern exceptionalism to absolve themselves of the burden of racism, just as their ancestors used it to absolve themselves of the burden of slavery. So today many white southerners still embrace the mantras of "honor" and "states' rights," and they still use it to justify southern policies that led to the Civil War, just as their nineteenth-century forebears embraced their Lost Cause myth and used it for regional self-justification. So strongly embedded are these shibboleths in the southern psyche that presidential candidate Ronald Reagan could place his capstone on the Republican Party's "southern strategy" by opening his 1980 national campaign in Philadelphia, Mississippi—site of the notorious, and at that time unpunished, murders of civil rights activists—and speak not about racial violence and oppression but about Dixie's cherished concept of states' rights before a wildly appreciative white audience. And in the year 2000, white South Carolinians could defend the flying of the Confederate flag over their state capitol by proudly referencing southern honor, courage, and heritage.

Recent events suggest that southerners, especially those living in the Deep South, have not yet entirely decided that they want to be a seamless part of the national fabric. The specter of race still hovers over the region, and many southern whites remain unreconciled to the idea of racial equality, as the phenomenal success of Republican political strategy in the region over the last thirty years attests. Southerners have historically employed their aristocratic racial myths in defense of white supremacy, and there is ample reason to suspect that their continuing urge to see themselves as a distinctive people within the contemporary American Union is tainted by similar white supremacist convictions. Dixie's antebellum Norman-Saxon race myth may be dead, but the white southerner's sense of being descended from a unique, superior, and aristocratic people is far from dead. Randall Jimerson's observations seem just as apposite today as when he made them in 1988. The Civil War, he wrote, perpetuated rather than destroyed "the conviction that northerners and southerners were two different peoples. More than a century after reunion and reconciliation, this sectional consciousness remains a troubling legacy."[30]

NOTES

INTRODUCTION

1. Preston Brooks, "Statement to Sumner," *Congressional Globe*, 34th Cong., 1st sess., 1349–50; Robert L. Meriwether, "Preston S. Brooks on the Caning of Charles Sumner," *South Carolina Historical and Genealogical Magazine* 52 (1951), 2–3.
2. Meriwether, "Preston S. Brooks on the Caning of Charles Sumner," 3.
3. David Donald, *Charles Sumner and the Coming of the Civil War* (New York: Knopf, 1974), 297.
4. Charles Sumner, *The Crime against Kansas* (1856; rpr. New York: Arno, 1969), 8.
5. Ibid., 9–10.
6. Donald, *Sumner and the Coming of the Civil War*, 286; Sumner, *Crime against Kansas*, 85.
7. Sumner, *Crime against Kansas*, 87.
8. Donald, *Sumner and the Coming of the Civil War*, 209.
9. Ibid., 280.
10. Ibid., 388.
11. Sumner, *Crime against Kansas*, 89; Donald, *Sumner and the Coming of the Civil War*, 287.
12. Horace Greeley, *New York Daily Tribune*, 21 May 1856, 4; Donald, *Sumner and the Coming of the Civil War*, 288.
13. Donald, *Sumner and the Coming of the Civil War*, 288–89.
14. Ibid., 290; Jack Kenny Williams, "The Code of Honor in Ante-Bellum South Carolina," *South Carolina Historical Magazine* 54 (1953), 115.
15. Charles S. Sydnor, "The Southerner and the Laws," *Journal of Southern History* 6 (1940), 19.
16. Williams, "Code of Honor in Ante-Bellum South Carolina," 114.
17. Donald, *Sumner and the Coming of the Civil War*, 291.
18. Williams, "Code of Honor in Ante-Bellum South Carolina," 125.
19. Donald, *Sumner and the Coming of the Civil War*, 291.
20. Sydnor, "The Southerner and the Laws," 23; Donald, *Sumner and the Coming of the Civil War*, 301, 304.
21. Henry Wadsworth Longfellow, letter to Charles Sumner, 24 May 1856, Longfellow Letters, Harvard University; John Palfrey, letter to Charles Sumner, 11 June 1856, Palfrey Family Papers, Harvard University; Donald, *Sumner and the Coming of the Civil War*, 299.
22. "The Sumner Case," *Littel's Living Age* 50 (1856), 376.
23. William Lloyd Garrison, *The Liberator* 26 (June 13, 1856), 95; Garrison, "Southern Degradation," in *William Lloyd Garrison and the Fight against Slavery: Selections from the Liberator*, ed. William E. Cain (Boston: Bedford Books, 1995), 148.
24. *The Selected Letters of Charles Sumner*, ed. Beverly Wilson Palmer (Boston: Northeastern University Press, 1990), 1:463.
25. Ibid.

26. Ralph Waldo Emerson, "The Assault upon Mr. Sumner," in *Centenary Edition, The Complete Works of Ralph Waldo Emerson* (1904; rpr., New York: AMS, 1968), 11:248; Ralph Waldo Emerson, "Assault on Charles Sumner," in *Emerson's Antislavery Writings*, ed. Joel Myerson (New Haven: Yale University Press, 1995), 108.

27. Bertram Wyatt-Brown, *Yankee Saints and Southern Sinners* (Baton Rouge: Louisiana State University Press, 1985), 186, 192. For Wyatt-Brown's assessment of the Brooks-Sumner confrontation, see his *The Shaping of Southern Culture* (Chapel Hill: University of North Carolina Press, 2001), 195–98.

28. Emerson, "Assault on Charles Sumner," 109.

29. Ibid., 108; Emerson, "Assault upon Mr. Sumner," 247.

30. *The Letters of Ralph Waldo Emerson*, ed. Ralph L. Rusk (New York: Columbia University Press, 1939), 1:107; *The Journals and Miscellaneous Notebooks of Ralph Waldo Emerson*, ed. William Gilman (Cambridge: Harvard University Press, 1960), 14:169–70.

31. Donald, *Sumner and the Coming of the Civil War*, 306, 307, 304–5.

32. Meriwether, "Preston S. Brooks on the Caning of Charles Sumner," 3, 4.

33. Donald, *Sumner and the Coming of the Civil War*, 308.

34. Ibid., 308-309.

35. *Reception and Speech: Reception of P. S. Brooks* (Boston: Jewett and Co., 1856), 4.

36. Ibid., 5.

37. Ibid., 6, 10.

38. Ibid., 10.

39. Sydnor, "The Southerner and the Laws," 14.

40. Horace Greeley, *New York Daily Tribune*, 23 May 1856, 4; Longfellow, letter to Charles Sumner, 24 May 1856, Longfellow Letters, Harvard University; Garrison, "More of Southern Chivalry," *The Liberator* 26 (27 June 1856).

41. Donald, *Sumner and the Coming of the Civil War*, 311; Emerson, "Assault upon Mr. Sumner," 247.

42. "A Tribute of Respect, Commemorative of the Worth and Sacrifice of John Brown, of Ossawatomie" (Cleveland, 1859), 58.

CHAPTER 1: Race Mythology, Science, and Southern Nationalism

1. "The Basis of Northern Hostility to the South," *DeBow's Review* 28 (Jan. 1860), 9.

2. Ibid., 10.

3. Ibid., 10, 9.

4. Ibid., 10–11.

5. Ibid., 9.

6. Edward Pessin, "How Different from Each Other Were Antebellum North and South?" *American Historical Review* 85 (1980), 1149; David M. Potter, *The Impending Crisis, 1848–1861*, ed. Don E. Fehrenbacher (New York: Harper and Row, 1976), 472; William R. Taylor, *Cavalier and Yankee: The Old South and the American National Character* (New York: George Braziller, 1961), 335.

7. Taylor, *Cavalier and Yankee*, 15.

8. *The Papers of Thomas Jefferson*, ed. Julian P. Boyd (Princeton: Princeton University Press, 1953), 8:468.

9. Quoted in "The Great Issue: Our Relation to It," *Southern Literary Messenger* 34 (1861), 161.

10. Henry Van Der Lyn, Journal, vol. 1, 27 Feb. 1828, New-York Historical Society.

11. Charles Sydnor, *The Development of Southern Sectionalism, 1819-1848* (Baton Rouge: Louisiana State University Press, 1948), 220.

12. George Featherstonhaugh, *Excursion through the Slave States* (1844; rpr. New York: Negro Universities Press, 1960), 155-56.

13. Ibid., 157.

14. "Progress of the Great West," *DeBow's Review* 4 (Sept. 1847), 31; B. F. Porter, "The Mission of America," *DeBow's Review* 4 (Sept. 1847), 122, 117.

15. Thomas Hart Benton, "Speech of Mr. Benton of Missouri on the Oregon Question," *Congressional Globe*, 29th Cong., 1st sess., 917.

16. "Speech of Jefferson Davis, February 13 and 14, 1850," in *Arguments Illustrating the Compromise of 1850*, ed. Frank W. Prescott (Madison: University of Wisconsin Press, 1926), 16.

17. "Plain Words for the North," *American Whig Review* 12 (Dec. 1850), 556.

18. For a concise account of James D.B. DeBow and his *DeBow's Review*, see John McCardell's *The Idea of a Southern Nation: Southern Nationalists and Southern Nationalism, 1830-1860* (New York: W. W. Norton, 1979), 119-26.

19. Jared Gardner, *Master Plots: Race and the Founding of an American Literature, 1787-1845* (Baltimore: Johns Hopkins University Press, 1998), 99-100.

20. Michael O'Brien, *Conjectures of Order: Intellectual Life and the American South* (Chapel Hill: University of North Carolina Press, 2004), 1:285-304; David Hackett Fischer, *Albion's Seed: Four British Folkways in America* (New York: Oxford University Press, 1989), 3-11.

21. Fischer, *Albion's Seed*, 6, 253, 216.

22. Ibid., 613, 633-34.

23. Ibid., 615.

24. W. J. Cash, *The Mind of the South* (1941; rpr. New York: Knopf, 1983), 31, 63.

25. Henry Clay Lewis, *Odd Leaves from the Life of a Louisiana Swamp Doctor* (1843; rpr. Upper Saddle River: Literature House, 1969), 87.

26. Elizabeth Fox-Genovese and Eugene D. Genovese, *Fruits of Merchant Capital: Slavery and Bourgeois Property in the Rise and Expansion of Capitalism* (New York: Oxford University Press, 1983), 249, 255-56.

27. Ibid., 263.

28. James M. McPherson, *Ordeal by Fire: The Civil War and Reconstruction* (New York: Knopf, 1982), 33. See also James Oakes, *Slavery and Freedom: An Interpretation of the Old South* (New York: Knopf, 1990), 129-32.

29. "The Difference of Race between the Northern and Southern People," *Southern Literary Messenger* 30 (1860), 404-5.

30. Ibid., 407.

31. "Northern Mind and Character," *Southern Literary Messenger* 31 (Nov. 1860), 346.

32. James M. McPherson, *Is Blood Thicker Than Water? Crises of Nationalism in the Modern World* (New York: Vintage Books, 1998), 31.

33. Ibid., 51; Drew Gilpin Faust, *The Creation of Confederate Nationalism: Ideology and Identity in the Civil War South* (Baton Rouge: Louisiana State University Press, 1988), 10.

34. Kwame Anthony Appiah, "Race," in *Critical Terms for Literary Study*, ed. Frank Lentricchia and Thomas McLaughlin (Chicago: University of Chicago Press, 1995), 276.

35. Ibid., 275–76.

36. Nicholas Hudson, "From 'Nation' To 'Race': The Origins of Racial Classification in Eighteenth Century Thought," *Eighteenth Century Studies* 29, no. 3 (1996), 248.

37. William Stanton, *The Leopard's Spots: Scientific Attitudes toward Race in America, 1815–59* (Chicago: University of Chicago Press, 1960), 11.

38. Hudson, "From 'Nation' to 'Race,'" 252.

39. Nancy Stepan, *The Idea of Race in Science: Great Britain, 1800–1960* (Hamden, Conn.: Anchor Books, 1982), 2; Robert Knox, *The Races of Men: A Fragment*, 2nd ed. (London: Henry Renshaw, 1862), 6.

40. Stanton, *Leopard's Spots*, 20–44.

41. Ibid., 51–53.

42. Charles Pickering, *The Races of Man and Their Geographical Distribution* (1848; rpr. London: H. G. Bohn, 1854), 12, 3.

43. Stanton, *Leopard's Spots*, 69.

44. Ibid., 71.

45. Josiah C. Nott and George R. Gliddon, *Types of Mankind; or, Ethnological Researches* (Philadelphia: Lippincott, Grambo, and Co., 1854), 80, 81.

46. Count Arthur de Gobineau, *The Moral and Intellectual Diversity of Races*, trans. Henry Hotze (1856; rpr. New York: Garland, 1984), 91.

47. Ibid., 15-16.

48. Stanton, *Leopard's Spots*, 155.

49. Stepan, *Idea of Race in Science*, 9; Appiah, "Race," 280.

50. Reginald Horsman, *Race and Manifest Destiny: The Origins of American Racial Anglo-Saxonism* (Cambridge: Harvard University Press, 1981), 140.

51. Harvey Lindsly, "Differences in the Intellectual Character of the Several Varieties of the Human Race," *Southern Literary Messenger* 5 (1839), 616–20; "Nott's 'Caucasism and Negro Races,'" *Southern Quarterly Review* 8 (1845), 148–90; Nott and Gliddon, *Types of Mankind*, 402.

52. "The Common Origin of the Human Races," *DeBow's Review* 17 (1854), 39; "The Indian Tribes of the United States," *DeBow's Review* 17 (1854), 69; "The Black Race in North America," *Southern Literary Messenger* 21 (1855), 676.

53. Elizabeth Fox-Genovese and Eugene D. Genovese, *The Mind of the Planter Class: History and Faith in the Slaveholder's Worldview* (New York: Cambridge University Press, 2005), 410, 442.

54. Robert L. Dabney, *A Defense of Virginia, and through Her, of the South, in Recent and Pending Contests against the Sectional Party* (1867; rpr. Dahlonega, Ga.: Crown Rights, 1997), 100, 207–8.

55. Stanton, *Leopard's Spots*, 71; John Fletcher, *Studies in Slavery, in Easy Lessons* (Natchez, Miss.: Jackson Warner, 1852), 23, 12; Nott and Gliddon, *Types of Mankind*, 402.

56. "Indian Tribes of the United States," 69; "Black Race in North America," 676.

57. S. A. Cartwright, "Slavery in the Light of Ethnology," in *Cotton Is King, and Pro-Slavery Arguments*, ed. E. N. Elliott (Augusta: Pritchard, Abbot, and Loomis, 1860), 694, 695–96, 698.

58. Ibid., 718; Chancellor Harper, "Slavery in the Light of Social Ethics," in *Cotton Is King*, ed. Elliott, 593–94.

59. Alexander H. Stephens, "The Chief Stone of the Corners of our New Edifice," in *Slavery as a Cause of the Civil War*, ed. Edwin C. Rozwenc (Boston: Heath, 1949), 45.

60. Robert Knox, *The Races of Men: A Fragment* (London: Henry Renshaw, 1850), 46.
61. Ibid., 318, 329, 18–19.
62. "Schlegel's Philosophy of History," *Southern Quarterly Review* 3 (1843), 311; "The Study of History," *Southern Quarterly Review* 10 (1846), 147.
63. "Mines of California," *Southern Quarterly Review* 17 (1850), 27.
64. Hudson, "From 'Nation' to 'Race,'" 258.
65. Boyd Shafer, *Faces of Nationalism: New Realities and Old Myths* (New York: Harcourt, Brace, Jovanovich, 1972), 154.

CHAPTER 2: *Ivanhoe*, Race Myth, and the Walter Scott Cultural Syndrome

1. "A Virginia Watering Place," *Richmond Enquirer*, 2 Sept. 1845; Rollin G. Osterweis, *Romanticism and Nationalism in the Old South* (New Haven: Yale University Press, 1949), 4–5.
2. Osterweis, *Romanticism and Nationalism*, 216, 41–53.
3. Ibid., 46–48, 203.
4. Hamilton James Eckenrode, "Sir Walter Scott and the South," *North American Review* 206 (October, 1917), 601; W. J. Cash, *The Mind of the South* (1941; rpr. New York: 1983), 65.
5. Samuel L. Clemens, *Life on the Mississippi* (1883; rpr. New York: Oxford University Press, 1996), 467–69.
6. Jay B. Hubbell, *The South in American Literature, 1607–1900* (Durham: Duke University Press, 1954), 192.
7. G. Harrison Oriens, "Walter Scott, Mark Twain, and the Civil War," *South Atlantic Quarterly*, 40 (October, 1941), 359; Michael O'Brien, *Rethinking the South: Essays in Intellectual History* (Baltimore: Johns Hopkins University Press, 1988), 53.
8. "Charge to the Knights in the Late Tournament at Hampton," *Richmond Enquirer*, 15 Jan. 1859.
9. Ibid.
10. Ibid.
11. Review of *Ivanhoe* in *The Western Review and Miscellaneous Magazine* 2 (May 1820), 204; Hubbell, *The South in American Literature*, 189.
12. Mary Boykin Chesnut, *Mary Chesnut's Civil War*, ed. C. Vann Woodward (New Haven: Yale University Press, 1981), 191.
13. William Gilmore Simms, "History for the Purposes of Art," in *Views and Reviews in American Literature, History, and Fiction*, 1st ser., ed. C. Hugh Holman (1845; rpr. Cambridge: Harvard University Press, 1962), 46.
14. Michael Banton, *The Idea of Race* (Boulder: Westview, 1978), 16; Richard Verstegan, *A Restitution of Decayed Intelligence* (1605; rpr. Norwood, N.J.: W. J. Johnson, 1979), 1.
15. Verstegan, *Restitution of Decayed Intelligence*, 25, 42, 46–50.
16. Ibid., 57, 62.
17. Banton, *Idea of Race*, 16–17.
18. Walter Scott, *Ivanhoe* (1819; rpr. New York: Heritage, 1950), ix, hereinafter cited in the text by page number only.
19. Augustin Thierry, *History of the Conquest of England by the Normans: With Its Causes from the Earliest Times, and Its Consequences to the Present Time*, 3 vols. (London: G. B. Whittaker, 1825), 1:13.

20. Simms, "History for the Purposes of Art," 46.

21. Mark Girouard, *The Return to Camelot: Chivalry and the English Gentleman* (New Haven: Yale University Press, 1981), 34, 30.

22. Thierry, *History of the Conquest of England by the Normans*, 548-49.

23. Susan Dabney Smedes, *Memorials of a Southern Planter*, ed. Fletcher M. Green (1887; rpr. New York: Knopf, 1965), 61, 21.

24. Anne Firor Scott, *The Southern Lady: From Pedestal to Politics, 1830-1930* (Chicago: University of Chicago Press, 1970), 17.

25. Elizabeth Fox-Genovese, *Within the Plantation Household: Black and White Women of the Old South* (Chapel Hill: University of North Carolina Press, 1988), 43, 38; Elizabeth Varon, *We Mean to Be Counted: White Women and Politics in Antebellum Virginia* (Chapel Hill: University of North Carolina Press, 1998), 1, 9.

26. Cash, *Mind of the South*, 86.

27. Nathaniel Beverley Tucker, *The Partisan Leader: A Tale of the Future* (1836; rpr. Chapel Hill: University of North Carolina Press, 1971), 130.

28. B. M. Wharton, "Women's Rights," *Southwestern Monthly* 1 (1852), 147, 149; Tucker, *Partisan Leader*, 123.

29. Review of *Ivanhoe* in *The Port Folio* 9 (1820), 301-2.

30. Review of *Ivanhoe* in *The Western Review and Miscellaneous Magazine* 2 (May, 1820), 224.

31. Banton, *Idea of Race*, 20; Kwame Anthony Appiah, "Race," in *Critical Terms for Literary Study*, 2nd ed., ed. Frank Lentricchia and Thomas McLaughlin (Chicago: University of Chicago Press, 1995), 280.

32. J. Quitman Moore, "Southern Statesmanship," *DeBow's Review* 29 (Oct. 1860), 402-3.

CHAPTER 3: A Slaveholding Race

1. "Direct Trade of Southern States with Europe," *DeBow's Review* 4 (1847), 350.

2. Ellwood Fisher, "The North and the South," *DeBow's Review* 7 (1849), 137.

3. Ibid., 141-42; John Forsyth, "The North and the South," *DeBow's Review* 17 (1854), 366.

4. "Slavery and the Abolitionists," *Southern Quarterly Review* 15 (1849), 199.

5. "The Destinies of the South," *Southern Quarterly Review*, n.s., 7 (1853), 186; *Richmond Enquirer* quoted in "Destiny of the Slave States," *DeBow's Review* 17 (1854), 284.

6. James D. B. DeBow, "The Interest in Slavery of the Southern Non-Slaveholder," in *Southern Pamphlets on Secession*, ed. Jon L. Wakelyn (Chapel Hill: University of North Carolina Press, 1996), 83-84.

7. "The Black Race in North America," *Southern Literary Messenger* 21 (1855), 664.

8. Edmund Ruffin, *Address to the Virginia State Agricultural Society, December 16, 1852* (Richmond: P. D. Bernard, 1853), 7; George Fitzhugh, *Sociology for the South; or, The Failure of Free Society* (1854; rpr. New York: Burt Franklin, 1965), 184.

9. James Henry Hammond, "Slavery at the South," *DeBow's Review* 7 (1849), 295.

10. George Fitzhugh, "Slavery Aggressions," *DeBow's Review* 28 (1860), 138; Fitzhugh, *Sociology for the South*, 181, 179.

11. Fitzhugh, "Slavery Aggressions," 138; Fitzhugh, *Cannibals All! or, Slaves without Masters* (1857; rpr. Cambridge: Harvard University Press, 1960), 69.

12. J. Quitman Moore, "Feudalism in America," *DeBow's Review* 28 (1860), 619.

13. Daniel R. Hundley, *Social Relations in Our Southern States* (New York: H. B. Price, 1860), 77, 81, 91, 193–201, 226, 273.

14. J. T. Wiswall, "Causes of Aristocracy," *DeBow's Review* 28 (1860), 557, 564.

15. Maria J. McIntosh, "The South," *Home Circle* 1 (1855), 539.

16. Wiswall, "Causes of Aristocracy," 565, 566.

17. "The Mines of California," *Southern Quarterly Review* 17 (1850), 27; Muscoe Russell Hunter Garnett, *The Union, Past and Future: How It Works, and How to Save It* (Washington: John T. Towers, 1850), 27.

18. Reginald Horsman, *Race and Manifest Destiny: The Origins of American Racial Anglo-Saxonism* (Cambridge: Harvard University Press, 1981), 166.

19. "The Destinies of the South," *Southern Quarterly Review*, n.s., 7 (1853), 200; J. N. Maffit, "The Almighty Dollar," *Southern Lady's Companion* 6 (1852), 76; Ruffin, *Address to the Virginia State Agricultural Society*, 12.

20. "Destinies of the South," 200; Maffit, "Almighty Dollar," 76.

21. Claudian B. Northrup, *Political Remarks by "N"* (Charleston: Evans and Cogswell, 1861), 9.

22. A. Clarkson, "The Basis of Northern Hostility to the South," *DeBow's Review* 28 (1860), 9–10; "The Edinburgh Review and the Southern States," *DeBow's Review* 10 (1851), 519.

23. Fitzhugh, *Sociology for the South*, 201, 197–98.

24. Fitzhugh, *Cannibals All!* 103; "Northern Mind and Character," *Southern Literary Messenger* 31 (1860), 345.

25. "Destinies of the South," 195; "New England and the Union," *The Liberator* 28 (23 April 1858), 65.

26. William John Grayson, *The Hireling and the Slave, Chicora, and Other Poems* (1856; rpr. Miami: University of Miami Press, 1969), 38, 39.

27. "Shorter's Opinion of the Pilgrim Fathers," *The Liberator* 28 (23 April 1858), 65; "New England and the Union," 65.

28. Clarkson, "Basis of Northern Hostility to the South," 13; "Northern Mind and Character," 343.

29. Clarkson, "Basis of Northern Hostility to the South," 13.

30. Grayson, *The Hireling and the Slave*, 42; Fitzhugh, *Sociology for the South*, 217.

31. "Northern Mind and Character," 345.

32. Ibid., 347.

33. Ruffin, *Address to the Virginia State Agricultural Society*, 16–17, 19.

34. "The Northman's Cause," *Southern Literary Messenger* 31 (1860), 415.

35. Northrup, *Political Remarks by "N,"* 9, 13.

36. Fitzhugh, *Sociology for the South*, 203.

37. "Southern Civilization; or, The Norman in America," *DeBow's Review* 32 (1862), 4–5, hereinafter cited in the text by page number only.

CHAPTER 4: Race Mythology and Antebellum Fiction

1. John Esten Cooke, *Virginia: A History of the People* (1883; rpr. Boston: Houghton Mifflin, 1894), 230.

2. Carl Bridenbaugh, *Myths and Realities: Societies of the Colonial South* (Baton Rouge: Louisiana State University Press, 1952), 53; Robert E. Brown and Katherine Brown, *Virginia, 1705–1786: Democracy or Aristocracy* (East Lansing: Michigan State University Press, 1964), 307; Robert Beverley, *The History and Present State of Virginia*, ed. Louis B. Wright (1705; rpr. Chapel Hill: University of North Carolina Press, 1947), 287–88.

3. David Hackett Fischer, *Albion's Seed: Four British Folkways in America* (New York: Oxford University Press, 1989), 3–11.

4. Louis B. Wright, *The First Gentlemen of Virginia: Intellectual Qualities of the Early Colonial Ruling Class* (San Marino, Calif.: Huntington Library, 1940), 37.

5. Philip Fithian, *Journal and Letters of Philip Vickers Fithian, 1773–1774: A Plantation Tutor of the Old Dominion*, ed. Hunter Dickinson Farish (Charlottesville: University Press of Virginia, 1957), 161.

6. James Reid, "The Religion of the Bible and the Religion of K[ing] W[illiam] County Compared," in *The Colonial Virginia Satirist: Mid-Eighteenth Century Commentaries on Politics, Religion, and Society*, ed. Richard Beale Davis (Philadelphia: American Philosophical Society, 1967), 48–49.

7. "Essay on Honor," *Virginia Gazette*, 27 July–3 August 1789, 1; "To the Printer," *Virginia Gazette*, 11 July 1751, 1; "London," *Virginia Gazette*, 4 April 1751, 2.

8. Charles S. Sydnor, *Gentlemen Freeholders: Political Practice in Washington's Virginia* (Chapel Hill: University of North Carolina Press, 1952), 10.

9. Marquis de Chastellux, *Travels in North America in the Years 1780, 1781, and 1782*, trans. Howard C. Rice Jr. (Chapel Hill: University of North Carolina Press, 1963), 2, 429, 435.

10. George Tucker, *The Valley of Shenandoah; or, The Memoirs of the Graysons*, 2 vols. (1824; rpr. Chapel Hill: University of North Carolina Press, 1970), 2:105.

11. Ibid., 106.

12. Ibid., 1:3.

13. Ibid., 307.

14. James Ewell Heath, *Edge-Hill; or, The Family of the Fitzroyals* (Richmond: T. W. White, 1828), 100.

15. John Pendleton Kennedy, *Swallow Barn: A Sojourn in the Old Dominion*, rev. ed. (Philadelphia: Lippincott, 1861), 149.

16. Ibid., 71.

17. William Alexander Caruthers, *The Cavaliers of Virginia; or, The Recluse of Jamestown: An Historical Romance of the Old Dominion*, 2 vols. (1834; rpr. Ridgewood, N.J.: Gregg, 1968), 1:164.

18. Ibid., 169.

19. Ibid., 5, 94.

20. Ibid., 4, 23.

21. Charles Sydnor, *Development of Southern Sectionalism, 1819–1848* (Baton Rouge: Louisiana State University Press, 1971), 220.

22. Nathaniel Beverley Tucker, *The Partisan Leader: A Tale of the Future* (1836; rpr. Chapel Hill: University of North Carolina Press, 1971), 89.

23. William Alexander Caruthers, *The Knights of the Golden Horse-shoe: A Traditionary Tale of the Cocked Hat Gentry in the Old Dominion* (1845; rpr. Chapel Hill, University of North Carolina Press, 1970), 28–29.

24. Ibid., 161.

25. Ibid., 245.

26. John Esten Cooke, *The Virginia Comedians; or, Old Days in the Old Dominion*, 2 vols. (1854; rpr. Ridgewood, N.J.: Gregg Press, 1968), 2:106–7.

27. Ibid., 148.

28. John Esten Cooke, *Henry St. John, Gentleman, of "Flowers of Hundreds," in the County of Prince George: A Tale of 1774–75* (New York: Harper and Brothers, 1859), 59.

29. Joseph Holt Ingraham, *The Southwest, by a Yankee*, 2 vols. (1835; rpr. New York: Negro Universities Press, 1968), 2:192; Ingraham, *The Sunny South; or, The Southerner at Home* (Philadelphia: G. G. Evans, 1860), 523.

30. *Faulkner in the University: Class Conferences at the University of Virginia, 1957–1958*, ed. Frederick L. Gwynn and Joseph L. Blotner (Charlottesville: University of Virginia Press, 1959), 212.

31. Caroline Lee Hentz, *The Planter's Northern Bride* (1854; rpr. Chapel Hill: University of North Carolina Press, 1970), 152.

32. Ibid., 30.

33. Ibid., 215.

34. Ibid., 521.

35. Michael Kreyling, *Figures of the Hero in Southern Narrative* (Baton Rouge: Louisiana State University Press, 1987), 16–18; Hentz, *Planter's Northern Bride*, 230.

36. Hentz, *Planter's Northern Bride*, 331–32.

37. William L. G. Smith, *Life at the South; or, "Uncle Tom's Cabin" as It Is, Being Narratives, Scenes, and Incidents in the Real "Life of the Lowly"* (Buffalo: George Derby, 1852), 13–14.

38. Robert Criswell, *"Uncle Tom's Cabin" Contrasted with Buckingham Hall, the Planter's Home; or, A Fair View of Both Sides of the Slavery Question* (New York: D. Fanshaw, 1852), 10.

39. J. Thornton Randolph [Charles Jacobs Peterson], *The Cabin and Parlor; or, Slaves and Masters* (Philadelphia: T. B. Peterson, 1852), 11.

40. Ibid., 12.

41. Ingraham, *Sunny South*, 26–27, 198.

42. Ibid., 31.

43. Ibid., 66.

44. Ibid., 118, 123.

45. Ibid., 31, 37, 112.

46. [St. Leger Landon Carter (?)], "Interesting Ruins on the Rappahannock," *Southern Literary Messenger* 1 (1834), 9–10.

47. Mrs. Henry R. Schoolcraft, *The Black Gauntlet: A Tale of Plantation Life* (Philadelphia: J. B. Lippincott, 1861), 11, 12, 19, 20, 159.

48. Ibid., 7.

49. Charles Sealsfield, *The Cabin Book; or, National Characteristics*, trans. Sarah Powell (1841; rpr. Austin: Eakin, 1985), 82, 83–84, 85.

50. Ibid., 85, 87.

51. Ibid., 86.

CHAPTER 5: A Universal Yankee Nation

1. Quoted in Shaw Livermore, *The Twilight of Federalism: The Disintegration of the Federalist Party, 1815–1830* (Princeton: Princeton University Press, 1962), 96.

2. Reginald Horsman, *Race and Manifest Destiny: The Origins of American Racial Anglo-Saxonism* (Cambridge: Harvard University Press, 1981), 177.

3. George Perkins Marsh, *The Goths in New England: A Discourse Delivered at the Anniversary of the Philomathesian Society of Middlebury College* (Middlebury, Vt.: J. Cobb, 1843), 10.

4. Ibid., 22.

5. Audrey Smedley, *Race in North America* (Boulder: Westview, 1993), 189.

6. Quoted in James Elliot Cabot, *A Memoir of Ralph Waldo Emerson* (Boston: Houghton Mifflin, 1888), 2:748–49.

7. Ibid., 749.

8. Ibid., 750.

9. Theodore Parker, "The Destination of America," in *The Slave Power*, ed. James K. Hosmer (1910; rpr. New York: Arno, 1969), 121.

10. Ibid., 121–22.

11. Ibid., 122–23.

12. Ibid., 126.

13. Ralph Waldo Emerson, *English Traits*, ed. Howard Mumford Jones (Cambridge: Harvard University Press, 1966), 38.

14. Ibid., 75.

15. Ibid., 201.

16. Ibid., 30.

17. Henry Ward Beecher, "Puritanism," in *Lectures and Orations*, ed. Newell Dwight Hillis (1913; rpr. New York: AMS, 1970), 12, 22, 18.

18. Ibid., 18, 30.

19. Charles Lyell, *A Second Visit to the United States of North America* (New York: Harper and Brothers, 1850), 1:81.

20. "William H. Seward's Higher Law Speech," in *The Compromise of 1850*, ed. Edwin C. Rozwenc (Boston: Heath, 1957), 47.

21. "The South: Slavery in Its Effects on Character, and the Social Relations of the Master Class," in *The Leaven of Democracy*, ed. Clement Eaton (New York: Harper, 1963), 485–86.

22. Horace Greeley, *New York Daily Tribune*, 7 March 1854, 1.

23. Horace Greeley, *New York Daily Tribune*, 15 April 1854, 4.

24. Horace Greeley, *New York Daily Tribune*, 21 April 1854, 4.

25. Horace Greeley, *New York Daily Tribune*, 9 Jan. 1855, 4; 9 Feb. 1855, 4.

26. Quoted in "The War against the South," *DeBow's Review* 21 (1856), 273.

27. Henry Ward Beecher, *Defense of Kansas* (Washington: Buell and Blanchard, 1856), 4.

28. William Lloyd Garrison, "Southern Degradation," in *William Lloyd Garrison and the Fight against Slavery: Selections from "The Liberator,"* ed. William E. Cain (Boston: Bedford Books, 1995), 147.

29. William Lloyd Garrison, "Review of Fitzhugh's *Cannibals All!*" *The Liberator*, 6 March 1857, 38.

30. Sloan quoted in William Lloyd Garrison, "Speech of Rev. J. R. W. Sloane," *The Liberator*, 1 June 1860, 85; Mayo quoted in William Lloyd Garrison, "The Herod of America," *The Liberator*, 4 May 1860, 69.

31. William Lloyd Garrison, "No 'Covenant with Death,'" *The Liberator*, 5 Dec. 1856, 194.

32. Howard Floan, *The South in Northern Eyes* (Austin: University of Texas Press, 1956), 186.

33. Theodore Parker, "Slave Power in America," in *Speeches, Addresses, and Occasional Sermons* (Boston: R. Leighton Jr., 1860), 3:41–42.

34. Ralph Waldo Emerson, "Attempted Speech—24 January 1861," in *Emerson's Antislavery Writings*, ed. Joel Myerson (New Haven: Yale University Press, 1995), 126; Henry Wadsworth Longfellow, letter to Charles Sumner, 12 Dec. 1860, Longfellow Letters, Harvard University.

35. *The Journals and Miscellaneous Notebooks of Ralph Waldo Emerson*, ed. William Gilman (Cambridge: Harvard University Press, 1960), 14:98; Ralph Waldo Emerson, "Assault on Charles Sumner," in *Emerson's Antislavery Writings*, 109.

36. Emerson, *Journals and Miscellaneous Notebooks*, 11:408, 14:169–70.

CHAPTER 6: A Proud, High-Toned People Repudiate the Scum of the North

1. Alexander Stephens, "Speech before the Georgia Convention," Facsimile Collection, Louisiana and Lower Mississippi Valley Collections, Louisiana State University Libraries; "The Address of the People of South Carolina, Assembled in Convention, to the People of the Slaveholding States of the United States," Joseph Jones Papers, Letter Filebook, 1860–61, Louisiana and Lower Mississippi Valley Collections, Louisiana State University Libraries.

2. Jabez Lamar Monroe Curry, "The Perils and Duty of the South," in *Pamphlets on Secession*, ed. Jon L. Wakelyn (Chapel Hill: University of North Carolina Press, 1996), 47.

3. "Epitaph on the United States of America" (Charleston, 1860), South Carolina Historical Society; Elise Rutledge Scrapbook, Southern Historical Collection, University of North Carolina.

4. "The Great Issue: Our Relation to It," *Southern Literary Messenger* 34 (1861), 187.

5. "Cuba: The March of Empire and the Course of Trade," *DeBow's Review* 30 (1861), 41, 42.

6. *Charleston Mercury* and Ellwood Fisher quoted in "Northern and Southern Nations," *Savannah Daily Morning News*, 11 Feb. 1861, 1.

7. "National Characteristics: The Issue of the Day," *DeBow's Review* 30 (1861), 45–46.

8. Ibid., 45, 47.

9. Ibid., 45.

10. Ibid., 53.

11. Quoted in "Northern Rule," *Charleston Mercury*, 12 Jan. 1861, 1.

12. "Union with the Northern States Necessarily Destructive of Southern Liberty," *Charleston Mercury*, 18 Jan. 1861, 1.

13. John M. Daniel, *The Richmond Examiner during the War* (1868; rpr. New York: Arno, 1970), 6.

14. *Richmond Dispatch*, April 1861, Elise Rutledge Scrapbook, Southern Historical Collection, University of North Carolina.

15. *Charleston Mercury*, 15 April 1861, 1.

16. "The War News," *Charleston Mercury*, 18 April 1861, 1.

17. "The Crisis," Cheves Papers, Civil War Clippings, Southern Historical Collection, University of North Carolina.

18. "The War," *New Orleans Bee*, 1 May 1861, in *Southern Editorials on Secession*, ed. Dwight Lowell Dumond (New York: Century, 1981), 513.

19. "Conflict of Northern and Southern Races," *DeBow's Review* 31 (1861), 391, 393, 394.

20. *New York Herald*, 3 Feb. 1861, Elise Rutledge Scrapbook, Southern Historical Collection, University of North Carolina.

21. Ibid.

22. Quoted in *Charleston Mercury*, 17 Nov. 1860, 1.

23. Quoted in "Complimentary View of the South," *Savannah Daily Morning News*, 25 March 1861, 1.

24. *New York Herald*, 6 April 1861, 4.

25. Horace Greeley, *The American Conflict: A History of the Great Rebellion in the United States of America, 1860–64* (Hartford: D. D. Case and Co., 1865), 1:448.

26. "The People and the Issue," *New York Times*, 15 Apr. 1861, 4.

27. "Southern Chivalry," *New Haven Daily Palladium*, 29 April 1861, in *Northern Editorials on Secession*, ed. Howard Cecil Perkins (New York: D. Appleton-Century, 1942), 1:526.

28. "Northern Homage to Southern Humbug," *Peoria Daily Transcript*, 8 May 1861, in *Northern Editorials on Secession*, 1:528–29; "The Sepoys of Montgomery," *Albany Evening Journal*, 10 May 1861, in *Northern Editorials on Secession*, 1:530.

29. "Are We One People?" *Burlington (Vt.) Daily Times*, 14 May 1861, in *Northern Editorials on Secession*, 1:531.

30. Ibid., 532, 533.

31. Samuel May, letter to Richard Davis Webb, 6 Nov. 1860, May Papers, Boston Public Library.

32. Letter, Feb. 1861, John Bigelow Papers, New York Public Library.

33. William Furness, letter to Samuel May, 20 May 1861, May Papers, Boston Public Library.

34. *Life and Letters of Edmund Clarence Stedman*, ed. Laura Stedman and George M. Gould (New York: Moffat, Yard, and Co., 1910), 243.

35. Thomas Atkinson, "On the Causes of Our National Troubles" (Wilmington, N.C., 1861), 9–10, pamphlet found at University of North Carolina Rare Book Collection.

36. "Draft of Speech," Jan. 1861, Thomas O. Moore Papers, Louisiana and Lower Mississippi Valley Collections, Louisiana State University Libraries.

37. Nathaniel Francis Cabell, letter to Henry Stephens Randell, 6 Jan. 1860, Virginia Historical Society.

38. Quoted in Robert Manson Myers, *The Children of Pride: A True Story of Georgia and the Civil War* (New Haven: Yale University Press, 1972), 665.

39. A. C. Haskell, letter to his mother, 13 Feb. 1861, A. C. Haskell Papers, Southern Historical Collection, University of North Carolina; Jones quoted in Myers, *Children of Pride*, 694–95, 968.

40. George A. Mercer Diary, 11 Aug. 1861, Southern Historical Collection, University of North Carolina.

41. Henry St. John Dixon, letter to his father, 21 Mar. 1861, Henry St. John Dixon Papers, Southern Historical Collection, University of North Carolina; George A. Mercer Diary, 30 April 1861.

42. George A. Mercer Diary, 2 Feb. 1861.

43. Laurence M. Keitt, letter, 4 March 1861, Keitt Papers, Duke University.

44. R. F. W. Allston, letter, 11 April 1861, Factors' Letters, South Carolina Historical Society; A. McCall, letter, 23 Feb. 1861, Ebenezer Mariam Papers, New-York Historical Society.

45. Laurence M. Keitt, letter to Mrs. Frederick Brown, 4 March 1861, Keitt Papers, Duke University.

46. *Marion Harland's Autobiography: The Story of a Long Life* (New York: Harper and Brothers, 1910), 366.

47. John Preston, "Address of John Preston of South Carolina," in *Addresses Delivered before the Virginia State Convention*, ed. Fulton Anderson (Richmond: W. M. Elliott, 1861), 56–57.

48. Mary Boykin Chesnut, *Mary Chesnut's Civil War*, ed. C. Vann Woodward (New Haven: Yale University Press, 1981), 245.

49. Ibid., 25.

50. Ibid.

51. George A. Mercer Diary, 25 Jan. 1861.

52. Sophia Haskell, letter, 28 March 1861, Cheves Papers, South Carolina Historical Society.

53. Ben Allston, letter to Robert Allston, 14 April 1861, Robert F. W. Allston Papers, South Carolina Historical Society; A. C. Haskell, letter, 17 April 1861, A. C. Haskell Papers, Southern Historical Collection, University of North Carolina.

54. Adele Allston, letter to Charley Allston, 14 Apr. 1861, Robert F. W. Allston Papers, South Carolina Historical Society.

55. Sarah Butler, letters, 16 Apr. 1861, 7 June 1861, Margaret Butler Correspondence, Louisiana and Lower Mississippi Valley Collections, Louisiana State University Libraries; George A. Mercer Diary, 22 April 1861.

56. John Coles Rutherfoord Diary, 15 April 1861, Virginia Historical Society; Jones quoted in Myers, *Children of Pride*, 648; Preston, "Address of John Preston," 61, 62.

57. Wigfall quoted in G. G. Vest, "A Senator of Two Republics: Ben Hill, Toombs, Yancey, and Wigfall," *Saturday Evening Post*, 17 Oct. 1903, 4; Ewing quoted in Randall C. Jimmerson, *The Private Civil War: Popular Thought during the Sectional Conflict* (Baton Rouge: Louisiana State University Press, 1988), 127.

58. "Epitaph on the United States of America" (Charleston: Evans and Cogswell, 1860), one-page broadside found at South Carolina Historical Society.

59. "The Great Issue: Our Relation to It," *Southern Literary Messenger* 34 (1861), 166.

60. Ibid., 165.

61. George A. Mercer Diary, 30 March 1861.

62. Percival Drayton, letter to Lydig Hoyt, 19 May 1861, Percival Drayton Letters, New York Public Library.

63. James M. McPherson, *For Cause and Comrades: Why Men Fought in the Civil War* (New York: Oxford University Press, 1997), 20–21.

64. "Yankee Despotism at Washington," *Richmond Whig*, Elise Rutledge Scrapbook, Southern Historical Collection, University of North Carolina; Henry St. John Dixon, letter to his father, 15 Apr. 1861, Henry St. John Dixon Papers, Southern Historical Collection, University of North Carolina.

65. *I Wrote You Word: The Poignant Letters of Private Holt*, ed. James A. Mumper (Lynchburg: H. E. Howard., 1993), 79.

66. Louis B. Wright, *The First Gentlemen of Virginia: Intellectual Qualities of the Early Colonial Ruling Class* (San Marino, Calif.: Huntington Library, 1940), 1–37.

67. Bertram Wyatt-Brown, *Yankee Saints and Southern Sinners* (Baton Rouge: Louisiana State University Press, 1985), 187.

68. Edwin Harrison Cady, *The Gentleman in America: A Literary Study in American Culture* (Syracuse, N.Y.: Syracuse University Press, 1949), 4; Clement Eaton, *The Growth of Southern Civilization, 1790–1860* (New York: Harper, 1961), 2.

69. John Elliott Cairnes, *The Slave Power: Its Character, Career, and Probable Designs* (1863; rpr. New York: A. M. Kelley, 1968), 186; Clement Eaton, *The Mind of the Old South* (Baton Rouge: Louisiana State University Press, 1964), 241–42.

70. Wyatt-Brown, *Yankee Saints*, 201, 205.

71. Douglas Southall Freeman, *R. E. Lee: A Biography* (New York: Scribner's, 1944), 1:447; Harold Earl Hammond, ed., *Diary of a Union Lady, 1861–1865* (New York: Funk and Wagnalls, 1967), 359.

72. Wyatt-Brown, *Yankee Saints*, 191.

73. "Southern Convention at Savannah," *DeBow's Review* 22 (1857), 87.

74. James Hamilton Couper, letter to Francis Corbin, 20 Nov. 1860, Francis P. Corbin Papers, New-York Historical Society; J. Quitman Moore, "Southern Statesmanship," *DeBow's Review* 29 (1860), 409.

75. Quoted in Horace Greeley, *The American Conflict: A History of the Great Rebellion in the United States of America, 1860–64* (Hartford: O. D. Case and Co., 1865), 1:331.

76. Weldon Edwards, letter to George Barksdale, 21 Dec. 1860, Weldon N. Edwards Papers, Virginia Historical Society.

77. Quoted in James I. Robertson Jr., *Soldiers Blue and Gray* (Columbia: University of South Carolina Press, 1988), 7.

78. McPherson, *For Cause and Comrades*, 22–23.

79. David Pierson, letter to his father, 19 Apr. 1861, David Pierson Letters, Louisiana and Lower Mississippi Valley Collections, Louisiana State University Libraries.

80. Bertram Wyatt-Brown, *Southern Honor: Ethics and Behavior in the Old South* (New York: Oxford University Press, 1982), 20.

CHAPTER 7: **Northern Vandals versus Southern Ruffians**

1. John M. Daniel, *The Richmond Examiner during the War* (1868; rpr. New York: Arno, 1970), 19.

2. Ibid., 17. Preston Brooks had continued to represent his South Carolina district until his death in Washington on January 27, 1857, less than a year after his assault upon Charles Sumner.

3. Elise Rutledge Scrapbook, Southern Historical Collection, University of North Carolina; Daniel, *Richmond Examiner*, 17–18.

4. Chester G. Hearn, *When the Devil Came Down to Dixie: Ben Butler in New Orleans* (Baton Rouge: Louisiana State University Press, 1997), 103.

5. Daniel, *Richmond Examiner*, 66–68.

6. "Can the United States Be Restored?" *Richmond Daily Dispatch*, 7 Feb. 1863, 2.

7. Elise Rutledge Scrapbook, Southern Historical Collection, University of North Carolina.

8. Cheves Papers, Civil War Clippings, South Carolina Historical Society.

9. "Southern Civilization; or, The Norman in America," *DeBow's Review* 32 (1862), 2.

10. Ibid., 19.

11. Virginia Sherwood, "Southern Hate of the North," *Continental Monthly* 2 (1862), 448.

12. Virginia Sherwood, "Southern Hate of New England," *Continental Monthly* 4 (1863), 244; "Chivalry," *Columbus Daily Ohio State Journal*, 3 June 1861, in *Northern Editorials on Secession*, ed. Howard Cecil Perkins (New York: D. Appleton-Century, 1942), 1:536.

13. Evan W. Evans, "The American Cavaliers," *The New Englander* 23 (1864), 651–52, 655.

14. Ibid., 655–56.

15. Ibid., 658–59.

16. Sherwood, "Southern Hate of New England," 244.

17. Ibid., 247–48.

18. Ibid., 245, 246.

19. Ibid., 250, 249.

20. Ibid., 244; *Abraham Lincoln: Speeches and Writings, 1859–1865* (New York: Library of America, 1989), 687.

21. W. H. Whitmore, "The Cavalier Theory Refuted," *Continental Monthly* 4 (1863), 60, 68, 69.

22. Ibid., 70–71.

23. Ibid., 69; "Look at Home," *New Orleans Bee*, 29 March 1861, 1.

24. *The Letters of Ralph Waldo Emerson*, ed. Ralph L. Rusk, 6 vols. (New York: Columbia University Press, 1939), 5:253.

25. George Templeton Strong, *Diary of the Civil War, 1860–1865* (New York: Macmillan, 1962), 103, 170.

26. *The Correspondence of John Lothrop Motley*, ed. George William Curtis (New York: Harper and Brothers, 1900), 2:214; Strong, *Diary of the Civil War*, 332.

27. *The Letters of Francis Parkman*, ed. Wilbur R. Jacobs (Norman: University of Oklahoma Press, 1960), 1:160–61.

28. Ibid., 165.

29. Ibid., 163, 164–65.

30. Ibid., 163, 165.

31. William Chauncey Fowler, *The Sectional Controversy* (New York: Charles Scribner, 1863), 7.

32. George A. Mercer Diary, 5 May 1861, Southern Historical Collection, University of North Carolina.

33. David Schenck Diary, 16 June 1862, Southern Historical Collection, University of North Carolina.

34. Mary Boykin Chesnut, *Mary Chesnut's Civil War*, ed. C. Vann Woodward (New Haven: Yale University Press, 1981), 87.

35. "Clippings from a Diary of the War: General Van Dorn's Raid into Holly Springs [Mississippi], Dec. 20, 1863," Boston Public Library.

36. George A. Mercer Diary, 18 Aug. 1861.

37. Clara Solomon Diary, 8 May 1862, Louisiana and Lower Mississippi Valley Collections, Louisiana State University Libraries.

38. Ibid., 17 May 1862; Leila Habersham Scrapbook, Georgia Historical Society.

39. *Letters of Warren Akin, Confederate Congressman*, ed. Bell Irvin Wiley (Athens: University of Georgia Press, 1959), 54; *When the World Ended: The Diary of Emma Le Conte*, ed. Earl Schenck Miers (Lincoln: University of Nebraska Press, 1987), 44, 49.

40. *The Private Journal of Henry William Ravenel, 1859–1867*, ed. Arney Robinson Childs (Columbia: University of South Carolina Press, 1947), 66.

41. *Letters of Warren Akin*, 33; *Brokenburn: The Journal of Kate Stone, 1861–1868*, ed. John Q. Anderson (Baton Rouge: Louisiana State University Press, 1995), 339.

42. Ella Gertrude Thomas Papers, Journal, 1 Jan. 1862, Duke University; Clara Hoyt to Fannie Hamilton, 1 Feb. 1862, Ruffin, Roulhac, and Hamilton Family Papers, Southern Historical Collection, University of North Carolina.

43. Leila Habersham Scrapbook; David Schenck Diary, 16 June 1862.

44. "The Israelites of South Carolina," *Charleston Mercury*, 1 Feb. 1861, 1. For a full analysis of Jewish support for the Confederacy, see Robert N. Rosen, *The Jewish Confederates* (Columbia: University of South Carolina Press, 2000).

45. Clara Solomon Diary, 4 May 1862, 13 June 1862, 31 May 1862.

46. George A. Mercer Diary, 16 April 1865.

47. Kate Garland Diary, 6 June 1865, Louisiana and Lower Mississippi Valley Collections, Louisiana Sate University Libraries; Lucy Muse Fletcher Diary, 9 April 1865, Lucy Muse Fletcher Papers, Duke University.

48. Lucy Muse Fletcher Diary, 25 April 1865.

49. Quoted in Avery Craven, *Edmund Ruffin, Southerner: A Study in Secession* (New York: D. Appleton-Century, 1932), 259.

50. Bell Irvin Wiley, *The Common Soldier in the Civil War* (New York: Grosset and Dunlap, 1958), 361.

51. Ibid., 347–48; *The Civil War Letters of General Robert McAllister*, ed. James I. Robertson Jr. (New Brunswick: Rutgers University Press, 1965), 558; *A Politician Goes to War: The Civil War Letters of John White Geary*, ed. William Alan Blair (University Park: Pennsylvania State University Press, 1995), 65; Spooner quoted in *Yankee Correspondence: Civil War Letters between New England Soldiers and the Home Front*, ed. Norris Silber and Mary Beth Sievens (Charlottesville: University Press of Virginia, 1996), 55–56.

52. *War Letters of William Thompson Lusk* (New York: Privately printed, 1911), 97; second letter by Lusk quoted in Randall C. Jimerson, *The Private Civil War: Popular Thought during the Sectional Conflict* (Baton Rouge: Louisiana State University Press, 1988), 131.

53. *War Letters of William Thompson Lusk*, 100.

54. Ibid., 102.

55. Uriah Parmelee, letter to his mother, 28 Sept. 1863, Parmelee Papers, Duke University.

56. Constant C. Hanks, letter, 18 June 1864, Constant C. Hanks Papers, Duke University; Henry Thompson, letter to his wife, 14 Oct. 1863, Henry Thompson Papers, Duke University.

57. *Civil War Letters of Robert McAllister*, 230; Webb quoted in Jimerson, *Private Civil War*, 159.

58. *Civil War Letters of Robert McAllister*, 132; Hall quoted in *Yankee Correspondence*, ed. Silber, 88.

59. *Civil War Letters of John White Geary*, 149, 150.

60. Wiley, *Common Soldier in the Civil War*, 309; Alexander Cheves Haskell, letter, 4 May 1861, A. C. Haskell Papers, Southern Historical Collection, University of North Carolina.

61. Haskell, letter, 8 May 1861; Peter Hairston, letter to Fanny, 22 Sept. 1861, Peter Hairston Papers, Southern Historical Collection, University of North Carolina.

62. Haskel, letter, 25 May 1861; Sam Watkins, *"Company Aytch"; or, A Side Show of the Big Show and Other Sketches*, ed. M. Thomas Inge (New York: Plume, 1999), 67.

63. William L. Nugent, *My Dear Nellie: The Civil War Letters of William L. Nugent to Eleanor Smith Nugent*, ed. William M. Cash and Lucy Somerville Howorth (Jackson: University Press of Mississippi, 1977), 71; W. C. Kendrick, letter to his father, June–July 1863, H. C. Kendrick Papers, Southern Historical Collection, University of North Carolina.

64. Quoted in Wiley, *Common Soldier in the Civil War*, 360–61.

65. Peter Hairston, letter, 9 May 1861, Peter Hairston Papers, Southern Historical Collection, University of North Carolina.

66. Nugent, *My Dear Nellie*, 71; *Ham Chamberlayne Virginian: Letters and Papers of an Artillery Officer*, ed. C. G. Chamberlayne (Richmond: Dietz, 1932), 186.

67. Henry Higginbotham, letter, 30 June 1864, Dore Schary Collection, New York Public Library; Watkins, *"Company Aytch,"* 66–67.

68. Watkins, *"Company Aytch,"* 3.

69. Nugent, *My Dear Nellie*, 80; Edmund Dewitt Patterson, *Yankee Rebel: The Civil War Journals of Edmund Dewitt Patterson*, ed. John G. Barrett (Chapel Hill: University of North Carolina Press, 1966), 11.

70. Chamberlayne, *Ham Chamberlayne Virginian: Letters and Papers*, 105.

71. Ibid.

72. Watkins, *"Company Aytch,"* 102.

73. Ibid., 81.

74. "Clippings from a Diary of the War," Boston Public Library.

75. Haskell, letter, 4 May 1861, A. C. Haskell Papers, Southern Historical Collection, University of North Carolina.

76. Nugent, *My Dear Nellie*, 149.

77. John S. Mosby, letter, 4 Feb. 1864, John S. Mosby Papers, Library of Congress.

78. W. C. Kendrick, letter to his sister, 18 Nov. 1861; Edward O. Guerrant, War Journal, 8 Feb. 1865, Southern Historical Society, University of North Carolina.

79. *Reluctant Rebel: The Secret Diary of Robert Patrick*, ed. F. J. Taylor (Baton Rouge: Louisiana State University Press, 1959), 196.

80. Henry St. John Dixon, letter to his father, 7 May 1865, Henry St. John Dixon Papers, Southern Historical Collection, University of North Carolina.

CHAPTER 8: Poetry Fights the Civil War

1. Walt Whitman, "The Wound Dresser," in *Leaves of Grass*, ed. Harold W. Blodgett and Sculley Bradley (New York: New York University Press, 1965), 310–11.

2. Edmund Wilson, *Patriotic Gore: Studies in the Literature of the American Civil War* (New York: Oxford University Press, 1962), 482.

3. Ibid., 466.

4. F. Scott Fitzgerald, *The Crack-Up*, ed. Edmund Wilson (New York: New Directions, 1945), 69.

5. Howard Brownell, "The Bay Fight," quoted in Wilson, *Patriotic Gore*, 468–69.

6. Mrs. C. A. Warfield, "Southern Chant of Defiance," in *The Southern Poems of the War*, ed. Emily V. Mason (Baltimore: John Murphy and Co., 1867), 17; Kate Brownlee Sherwood,

"Albert Sidney Johnston," in *Poems and Songs of the Civil War*, ed. Lois Hill (New York: Fairfax, 1990), 87; Anne Pryre Dennies, "Carolina," in *Southern Poems*, ed. Mason, 86.

7. "A Ballad for the Young South," in Confederate Papers, Scrap-book Clippings, folder 12, Southern Historical Collection, University of North Carolina.

8. "The South," in Confederate Papers, Scrap-book Clippings, folder 12; "Chivalrous C.S.A.," in *Confederate Scrap-book*, ed. Lizzie Cary Daniel (Richmond: J. H. Hill, 1893), 251.

9. Frank Ticknor, "The Virginians of the Valley," in *Confederate Scrap-book*, ed. Daniel, 232; Margaret Junkin Preston, "Stonewall Jackson's Grave," in *Southern Poems*, ed. Mason, 310.

10. "'Southrons On!'—Southern Battle Chorus," in Cheves Papers, Civil War Clippings, 12/104/10, South Carolina Historical Society.

11. Henry Timrod, "Carolina," in *Bugle-Echoes: A Collection of the Poetry of the Civil War, Northern and Southern*, ed. Francis F. Browne (New York: Frederick A. Stokes, 1886), 103; Albert Pike, "Dixie," in *Poems and Songs of the Civil War*, ed. Hill, 199; "God Save the South," in *Confederate Scrap-book*, ed. Daniel, 215.

12. Blackford Mason, "The Cavalier's Glee," in *Confederate Scrap-book*, ed. Daniel, 205; Susan Tally, "Rallying Song of the Virginians," in *Southern Poems*, ed. Mason, 27.

13. "My Order," in *Southern Poems*, ed. Mason, 236; "The Homespun Dress," ibid., 251.

14. "The Fall of Fort Sumter," in *Southern Poems*, ed. Mason, 236.

15. "Invocation," in Confederate Papers, Scrap-book Clippings, folder 12; John R. Thompson, "A Word with the West," in *Bugle Echoes*, ed. Browne, 142; James Brewer, "Are We Free?" in *Southern Poems*, ed. Mason, 69.

16. John Dickson Bruns, "The Foe at the Gates," in *Bugle Echoes*, ed. Browne, 273; Paul Hamilton Hayne, "Away with the Dastards Who Whine of Defeat," in *Southern Poems*, ed. Mason, 136.

17. "Virginia Dead," in *Southern Poems*, ed. Mason, 234.

18. John Reuben Thompson, "Ashby," in *Poems and Songs of the Civil War*, ed. Hill, 81; "Dirge for Ashby," in *Southern Poems*, ed. Mason, 227.

19. "Riding a Raid," in *Southern Poems*, ed. Mason, 292.

20. Winston Fontaine, "Stuart," in *Southern Poems*, ed. Mason, 345–46.

21. John R. Thompson, "Obsequies of Stuart," in *Bugle Echoes*, ed. Browne, 211.

22. Mrs. C. A. Warfield, "On the Death of Lieut.-Gen. Jackson: A Dirge," in *Southern Poems*, ed. Mason, 295; H. L. Flash, "Stonewall Jackson," ibid., 304.

23. "General Lee at the Battle of the Wilderness," in *Southern Poems*, ed. Mason, 342.

24. "General Robert E. Lee," in *Southern Poems*, ed. Mason, 367.

25. Dixon Wecter, *The Hero in America: A Chronicle of Hero Worship* (New York: C. Scribner's Sons, 1941), 251; Florence Anderson, "The Surrender of the Army of Northern Virginia," in *Southern Poems*, ed. Mason, 364.

26. Quoted in *Lyrics of Loyalty*, ed. Frank Moore (New York: George P. Putnam, 1864), 275.

27. "South Carolina's Justification to the North," in Confederate Papers, Scrap-book Clippings, folder 12.

28. "A Ballad for the Young South," in Confederate Papers, Scrap-book Clippings, folder 12. Sumner is Massachusetts's Senator Charles Sumner, and Hale is Unitarian clergyman and abolitionist Edward Everett Hale.

29. "The Cotton States' Farewell to Yankee Doodle," in *Confederate Scrap-book*, ed. Daniel, 248.

30. "Song of the Southern Soldier," in *Confederate Scrap-book*, ed. Daniel, 213.

31. "Written after the Battle of Manassas," in Confederate Papers, Scrap-book Clippings, folder 12.

32. "Lines" and "Camp Song," Confederate Papers, Scrap-book Clippings, folder 12; Henry Timrod, "Carolina," in *Columbia Book of Civil War Poetry*, ed. Richard Marius (New York: Columbia University Press, 1994), 60; R. E. Blackmar, "The Southern Marseillaise," in *Poems and Songs of the Civil War*, ed. Hill, 208; John R. Thompson, "A Word with the West," in *Bugle Echoes*, ed. Browne, 141; James R. Randall, "My Maryland," in *Columbia Book of Civil War Poetry*, ed. Marius, 61; Blackmar, "Southern Marseillaise," 209.

33. Randall, "My Maryland," in *Columbia Book of Civil War Poetry*, ed. Marius, 61; "War Song," in Confederate Papers, Scrap-book Clippings, folder 12.

34. Chester G. Hearn, *When the Devil Came Down to Dixie: Ben Butler in New Orleans* (Baton Rouge: Louisiana State University Press, 1997), 103.

35. Rosa Vertner Jeffrey, "The Southern Oath," in *Southern Poems*, ed. Mason, 261; Paul Hamilton Hayne, "Butler's Proclamation," ibid., 209.

36. Charles Royster, *The Destructive War: William Tecumseh Sherman, Stonewall Jackson, and the Americans* (New York: Knopf, 1991), 353, 358.

37. L. Virginia French, "Shermanized," in *Southern Poems*, ed. Mason, 361–62.

38. "Ho! Sons of the Puritan," in *Lyrics of Loyalty*, ed. Moore, 275.

39. John Greenleaf Whittier, "To Englishmen," in *The Complete Poetical Works of John Greenleaf Whittier* (Boston: Houghton Mifflin, 1894), 336.

40. Ralph Waldo Emerson, "Boston Hymn," in *Bugle Echoes*, ed. Browne, 149; Charles Godfrey Leland, "Northmen, Come Out!" in *Lyrics of Loyalty*, ed. Moore, 91.

41. William O. Bourne, "The New Reveille," in *Lyrics of Loyalty*, ed. Moore, 244.

42. Bertram Wyatt-Brown, *Yankee Saints and Southern Sinners* (Baton Rouge: Louisiana State University Press, 1985), 191.

43. Josiah Gilbert Holland, "The Heart of the War," in *Bugle Echoes*, ed. Browne, 128–29.

44. Francis Janvier, "The Union," in *Lyrics of Loyalty*, ed. Moore, 59; William Cullen Bryant, "Not Yet," in *Bugle Echoes*, ed. Browne, 136.

45. Deborah Pickman Clifford, *Mine Eyes Have Seen the Glory: A Biography of Julia Ward Howe* (Boston: Little, Brown, 1978), 139; W. W. Story, "War Song," in *Lyrics of Loyalty*, ed. Moore, 79; E. D. Baker, "Bring the Hero Home," ibid., 145; Emerson, "Boston Hymn," in *Bugle Echoes*, ed. Browne, 150.

46. Clifford, *Mine Eyes Have Seen the Glory*, 144.

47. John Greenleaf Whittier, "The Watchers," in *Bugle Echoes*, ed. Browne, 251.

48. Revelations 14:19; Genesis 3:14–15.

49. Clifford, *Mine Eyes Have Seen the Glory*, 144–46.

50. Ibid., 146.

51. Ibid., 147.

52. James Russell Lowell, "Ode Recited at the Harvard Commemoration, July 21, 1865," in *The Complete Poetical Works of James Russell Lowell* (Boston: Houghton Mifflin, 1899), 461.

53. Ibid.

54. Annie Ketchum Chambers, "April Twenty-sixth," in *Southern Poems*, ed. Mason, 368–69; "Lines Written July 15, 1865," ibid., 385–86.

55. Margaret Junkin Preston, "Virginia," in *Southern Poems*, ed. Mason, 380; Rose Vertner Jeffrey, "Dixie," ibid., 371.

56. Abram J. Ryan, "Our Dead," in *Confederate Scrap-book*, ed. Daniel, 234.

57. Daniel B. Lucas, "In the Land Where We Were Dreaming," in *Confederate Scrap-book*, ed. Daniel, 33.

58. Ibid.

59. Ibid., 34–35.

60. Ibid., 35.

61. Sidney Lanier, "The Tournament," in *Civil War Poems*, ed. Hill, 176–77.

62. A. J. Requier, "Ashes of Glory," in *Confederate Scrap-book*, ed. Daniel, 19–20.

63. Paul Hamilton Hayne, "Heroes of the South," in *Bugle Echoes*, ed. Browne, 320.

64. James Barron Hope, "Memoriae Sacrum," in *Confederate Scrap-book*, ed. Daniel, 63.

65. Ibid., 68.

66. James Branch Cabell, "Almost Touching the Confederacy," in Cabell, *Let Me Lie* (New York: Farrar, Straus and Co. 1947), 153–54; Abram J. Ryan, "The Conquered Banner," in *Southern Poems*, ed. Mason, 382.

CONCLUSION

1. Edward W. Gantt, *The Two Ways of Reason; or, The Open Traitor of the South Face to Face with His Skulking Abettor at the North* (New York: W. C. Bryant, 1863), 8.

2. Colonel George Alexander Martin Memoir, Virginia Historical Society.

3. William Basinger, letter to George Washington Custis Lee, 3 March 1866, Brock Collection, Huntington Library; William Rasin, letter to Robert Brock, 17 April 1900, Brock Collection, Huntington Library.

4. Benjamin H. Rutledge, letter to Benjamin Williams, 24 June 1886, B. H. Rutledge Letters, South Carolina Historical Society.

5. Ibid.

6. Sophia Haskell Cheves Papers, Essays, 1909, South Carolina Historical Society.

7. Ibid.

8. Speech of A. Burnett Rhett on Confederate Memorial Day, 10 May 1938, Robert B. Rhett Papers, South Carolina Historical Society.

9. Ibid.

10. Journal, Lucy Muse Fletcher Papers, Duke University.

11. "South Carolina Society," *Atlantic Monthly* 39 (1877), 670.

12. Ibid.

13. Ibid., 684.

14. Joyce Appleby, "Reconciliation and the Northern Novelist, 1865–1880," *Civil War History* 10 (1964), 120, 129.

15. C. Vann Woodward, *The Burden of Southern History* (Baton Rouge: Louisiana State University, 1968), 110–11.

16. Jay Martin, *Harvests of Change: American Literature, 1865–1914* (Englewood Cliffs: Prentice Hall, 1967), 83; Rollin G. Osterweis, *The Myth of the Lost Cause, 1865–1900* (Hamden: Anchor Books, 1973), 152.

17. Albion W. Tourgée, "The South as a Field for Fiction," *Forum* 6 (1888), 405, 408.

18. John Cussons, *United States "History," as the Yankee Makes It and Takes It* (Glen Allen, Va.: Cussons, May, and Co., 1900), 52–53.

19. Percy Greg, *History of the United States from the Foundations of Virginia to the Reconstruction of the Union* (1887; rpr., Richmond: West and Johnston, 1892), 1:105.

20. Ibid., 2:145, 157.

21. William Hepworth Dixon, *The White Conquest* (London: Chatto and Windus, 1876), 2:141.

22. Ibid., 141–43.

23. "South Carolina Society," 673.

24. Tony Horwitz, *Confederates in the Attic: Dispatches from the Unfinished Civil War* (New York: Pantheon Books, 1998), 53.

25. Ibid., 53, 49, 53.

26. *Faulkner in the University: Class Conferences at the University of Virginia, 1957–1958*, ed. Frederick L. Gwynn and Joseph L. Blotner (Charlottesville: University of Virginia Press, 1959), 212.

27. Horwitz, *Confederates in the Attic*, 68–69.

28. Barry Reid McCain, "The Anglo-Celts," *League of the South Homepage* (20 Aug. 2004), www.leagueofthesouth.com/spatriot/vol13no5/member13.html.

29. Grady McWhiney, *Cracker Culture: Celtic Ways in the Old South* (Tuscaloosa: University of Alabama Press, 1988), 7, 22.

30. Randall C. Jimerson, *The Private Civil War: Popular Thought during the Sectional Conflict* (Baton Rouge: Louisiana State University Press, 1988), 1.

INDEX

Abolitionism: and caning of Sumner by Brooks, 2–3, 9–10, 13–17; as cause of Civil War, 144; in 1850s, 130–31; and Manifest Destiny, 25; *New York Herald* on, 143; poetry on, 215; on southern aristocratic myth, 130–31; southerners on, 12, 84–85, 88, 215. *See also* Slavery; specific abolitionists
Absalom! Absalom! (Faulkner), 108
Adams, Henry, 242
African Americans. *See* Freed blacks; Slavery
Agrarianism, 73
Akin, Warren, 183, 184
Alabama, 163–64
Albion's Seed (Fischer), 94
Allston, Adele, 156
Allston, Ben, 155–56
American Anti-slavery Society, 131
American Civil War. *See* Civil War
American Revolution. *See* Revolutionary War
Anderson, Major, 155–56
Anglo-Saxon race: barbarism of, 142; Emerson on, 121–24; Lowell's poem on, 226; McCain on, 250; and northern racial mythmaking, 119–25, 127; Parker on, 122–23; terminology on, 20–21, 22, 45–46, 80–81; Whittier's poem on, 220–21. *See also* Norman-Saxon race myth; Puritanism; Yankees
Animal imagery: for southerners, 177–78, 192–93; for Union soldiers, 170, 193
Antebellum fiction. *See* Fiction; Plantation romance novels
Appiah, Kwame, 34, 39, 69
"April Twenty-sixth" (Chambers), 226–27
Aristocratic myth: in colonial Virginia, 93–99, 109, 162, 232–33, 240; and Confederate soldiers, 198, 199; Greeley on, 128–29; and Lost Cause myth, 236–39; northern repudiation of, 79, 127–33, 144–49, 173–74, 176, 178–79, 188, 191; in plantation romance novels, 99–116; poetry on, 203–13, 232–33; in postbellum period, 236–47; and slavery, 174; of southerners, 15–16, 18, 71, 76, 79–80, 94–99, 109, 127–29, 162; in twenty-first century, 248–51. *See also* Cavaliers; Chivalry; Honor
Arkansas, 163, 206, 235
Ashby, Turner, 209–10
"Ashes of Glory" (Requier), 231–32
"Assault on Charles Sumner" (Emerson), 10–12, 133
Atkinson, Rev. Thomas, 149
Atlantic Monthly, 225–26, 240–43
Avarice of northerners, 151, 154, 169, 179, 181–82, 195, 197, 215–16
"Away with the Dastards Who Whine of Defeat" (Hayne), 209

Baker, E. D., 224
"A Ballad for the Young South," 204, 214
Banton, Michael, 53, 69
Barbarism: and caning of Sumner by Brooks, 9–10, 146, 173; of Cavaliers, 173, 180; of Confederate soldiers, 178, 188; of Saxon race, 142; in Scott's *Ivanhoe*, 56, 71; of slaves, 81; of southerners, 9–10, 16, 17, 22, 32–33, 61, 87, 124, 130–33, 137, 144, 146–48, 153, 173, 177–78, 180, 188; of Union soldiers, 155, 170, 180–88, 193–94, 216–17; of Yankees, 48, 71, 141–42, 150, 155, 156, 169, 170, 180–88, 193–94, 216–17
Basinger, William, 236
"The Basis of Northern Hostility to the South," 19–21, 22, 27
"Battle Hymn of the Republic" (Howe), 224–26
The Bear (Faulkner), 108
Beauregard, G. T., 156, 183, 193
Beecher, Henry Ward, 125–26, 130, 143
Benton, Thomas Hart, 25–26, 27
Beverley, Robert, 94, 176
Bible: and Confederacy, 160, 185, 191; and Creation myth, 35, 36, 42; and Howe's "Battle Hymn of the Republic," 225; and polygenesis race theory, 39, 40; and Puritans, 126; and slavery defense, 41, 130
Bigelow, John, 148
The Black Gauntlet (Schoolcraft), 114–15

275

Blackmar, A. E., 216–17
Blacks. *See* Freed blacks; Slavery
"Bloody Kansas," 2–5, 8, 27, 130
Boone, Daniel, 107
Boston Chronicle, 129–30
Boston Daily Advertiser, 178–79
"Boston Hymn" (Emerson), 221
The Bostonians (James), 242
Bourne, William, 222
Brewer, James, 208
The Bride of Lammermoor (Scott), 52–53
Bridenbaugh, Carl, 94
"Bring the Hero Home" (Baker), 224
Brooks, John Hampton, 13
Brooks, Preston: caning of Sumner by, 1–17, 27, 129–30, 133–34, 146, 162, 173; censure vote against, in House of Representatives, 13–14; and "Crime against Kansas" speech by Sumner, 1, 2, 5; and dueling, 6–7; northern reactions to caning of Sumner by, 8–12, 13; on northerners, 14; and southern code of chivalry and personal honor, 3, 4, 6–8, 11, 14; southern reactions to caning of Sumner by, 9, 12–15
Brown, John, 2, 16–17, 19, 27, 144, 214
Brown, Robert and Katherine, 94
Brownell, Howard, 203
Bruns, John Dickson, 208
Bryant, William Cullen, 223
Buckingham, James, 7
Bull Run, Battle of, 178, 182
The Burden of Southern History (Woodward), 242
Burke, Edmund, 52
Burlingame, Anson, 10
Butler, Andrew P., 3, 4, 6, 14
Butler, Benjamin Franklin, 170, 183, 217–18
Butler, Sarah, 156
Byrd, William, II, 97–98
Byron, George Gordon Lord, 216

Cabell, James Branch, 234
Cabell, N. F., 149–50
Cabin and Parlor; or, Slaves and Masters (Randolph), 112–13
The Cabin Book (Sealsfield), 116–18
Cady, Edwin, 162–63
Cairnes, John Elliott, 163
Calhoun, John C., 24
California, 26, 45, 127

Caning of Charles Sumner, 1–17, 27, 129–30, 133–34, 146, 162, 173
"Carolina" (Timrod), 206
Carter, Robert, 95–96
Cartwright, S. A., 42
Caruthers, William Alexander, 103–7
Cash, W. J., 30–31, 40, 48, 64
Caucasian and Negro Race (Nott), 37, 39–40
"The Cavalier Theory Refuted" (Whitmore), 176
Cavaliers: barbarism of, 173, 180; Emerson on, 133; and English Civil War, 22, 53–55, 83, 84, 90–91, 93, 139, 219–20; Jefferson on, 168; in late-twentieth century writings, 248–51; and Lost Cause myth, 237; northerners' views of, 133, 147, 176, 180; in plantation romance novels, 99–116; poetry on, 203–13, 233; in postbellum writings, 240, 245–46; Puritans versus, 19–21, 22, 29–33, 75–80, 82–99, 138–39, 142, 146–47, 175–77, 180, 226. *See also* Aristocratic myth; Norman-Saxon race myth; Southerners
"The Cavalier's Glee" (Mason), 206
The Cavaliers of Virginia (Caruthers), 103–4
Celtic race, 44–45, 86–88, 249–51
Cervantes, Miguel de, 3
Chamberlayne, John Hampden, 195, 196–97
Chambers, Annie Ketchum, 226–27
Charles I, King, 55, 101, 219, 221
Charles II, King, 78, 93
Charleston Courier, 171
Charleston Mercury, 131–33, 137, 140, 144, 185
Chastellux, Marquis de, 98–99
Chesnut, James, 52–53, 165–66
Chesnut, Mary Boykin, 52, 154–55, 165
Cheves, Langdon, 140
Chicago Democrat, 143, 147
"Chivalrous C. S. A.," 204–5
Chivalry: and American Civil War, 155, 157, 197–98; code of, and personal honor, 3, 4, 6–8, 11, 14–16, 77–78, 162–67, 207; and duels, 6–7, 10, 12, 103, 163, 165; and knightly tournaments in the South, 47, 50–52, 67; Lee as representative of, 245; and Lost Cause myth, 229–31; northerners and genuine chivalry, 178; northerners' view of southern chivalry, 16, 130, 145–46, 178, 188, 191; in plantation romance novels, 110, 114–15; poetry on, 204–7, 212–13, 229–31; and Scott's *Ivanhoe*, 49, 52–71; and selflessness of southerners, 151; and slavery defense, 165; and Southern Womanhood,

63–66; and Walter Scott cultural syndrome, 47–71, 155, 163, 209–10. *See also* Aristocratic myth; Honor

Christianity: and Confederacy, 160, 185, 186, 197; of Confederate soldiers, 189; and division of northern and southern races, 157; and Howe's "Battle Hymn of the Republic," 224–26; and Puritanism, 175; and race theory, 35, 36, 39, 40–41; and slavery defense, 41–42, 81, 115, 130; and southerners as anti-Christ, 131, 132; and superiority of southerners, 87; and Union cause during Civil War, 176; and yeoman farmers in the South, 29, 40. *See also* Bible

Civil War: and barbarism of Confederate soldiers, 178, 188; and barbarism of Union soldiers, 155, 170, 180–88, 193–94, 216–17; and barbarism of Yankees, 142; Battle of Bull Run during, 178, 182; Battle of Gettysburg during, 193, 226, 235; Battle of Vicksburg during, 235; causes of, 142, 144, 148–51, 213–14, 236; and chivalry of southerners, 155, 157, 197–98; Confederacy's superior military spirit during, 178–79; Confederate heroes of, 209–13, 232–33, 237, 238; correspondence from soldiers during, 188–200; and cowardice of Union soldiers, 141, 145, 155–56, 169, 170, 171, 179, 182, 183, 216; defeat of Confederacy in, 186–87, 199–200, 209, 226–27, 235–36; and disgrace of submission to North, 160–61, 165–66, 183–84, 198, 207–9; duty as motive of Union soldiers in, 166; fighting of, in South, 192; and First Battle of Manassas, 169–70, 182, 216; and Fort Sumter attack, 144–45, 150, 155–56, 166, 182, 187, 206, 208, 237; hatred of Yankees by Confederate soldiers during, 192–200; honor as motive of Confederate soldiers in, 166–67, 183–84, 198–99; northern reasons for fighting, 157–58, 166, 223–24; poetry on, 201–34; predictions of southern victory in, 140–42, 150, 157, 199; and Puritanism, 141, 149–50, 171–72, 195–97; and race mythology, 147–57; and sectional consciousness in twenty-first century, 251; Shenandoah Valley campaigns of, 205; and Sherman's march through Georgia and South Carolina, 183, 218–29; similarities between northern and southern soldiers in, 187–88; and slavery, 142, 148, 158–60, 165–68, 188, 198, 207, 223–24, 235, 236, 238; and southern honor, 162–67;

183–84, 198–99; southern reasons for fighting, 158–68, 251; and states' rights, 236, 237, 238; Union military defeats in, 178–79; Union occupation of southern cities and towns during, 170, 181–82, 187, 189, 217–18; and Union soldiers debased by hybridization, 181; Union soldiers on conditions in South during, 188–92. *See also* Confederacy

Clarel (Melville), 242

Clarkson, A., 85–86

Clay, Henry, 26

Clifford, Deborah, 223

Code duello, 6–7, 10, 103, 163, 165

Columbia Guardian, 141–42

The Common Soldier in the Civil War (Wiley), 187–88

Compromise of 1820, 2, 13, 23

Compromise of 1850, 13, 26–27, 73, 121

"Concord Hymn" (Emerson), 222

Confederacy: defeat of, 186–87, 199–200, 209, 226–27, 235–36; God's support for, 160, 185, 186, 197; heroes of, 209–13, 232–33, 237, 238; and Jews, 185–86; and northern view of southern chivalry, 145–46; poetry by southerners on, 203–13; predictions of victory for, 140–42, 150, 157, 199; and race mythology, 33–34, 46; and states' rights, 236, 237, 238; underlying truths of, 159–60. *See also* Civil War; Lost Cause myth; Neo-Confederates; Secession; Southerners

Confederates in the Attic (Horwitz), 248–49

Conjectures of Order (O'Brien), 28

Constitution, U.S., 138–40, 175, 223

Cooke, John Esten, 93–94, 107–8

"The Cotton States' Farewell to Yankee Doodle," 215

Couper, James Hamilton, 165

Cowardice: of southerners, 8, 9–10, 14, 16, 128, 130, 131, 147; of Yankees, 6, 7, 13, 110, 141, 145, 155–56, 169, 170, 171, 179, 182, 183, 216

Crania Aegyptiaca (Morton), 36

Crania Americana (Morton), 36

Creation myth, 35, 36, 42. *See also* Bible

"Crime against Kansas" speech (Sumner), 1, 2–6, 9, 11, 131

Criswell, Robert, 112

Cromwell, Oliver, 83, 84, 93, 139, 152, 171, 213, 220, 244

Crooks, Rev. A., 17

Cult of medievalism, 47–71, 72, 77–78

Curry, Jabez, 136
Cussons, John, 244

Dabney, Robert L., 41
Daly, Charles, 164
Dana, Richard Henry, 9
Daniel, John M., 140, 169–70
Davis, Jefferson, 26, 237
De Gobineau, Count Arthur, 37–38
"The Death of the Ball Turret Gunner" (Jarrell), 201
DeBow, James, 75
DeBow's Review: "The Basis of Northern Hostility to the South" in, 19–21, 22, 27, 32, 33; commercial boosterism in, 72, 73; on diversification of plantation economy, 72; on feudalistic spirit in America, 77–78; on "free-love" societies and spiritualism in the North, 85–86; on Hundley's *Social Relations in Our Southern States,* 79; on Lincoln's presidential candidacy, 165; on Manifest Destiny, 25–26, 27; on Norman race myth and Cavaliers versus Puritans, 19–21, 22, 32, 33, 34, 90–92, 138–40; "The North and the South" in, 72–73; on plantation system, 72–73; on Puritans, 83; on race and polygenesis, 40, 42; on Sir Walter Scott, 52; and secession, 136–37; on southern American race compared with Mediterranean races, 137; "Southern Civilization; or, The Norman in America" in, 89–92; "Southern Statesmanship" in, 71; on tyranny, 139, 140
Declaration of Independence, 77, 175. *See also* Revolutionary War
Democracy (Adams), 242
Democratic party, 243
Dennies, Anne Pryre, 204
"The Destination of America" (Parker), 122–23
"Dirge for Ashby," 210
"Dixie" (Jeffrey), 228
"Dixie" (Pike), 206
Dixon, Henry St. John, 151, 161, 200
Dixon, William H., 246–47
Don Quixote (Cervantes), 3
Donald, David, 3, 6, 16
Douglas, Stephen A., 2
Drayton, Percival, 160
Dred Scott decision, 27
Drum Taps (Whitman), 201, 202, 203
Duels, 6–7, 10, 12, 103, 163, 165

Eaton, Clement, 163
Eckenrode, Hamilton, 48
Edge-Hill; or, The Family of the Fitzroyals (Heath), 101
Edwards, Weldon, 166, 168
Emancipation of slaves, 187, 208
Emerson, Ralph Waldo: on Anglo-Saxon race, 121–24; and animal imagery for southerners, 177–78, 192–93; on caning of Sumner by Brooks, 10–11, 133–34, 177; on civil war, 134; on differences between southerners and northerners, 12, 16, 17, 22, 132–34; *English Traits* by, 123–24; Evans compared with, 173; poetry by, 221, 222, 224; "Self Reliance" by, 122; on slavery, 132–33; southerners on, 85, 154
English Civil War: immigration to America following, 22, 83, 84, 93; northern poetry on, 219–20; and race mythology, 53–55; southern writers on, 22, 83, 84, 90–91, 93, 139, 150, 171
English Traits (Emerson), 123–24
Equality: Jefferson on, 76; southerners' rejection of, 76–77, 170
Essay on the Inequality of Human Races (de Gobineau), 38
Evans, Evan, 173–74
Everett, Edward, 6, 9
Ewing, Henry, 157

A Farewell to Arms (Hemingway), 201
Farmers. *See* Yeoman farmers
Faulkner, William, 108, 109, 249
Faust, Drew Gilpin, 34
Featherstonhaugh, George, 24
Feudalism. *See* Medievalism
Fiction: northern fiction with pro-southern views, 109–14; plantation romance novels of Old Southwest, 108–9; plantation romance novels of Virginia, 99–109, 115–16; in postbellum period, 242, 243–44; race mythology and antebellum fiction, 93–118; Sealsfield's *The Cabin Book,* 116–18; and slavery defense, 109–11, 115. *See also* specific writers and novels
Fischer, David Hackett, 28–30, 94
Fisher, Ellwood, 72–73, 137
Fithian, Philip, 95–96
Fitzgerald, F. Scott, 202
Fitzhugh, George, 76–77, 79, 83–84, 86, 89, 131
Flash, H. L., 212
Fletcher, John, 41–42

Fletcher, Lucy Muse, 187, 239–40
Floan, Howard, 132
"The Foe at the Gates" (Bruns), 208
Fontaine, Winston, 210–11
Forsyth, John, 73
Fort Pulaski, 151
Fort Sumter: beginning of Civil War at, 144–45, 150, 237; defeat of Union soldiers at, 141, 155–56, 182; northern media on, 144–45; poetry on, 206, 208; Ruffin's firing of first shell at, 187; southern media on, 141
Fowler, William Chauncey, 180
Fox-Genovese, Elizabeth, 31, 40, 63
"Free-love" societies, 85–86
Freed blacks, 187, 208, 246–47
French, Virginia, 219
French Revolution, 77
Fugitive Slave Act, 26
Furness, William, 148

Gantt, Edward W., 235
Gardner, Jared, 28
Garland, Kate, 186
Garnett, Hunter, 81
Garrison, William Lloyd, 9–10, 16, 84, 130–32, 133
Geary, John White, 188, 191
"General Lee at the Battle of the Wilderness," 212
"General Robert E. Lee," 212
"Genius of the Anglo-Saxon Race" (Emerson), 121–22
Genovese, Eugene, 31, 40
Georgia, 135, 183
Gettysburg, Battle of, 193, 226, 235
Giddings, Joshua, 10, 84–85
Girouard, Mark, 60
Gliddon, George, 37, 38, 40
"God Save the South," 206
Gone with the Wind (Mitchell), 234, 248
Goths and Vandals. See Vandals and Goths
The Goths in New England (Marsh), 120–21
Grant, Ulysses, 197–98, 209, 213
Grayson, William John, 84–85, 86
Greeks, 137
Greeley, Horace, 5, 16, 85, 128–29, 144–45, 154
Greg, Percy, 244–46
Guerrant, Edward, 199

Hairston, Peter, 193, 194
Hall, Edward, 191
Hamilton, Fannie, 184–85

Hamlin, Hannibal, 153
Hammond, James, 76, 77, 79
Hanks, Constant, 190
Harland, Marian, 153
Harper, Chancellor, 42–43
Harpers Ferry raid, 16–17, 27, 144
Harrison, Benjamin, 98–99
Haskell, A. C., 150, 156, 192–93, 198
Haskell, Sophia, 155, 237–38
Hawthorne, Nathaniel, 85
Hayes, Rutherford B., 243
Hayne, Paul Hamilton, 209, 218, 232
"The Heart of the War" (Holland), 222–23
Heath, James Ewell, 101
Hemingway, Ernest, 201
Henry St. John, Gentleman (Cooke), 108
Hentz, Caroline Lee, 109–11
"Heroes of the South" (Hayne), 232
Hindman, T. C., 194
The Hireling and the Slave (Grayson), 84–85
History and Present State of Virginia (Beverley), 94
History of the Conquest of England by the Normans (Thierry), 59
History of the United States from the Foundation of Virginia to the Reconstruction of the Union (Greg), 244–46
Holland, Josiah Gilbert, 222–23
Holmes, Oliver Wendell, 178, 202
Holmes, Oliver Wendell, Jr., 178
Holt, Ellen, 161
Holt, John Lee, 161
"The Homespun Dress," 207
Honor: and American Civil War, 162–67, 183–84, 198–99; Brooks on, 14; in colonial Virginia, 97, 162; and Confederate soldiers, 166–67; and duels, 6–7, 10, 12, 103, 163, 165; Emerson on, 10–12; and Robert E. Lee, 164, 165, 167; of Norman-descended aristocrats, 90; northerners on, 10–11, 15, 164, 222–23; in poetry by northerners, 222–23; in poetry by southerners, 205–8, 209, 213; and slavery defense, 165; and southerners' code of chivalry, 3, 4, 6–8, 11, 14–16, 50–51, 162–67, 183–84; Wyatt-Brown on, 11, 162, 163–64, 167, 222; and yeoman farmers, 162–63, 222–23. See also Aristocratic myth; Chivalry
Hope, James Barron, 232–33
Horsman, Reginald, 39, 81, 119–20
Horwitz, Tony, 248–49

Hotze, Henry, 37–38
Howe, Julia Ward, 224–26
Hoyt, Clara, 184–85
Hubbell, Jay B., 49–50
Hudson, Nicholas, 46
Huguenots, 61, 75, 91, 142, 169, 180, 197, 204, 213
Hundley, Daniel R., 78–79

Illiteracy, 129
Immigrants, 29–30, 74, 79, 87, 102, 176, 181, 194
"In the Land Where We Were Dreaming" (Lucas), 228–30, 231
Industry and commerce, 71, 72, 81–82, 88–89, 179, 181–82
Ingraham, Joseph Holt, 109, 113–14
"Invocation," 208
Irish immigrants, 87
Ivanhoe (Scott): conclusion of, 68–69; Emerson on, 123–24; female characters in, 62–71; and nineteenth-century racism, 69–71; and Norman-Saxon race myth, 53, 55–62, 69–71, 209–10; northern reviewer on, 65; reaction of southern farmer to, 49–50; southern reviewers on, 52, 65; theme of, 68–69

Jackson, Andrew, 104, 139
Jackson, Stonewall, 185, 205, 211–12, 237
James, Henry, 242
Janvier, Francis, 223
Jarrell, Randall, 201
Jefferson, Thomas: agrarianism of, 73; on differences between northerners and southerners, 22, 168; on equality of all men, 76; and monogenism, 35; political principles of, 77, 140, 143, 158, 175; as slave owner, 139; support for, during Revolutionary period, 98–99
Jeffrey, Rose Vertner, 218, 228
Jews, 163, 182, 185–86
Jimerson, Randall, 251
Johnson, Samuel, 52
Jones, Charles C., 150, 157
Justices of the peace, 98

Kansas: slavery dispute in ("Bloody Kansas"), 2–5, 8, 27, 130; Sumner's speech on, 1, 2–6, 9, 11, 131
Kansas-Nebraska Act (1854), 2, 27
Keitt, Laurence, 152, 153
Kendrick, H. C., 193, 199

Kennedy, John Pendleton, 101–3
Kentucky, 208
The Knights of the Golden Horse-shoe (Caruthers), 105–7
Knox, Robert, 35, 44–45, 46, 53
Kreyling, Michael, 111

Languages of North and South, 171
Lanier, Sidney, 202, 230–31
Le Conte, Emma, 183
Lee, George Washington Custis, 236
Lee, Harper, 248
Lee, Richard Henry, 98–99
Lee, Robert E.: and chivalry, 245; and honor, 164, 165, 167, 213; and Lost Cause myth, 237, 238; monument to, in Richmond, 232–33; in Pennsylvania, during Civil War, 192; poetry on, 212–13, 229, 232–33; surrender of, at Appomattox, 199, 209, 213, 235
Leland, Charles Godfrey, 221
Lewis, Henry Clay, 30
The Liberator, 16, 130
Life at the South; or, "Uncle Tom's Cabin" as It Is (Smith), 111–12
Life on the Mississippi (Twain), 48–49, 52
Lincoln, Abraham: and "Battle Hymn of the Republic," 226; and Civil War, 161, 175, 176; northerners on, 142–43, 147–48; second inaugural address of, 176; southern reactions to, 135, 139–40, 149, 150–51, 153, 158, 161, 165–66, 207
"Lines Written July 15, 1865," 227
Linnaeus, Carolus, 35
Literacy, 129
Longfellow, Henry Wadsworth, 8, 9, 85, 132, 133
Lost Cause myth: and aristocratic myth, 236–39; and neo-Confederates, 251; poetry on, 228–34; and racism, 246–47; tenets of, 236–37; in twentieth century, 237–39
Louisiana: and Civil War, 156; farmers in, 30; French and Spanish settlers in, 91; Jews in, 186; and Lincoln's election, 149; New Orleans before the city's surrender, 186; Sealsfield on, 116; and secession, 161; women in New Orleans during Union occupation, 170, 182–83, 217–18
Louisiana Territory, 2, 23
Lovelace, Richard, 207
Lowell, James Russell, 132, 226

Lucas, D. B., 228–30
Lusk, William Thompson, 188–89
Lyell, Charles, 126
Lyons, Jason, 165

Madison, James, 143, 175
Maffit, J. N., 82
Manassas, First Battle of, 169–70, 182, 216
Manifest Destiny, 25–26, 27, 45–46, 106–7
Marsh, George Perkins, 120–21, 123
Martin, George Alexander, 235–36
Martin, Jay, 242–43
Maryland, 75, 196, 208, 217
Mason, Blackford, 206
Mason, James, 5
Matthews, Martha, 181–82, 185
May, Rev. Samuel, 147, 148
Mayo, Rev. A. D., 131, 132
McAllister, Robert, 188, 191
McCain, Barry Reid, 250
McCall, A., 153
McIntosh, Maria, 79–80
McPherson, James, 31, 33, 160, 166
McWhiney, Grady, 249–51
Media. *See* specific newspapers
Medievalism: in plantation romance novels, 110, 114–15; poetry on, 212; southern cult of, 47–71, 72, 77–78; and Walter Scott cultural syndrome, 47–71, 155, 163
Mediterranean races, 137
Melville, Herman, 242
"Memoriae Sacrum" (Hope), 232–33
Memorials of a Southern Planter (Smedes), 60–61
Memories of President Lincoln (Whitman), 202
Mercer, George, 151, 155, 156, 159–60, 180–82, 186, 187
Mexican-American War, 25, 26, 45, 106
Middle class, in the South, 78, 79
The Mind of the South (Cash), 30–31, 40, 48, 64
Mississippi, 108, 109, 181–82
Missouri, 2
Missouri Compromise, 2, 22–23, 119
Mitchell, Margaret, 234, 248
Monogenism, 34–35, 36, 38, 40
Moore, J. Quitman, 71, 77, 80, 165
Moore, Thomas O., 149
The Moral and Intellectual Diversity of Races (de Gobineau), 37–38
Morton, Samuel George, 36, 38, 39, 43, 46

Mosby, John S., 199
Motley, John Lothrop, 178
"My Maryland" (Randall), 217
"My Order," 207
Myths and Realities (Bridenbaugh), 94

Nebraska territory, 2, 27
Neo-Confederates, 249–51
New England. *See* Northerners; Puritanism; Yankees
The New Englander (Evans), 173–74
New media. *See* specific newspapers
New Orleans Bee, 142
New Orleans Medical and Surgical Journal, 42
"The New Reveille" (Bourne), 222
New York Daily Times, 15, 127–28
New York Daily Tribune, 5, 16, 128
New York Evening Post, 5
New York Herald, 143, 144
New York Times, 144, 145, 148
Norman-Saxon race myth: and American Civil War, 155, 157, 197; and Anglo-Norman as term, 81, 86; and Anglo-Saxon as term, 20–21, 22, 45–46, 80–81; and Celtic race, 44–45, 86–88, 249–51; characteristics of German race, 54–55; Emerson on, 123–24; Fitzhugh on, in *DeBow's Review,* 89–92; and *Ivanhoe* by Scott, 55–62, 69–71, 123–24; and neo-Confederates, 250; Parker on, 123; in plantation romance novels, 108, 113; poetry on, 203–13, 228, 232–33; in postbellum period, 239–40; and scientific theory of race, 43–46; in Sealsfield's *The Cabin Book,* 116–18; of southerners, 18, 21, 22, 28–34, 89–92, 119, 142, 180–81; in twenty-first century, 248–51; and Verstegan, 53–55; and Walter Scott cultural syndrome, 53–61, 155, 163, 209–10. *See also* Anglo-Saxon race; Cavaliers; Race mythology
North American Review, 48
"The North and the South," 72–73
North Carolina, 166, 190–91
"Northern Mind and Character," 33
Northerners: avarice of, 151, 154, 169, 179, 181–82, 195, 197, 215–16; barbarism of, 48, 71, 141–42, 150, 155, 156, 169, 170, 180–87, 193–94; Brooks on, 14; on caning of Sumner by Brooks, 8–12, 13, 129–30, 133–34, 146, 173; and censure vote against Brooks, 13–14; and duels, 10; Emerson on, 12, 16, 17, 22; and "free-

Northerners *(continued)*
  love" societies, 85–86; on Harpers Ferry raid by John Brown, 17, 144; and honor, 10–11, 15, 164, 222–23; and illiteracy, 129; and individualism, 71; and industry and commerce, 71, 72, 81–82, 88–89, 179, 181–82; Jefferson on, 22; laissez-faire economic principles of, 83; language of, 171; manners of, 178; moral condemnation of southerners by, 128–33; and progress in postbellum period, 242–43; similarities between southerners and, 21–22; and spiritualism, 85, 86; on Sumner's "Crime against Kansas" speech, 5–6; sympathy for South in postbellum period, 240–47; tyranny of, over South, 139–40, 161; Yankee nation as defined by northerners, 119–34; Yankee race as defined by southerners, 81–89, 149–55, 187. *See also* Civil War; Norman-Saxon race myth; Puritanism; Women; Yankees
"The Northman's Cause," 88
"Northmen, Come Out!" (Leland), 221
Northrup, Claudian, 82, 88–89
Nott, Josiah Clark, 37, 38, 39–40, 41, 46, 53
Nugent, William, 193, 194–95, 196, 198–99

O'Brien, Michael, 28, 51, 69
"Obsequies of Stuart" (Thompson), 211
"Ode Recited at the Harvard Commemoration, July 21, 1865" (Lowell), 226
Oregon Territory, 25, 126–27
Oriens, G. Harrison, 50
Osterwies, Rollin, 47–48, 50, 243

Palfrey, John, 8–9
Parker, Theodore, 85, 122–23, 125, 132
Parkman, Francis, 178–80
Parmelee, Uriah, 190
The Partisan Leader (Tucker), 64, 104–5
Patrick, Robert, 199–200
Patriotic Gore (Wilson), 202
Patterson, Edmund Dewitt, 196
Pessen, Edward, 21
Peterson, Charles Jacobs, 112–13
Pickering, Charles, 36, 43
Pierson, David, 167
Pike, Albert, 206
Plantation romance novels: chivalry in, 110, 114–15; by northern writers, 109–14; in Old Southwest, 108–9; slavery in, 109–11, 114; in Virginia, 99–109, 115–16; women characters in, 100–101, 103, 108, 110, 113; Yankee characters in, 100, 110, 113
Planters and plantation system. *See* Aristocratic myth; Cavaliers; Chivalry; Honor; Norman-Saxon race myth; Slavery; Southerners
The Planter's Northern Bride (Hentz), 109–11, 112, 114
Poetry: anti-slavery poetry, 223–24; on Cavaliers and aristocratic myth of southerners, 203–13, 233; on chivalry, 204–7, 212–13, 229–31; on Civil War, 201–34; on Confederate heroes, 209–13, 232–33; on disgrace of submission to North, 207–9; on honor of northerners, 222–23; on honor of southerners, 205–8, 209; Howe's "Battle Hymn of the Republic," 224–26; Lost Cause myth in, 228–34; northern Civil War poetry, 203, 219–26; on Puritanism, 203–4, 213–14, 219–22, 226; on slavery, 84–85, 223–24; southern Civil War poetry, 203–19; southern postbellum poetry, 226–34; on Southern Womanhood, 206, 207; on Union generals by southerners, 217–19; by Whitman, 201–2, 203; on Yankees by southerners, 213–19; on yeoman farmers, 221–23
Polygenism, 34, 35–43
Population of South, 73, 74
The Port Folio, 65
Post, Karl. *See* Sealsfield, Charles
Preston, John, 153, 157
Preston, Margaret Junkin, 205, 227–28
Puritanism: and American Civil War, 141, 149–50, 171–72, 195–97; and America's national character, 173, 174–77; Beecher on, 125–26, 143; Cavaliers versus, 19–21, 22, 29–33, 75–80, 82–99, 138–39, 146–47, 175–77, 180, 226; character traits and stereotypes of, 9, 18, 20, 90, 120, 141–42, 143, 146–47, 149–52, 171–72, 174–77, 180, 195–96, 213–14, 244; *DeBow's Review* on Cavaliers versus, 19–21, 22, 32, 33, 34, 83, 90–92; Emerson on, 121–22; and English Civil War, 22, 53–55, 83, 84, 90–91, 93, 139, 150, 171, 219–20; and Gothic racial strain, 120–21; and industry and commerce, 72, 81–82, 88–89, 179, 181–82; and laissez-faire economic principles, 83; Parker on, 122–23; poetry on, 203–4, 213–14, 219–22, 226; postbellum writings on, 244–46; Sealsfield on, 117; Sumner as voice of, 5; superiority of Puritan blood, 143; of Union soldiers, 195–97. *See also* Anglo-Saxon race; Yankees

Quincy, Josiah, 9

Race: Appiah on, 34, 39, 69; biological determination of, and polygenism, 34, 35–43; Cartwright on Negro race, 42; Celtic and Saxon races, 44–45, 86–88, 249–51; de Gobineau on, 37–38; environmental influences on, and monogenism, 34–35, 36, 38, 40; Greek view of, 34; Harper on Negro race, 42–43; Hebrew view of, 34; Knox on, 35, 44–45, 46, 53; medieval Europeans' view of, 34; Nott on, 37, 38, 39–40, 41, 46, 53; number of races, 38, 43; and Scott's *Ivanhoe*, 69–71, 123–24; and skull measurements, 36, 38, 39; southern scientists on, 36–46; Teutonic race, 45, 120–21, 126; Verstegan on German race, 54–55. *See also* Anglo-Saxon race; Norman-Saxon race myth; Race mythology

Race mythology: and American Civil War, 147–57, 197; and Anglo-Norman as term, 81, 152; and Anglo-Saxon as term, 20–21, 22, 45–46, 80–81; Anglo-Saxon race and northern race mythmaking, 119–25, 127; and antebellum fiction, 93–118; Beecher on superiority of Puritan blood, 143; Benton's national racial myth, 25–26, 27; and Confederacy, 33–34, 46; and English Civil War, 53–55; and German/Teutonic race, 45, 54–55, 120–21, 126, 196–97; Gothic racial strain, 120–21; and Latin races, 148; and Lost Cause, 246–47; Mediterranean races compared with southern American race, 137; and neo-Confederates, 249–51; Norman-Saxon race myth of southerners, 18, 21, 22, 28–34, 43–46, 86–88; northern racial mythmaking, 119–34; and secession, 74, 136–37, 147–57; in slavery defense, 33, 37, 39, 41–43; southern slaveholding race as unique and homogeneous, 73–81, 89–92; and twentieth-century southern sectionalism, 235–51; in twenty-first century, 248–51; Vandals and Goths compared with Yankees, 155, 180–87, 192, 193–94, 217; and Walter Scott cultural syndrome, 47, 53; and white supremacy, 77, 81, 115, 159, 169; Yankee race as defined by southerners, 81–89, 149–55, 187; Yankees as mongrel mixture of races, 152–55, 170–71, 181, 194–95. *See also* Anglo-Saxon race; Norman-Saxon race myth; Race

Races of Man and Their Geographical Distribution (Pickering), 36

The Races of Man (Knox), 35, 44–45, 46, 53
Randall, James Ryder, 217
Randolph, J. Thornton, 112–13
Randolph, John, 12
Rasin, William, 236
Reagan, Ronald, 251
Reconstruction, 228, 238, 239, 243
Reid, James, 96
Republican Party: and caning of Sumner by Brooks, 8; and Hayes's election, 243; and Lincoln's election, 158, 165; and Reagan's southern strategy, 251; southerners on, 136, 150, 152, 158–59, 165; view of southerners by, 132. *See also* Lincoln, Abraham
Requier, A.J., 231–32
Restitution of Decayed Intelligence (Verstegan), 54–55
Return to Camelot (Girouard), 60
Revolutionary War: compared with North's tyranny over South, 88; and Declaration of Independence, 77, 175; and equality for all men, 76–77; in fiction, 101, 102, 107; Greg on, 244–45; pride in, 21, 75; and Puritanism, 175; and Virginians, 101, 102, 107, 139–40, 175
Rhett, A. Burnett, 238–39
Richmond Daily Dispatch, 170–71
Richmond Enquirer: on aristocratic myth of southerners, 129; on caning of Sumner by Brooks, 12; on First Battle of Manassas, 169–70; on knightly tournament in Virginia, 47, 51–52; on Lincoln, 140; on predictions of southern victory in Civil War, 141; on secession, 136; on slaveholding race, 74
Richmond Whig, 161, 171–72
"Riding a Raid," 210
Romance novels. *See* Plantation romance novels
Romans, 137, 197–98
Romanticism and Nationalism in the Old South (Osterweis), 47–48, 50
Roundheads, 22, 53–55, 84, 90, 139, 180, 219–20, 226
Royster, Charles, 218
Ruffin, Edmund, 76, 80, 82, 87, 187
Rutherford, John Coles, 157
Rutledge, Benjamin, 236–37
Ryan, Abram J., 228, 234

Savannah Daily Morning News, 144
Saxon Chronicle, 56

Saxons. *See* Anglo-Saxon race; Norman-Saxon race myth
Schenck, David, 181, 185
Schoolcraft, Mary Howard, 114–15
Scott, Anne Firor, 62–63
Scott, Sir Walter: *The Bride of Lammermoor* by, 52–53; female characters of, 62–70; influence of, on southern imagination, 47–71, 114, 163; *Ivanhoe* by, 49, 52–71, 123–24, 155, 209–10; and nineteenth-century racism, 69–71; Twain on, 48–50, 52–53; twentieth-century critics on, 49–51; word coinages of, 48
Sealsfield, Charles, 116–18
Secession: abolitionists on, 147; and Alabama, 163–64; Fitzhugh on, in 1850s, 89; and Georgia, 135; and honor, 165–66; and Louisiana, 161; and North Carolina, 166; northern reactions to, 143–44; ordinances of, 46; in plantation romance novels, 104; and race mythology, 74, 136–37, 147–57; and secessionists in 1850s, 27, 89; and slavery, 158, 160; of South Carolina, 135, 136; southern opposition to, 135, 167; and southern reaction to Lincoln's election, 135, 139–40, 158, 165–66; and southerners of Unionist persuasion, 156; and Virginia, 136, 153–54, 166. *See also* Confederacy
Sectionalism. *See* Northerners; Southerners
"Self Reliance" (Emerson), 122
Seward, William, 127, 128
Shafer, Boyd, 46
Shenandoah Valley campaigns, 205
Sherman, William Tecumseh, 183, 218–19
"Shermanized" (French), 219
Sherwood, Kate Brownlee, 203–4
Sherwood, Virginia, 174–76
Simms, William Gilmore, 53, 59, 81
Slavery: and aristocratic myth, 80, 174; and "Bloody Kansas," 2–5, 8, 27, 130; Christian defense of, 41–42, 81, 115, 130; and Civil War, 142, 148, 158–60, 165–68, 188, 198, 207, 223–24, 235, 236, 238; Constitution on, 138; Jefferson Davis on, 26; Dred Scott decision on, 27; Emerson on, 132–33; fictional defense of slavery, 109–11, 115; freedom for slaves, 187, 208; and Fugitive Slave Act, 26; Garrison on defenses of, 131; Greeley on, 128–29; honor defense for preservation of, 165; in plantation romance fiction, 109–11, 114; poetry on, 84–85, 223–24; and prosperity in the South, 73; race myth defense of, 33, 37, 39, 41–43;

and secession, 158, 160; Seward's repudiation of, 127; and slave trade, 144; and Southern Womanhood, 63–64; in territories, 2–5, 8, 23, 26, 27, 127; and unique southern slaveholding race, 76; Van Der Lyn on, 23; and Walter Scott cultural syndrome, 51; and white supremacy, 81, 115, 159, 169. *See also* Abolitionism
Sloane, Rev. J. R. W., 131
Smedes, Susan Dabney, 60–61
Smedley, Audrey, 120–21
Smith, William L. G., 111–12
Social Relations in Our Southern States (Hundley), 78–79
Sociology for the South (Fitzhugh), 83–84
Solomon, Clara, 182–83, 186
South Carolina: aristocracy in, 240; *Atlantic Monthly* on, 240–43; attack on Fort Sumter in, 144–45, 150, 155–56, 166, 182, 187, 206, 208; Beaufort mansions in, 188–89; and caning of Sumner by Brooks, 12–15; during Civil War, 183, 188–89, 191, 218–19; colonial charter of, 115; and Confederate flag in 2000, 251; duels in, 7, 10; Garrison on, 9–10; Greeley on, 129; Horwitz on, in late twentieth century, 248–49; Huguenots of, 91, 142, 169, 180; Jews in, 185; plantation romance novels from, 114–15; secession of, 135, 136; Sumner on, 3–4; Union soldiers on, 191
"South Carolina Society," 240–43, 247
"South Carolina's Justification to the North," 214
The South in American Literature (Hubbell), 49–50
Southern and Western Magazine, 59
"Southern Battle Chorus," 205
"Southern Chant of Defiance" (Warfield), 203
"Southern Civilization; or, The Norman in America" in, 89–92
"Southern Hate of New England" (Sherwood), 174–75
The Southern Lady: From Pedestal to Politics (Scott), 62–63
Southern Literary Messenger: on California, 45; on Cavalier-descended southerners, 32–33, 75–76; on Confederacy, 159–60; on inferiority of blacks, 42; on Norman-descended southern race, 34; on northern Yankee race, 84, 86–87; "The Northman's Cause" in, 88; on race theories, 39, 40, 42; and secession, 136; on slavery as justification for Civil War, 158–59

"The Southern Marseillaise" (Blackmar), 216–17
"The Southern Oath" (Jeffrey), 218
Southern Quarterly Review: Anglo-Norman as term used by, 81; on Anglo-Saxon race, 45; on northern Yankee race, 81–82; on Puritanism, 84; on race theories, 39, 45; on southern race as unique and homogeneous, 46, 73–74; on superiority of southern race, 73–74
"Southern Statesmanship" (Moore), 71
Southerners: barbarism of, 9–10, 16, 17, 22, 32–33, 61, 87, 124, 130–33, 137, 144, 146–48, 153, 173, 177–78, 180; on caning of Sumner by Brooks, 9, 12–15; Cavaliers as ancestors of, 19–20, 22, 29–33, 75–80, 82–83, 90–99, 133; and censure vote against Brooks, 14; characteristics of southern civilization, 92, 154, 157; cowardice of, 8, 9–10, 14, 16, 128, 130, 131, 147; and cult of medievalism, 47–71, 72, 77–78; and cultural and political isolation of the South, 23–24; and duels, 6–7, 10, 12, 163, 165; Emerson on, 12, 16, 17, 22; on equality, 76–77, 170; and illiteracy, 129; and industry, 72; Jefferson on, 22; language of, 171; middle class of, 78, 79; northern sympathy for, in postbellum period, 240–47; northerners' condemnation of, 127–33, 144–49; political dominance of, in 1840s, 126–27; population of, 73, 74; pride and sense of superiority of, 24, 73–74, 87, 89, 91–92, 126–27, 157, 169–70, 180–81, 190, 191, 238–40; race as viewed by southern scientists, 36–46; regional versus national identity of, 24–25, 45, 81; and selflessness of, 151; siege mentality of, 104, 119; similarities between northerners and, 21–22; and Southern Womanhood, 63–66, 79–80, 206, 207; on Sumner's "Crime against Kansas" speech, 6, 10; on tyranny of North over South, 139–40, 161; and Walter Scott cultural syndrome, 47–71, 155, 163, 209–10; as yeoman farmers versus planters, 28, 29–32, 40, 78–79, 95, 98, 162–63. *See also* Aristocratic myth; Cavaliers; Chivalry; Civil War; Confederacy; Honor; Norman-Saxon race myth; Race mythology; Secession; Women
The Southwest, by a Yankee (Ingraham), 109
Spiritualism, 85, 86
Spooner, Fred, 188
Stanley, Henry, 163
Stanton, William, 35, 38

States' rights, 236, 237, 238, 251
Stedman, Edmund Clarence, 148
Stepan, Nancy, 38
Stephens, Alexander, 43, 135
Stoics, 227–28
Stone, Kate, 184
"Stonewall Jackson" (Flash), 212
Story, W. W., 224
Stowe, Harriet Beecher, 86, 109, 111, 154
Strong, George Templeton, 178
Stuart, J. E. B. "Jeb," 205, 209, 210–11
Sumner, Charles: caning of, by Brooks, 1–17, 27, 129–30, 133–34, 146, 162, 173; convalescence of, 8–9; "Crime against Kansas" speech by, 1, 2–6, 9, 11, 131; and Longfellow on divisions between North and South, 133; Mason on, 5; northern reactions to caning of, 8–12, 13; northern reactions to speech by, 5–6; personality of, 4; and Puritanism, 5; southern reactions to caning of, 9, 12–15; southerners on, 6, 10, 154
The Sunny South; or, The Southerner at Home (Ingraham), 113–14
Swallow Barn (Kennedy), 101–3
Sydnor, Charles, 24, 26–27, 98, 104

Tally, Susan, 206
Taylor, William R., 22
Tennessee, 191–92, 197
Territories and slavery, 2–5, 8, 23, 26, 27, 127
Texas, 116–17
Thierry, Augustin, 59, 60
Thomas, Ella Gertrude, 184
Thompson, Henry, 190
Thompson, John Reuben, 208, 209–10, 211
Thoreau, Henry David, 132, 154
Ticknor, Frank, 205
Timrod, Henry, 206
"To Englishmen" (Whittier), 220–21
To Kill a Mockingbird (Lee), 248
Tourgée, Albion, 243
"The Tournament" (Lanier), 230–31
Tucker, George, 99–101, 103, 104–5
Tucker, Nathaniel Beverley, 64, 65
Twain, Mark, 48–53
Two Lectures on the Natural History of the Caucasian and Negro Races (Nott), 37, 39–40
Types of Mankind (Nott and Gliddon), 37, 38, 40
Tyranny of North, 139–40, 161

Uncle Tom's Cabin (Stowe), 86, 109, 111
"Uncle Tom's Cabin" Contrasted with Buckingham Hall, the Planter's Home (Criswell), 112
Union soldiers. *See* Civil War
University of Virginia, 12, 109
Usher, Archbishop, 35, 36

The Valley of Shenandoah (Tucker), 99–101, 103
Van Buren, Martin, 104–5
Van Der Lyn, Henry, 23
Van Dorn, General, 197–98
Vandals and Goths, compared with Yankees, 155, 180–87, 192, 193–94, 217
Varon, Elizabeth, 63
Verstegan, Richard, 53–55
Vicksburg, Battle of, 235
Virginia: aristocratic origins of colonial Tidewater Virginia, 93–99, 109, 162, 180, 232–33, 240; and caning of Sumner by Brooks, 12; during Civil War, 187, 190, 191; execution of John Brown in, 17; Greeley on, 128; Harpers Ferry raid by John Brown in, 16–17, 27, 144; heterogeneous nature of settlement of, 176; Robert E. Lee monument in Richmond, 232–33; occupation of Richmond by Union Army, 187; plantation romance novels from, 99–109, 115–16; poets from, 205; and secession, 136, 153–54, 166; Union soldiers on, 190, 191. *See also Richmond Enquirer*
The Virginia Comedians (Cooke), 107–8
"Virginia Dead," 209
Virginia Gazette, 97

Walsh, Robert, 119, 125, 126
"War Song," 217
Warfield, Mrs. C. A., 203, 211
Washington, George, 139, 143, 158, 161, 175
Washington Star, 6
"The Watchers" (Whittier), 224–25
Watkins, Sam, 195, 196, 197
Webb, Nathan, 191
Webb, Richard Davis, 147
Webster, Daniel, 26
Whig Party, 8, 12
The White Conquest (Dixon), 246–47
White supremacy: Fitzhugh on, 77; in postbellum writings, 246–47; and slavery, 81, 115, 159, 169; in twenty-first century, 251
Whitman, Walt, 201–2, 203
Whitmore, W. H., 176–77
Whittier, John Greenleaf, 132, 202, 220–21, 224–25
Wigfall, Louis T., 157
Wiley, Bell Irvin, 187–88, 192
William the Conqueror, 33, 54, 56, 116–17, 204
Williams, Benjamin, 236
Wilson, Edmund, 202
Winthrop, Robert, 8
Wiswall, J. T., 79, 80
Women: Civil War and southern women, 199; in colonial Virginia, 97; northern women as described by southerners, 80, 83, 85–86, 154–55; in plantation romance novels, 100–101, 103, 108, 110, 113; poetry on, 206, 207; in Scott's *Ivanhoe*, 62–71; Southern Womanhood, 63–66, 79–80, 206, 207; in Union-occupied cities and towns, 170, 181–83, 187, 217–18. *See also* specific women
Woodward, C. Vann, 242
"The Wound Dresser" (Whitman), 201–2
Wright, Louis, 95
"Written after the Battle of Manassas," 216
Wyatt-Brown, Bertram, 11, 162, 163–64, 167, 222

Yankees: barbarism of, 48, 71, 141–42, 150, 155, 156, 169, 170, 180–87, 193–94, 216–17; Beecher on, 125–26; character traits and stereotypes of, 141–42, 143, 146–47, 149–55, 169–71, 181–82, 191, 192; cowardice of, 6, 7, 13, 110, 141, 145, 155–56, 169, 170, 171, 179, 182, 183, 216; as debased and racially hybridized, 152–55; hatred of, by Confederate soldiers, 192–200; as mongrel mixture of races, 152–55, 170–71, 181, 194–95; nation of, as defined by northerners, 119–34; in plantation romance novels, 100, 110, 113; poetry on, by southerners, 213–19; race of, as defined by southerners, 81–89, 149–55, 187; Universal Yankee Nation, 119, 125, 126, 133, 180; as Vandals, 155, 180–87, 192, 193–94, 217. *See also* Anglo-Saxon race; Northerners; Puritanism
Yeoman farmers: in North, 221–23; in South, 28, 29–32, 40, 78–79, 95, 98, 162–63